PARLIAMENT
THE BIOGRAPHY
VOLUME 2: REFORM

CHRIS BRYANT

BLACK SWAN

TRANSWORLD PUBLISHERS
61–63 Uxbridge Road, London W5 5SA
www.transworldbooks.co.uk

Transworld is part of the Penguin Random House group of companies
whose addresses can be found at global.penguinrandomhouse.com

Penguin
Random House
UK

First published in Great Britain in 2014 by Doubleday
an imprint of Transworld Publishers
Black Swan edition published 2015

A CIP catalogue record for this book
is available from the British Library.

ISBN
9780552779968

Typeset in Minion by Falcon Oast Graphic Art Ltd.
Printed and bound by Clays Ltd, Bungay, Suffolk.

Penguin Random House is committed to a sustainable
future for our business, our readers and our planet. This book is made from Forest
Stewardship Council® certified paper.

MIX
Paper from
responsible sources
FSC® C018179

1 3 5 7 9 10 8 6 4 2

JACOB

Politics, they say, is the art of the possible. In half a century of public and professional life I have not found it so. The limits of the possible constantly shift, and those who ignore them are apt to win in the end. Again and again I have had the satisfaction of seeing the laughable idealism of one generation evolve into the accepted commonplace of the next. But it is from the champions of the impossible rather than the slaves of the possible that evolution draws its creative force.

Barbara Wootton (Baroness Wootton of Abinger),
In a World I Never Made

Contents

Acknowledgements

I am indebted to many people for their help with this book and its sister first volume. In particular, my agent Jim Gill steered me through the early stages, my editor Doug Young provided sage advice at every turn, Gillian Somerscales spotted errors and unintended ambiguities aplenty, Sheila Lee researched the illustrations, and several friends read individual chapters and put me back on the straight and narrow, including Professor Sir Diarmaid MacCulloch, Gregg McClymont MP, Chris Skidmore MP, Hywel Francis MP, Lynn Brown MP, Tristram Hunt MP, Jesse Norman MP and David Natzler. The printed and online publications of the History of Parliament Trust have been invaluable, as have several of its staff who also reviewed chapters, including Stuart Handley, Andrew Thrush, Stephen Roberts, Ruth Paley and Paul Seaward. While I have often relied on the scholarship of others, I have been fortunate in being able to access primary sources in the collections of the British Library, Lambeth Palace, the Middle Temple, the Bodleian Library at Oxford University, the National Archives at Kew and the Parliamentary Archives in the Victoria Tower, whose staff members Simon Gough, Adrian Brown and Caroline Shenton also cleared up some specific queries for me. The House of Commons and House of Lords Library staff have been universally superb.

An interest in history and religion was sparked in me by my parents Anne and Rees, and by three beautiful sisters who lived together all their lives and were my cousins twice removed, Isobel, Jean and Alison Gracie, but that interest was brought alive by many school-teachers and college lecturers, including the Revd Sam Salter, Tim Pearce, Jack Ralphs, Tim Brown, Bill Simpson, Professor John Creaser and Professor Donald Sykes. Colleagues at Ripon College Cuddesdon, at ISEDET in Buenos Aires, and in the dioceses of Oxford and Peterborough weaned me off conservatism and schooled me in the pursuit of justice and freedom; they include Colin Manley, Jon and Penny Inkpin, Christopher Evans, Michael Roberts, John MacQuarrie and Bishops Rowan Williams, David Willcox, Richard Harries, Richard Holloway and Peter Selby. And members of the Labour Party in High Wycombe, Northampton, Hackney and South Wales, and in the Christian Socialist Movement, made me realize that justice won't roll down like a river without the dedication of those who are prepared to deliver leaflets in the pouring rain, listen to speeches into the small hours, pay their party dues and turn up for the vote. Those volunteer members of every party are the rock and solid place on which our parliamentary system stands.

I am enormously grateful to those among my friends and family (and my office staff Rhys Goode, Kevin Morgan, Mark Norris, Jack Jones and Matt Reilly) who have put up with me while I have recounted endless parliamentary anecdotes at them or disappeared into the library for hours on end. Above all, I would not have been able to write this book without the forbearance of the people of the Rhondda, whose voice in parliament I try faithfully to be. In that, and in this, all mistakes are my own.

The thirteenth-century chapel of St Stephen's had been the very cramped home of the House of Commons since 1548. When work was being done to make room for 100 additional MPs following the Act of Union with Ireland, beautiful medieval murals were discovered, but as fast as the antiquarian John Smith could draw them, the architect, James Wyatt, had them destroyed. This is one of John Smith's drawings.

Prologue

WHEN PARLIAMENT GATHERED IN January 1801, the House of Commons was still sitting in the thirteenth-century Chapel of St Stephen's, as it had been since 1547. In an attempt to accommodate the additional one hundred Irish MPs who arrived with the Act of Union, the surveyor-general James Wyatt had been asked to try to cram a few more seats into the chapel, which measured barely 50 feet by 33 (compared to the modern Chamber which, including the public galleries, is 103 feet by 48). Wyatt removed the wainscoting that had been added by the architect and MP Sir Christopher Wren in 1692 and skimmed a couple of feet off the ancient three-foot-thick walls between the buttresses so as to fit in an extra row of benches. These, which had been clad in green morocco leather since 1791, could, at a pinch, take 342, and the larger new side galleries he created could pack in another 150. Yet even after these alterations there was nowhere near enough standing room for the rest of the 658 members, and such was the fug that an 'air machine' had been installed in the attic above the false ceiling along with thermometers to monitor conditions. Still there were constant complaints that the Chamber was unhealthy, not least from the journalists whose gallery had been so reduced in the modifications that they had to queue for hours to be sure of finding places. One such, the poet Samuel Taylor Coleridge, a reporter for the *Morning Post* from 1799, complained that the first time he attended the Commons he was there for twenty-five 'very unpleasant' hours in a row, that the next time he was there from ten in the morning till four o'clock the next morning, and that in consequence he believed 'we Newspaper Scribes are true Galley Slaves' and was determined to 'give up this newspaper business [as] it is too, too fatiguing'.[1]

Wyatt's alterations did more than irritate the press: they involved an extraordinary act of architectural vandalism. While the work on St Stephen's was being undertaken, the Commons was temporarily housed in another building on the Palace estate, the thirteenth-century Painted Chamber, which had variously served as a royal bedchamber, the Court of Star Chamber and a reception room. When its old tapestries were taken down to allow some redecoration in preparation for the MPs' arrival, a series of medieval paintings were revealed. Angels, warriors, Latin texts, all in remarkably good condition, covered every inch of the walls. Unimpressed, Wyatt had the priceless works of art whitewashed over, to the utter chagrin of the Society of Antiquaries. When he came to start work on the Chapel of St Stephen's, the removal of Wren's panelling revealed another series of bright, unvarnished medieval paintings. There were murals of a medieval woman kneeling in prayer, a king in procession, a couple of knights named Eustace and Mercure, two young men carrying a thurible and a taper, and a representation of the adoration of the shepherds. These too were in good condition and covered in gilt, but Wyatt remained unmoved. The antiquarian John Carter, who had been so desperate to preserve whatever was left of the original Gothic building that he had previously scrabbled around under the Commons benches to record every detail and wrote 212 pieces attacking Wyatt in the press, was barred entry as the work went on. A colleague, John Smith, was allowed in, though – and he had to sketch fast, as 'the workmen very often followed him so close in their operations, as to remove, in the course of the same day on which he had made his drawing, the painting which he had been employed in copying that very morning'.[2] In all, Smith reckoned that 122 medieval artworks were destroyed.

Subsequent parliamentary architects called Wyatt a 'destroyer', and Augustus Pugin referred to him as a 'monster of architectural depravity';[3] but, as the first volume of this two-part history of parliament sought to show, an overly sentimental approach to Britain's history has seriously misled many commentators – and so it has been in this case too. The artworks were not by the Old Master Jan Van Eyck, as used to be claimed, and unless they had been extracted from the chapel and preserved elsewhere, they would certainly have been destroyed by fire in 1834 or by bombs in the Second World War. Yet a central theme of these two volumes is that we cannot fully comprehend our modern system of governance – a hereditary monarchy prevented from acting arbitrarily by the will and wilfulness of parliament – without understanding the path we travelled to get here. What lies beneath, what has been whitewashed over and what has been discarded as political or philosophical fashion has changed: all this is part of what gives a modern constitution its lustrous patina.

The first volume, *Ancestral Voices*, started with the teenage Mauger le Vavasour coming to Westminster in 1258 and ended with the 1801 Act of Union. That history rarely, if ever, proceeded on a straight path: for every positive medieval, Tudor or Stuart parliamentary innovation there was a reversal. The decisions of the parliament of 1376, for instance, were thought so significant that it was ever thereafter known as the 'Good Parliament', yet they were entirely reversed the following year. Many of the MPs and peers who voted for Edward VI's Protestant religion also voted just a few years later for a return to the old Catholic faith under Mary. The civil wars saw a period of exceptional constitutional turbulence in the three kingdoms of England, Scotland and Ireland; and even when people might have thought that the constitution had reached a permanent settlement, after the restoration of the monarchy in 1660, after the Glorious Revolution in 1688 or after the arrival of the Hanoverians in 1714, there were new battles over religion and the respective powers of the monarch and parliament.

Fixed parts of the much-vaunted canon of British freedoms, including habeas corpus, the right to a fair trial, free elections and freedom of speech, were regularly rescinded or ignored.

The history of the two centuries covered by this volume (up to the fall of Mrs Thatcher) may seem more familiar to readers. By 1801, several of the features of today's constitution, including political parties, the Prime Minister, the Cabinet and term limits for parliaments, were already part of the furniture. The premiers covered here – the duke of Wellington, Earl Grey, Sir Robert Peel, William Ewart Gladstone, Benjamin Disraeli, the marquess of Salisbury, David Lloyd George, Winston Churchill – are far better known than most of their eighteenth-century predecessors. Yet many of the themes of volume 1 recur: the significance of chance, hazard and the caprice of history; the role of personal predilections, antipathies and tragedies in shaping events; the never-ending cycles of reaction and reform, of experiment and improvisation; the humanity and weakness of many of the protagonists, including the heroic ones; and the extraordinary effectiveness of many a now-forgotten individual bishop, lord or MP.

Some elements of this volume's story, though, are quite different. In 1801 the vast majority of the population was excluded from voting, and many politicians considered 'democracy' a menace outranked in villainy only by those other French innovations, revolution and Napoleon. Yet as the landed aristocracy, who once equally dominated the Commons, the lords temporal and the lords spiritual, slowly departed the scene (or were evicted from it), so the businessmen, the financiers, the merchants, the teachers, the miners, the labourers and the nurses came into their own. As the formal powers of the crown diminished, so the parliamentary grip of its proxy, the government, strengthened. The press became the Fourth Estate, private lives became public, working men and women got the vote, parliament surrendered its sinews to the demands of total war, the roar of faith subsided down the beach, the struggles for home rule and devolution bore bloody and limited fruit, and women finally made the journey from the seats in the Strangers' Gallery to the green and red Treasury benches of the Commons and the Lords. This volume charts that passage in both chronological and thematic chapters.

There is one theme above all others that fascinates every politician (apart perhaps from the exceptionally venal, of whom a number feature in this volume). Some call themselves reformers; others declare their desire to change the world or at least make a mark. All urge the bells to chime 'ring out the old, ring in the new'. But the art throughout these two centuries has been to fashion the new without whitewashing over or destroying the best of the old, and to respond to immediate crises without creating hostages to future fortune. Swift innovators when it came to the industrial revolution, we in these isles have tended to be far slower adopters of political innovation. An obsessive respect for the past and a dedication to constitutional evolution rather than revolution has led to piecemeal reform and a fudged constitution perilously dependent on custom, convention and gentlemen's agreements.

The question is whether, like Wyatt, the United Kingdom has in every generation been too indifferent to ancient freedoms, too blind to historic truth, too deaf to ancestral voices; or whether we have just been too lazy, cowardly, patient or politically pedestrian to build or vote for something better.

The early nineteenth-century campaign for parliamentary reform sharply divided the country. Here King William IV, surrounded by Whig and Radical politicians, looks down benignly as Britannia slays the dragon of the 'old corruption' and the Tories are put to flight.

1

The Voice of a Nation

AT A QUARTER PAST FIVE on the afternoon of Monday, 11 May 1812 the diminutive, balding Prime Minister walked into the ante-room of the thirteenth-century chapel of St Stephen's, which since 1547 had served as the lobby and Chamber of the House of Commons. The lobby was busy, full of lawyers, merchants and shippers gathered for the opening of an inquiry into the government's controversial Orders in Council of 1807 which, designed to enforce a naval blockade on Napoleon Bonaparte's France, had led to a worldwide trade crisis. There were MPs too, of course. The anti-slavery members William Smith and Francis Phillips were about to join the debate, and the pro-slavery Liverpool member General Isaac Gascoyne was in the committee room above the lobby. The Prime Minister was late. In the Chamber the excitable Scottish MP for Camelford, Henry Brougham, had angrily demanded why he was not present, and the chairman of the session, the earnest Christian philanthropist MP for Leicester, Thomas Babington, had sent urgently to Downing Street for him. But Spencer Perceval seemed relaxed when he finally arrived, laughing and chatting, dressed smartly in a blue jacket, white waistcoat and charcoal trousers. His penalty for tardiness was a severe one, for if he had been on time he might never have come across John Bellingham, a 41-year-old heavily indebted former employee of the East India Company who nursed a grievance against the government and lay in wait for him, armed with two nine-shilling pistols. As Perceval made his way to the Chamber, Bellingham, who had spent weeks mastering the layout of the building, got as close as he could before drawing a pistol, thrusting it into Perceval's chest and firing. The Prime Minister slumped to the floor at Smith's feet, gasping, 'Murder, oh, murder!' In the ensuing pandemonium Bellingham was seized while Smith and Phillips carried Perceval into an adjacent room, where he died in Phillips' arms. The Commons acted swiftly. Just a week after the murder Bellingham, who had unsuccessfully pleaded insanity, was executed. Barring the assassination of the proto-Prime Minister Buckingham in 1628, Perceval's murder remains unique in British history.*

Perceval was killed at the height of his powers. The impoverished seventh son of an Irish earl,† he had first entered parliament in 1796 as MP for Northampton, and joined the Cabinet as Solicitor-General and then Attorney-General between 1801 and 1806. When the Prime Minister William Pitt the Younger had died at the end of January 1806 (after nearly two decades as premier, with just a brief hiatus between 1801 and 1804) everyone had expected the Home Secretary, Robert Jenkinson, the 2nd Lord Hawkesbury, to take over; but when Hawkesbury was offered the premiership by George III he declined it, telling his sister-in-law that after a mere two hours of thinking about it he knew he did not have the courage to go on. The king reluctantly turned to Pitt's cousin and former Foreign Secretary William, Lord Grenville, who had resigned with Pitt in 1801 when the king refused

---

* There were two other attempts to assassinate a Prime Minister. In 1842 Sir Robert Peel's secretary Edward Drummond was mistaken for his master and murdered in his place, and on 12 October 1984 the IRA attempted to murder Margaret Thatcher during the Conservative party conference in Brighton.

† According to the History of Parliament Trust, though his entry in the *New Oxford Dictionary of National Biography* mentions only three step-brothers, one step-sister and one elder full brother.

to countenance Catholic emancipation. Conscious that the country was tired of the old Pitt team, Grenville now led a new 'Ministry of All the Talents', which included the pedestrian Henry Addington, Viscount Sidmouth (who had filled the Pitt interregnum as Prime Minister from 1801 to 1804), and Pitt's sparring partner Charles James Fox, but not Perceval. The ministry gained twenty-five seats in an autumn election in 1806 and secured the abolition of the transatlantic slave trade (although not yet slavery itself), but itself came to an end when Grenville's proposal to make Catholics eligible for commissions in the army up to the rank of general was turned down by the king and Grenville again resigned.

In the new ministry of Pittites brought together under yet another former premier, the veteran of 1783, the 3rd duke of Portland, Perceval was Chancellor of the Exchequer and Leader in the Commons (with 10 Downing Street as his official residence*), and when Portland stepped down in 1809 following a severe stroke, a stand-off between Perceval and the Foreign Secretary George Canning led to the Cabinet resolving that their opponents, Grenville and Charles Grey, be asked to join a larger administration. When the two Gs refused even to discuss the matter, the Cabinet moved to Plan B, recommending that Perceval take over, which he did on 4 October 1809, together with a band of new ministers, many of them young and untried.

He had already accumulated problems. Just one of his new Cabinet members was an MP – Richard Ryder, the Home Secretary – and, having failed to persuade anyone else to take on the post, Perceval himself had to remain as Chancellor of the Exchequer. The 1809 session of parliament had been difficult enough, as on 20 January Colonel

---

* George II offered 10 Downing Street to Robert Walpole as a personal gift, but he refused it and suggested instead that it be the official residence of the First Lord of the Treasury, the primary title of the king's chief minister. Walpole lived there from 1735, but several prime ministers preferred to live in their own houses, including Pelham, Newcastle, Portland, Wellington, Melbourne and Palmerston. No. 11 Downing Street became the official residence of the Chancellor of the Exchequer in 1828.

Gwyllym Wardle had tabled a resolution that was deeply critical of the king's second son, Frederick, the duke of York, who was commander-in-chief of the army. Wardle had then alleged that one of the duke's mistresses, Mrs Mary Clarke, had sold commissions in the army, and that the duke had profited from this corrupt trade. The ensuing parliamentary inquiry had lasted twelve titillating days, including risqué evidence from Mrs Clarke; Wardle had triumphed when the duke was forced to resign, and for much of the summer the colonel was the toast of every radical coffee-house. But Wardle's fame soon turned to notoriety when a separate court case revealed that he had actually bought Mrs Clarke's evidence, and he collapsed into debt. Then another minister, the War Secretary, Robert Stewart, Viscount Castlereagh,* came under attack both verbally, from radical MPs over his conduct of the Peninsular War, and physically, from his own Cabinet colleague George Canning, with whom he fought a duel on Putney Heath on 21 September. Such was the outrage at this flagrant breach of the law that both men resigned.

So when the 1810 session opened, Perceval had to field a ferocious attack from the wealthy radical baronet Sir Francis Burdett over the failure of the Walcheren expedition† with both a new Foreign Secretary and a new War Secretary. Charles Yorke, the MP for St Germans, robustly defended the expedition in the Commons and successfully ensured that the debate was conducted in secret (gaining himself by way of reward the £2,700 p.a. post of Teller of the Exchequer in February and then the even more lucrative first lordship of the Admiralty three months later). This so incensed Burdett that he condemned the secret sessions, demanded that Wellington's annuity be

* Stewart was known as 'Viscount' Castlereagh following his father's being granted an Irish title as marquess of Londonderry. As with all courtesy titles, this did not bar him from standing as an MP. Prior to the Union with Ireland, he held seats simultaneously in both the Irish and British Commons.

† In July 1809 the United Kingdom had sent a campaign force of 40,000 to the Netherlands to support the Austrian Empire against France. Led by Pitt's elder brother John, 2nd earl of Chatham, the ill-conceived expedition lost 4,000 British troops from disease and by the end of the year it was abandoned.

stopped, attacked the arrest of the publisher John Gale Jones for breach of parliamentary privilege and rushed into print in William Cobbett's *Political Register* with an attack on the House's abuse of its own privilege. This in turn infuriated the Commons, whose Tory Speaker, Charles Abbott, attempted to have Burdett arrested. He, however, barricaded himself into his house at 78 Piccadilly on 6 April as supportive crowds gathered outside. It was not until the ninth that troops managed to force their way in and he was carted off to the Tower, from which a national outcry (and the prorogation of parliament, beyond which the Commons had no power of arrest or imprisonment) ensured his release in the summer. So anxious was the government about social unrest at this time that despite Burdett's manifest contempt for the Speaker's arrest warrant he was not excluded from the House and continued to irritate the government throughout the autumn.

All this would have left Perceval vulnerable had it not been for divisions on the opposition benches. For Grey and Grenville despised Burdett's demagoguery and fell out with Charles James Fox's successor as leader of the Whigs in the Commons, Samuel Whitbread. Even more importantly, the longstanding alliance of Whigs with the king's profligate and estranged son, the Prince of Wales, had soured somewhat, so when George III subsided into his final bout of insanity in late 1810 Perceval was happy to hand the regency over to the prince in February 1811 without fear of being turned out of office in favour of the younger George's old ally Grenville. Indeed, when the Foreign Secretary – another Anglo-Irishman, Richard, Marquess Wellesley* – made a stand in favour of Catholic relief at the start of 1812, a position that might once have endeared him to the prince rather than his father the king, Perceval was easily able to replace him with a rehabilitated Castlereagh. It was clear that Perceval enjoyed both

---

* Wellesley was the eldest son of an Irish peer, the earl of Mornington, and therefore styled Viscount Wellesley until he inherited the Irish earldom in 1781. He was also granted an Irish marquessate and made a United Kingdom baron, with a seat in the House of Lords, in 1799. From 1784 to 1799 he was a Member of the British Parliament.

a stable majority in parliament and solid support from the palace. And then, just as the war was beginning to turn, he was shot dead.

Virtually every aspect of the regency parliament, including the buildings (apart from a new Palladian frontage added by James Wyatt in 1799), the procedures, the electoral system, the religious requirements and the type of person elected, would have been instantly recognizable not just to William Pitt the Younger, but even to his father and *his* father before him – and it was not just the longevity of George III (the first monarch since Edward III to reach a golden jubilee) that helped preserve the institution in aspic. The Commons Chamber, which had already felt full in the reign of Elizabeth I, when there were just 310 members, was now extremely crowded, with 45 MPs for Scotland and 100 for Ireland (since the two Acts of Union), plus two each for Oxford and Cambridge universities, as well as the 92 knights of the shires and 417 burgesses representing the towns and villages for England and Wales – 658 in all. As with many institutions that have grown by steady accretion, there was little coherence to the electoral system. Since 1430 the law had stipulated that only those who held land that could bring in an annual rent of forty shillings or more – of whom there were some 190,000 in the early 1800s – could vote in county elections for the knights of the shire. But there was no uniform franchise for the borough seats. In some the electorate consisted of all the freemen of the borough; in others you had to pay scot and lot,* or hold a burgage tenement,† or be a member of the borough corporation, or be a forty-shilling freeholder to qualify as a voter. Yet other seats were known as 'potwalloper' boroughs, where you could vote if you were a householder, defined as a man with a hearth on which to boil a pot. Only the Irish MPs felt like much of an innovation

---

* A form of local taxation, deriving from the Old English for a payment, *sceot*, and for a share, *lot*. Those who did not have to pay got off 'scot-free'.

† Burgage was a medieval form of rental property in boroughs. Fixed in number, burgage tenements could be conveyed to a candidate or his agent for the period of an election, along with its right to a vote.

– and the same was true in the Lords, which from 1801 sat in the Lesser Hall, formerly the Court of Requests. Centuries of evolving tradition and precedent had resulted in an upper house that now consisted of the twenty-six English and Welsh bishops, who sat for life and could not retire; one Irish archbishop and three bishops, who were chosen in rotation from among the larger number and changed each session; sixteen 'representative peers' elected from among the Scottish nobility at the start of each parliament; twenty-eight Irish peers, elected for life; and a host of dukes, marquesses, viscounts, earls and barons, whose number grew by 209 between 1776 and 1831. In total, the Lords had 334 members in 1801.

True, the undercurrents of religious dissent had brought a new kind of member into the Commons. In the old days Tories had been ardent Anglicans or Scottish Episcopalians (with a few undeclared Catholics for leavening) and Whigs had been avowedly anti-Catholic supporters of the established Protestant church (with a few taciturn supporters of dissenting chapel-goers). The Test Acts still stipulated that all MPs had to take an oath of allegiance to the Protestant faith as established by law. But by the time of the French Revolution the Church of England, debilitated by successive generations of weak and ineffectual bishops, was facing a crisis of faith and the monolith of British confessional politics had split. As early as the 1730s the Welsh MP John Philips, whose son-in-law was the revivalist preacher Griffith Jones, was actively supporting the Wesley brothers and George Whitefield in their 'methodist' lifestyle at Oxford, and by the 1780s John and Charles Wesley were busily converting a large part of the Church of England to their cause. Several MPs and peers were inspired by them, the former including Samuel Gumley and Richard Hill, the 'upright, disinterested and honest' heir to the Tory family estate of Hawkestone, who regularly attracted ridicule in the Commons for his evangelism, declaring, for instance, in a debate on America at the end of Lord North's administration that if the nation wished to be saved, it should turn to Jehovah 'and appease his wrath'. James Adair was buried in the dissenter graveyard at Bunhill

Fields, and the radical anti-corruption campaigner Frederick Bull was a Baptist.

Even more outré, to the conventional Anglican mind, were the Unitarians, who, contrary to the law of the land, denied the doctrine of the Trinity.[1] They too attracted a sprinkling of politicians, including Sir Francis Dashwood, who in addition to forming the Hellfire Club and drafting an abbreviated version of the Book of Common Prayer with Benjamin Franklin, helped build the Unitarians' first chapel in Essex Street off the Strand; and Thomas Brand Hollis, who purchased the seat of Hindon in 1774 only to find his 'election' overturned and himself convicted, fined and jailed for six months. Brand Hollis's subsequent membership of the Society for Constitutional Information and the Revolution Society, and his campaigns for annual elections, equal districts and universal male suffrage, undoubtedly owed much to his religious nonconformity. Also among the supporters of the Essex Street chapel were John Lee, an immensely partisan Solicitor-General in the marquess of Rockingham's second administration in 1782, whose motto was 'never speak well of a political enemy',[2] James Martin, the independently minded MP for Tewkesbury,* whose family ran the Grasshopper bank, and, even more surprisingly, the Prime Minister, the duke of Grafton. The embodiment of this spirit of standalone independence on all fronts, religious, constitutional and political, was another Essex Street adherent, the eminent Cornish barrister John Glynn, who sat for nearly eleven years for Middlesex alongside his client John Wilkes. The freedom of the press, the rights of juries, the administration of justice, American independence: these were his ideological stomping ground, as indeed they were Wilkes's – although Wilkes mischievously told George III: 'Sir, [Glynn] was my counsel – one must have a counsel; but he was no friend; he loves sedition and licentiousness, which I never delighted in. In fact, Sir, he was a Wilkite, which I never was.'[3] In a nation governed according to the rites and

---

* He was nicknamed 'Starling' after a particularly vicious and unexpected speech in 1783.

theology of the established churches of England, Scotland and Ireland, these dissenters were making not just a private declaration of preference, but a very public and ultimately political declaration of allegiance.

Within the Anglican fold, there were the evangelical MPs, too: the likes of Walter Spencer Stanhope, who was first elected in 1775 and remained in parliament until 1812; the Scottish jurist Sir James Mackintosh, who notably defended the French Revolution; Edward Eliot, a minister in Pitt's government from 1783 until his death in 1797; Sir Charles Middleton, a naval commander who turned against the slave trade; Charles Grant; the three Thornton brothers, Henry, Samuel and Robert; the brewer Thomas Buxton, who secured the abolition of the death penalty for forgery; and, most famously, William Wilberforce, who did not experience his personal conversion until 1785 (by which time he had already been an MP for five years) and who went on to be the brightest of lights around whom a whole range of campaigns coalesced. Wilberforce tends to get the attention, but this 'Clapham Sect' of 'Saints' was a tight-knit and well-connected group. Wilberforce was cousin to the three Thornton brothers, Eliot was brother to the earl of St Germans and brother-in-law to Pitt the Younger, and the group had the support of the abolitionist turn-of-the-century bishop of London, Beilby Porteous. These were men for whom independence of mind was not just a personality trait or a political posture but a religious imperative. In debate after debate their zeal was to act as a catalyst for others in the mainstream parties. Sometimes their battles were overtly religious (as in Henry Hoghton's Bill for relief for Protestant dissenters in 1779, or the regular attempts to repeal the Test and Corporation Acts), but often they were ethical (opposition to flogging in the armed forces, or the campaigns for penal reform and the abolition of slavery). Sometimes the piety would grate, and often their political aloofness would infuriate. Witness Robert Thornton's explanation of why he (unlike his two brothers) could not support Grey's parliamentary reform Bill in 1797: 'He would not say that some reform was not requisite; but these were unfriendly times for reformation. In a few years, he hoped it would be otherwise; but when a

House was on fire, a man should think only of extinguishing it.'[4] One can imagine Grey slapping his forehead with disdain (and we know that when Robert got into financial and legal troubles later his brother Henry was mightily upset, considering 'so many prayers have been sent up to the throne of God [on his behalf] and [he] was himself so abundantly furnished with religious instruction').[5] But what the evangelicals gave the pragmatists in parliament was the edge to slice through cynicism, an edge that was to prove vital in securing reform. Typical of their messianic energy was one exchange between Thornton and Wilberforce immediately after the abolition of slavery:

'Well, Henry, what shall we abolish next?'

'The lottery, I think.'[6]

Parliament itself, though, was profoundly resistant to change. The vast majority of MPs still took little interest in their constituents. Indeed, Edmund Burke attempted to make a virtue of such detachment. Having been bumped from his original seat of Wendover for the 1774 election, Burke focused his attentions on Britain's second port, Bristol, where there was a far more open contest. By the time he was nominated, polling had already started, with the radical Henry Cruger vying with two establishment candidates, Matthew Brickdale and Robert Nugent, earl of Clare; yet, despite Cruger's hesitation at running on a joint ticket with Burke, the two won. An elated but cautious Burke thereupon expounded his great theory of parliamentary representation to the electorate:

> It ought to be the happiness and glory of a representative to live in the strictest union, the closest correspondence, and the most unreserved communication with his constituents. Their wishes ought to have great weight with him; their opinion, high respect; their business, unremitted attention. It is his duty to sacrifice his repose, his pleasures, his satisfactions, to theirs; and above all, ever, and in all cases, to prefer their interest to his own. But his unbiased opinion, his mature judgment, his enlightened conscience, he ought not to sacrifice to you, to any man, or to any set of men living . . . Your

> representative owes you, not his industry only, but his judgment; and he betrays, instead of serving you, if he sacrifices it to your opinion.[7]

Whatever his new constituents thought of this at the time, Burke wrote to Rockingham the following year that an annual 'complimentary' visit to the constituency was necessary even in quiet times; but in 1780, just as the election was starting, he had to explain away a four-year absence. As he put it:

> To pass from the toils of a session to the toils of a canvass, is the furthest thing in the world from repose. I could hardly serve you as I have done, and court you too . . . My canvass of you was not on the 'Change nor in the county meetings nor in the clubs of this city: it was in the House of Commons; it was at the Custom House; it was at the Council; it was at the Treasury; it was at the Admiralty.[8]

As always with Burke, the phrases were good; but his absence and his hauteur did him no favours. Having come second in 1774 with 2,707 votes, in 1780 he came a distant fifth with just 18.

Constituencies, it is true, had often tried to rein in their MPs in previous decades, indeed centuries. Boroughs in particular had expected that the issues they valued would be addressed by their members, and in several cases MPs provided written reports of what they had been up to on behalf of their towns. Yet even Burke's declaration set a high threshold for parliamentary representation – a threshold not many MPs would have passed. Many had no constituents to speak of. Pitt the Elder, for instance, sat for Old Sarum, a burgage franchise seat which had returned two members ever since the days of Edward II. Since the cathedral town had moved to New Sarum (Salisbury) many centuries earlier, the only 'voters' were those people nominated to the qualifying tenancies by the owner of the seat, none other than Pitt's father, Thomas Pitt, Lord Camelford. Dunwich in Suffolk had never had a cathedral, but had at least been a thriving port until half its houses fell into the sea, leaving it with a population of 232. Here too, though, it was not resident constituents who chose the two MPs, as the franchise was limited to the borough's freemen, whose numbers could be supplemented by non-residents – as in 1670, when an additional 500 outsiders were dubiously granted freemanship. The Commons eventually took action against such overt rigging of the franchise by limiting the number of freemen to thirty-two, but by the middle of the eighteenth century eight each were appointed by Miles Barne and Joshua Vanneck, so between them they could guarantee that a Barne sat from 1764 to 1832 and a Vanneck from 1768 to 1819. Likewise, Fowey in Cornwall had sent MPs to Westminster since 1571, but under its peculiar arrangements the vote lay with those three hundred or so tenants who paid scot and lot, a list that was determined by the Rashleigh family (who sent seven men to the Commons for Fowey between 1588 and 1818) and that of the earl of Mount Edgcumbe, who accommodated their friends as much as their own kin. Cornwall, indeed, was the *sans pareil* in matters rotten, returning forty-two borough members in 1802, thirty-two of them for seats which since their enfranchisement under the Tudors had always had tiny populations.

Elections were often even less edifying when the constituents did get a look-in, as vying candidates bought votes with utter sangfroid. In 1770 it was discovered that eighty-one enfranchised electors in New Shoreham had set themselves up as a 'Christian Society' and sold their votes to the highest bidder. Since Thomas Rumbold came top of the poll with eighty-seven votes, it was clear that this was wholesale corruption; the franchise was changed and the seat enlarged. The same happened in Cricklade in 1782. The case of another borough, Grampound in Cornwall, shows quite how endemic was such electoral malfeasance. The franchise fell to the freemen who paid scot and lot, but the list of freemen was determined entirely by the corporation, consisting of a mayor and eight aldermen, and they owed their allegiance to Edward Eliot MP, the receiver-general for Cornwall, who in turn happily charged the government up to £3,000 apiece for

Grampound's two seats in each general election between 1761 and 1784. From 1796 onwards, though, this cosy arrangement fell apart, and instead of following the Eliot line the freemen effectively put their votes up for sale to the highest bidder. When they openly boasted of receiving three hundred guineas apiece in 1818, an inquiry led to criminal convictions for the 'borough-monger' Sir Manasseh Lopes and twenty-three electors. Yet even then, successive attempts at a Bill to disenfranchise Grampound, led by Lord John Russell,* were rebuffed before it was finally abolished in 1821 and its seats given to Yorkshire.

In other words, the problem was not just one of members' aloofness from those they represented; the very system was rotten. And attempts to change it met stubborn opposition. In April 1785 Pitt had introduced a modest Bill for piecemeal reform of thirty-six small boroughs and the redistribution of their seats among the counties and London, but it was defeated by a majority of seventy-four. Later attempts at reform launched in 1793 and 1797 by James Maitland, 8th earl of Lauderdale, and Charles Grey, while still an MP, failed by even larger margins of 200 and 150. And when Burdett tabled a motion on 15 June 1809 in favour of universal taxpayer suffrage and equalized constituencies he had the support of just fourteen MPs. Some measures aimed at penal or parliamentary reform did manage to scrape through. Pitt ended the king's election-time grants, and in 1809 a Bill proposed by the Carlisle MP John Curwen outlawed the sale of parliamentary seats. But the Commons was scarcely representative, let alone democratic.

By the time Perceval was succeeded by Lord Liverpool, though, there was a small band of campaigners as zealous for reform of the constitution as Wilberforce was for God. At the courageous forefront of these was Burdett, whose closest ally was the Scottish naval hero of the Napoleonic Wars, Lord Thomas Cochrane. The son of the

---

* Lord John Russell earned his courtesy title of 'Lord' as the third son of the 6th duke of Bedford. He was an MP from 1813 to 1861, when he was made an earl.

impoverished and eccentric earl of Dundonald, Cochrane initially got himself elected at Honiton at the second time of asking in 1806 by paying the 124 voters ten guineas each but went on to win the 1807 Westminster election alongside Burdett. A regular at Burdett's meetings for constitutional reform, in keeping with the wildcat style of his naval career he was the only MP to speak against Burdett's arrest in 1810 and offered to prevent it by mining his house with gunpowder. In January 1812, when Burdett came forth with yet another scheme for reform, he was the only MP to support it. There were other constitutional zealots. Thomas Brand tabled a scheme for reform in 1810 and attracted 115 votes against the government's 234; Thomas Creevey, the illegitimate son of a careless nobleman, advocated reform in the interests of saving government money; George 'Citizen' Tierney, who was elected in Southwark in 1796 under the banner 'peace and reform against war and corruption', lent Whig support to Burdett's regular motions for reform as leader of the opposition between 1816 and 1819; Samuel Whitbread pushed for parliamentary as well as economic reform; Henry Brougham, the Scottish co-founder of the radical *Edinburgh Review*, made constitutional reform the centrepiece of his political argument; and Grey, the *primum mobile* of reform in the 1790s, remained committed. These men regularly attended dinners and meetings to discuss reform at the Crown and Anchor, in Arundel Street by the Strand, though there were often sharp divisions among them, especially between those who urged greater ambition or moderation. For instance, Burdett seems to have loathed and distrusted Whitbread, calling him a 'wealthy brewer who, disappointed of a job, takes in consequence the independent line and bawls out against corruption';[9] and Tierney said of Burdett that he was 'a political seagull, screaming, and screeching and sputtering about foul weather which never arrived'.[10] Nevertheless, with the extra-parliamentary support of William Cobbett, busy publishing searing analyses of the political scene and a daily record of events in the Commons, and Major John Cartwright, elder brother of the inventor of the steam power loom, whose first work on reform, *Take Your Choice*, appeared in 1776,* they had a vehicle for the reform movement and people to drive it.

It is easy to see why some people were opposed to reform, for the system of 'pocket' and 'rotten' boroughs could be amazingly convenient. Of the prime ministers who sat in the unreformed Commons, Robert Walpole sat for Castle Rising, Henry Pelham for Aldborough and Bamber, Pitt the Elder for Aldborough, Pitt the Younger for Appleby, Canning for Newport on the Isle of Wight and Wendover – all of them purchasable boroughs. At one point Newport on the Isle of Wight was represented by two future prime ministers of Anglo-Irish stock: Arthur Wellesley, later duke of Wellington (whose Commons career embraced Rye, Mitchell and a string of safe Irish seats) and Henry Temple, Viscount Palmerston, who also took advantage of the kindness of Bletchingley and Boroughbridge. Other senior political players readily found commodious berths in several of these seats. Henry Fox and his son George sat simultaneously for Hindon in the 1730s; apart from periods as an Irish MP, Castlereagh needed Tregony in 1794–6, Orford in 1796–7, Boroughbridge in 1806, Plympton Erle from 1806 to 1812, Clitheroe in 1812 and Orford again from 1821 until his death; Nicholas Vansittart, a longstanding Chancellor of the Exchequer, briefly sat for Old Sarum and then East Grinstead; and Grey's and Melbourne's Chancellor of the Exchequer John Spencer, Viscount Althorp, found his first seat in Okehampton. Even the reformers were not above taking advantage of the system. Burdett, Sheridan, Tierney, Romilly, Brougham: all sat for borough seats that were eventually abolished, and Thomas Creevey was the sitting member for Downton when it was removed.

So the rotten and pocket boroughs were just part of the system. They greased the political wheels by allowing would-be parliamentarians to start their careers and those already established to continue

* This work led on to the creation of the London Corresponding Society in 1792 and, after its suppression, to Cartwright's formation of the Hampden Clubs in 1812, which were devoted to political and economic reform and were named after the Civil War parliamentary leader, John Hampden.

should one set of voters inconveniently reject them. It also gave the crown a significant advantage, which under George III and during the Regency meant perpetuating an expressly Tory government.

What finally provided the impetus for reform? First, a rising tide of national disaffection with the government throughout the long, fifteen-year term in office (1812–27) of Robert Jenkinson, the 2nd earl of Liverpool. In later years Liverpool would be described by Disraeli as an 'arch-mediocrity', but this was unfair. Liverpool himself was not particularly the problem. Many thought him unobjectionable and insipid – but then, that was precisely why he secured the premiership, as it enabled him to bind together far stronger personalities. The worst his opponent Cobbett could do was ridicule him as Lord Picknose, recounting that he knew 'a Prime Minister who picks his nose and regales himself with the contents'.[11] In similar vein it was rumoured that a Frenchman said Liverpool was so opposed to change that if he had been present at the creation he would have said '*conservons-nous le chaos*'[12] – but then, the whole tenor of his premiership was deliberately conservative (a term first coined by the rebarbative Irish MP John Wilson Croker in an article in the *Quarterly Review* in 1830). Others complained, when he first refused the premiership and accepted the well-rewarded sinecure of Warden of the Cinque Ports instead, that 'the Jenkinson craving disposition will revolt the whole country'.[13]

More to the point was that Liverpool's period saw not just the successful completion of the Peninsular War and the defeat of Napoleon, but severe hardship in the country, thanks to a trade crisis and prolonged economic depression, which politicized a whole new class of workers. In 1811 the Luddites started smashing up the textile machines that they thought were depriving them of work in Nottinghamshire and Derbyshire, and in 1812 there were riots in Sheffield. In 1815 the government prohibited imports of corn until the price should rise above eighty shillings a quarter; following this measure and the subsequent bad harvest, in June 1816 there was a renewed bout of machine-breaking in Loughborough and agricultural workers went on a rampage across middle England – just as Henry Hunt, a friend of Burdett, who had tried to get elected in Bristol, started making a series of tub-thumping speeches in the Spa Fields in London, earning himself the derisive nickname of 'Orator'. Wilberforce wrote from a committee room in the Commons that 'the blasphemous songs and papers of the seditious will disgust all who have any religion, or any decency,'[14] and quietly urged his family to 'pray in earnest against sedition, privy conspiracy and rebellion', but the government's reaction was coercive. Machine-breaking was made a capital offence and seventeen men were executed in January 1813; the Combinations Act of 1801 was enforced against outlawed trade unions; and printers and publishers were arrested. Then, on 28 January 1817, Cochrane marched on the state opening of parliament with some 20,000 petitioners for reform and on the same day the Prince Regent's carriage was attacked en route back to the Palace. The government panicked. Home Secretary Sidmouth claimed in the Lords that the national danger had only been revealed by spies who could not appear openly in court; so habeas corpus was suspended on 3 March 1817 and yet another Treason Act and a Seditious Meetings Act were hurried on to the statute book.

The climax of all these disturbances came on 16 August 1819, when Hunt was invited by the Patriotic Union Society to speak at a meeting in St Peter's Fields in Manchester (a city which still had no parliamentary representation beyond the two Lancashire MPs), called expressly to consider how the people of the city could elect themselves an MP. It was less his (undelivered) speech than the authorities' reaction to the prospect of it that helped stir the parliamentary reformers into action, for the ensuing 'Peterloo massacre', which saw fifteen people killed and at least 400 injured, was widely blamed on the troops who were sent in to arrest Hunt, and the swift repression of the meeting comprehensively confirmed the Liverpool administration's reputation for authoritarianism. Despite widespread public revulsion, the Manchester authorities were exonerated and the organizers of the event imprisoned for sedition, Hunt getting thirty months. On parliament's reassembly that November, Sidmouth resorted yet again to the statute book with six more acts banning any gathering of more than fifty people and tightening the law on publications. When the one true conspiracy of the period, a plot to blow up the whole Cabinet and murder the new King George IV at dinner at Lord Harrowby's Grosvenor Square House (known as the Cato Street Conspiracy after the street off the Edgware Road where it was plotted), was discovered in February 1820, Sidmouth felt his actions had been amply justified.

Such draconian measures did not pass through parliament unchallenged. The poet Byron was particularly eloquent, defending the Luddites in his maiden speech in the Lords in 1812: 'Nothing but absolute want could have driven a large and once honest and industrious body of the people into the commission of excesses so hazardous to themselves, their families and their community,' he began. 'You may call the people a mob, but do not forget that a mob too often speaks the sentiments of the people,' he went on. 'Is there not blood enough upon your penal code, that more must be poured forth to ascend to heaven and testify against you? How will you carry this bill into effect? Can you commit a whole county to their own prisons? Will you erect a gibbet in every field and hang up men like scarecrows?'[15]

The second determining factor was a split within Tory ranks. The first crack had come with a significant Tory rebellion in 1816 over tax. Pitt had introduced income tax in December 1798 to pay for the war with France; Addington had repealed it in 1802, and then reinstated it in 1803 when war recommenced. With victory at Waterloo came an eager national expectation that wartime taxation would be repealed, and although the Chancellor of the Exchequer, Nicholas Vansittart, urged the need to retain it to meet the burgeoning national debt, some eighty MPs from the government benches joined the Whigs in over-throwing it by thirty-seven votes on 18 March 1816. Then, later that year, George Canning, who had been languishing in a minor ambassadorial post, was admitted to the Cabinet – notwithstanding his 'pro-Catholic' views – to be followed in 1819 by the war hero Arthur Wellesley, now duke of Wellington. At first there was the kind of intra-party harmony that only a national crisis can produce. For all their differences, Liverpool, Canning and Wellington formed a single phalanx. But when the general election necessitated by the death of George III on 29 January 1820 produced Whig gains, and when the new king's Bill of Pains and Penalties (by which he sought to divorce Queen Caroline, who was as popular with the country as she was unpopular with him) unravelled to shocking effect, the divisions opened up. Canning was a reluctant participant in the Bill, and Grey managed to corral forty Tory peers to vote with his opposition against the government at second reading. When the Bill struggled through the Lords by only nine votes Canning felt vindicated, as there was clearly little chance of its getting through the Commons; but when the king refused to include Caroline in the Book of Common Prayer's collects for the royal family, he resigned.

By the time of the general election of 1826 the battle-lines were drawn. On the one side stood the Home Secretary Robert Peel,* whose views on Catholicism had been framed by his upbringing in a Protestant household and by six years as Chief Secretary for Ireland. The Irish were poor, he thought, because of their religion. When prosperity arrived they would grow out of it; and in the meantime no relief should be granted them, no quarter given. This, in large measure, was the attitude he brought to the Home Office to which Liverpool appointed him in 1822. Law and order, from penal policy to the administration of prisons, was his forte, and although his consolidation of much penal legislation was long overdue, the number of executions remained high. In the other corner stood Canning, an 'Irishman born in London', as he referred to himself, who had started his political life with republican, Foxite views but had developed an enduring loyalty to Pitt, to whom he adhered until his mentor's death,

---

* Although often referred to as Sir Robert even at this point in his career, Peel did not inherit his father's baronetcy until 1830.

thereby earning himself promotion as Paymaster-General and Treasurer of the Navy. Twice Foreign Secretary, under Portland and Liverpool, he had embraced secessionist movements in Latin America and a style of liberal or at least Pittite Toryism at home, gathering under this banner a band of allies including William Huskisson, William Sturges Bourne, Henry Temple, Viscount Palmerston and Frederick Robinson. It was during a brief period out of office that Canning had secured the first Commons vote in favour of Catholic relief in March 1822, and as Foreign Secretary he had expressed support for those who sought mitigation of the harsh effects of the government's corn laws – thereby earning himself the angry disdain of fellow Cabinet members Peel and Wellington on the two issues that were to dominate the election. With Huskisson now President of the Board of Trade, Palmerston Secretary at War and Robinson Chancellor of the Exchequer, the Canningites were a force to be reckoned with. It was a flaw in the marble that was soon to split it apart.

The third and most important driver of change, though, was a string of untimely and inconvenient departures from the political stage. First, on Saturday, 17 February 1827, Liverpool was laid low by a massive stroke. A month later he was still barely able to speak and on 12 April, after prevaricating longer than was wise, the king reluctantly appointed Canning as Prime Minister, despite the fact that plenty of senior figures, including Wellington and Peel, refused to serve under him. By dint of appointing his brother-in-law the 4th duke of Portland as Lord Privy Seal, persuading three Whigs (the marquess of Lansdowne, Lord Carlisle and George Tierney) to join the Canningites (Robinson, Huskisson and Sturges Bourne), and promising the king that he would not enact parliamentary reform, Canning cobbled together a coalition government of moderates in his own liberal like-ness. But physically Canning was not in agood state: he had long suffered from gout, and in January he had caught a severe chill at the duke of York's funeral (a particularly icy affair which reputedly led to the death of the bishop of Lincoln, George Pelham). In July 1827 he fell ill again, just as parliament was prorogued, and on 8 August he died.*

On Canning's death, one Whig quipped that 'God has declared against us. He is manifestly for the Tories, and I fear the king also, which is much worse,'[16] but Canning's appointment had riven both political parties. The Tories were now split between the Canningites, who countenanced Catholic emancipation, and those for whom it was anathema; and the Whigs between those who were prepared to put parliamentary reform on the back burner and those for whom it was the primary goal. The king, who had taken exception to Wellington's and Peel's refusal to serve under Canning, decided to stick with the centrist coalition and appointed Robinson (who had been elevated to the Lords as Viscount Goderich in January and had been Canning's Leader in the Lords) as his mentor's successor, so that the more effective and more popular Huskisson had to content himself with the posts of Colonial Secretary and Leader of the Commons. But Canning was a hard act to follow and Goderich was not up to the task. When a mob had attacked his London home over his role as the architect of the corn laws, he had cried in parliament and earned himself the nickname the 'blubberer'. Now he led a feeble, lacklustre government, and by the turn of the year George IV had decided to draft in the duke of Wellington as Prime Minister with Peel as his leader in the Commons. Goderich's ministers had never even had to face parliament.

Although the old Canningites had misgivings about the direction of the new Wellington administration, they decided at first to remain in office; but when a minor parliamentary reform to reallocate the rotten seats of Penryn and East Retford to Manchester and Birmingham was defeated by the government, Palmerston and Huskisson tendered their resignations. For the two liberal Tories, it was the first time they had been out of office since 1809 and 1814 respectively. Portland's grandson Charles Greville wrote in his diary:

* Canning notched up a couple of records. His 119 days as Prime Minister is still the shortest tenure; and he was the last Foreign Secretary not to have a title until Arthur Balfour, the nephew of a marquess, in 1916 and Ramsay MacDonald in 1924.

'we have now got a Tory govt., and all that remained of Canning's party are gone.'[17]

The ability to count is a vital political skill. Wellington was a national hero, but the arithmetic was against him, both in parliament, where the reunited Whigs pushed through a motion to repeal the Corporation and Test Acts with a comfortable majority of forty-four (and another motion for Catholic relief), and in Ireland, where William Vesey-Fitzgerald, MP for Clare, lost the by-election caused by his appointment as President of the Board of Trade to the charismatic leader of the Catholic Association, Daniel O'Connell, who could not take his seat without swearing the specified oath 'that the sacrifice of the mass, and the invocation of the blessed Virgin Mary and other saints, as now practised by the Church of Rome are impious and idolatrous'. Even Peel now reckoned that full Catholic emancipation was the only answer, as the Protestant ascendancy in Ireland was no more and the Catholic majority, who could vote as forty-shilling freeholders, would not now return a Protestant MP. He was not alone in this dawning recognition: Burdett's attempt to introduce a Catholic relief measure just seven weeks before Liverpool's death had attracted the support of Canning but failed by just four votes. But when Wellington and Peel announced their change of mind, they faced considerable opposition on their own side from the likes of Sir Edward Knatchbull and the romantically inclined 29-year-old Cornish baronet Sir Richard Vyvyan. Knatchbull was the kind of sturdily pious man who would take pleasure in his own no-nonsense bluffness and not knowing too much about religion. Greville dismissed him as being 'anti-everything',[18] and Cobbett caustically thought him 'not gifted with much light'.[19] He may well have been motivated by Peel's failure to secure the Oxford Regius professorship of Hebrew for his brother Wyndham; either way, the Knatchbull brand of stubborn piety was the stuff of whips' nightmares. As he wrote to his second wife, Jane Austen's niece:

> To act upon a uniform and steady principle, to adhere to what is
> right and to abstain from what is wrong, to afford the best example

in my power, never to obtrude my opinions, but never upon proper occasions to be ashamed or afraid of avowing them – these have been the rules upon which I have acted, and I believe that they will bring peace at the last.[20]

This was stomach-turning self-indulgence, really, but in his mind true Toryism meant ardent protectionist defence of British agriculture and passionate anti-Catholicism; so over the coming months he and Vyvyan, who lived just a few doors apart in Great George Street in Westminster, built a Tory 'Ultra' faction on the back of opposition to Catholic relief. In the Lords the archbishop of Canterbury, William Howley, whom Wellington had only recently and reluctantly promoted from his see in London, openly attacked the measure, as did the archbishop of Armagh, the normally conciliatory Lord John Beresford, younger son of the marquess of Waterford. At the height of the row Peel, the member for Oxford University, which was universally opposed to emancipation, even suffered the double indignity first of having to fight a by-election, when his unwisely tendered resignation as MP was accepted by the university vice-chancellor, and then of losing it. As a result, Peel was only able to present the Roman Catholic Relief Bill to the Commons on 5 March 1829 thanks to the machinations of Sir Manasseh Lopes, who just a year after his imprisonment for electoral fraud at Grampound in 1819 had returned himself to parliament by purchasing the pocket borough of Westbury, another burgage seat; this he now vacated for Peel, in the expectation of a peerage (which failed to materialize).

However dodgy the means, Peel and Wellington secured their ends, as the Act was passed on 24 March 1829, abolishing the dis-criminatory oaths, enabling Catholics to vote in all elections and sit as peers or MPs, and raising the threshold for voters from forty shillings to ten pounds. The Tory Ultras howled that Peel was performing a hideous U-turn, but Peel confessed that he yielded only because he was 'too sincerely attached to the Protestant [faith] to push his resist-ance to concessions to that point which should endanger the very existence of the institutions that he wished to defend'.[21] He was not the last to have to declare that a good minister could not be bound by past declarations.

If Peel thought that the concessions on the Test and Corporation Acts and on Catholic relief would assuage the demands for constitutional change, he was wrong. If anything, the campaigners for parliamentary reform became bolder. The Whigs had been reunited by the collapse of the Goderich ministry and were now led by Charles, the 2nd Earl Grey, who had first advocated reform in 1793; when Peel had to see off 173 Tories in the Commons and 109 in the Lords and rely on the Whigs to get Catholic relief through, they knew the tide was with them. The Tories' divisions were further laid bare in February 1830 when the loyal address, the government's statement of its own *raison d'être*, was opposed by Knatchbull. Clearly the Ultras would risk a change of administration rather than assist a liberal Tory one.

And then death interposed itself in politics once again when George IV shuffled off his considerable mortal coil on 26 June 1830. His brother, the new and more popular King William IV, dissolved parliament on 23 July, precipitating another general election. Wellington, still a convinced opponent of parliamentary reform, faced it at the head of a divided party, with the old Canningites still excluded and Knatchbull's Ultra-Tories angry and disillusioned. The polls, which continued until 1 September, confirmed the awkward truth that Wellington needed the support of the Canningites if he was to continue in office. There was some hope that they might be wooed back, and on 15 September 1830 there was an informal opportunity for Wellington and Huskisson to bridge the gap when they were both in Huskisson's Liverpool constituency for the celebrations to launch the Liverpool-to-Manchester railway, along with the Tory chief whip, Billy Holmes, who was keen to effect a reconciliation between the two men. Wellington had ridden in his own carriage, and when the trains reached the mid-point at Parkside and stopped to take on water, at Holmes's urging Huskisson alighted (disregarding the instruction to the contrary) and made his way along the tracks in the light drizzle to the duke's carriage – only to notice, too late, that George Stephenson's *Rocket* was thundering towards him. The Staffordshire MP Edward Littleton dragged the Austrian ambassador, Prince Esterházy, to safety and Holmes, who had intended to join Huskisson, managed to hang tight to the side of the main carriage, but as Huskisson tried to scramble back into it, he was caught swinging on the open door and took the full force of the approaching engine. With his right leg horribly mangled, he died later that day of his injuries – and along with him died any attempt at an accommodation between Wellington's Tories and Huskisson's supporters.

The sole question now was what the Whigs would do. Henry Brougham had run a well-publicized and noisy election campaign in Yorkshire expressly on the platform of parliamentary reform, and by dint of his frequent repetition of the reform mantra (and his unexpected victory) he had managed to screw the Whig leadership's courage to the sticking point, so that by the time the last poll was in it was clear that the party and the country stood four-square behind reform. This meant that when it came to the loyal address debate in the Lords exactly two months after Huskisson's death, on 15 November, Wellington was signing his own political execution papers when he told the House:

> I am not only not prepared to bring in any measure of the description alluded to by the noble lord [Grey], but I will at once declare that as far as I am concerned, as long as I hold any station in the Government of the country, I will always feel it my duty to resist such measures when proposed by others.[22]

Wellington having thus declared himself implacably opposed to reform, Peel lost a Commons vote of no confidence on the civil list that same day (in which Knatchbull and the Ultras voted with the Whigs) by a margin of 233 to 204. Wellington dutifully resigned and was replaced by Grey, armed with a clear mandate for reform, a clean sweep of new ministers and the support of the Canningites Palmerston and Melbourne.

PARLIAMENT: THE BIOGRAPHY

*

Today Earl Grey stands forty metres above Newcastle upon Tyne on a pedestal as distinguished as that provided for Nelson in Trafalgar Square, and to many of his political friends he was equally unapproachable in real life. Like a surprising number of politicians he was that strange hybrid personality, an ambitious introvert, whose bouts of introspection, especially when he met failure, would turn to despondency. Often he was physically distant, tucked away on his estate in Howick in Northumberland, but even when he was in London he could seem cold and aloof, quite unlike his early ally Fox. Yet Grey had one quality above all others: perseverance. So the young man who pushed again and again for reform, addressed dinner after dinner and attended meeting after meeting, the middle-aged man who spent twenty-one years as an MP before inheriting his father's earldom, became Prime Minister at the age of sixty-six. He had complained to his wife after his maiden speech in the Lords: 'What a place to speak in! with just light enough to make darkness visible, it was like speaking in a vault by the glimmering light of a sepulchral lamp to the dead. It is impossible I should ever do anything there worth thinking of.'[23] Yet in leading the government from the Lords, while he had the difficult task of taking the Reform Bill through that House (along with the pugnaciously populist new Lord Chancellor Baron Brougham), the initial battle in the Commons was not in his hands, but in those of two of the more popular and amiable scions of the nobility: John Spencer, Lord Althorp, the genial eldest son of the 2nd Earl Spencer, and Lord John Russell, respectively Chancellor of the Exchequer and Paymaster-General. When a special committee chaired by John Lambton and led by Russell reported its findings, it was clear that the government had taken Brougham's injunctions to heart. Massive reform was planned, touching more than 150 parliamentary boroughs.

It was always going to be a tall order, steering the Bill through the two houses of parliament. In the Commons many MPs would be voting for the abolition of their own seats, and the Lords was stacked against reform. Ever since their arrival in 1707 the Scottish representative peers had tended to be government supporters. Mostly poorer than the English peers and forced to bear the expense of re-election every time a new parliament was called, they were perceived as vulnerable to offers of lucrative positions. Also, the block voting system which entitled each Scottish noble to vote for sixteen peers effectively created a ministerial slate. In the early days this meant a preponderance of Whigs with just a smattering of Tories, but by the mid-eighteenth century the majority were Tories (notably including the Prime Minister, the earl of Bute). The government's hold over the Lords was further strengthened in 1782 when the House repealed the rule that prevented a Scottish peer who received a British title (which would normally entitle him to a seat in the Lords) from sitting there, unless elected as a representative peer.* Just as Pitt had done when in need of extra votes in the Lords, Grey now had a few Scottish representative peers appointed as lords in the United Kingdom peerage, guaranteeing a few more votes by freeing up representative Scottish seats for other government supporters from the Scottish peerage. Similarly, after the Union with Ireland in 1801, the Irish representative peers (who unlike the Scots were elected for life) also tended to be government supporters; and additional Irish peers could be added to the supporting ranks by giving them UK peerages.

But the most acutely embarrassing opposition in the Lords came from the thirty bishops. In the normal course of things, they would be expected to vote with the supreme head of their church, the king; but Pitt had made thirty-three bishops, Liverpool twenty-four, Addington eight, Portland twelve and Wellington eight, so that by 1830 their graces were in the main a Tory bunch. At the time of the Reform Bill they were led by William Howley, archbishop of Canterbury from 1828, a haughty, illiberal man who had vigorously opposed Catholic emancipation and the Jewish civil disabilities Bill; and he was far from unique in his attitudes. Indeed, during Sir Samuel Romilly's campaign

---

*The rule had originally been instigated on the grounds that the Act of Union had fixed the number of Scots in the British House of Lords.

to restrict the application of the death penalty seven bishops voted against abolishing it for shoplifting; and in his sarcastic 1837 review of the peerage, William Carpenter said of Christopher Bethel, Wellington's appointee as bishop of Bangor, that 'he has, in his place in parliament, lent his aid to every illiberal and intolerant measure; in short, he has exhibited himself as a good Tory bishop'.[24] Disraeli later scathingly commented on Liverpool's episcopal appointments that 'he sought for the successors of the apostles, for the stewards of the mysteries of Sinai and of Calvary, among third rate hunters after syllables',[25] and he was right. One Liverpool appointee, Thomas Burgess, the bishop of Salisbury from 1825, wore his Tory heart ostentatiously on his sleeve, and one of Wellington's last appointments was Henry Phillpotts, the combative bishop of Exeter from November 1830, who had attacked Lambton's support for the Manchester rioters eleven years earlier. Many were drawn from the lower echelons of the aristocracy. Durham regularly had aristocratic bishops; Charles Manners-Sutton, archbishop of Canterbury from 1805, was the grandson of the duke of Rutland; George Pelham, at Lincoln, described as 'the weakest sycophant on the bench',[26] was the son of the earl of Chichester; George Murray of Rochester was nephew to the duke of Atholl; and John Banks Jenkinson at St David's was Liverpool's cousin. There were even two brother gentleman bishops, Charles Sumner of Winchester and John Bird Sumner of Chester. These last two voted for Catholic emancipation, but across the preceding fifty years just three bishops dipped their croziers in liberalism: Richard Watson of Llandaff (1782–1816); the longstanding Henry Bathurst at Norwich (1805–37); and Charles Blomfield, bishop of London from 1828. It was little wonder that Grey appointed the Regius professor of political economy at Oxford, Richard Whateley, as archbishop of Dublin in 1831 in the hope of diluting the Tory strength on the bench (though he later bitterly regretted the appointment of his own hopelessly ineffectual and frequently Tory brother Edward as bishop of Hereford in 1832).

The battle started in the Commons, where Russell presented the first Reform Bill on 1 March 1831, rising to speak at six o'clock in the evening and continuing for two hours. First the good news: the cities that were to be enfranchised for the first time, including Manchester, Birmingham and Leeds. Then the bad news: the seats to be abolished. Or, in the prim words of Hansard: 'The noble Lord accordingly read the following list, in the course of which he was frequently interrupted by shouts of laughter, cries of "Hear, Hear!" from Members for those boroughs and various interlocutions across the Table.'[27] Old England passed before the House's eyes as Great Bedwyn, Fowey, Tregony, Camelford were listed for the cull in two lengthy schedules detailing the borough seats to be abolished and those to be reduced to a single member. The anti-reformer John Wilson Croker's seat at Aldeburgh in Suffolk was to go, as was Boroughbridge, whose MP, Wellington's former Attorney-General Sir Charles Wetherell, 'threw down his notes with a mixture of despair and ridicule and horror'.[28] Seemingly the only concession to conservatism was the refusal to introduce triennial parliaments, as it was felt 'inexpedient to make the durations of parliament so short that the Members of this House are kept in a perpetual canvass'.[29]

It was revolutionary stuff, albeit spoken by an aristocrat, and it attracted a fierce and immediate reaction from the very man who had defeated Peel in his Oxford University by-election, Sir Robert Inglis – and then from Knatchbull, from Vyvyan, from Croker and a string of other Tories. The bibulous Wetherell, of whom the Speaker had once noted that 'the only lucid interval he had was the one between his waistcoat and his breeches', accused Althorp of acting as a new Cromwell, ejecting members like Oliver or hanging abbots like Thomas. And so it went on for seven days of sharp debate. 'Orator' Hunt, now MP for Preston, detailed some of the corrupt practices customary in elections in asserting his support for the Bill. The writer Thomas Babington Macaulay stood by it, too, declaring in his maiden speech that its whole aim was simply 'to admit the middle classes to a large and direct share in the Representation without any violent shock to the institutions of our country',[30] and demanding:

Does there remain any species of coercion which was not tried by Mr Pitt and Lord Londonderry [Castlereagh]? We have had laws, we have had blood. New treasons have been created. The press has been shackled. The Habeas Corpus Act has been suspended. Public meetings have been prohibited. The event has proved that these were mere palliatives. You are at the end of your palliatives. The evil remains.[31]

Peel, who might so easily have shut down debate with a simple demand for a vote the moment Russell finished speaking (and might have won it), saved his words for last. He excoriated the government for bringing forward constitutional innovation when the country was crying out for economic measures. He acknowledged that giving votes to half a million people would be popular. How could it not be? 'But these are vulgar arts of government,' he argued, warning: 'Others will outbid you, not now, but at no remote period – they will offer votes and power to a million of men, will quote your precedent for the concession, and will carry your principles to their legitimate and natural consequence.'[32]

Brougham had feared a sudden vote would lose the Bill and Billy Holmes reckoned on securing 356 votes against it, but when the second reading vote came on 22 March, there was a record attendance of 608 MPs. Members looked round nervously. Joseph Hume, the radical Scottish government whip, made a rough calculation, but when the division was called on Vyvyan's amendment to delay consideration by six months, the opponents of the Bill (the Ayes on the motion to delay) trooped out and the reformers remained seated.* The result was as tight as could be – the Noes had 302 and the Ayes 301. The Bill could proceed into committee, thanks to the absence of Knatchbull, who was ill, and the single vote of John Calcraft, who despite calling himself 'a reformer' had spoken virulently against the Bill's interfer-

* There were as yet no division lobbies: this innovation, in both Commons and Lords, was brought in when the new Palace of Westminster was built after the fire of 1834.

ence in the 'balance of the Constitution', but voted for it after an eleventh-hour conversion.

Russell was not out of the woods yet, though, for General Isaac Gascoyne's wrecking amendment, insisting that the total number of seats in England and Wales should not be reduced, was carried by eight votes on 19 April. At this point, Grey determined to go over the heads of both the Commons and the Lords (where he expected an even harder time), and persuaded William IV to turn up in person to dissolve parliament on 22 April and force an election. His gamble paid off. By the time the Commons met again the Tories had been wiped from the field like so much chaff and, with 370 MPs, Grey had a clear majority of 135. The second attempt was now assured success in the Commons, which carried the Bill in September with a majority of more than a hundred. This left the Lords, whose key debate started on Friday, 7 October 1831. Wise counsel would have urged caution on the Tory peers, but they behaved more like Ultras than Canningites. The debate was as torrid as ever, feelings probably raised rather than calmed by Lord Chancellor Brougham's late-night contribution, for all its erudition and passion. After a three-hour expostulation, he ended: 'I pray and exhort you not to reject this measure. By all you hold most dear; by all the ties that bind every one of us to our common order and common country, I solemnly adjure you – I warn you – I implore you – yea, on my bended knees, I supplicate you – reject not this bill.'[33] Brougham was not speaking metaphorically. He had got down on his knees, and remained there for some time as if in prayer, while his astonished peers looked on. Finally, fearing that he had drunk too much mulled port at dinner, they picked him up off the floor and deposited him safely on the Woolsack.

The vote came at six-thirty on the Saturday morning. Brougham and Grey had lost by just forty-one votes (199 to 158), with the proxies falling 49 to 30 against. The arithmetic was telling. Eleven Scottish peers voted against and three in favour, while among the Irish peers fifteen voted against and just four in favour. Even more strikingly, the bench of bishops turned out in force, and just one, Bathurst, voted for the Bill; twenty-one voted against. (One other bishop, Blomfield, who had spoken in favour of the Bill, was not present for the vote owing to his father's death.) It did not take people long to work out that if the bishops had voted with the government the Bill would have passed. That night there were riots in Derby, Nottingham and Bristol. The duke of Newcastle's home was attacked. So was that of Lord Middleton. But, as John Stuart Mill wrote, 'the first brunt of indignation has fallen upon the Prelacy. Every voice is raised against allowing them to continue in the House of Lords, and if I did not express my conviction of their being excluded from it before this day five years, it is only because I doubt whether the House itself will last so long.'[34] It was not just constitutional change that people sought, though, for revenge was on the mob's mind when the bishop of Exeter's palace was attacked and Bristol's palace was burned down. Russell put things more moderately in the Commons, stating that it was 'impossible that the whisper of a faction should prevail against the voice of a nation'.[35]

Mob violence might hope to change parliamentary minds but it could not change the rules of parliament, which stipulated that no Bill could be presented twice in the same session; so after the Commons passed a motion supporting Grey's ministry, the king prorogued parliament, a new session began in December and a third, very similar Bill was carried in the Commons in March 1832. This brought the matter back to the Lords. Their second reading debate, held over four days in April, was particularly heated, in no small measure thanks to the snide, incendiary contribution from the reactionary bishop of Exeter, Henry Phillpotts, who attacked Grey for 'ambition' and an assault on the church. Grey responded caustically in winding up, complaining that the bishop 'threw out insinuations about my ambition. Let me tell him calmly, that the pulses of ambition may beat as strongly under sleeves of lawn as under an ordinary habit.' Indeed, he continued,

a speech more unbecoming the situation of a Christian Bishop – a speech more inconsistent with the love of peace – a speech more remote from the charity which ought to distinguish a Clergyman of his order – a speech more replete with insinuations and charges, calculated to promote disunion and discord in the community, never was uttered within the walls of this or any other House of Parliament.[36]

The vote came at seven in the morning on 14 March. Notwithstanding the king's assertion that 'the bishops are in that house to defend my crown and not to follow vagaries of their own',[37] the thirty prelates divided twelve in favour (including those of York, London, and Bath and Wells, the last despite his nephew Lord Ellenborough being a prominent opponent) and fifteen against (including Canterbury, Armagh, Exeter, and both Carlisle and Oxford, who voted like their respective brothers, the earl of Beverley and Lord Bagot), the remaining three failing to vote. Two royal dukes also voted against. According to a swift computation appended to Hansard, the Scots and Irish were overwhelmingly against, by twenty-nine to eight, but the British peers (157:130) swung the day. Hansard's figures don't add up, but once the 105 proxy votes had been added in the second reading was carried by nine votes, by 184 to 175. The battle was still not over, though. Seventy-three peers swiftly signed a protest tabled by Wellington, and when the Bill moved into committee on 7 May the Lords agreed a wrecking amendment by a majority of thirty-five. The Cabinet met the next day and decided that the only way forward was the mass creation of peers. When William refused, Grey resigned on 9 May and Wellington was asked to try to form a new government, even though he could command just 235 members of the Commons. After five days, during which mass petitions were presented to the Commons, £1.5 million was withdrawn from the Bank of England in panic, and Peel refused to serve as Leader in the Commons lest he yet again have to assent to legislation against which he had fought in opposition, Wellington gave up and Grey was reappointed. As was to happen again in 1911, the king secretly asked Tory peers to desist from opposition; but when Wellington persisted in ranting at the ministry and refusing to let the Bill pass unamended, William allowed Grey subtly to let it be known that he had the means to ensure the Bill was passed if necessary and assiduously lobbied opponents of the Bill to stay away. The discreet royal arm-twisting finally gained purchase. The Bill made 'rapid and almost unobstructed progress' through its remaining stages,[38] with both Tory peers and bishops absent, and royal assent was granted to the Reform (England) Bill on 7 June. The Secretary at War, Sir John Hobhouse, happily proclaimed: 'Thus ends this great national exploit. The deed is done.'[39] But Wellington moaned that 'the government of England is destroyed', and the poet William Wordsworth charged the government with 'committing a greater polit- ical crime than any committed in history'.[40]

From the opposite perspective, too, for the likes of Orator Hunt the Bill was far from perfect. The vast majority of working men still had no vote, and the ballot was still not secret, nor even conducted on a single day. Moreover, the property qualifications for candidacy, at £600 p.a. for a county seat and £300 p.a. for a borough seat, excluded many. A number of rotten boroughs had gone, but some seats still had very few electors. Totnes, for instance, retained two MPs with an electorate of just 217, of whom 179 voted in 1832, and Reigate had only one MP, but only 165 electors – of whom in 1835 just 99 voted, so that 50 voters could still return a member. Yet in the newly enfranchised Liverpool, candidates for the two seats were chasing 11,300 voters (of whom 8,600 made it to the 1832 poll), and the south of England (with 174 seats) was still dramatically over-represented compared to the north (with 58).

But for all these caveats, nearly four decades after he had first advanced a scheme for moderate parliamentary reform, Charles Grey had landed his catch. His moderation had undoubtedly secured success; but he had hated the vitriolic debates, asserting that, 'much as I have been engaged, all my life, in political contention, there is no one to whom this kind of strife is more painful'.[41] Exhausted as he was by the struggle, he was not shy of taking advantage of the evident disarray in Tory ranks, though. Parliament was dissolved on

3 December 1832 and a general election was held under the new Act. The dogmatic Croker refused even to stand for the reformed House, an attitude that totally mystified his long-time friend Wellington. But even if he had stood, he would have made little impact. Grey was rewarded with a resounding victory for the Whigs, who returned 441 MPs, 109 of them unopposed. With Daniel O'Connell's party (devoted to the repeal of the Act of Union) securing 42 and the Tories 175, the Whigs alone had a technical majority of 224 and an effective one of 308. Reform was not just its own reward.

PAPA COBDEN TAKING MASTER ROBERT A FREE TRADE WALK.

The Conservative Prime Minister Sir Robert Peel had long supported the corn laws, but in 1846 he backed Richard Cobden's Anti Corn Law League and urged their repeal, against the wishes of many of his own party. Peel won the vote, but with his party split down the middle he was forced to resign three days later.

2

A Liberal and a Conservative

THE FIRE STARTED IN THE basement early in the evening of Thursday, 16 October 1834. That afternoon, workmen had been burning two cartloads of old wooden Exchequer tally sticks in the stoves underneath the House of Lords. At five o'clock, in a hurry to go home, they bundled the last of the tallies into the stoves and left them to burn themselves out. Somehow the stoves overheated and a chimney flue caught fire. At about six-thirty that evening, one of the doorkeepers' wives spotted flames under a closed door and raised the alarm. Within half an hour the Lesser Hall was engulfed, and by eight o'clock a strong south-westerly wind had fanned the blaze down a series of wood-panelled corridors into St Stephen's Chapel, where Wren's balcony and false ceiling and the medieval wall paintings under Wyatt's whitewash were rapidly consumed in the inferno. Suddenly there was a great crash as the roof caved in – loud enough to start rumours of a new gunpowder plot. Against the sky the crowds that gathered in boats and on the far bank of the river could see the conflagration making its way towards the Great Hall, where fire engines were brought into the hall itself so as to douse the wooden ceiling with as much water as possible. Parliament had been prorogued on 14 August, so few members of the government were in town; by the time the Prime

Minister and Speaker turned up, it was clear that most of the medieval palace had been destroyed. All that was saved was the Jewel Tower, the cloisters and chantry, the Speaker's dining room (which sat immediately beneath the old Commons and is now the Crypt chapel) and the Great Hall.

Some were not entirely upset by the loss of the old higgledy-piggledy palace. William Ewart Gladstone, for one, recalled the lack of facilities when he first arrived as a Tory MP in 1832: 'What I may term corporeal conveniences were . . . marvellously small. I do not think that in any part of the building it afforded the means of so much as washing the hands.'[1] Many a member was pleased that the king's offer of the dingy Buckingham Palace as a replacement was rejected and a design competition was launched for a comprehensive reconstruction of the whole site while work progressed with amazing celerity to provide an interim home for each of the two houses. As the walls of the Lesser Hall and Painted Chamber were sounder than those of St Stephen's, they were reroofed and fitted out for, respectively, the Commons and the Lords in time for the opening of a new parliament on 19 February 1835.

By then the government had also been undergoing major reconstruction. Despite the fact that there had been three general elections in three years and the parliament was due to last until 1839, William dissolved it on 29 December 1834. The battles over the Reform Act and the abolition of slavery throughout the dominions had worn Grey down. By the end of the parliamentary session in 1833 he confessed: 'I feel wearied and oppressed from the moment I get up till I go to bed, and I think it will be impossible for me to go through the work of another session.'[2] So when the Whigs started to implode the following summer, with a corridor of ministers resigning over plans to appropriate to the crown some of the revenues of the Irish church, Grey stood down in July, aged seventy. William IV turned to the Canningite Home Secretary, William Lamb, 2nd Viscount Melbourne, a louche but diffident man (one colleague thought him 'lax in morals, indifferent in religion and very loose and pliant in politics'[3]), whose first reaction was to worry that being Prime Minister might involve rather too much work.* It was only when his secretary told him: 'Why, damn it, such a position never was occupied by any Greek or Roman, and, if it only lasts two months, it is well worth while to have been Prime Minister of England,'[4] that he deigned to attend on the king. And indeed, Melbourne's first government did not last long: on 14 November 1834 William summarily sacked the government and asked the Opposition leader, Sir Robert Peel (who happened to be abroad at the time), to form a new Tory one. Overtures were made to some of the Whigs who had resigned, but it was clear that Peel could not last a parliamentary session unless the country overturned the Whigs' Commons majority. So, with the Palace of Westminster a building site, the parties went to the polls.

When the new parliament gathered on 19 February 1835, the numbers were tight. If the Whigs, the radicals and the Irish members could combine, they could probably defeat Peel. The first skirmish came on day one, as the sitting Speaker, Charles Manners-Sutton, son of an archbishop and scion of the earls of Rutland, was a Tory. In 1832 he had defeated the radicals' candidate, Edward Littleton, with Whig government support, but this time, thanks to anger about the way in which the king had tried to force a Peel government on the Commons, the Whigs turfed him out, after eighteen years in office, on a vote of 316 to 306 in favour of the Scottish lawyer James Abercromby. With just ten votes in it Peel must have thought all was to play for, but in the first week of April he was defeated three times in the Commons, and

* Although the term 'Prime' or 'First' Minister had been informally recognized since the days of Walpole, normally combined with the post of First Lord of the Treasury and Chancellor of the Exchequer, some still denied its existence well into the nineteenth century; it had no written legal status until 1878, when Disraeli signed the Treaty of Berlin as 'First Lord of the Treasury and Prime Minister of her Britannic Majesty', and statutory recognition of the post came even later, with the Chequers Estate Act 1917 and the Ministers of the Crown Act 1937. Gladstone and Balfour both bemoaned the fact that a man with so much power had so little to show for it in formal title or privilege; and indeed, the Prime Minister's powers are still largely a matter of convention.

after 120 days in office he resigned. Back came Melbourne as Prime Minister, a post he was to retain for six further years, four of them as avuncular mentor to the young Queen Victoria.

These years saw a fundamental reconstruction of the party political system in parliament. For although the 1832 Act had not extended the franchise to all that many voters, and many of the patronage seats still existed, it had effectively demolished the Tory party and created a new party in its stead. Even in prospect, parliamentary reform had challenged the central Tory tenets of protecting the inherited constitution, the right to property, and respect for the monarchy, the church and the Lords. When the Bill appeared it pushed the Tories into a defensive, reactionary posture and they began to think of themselves as conservators of the national interest, 'conservatives' rather than Tories. As one anonymous author put it in 1830: 'We now are, as we have always been, decidedly and conscientiously attached to what is called the Tory, and which might with more propriety be called the Conservative Party.'[5] And when the measure was enacted, the new electorate removed a whole swathe of Tory MPs. But the Act also gave them a chance to recover, for one of its provisions was that voters had to pay a shilling to register to vote, every year in the case of borough seats, once only in the counties. Suddenly registration campaigns became every bit as important as parliamentary debates or sound policy, and from now on party organization would matter at least as much as aristocratic patronage. In this fresh enterprise the new Conservatives took the lead: soon after the 1831 election fifteen Tories met in Charles Street off St James's Square and decided to set up a party headquarters, much in the mould of the new gentlemen's clubs that were springing up around the Mall, but designed expressly to oppose reform. This initial venture collapsed in debt, but on 10 March 1832 another meeting was held in the Thatched House Tavern in St James's Street, with the short, aggressive (and extremely fecund) James Gascoyne-Cecil, the 2nd (and least significant) marquess of Salisbury, in the chair. A week later the new club members took a short lease of 2 Carlton Terrace, the home of

William Edwardes, Lord Kensington, and named themselves the Carlton Club. Within three years the club had moved to new purpose-built premises in Pall Mall and counted virtually every Conservative peer and MP among its eight hundred members, as it housed the Conservative whips' office (initially under Billy Holmes); and it became the organizing base for registration drives and for the selection of Conservative candidates. The *Edinburgh Review* reckoned that 'from the first it was a political association organised for party and parliamentary purposes',[6] and so central did it become to Conservative fortunes that Gladstone joined as a young Tory MP in 1833, Benjamin Disraeli canvassed hard for membership when he lost in High Wycombe in 1835 and Anthony Ashley Cooper worried that he might have to resign when he voted against Conservative ministers on the Ten Hours Bill in 1842. In the days before the smoking room and the members' dining room of the Commons had been built, and before Conservative Central Office came into existence (in 1868), the Carlton was all a Conservative could desire – a place to eat, drink, socialize and pursue one's career with like-minded people. The Carlton was even to survive the Tory corn law schism, and when its rules were changed in 1857 so that all members had to prove that they held political views 'in accordance with those entertained by the great body of the Carlton Club',[7] it was established as the beating heart of Conservatism.

The 'Conservatives' had, then, plenty of the building blocks of a new party to hand. Edmund Burke had pointed the way with his exhortation that 'when bad men combine, the good must associate; else they will fall, one by one, an unpitied sacrifice in a contemptible struggle',[8] and his concept of party, namely 'a body of men united for promoting by their joint endeavours the national interest upon some particular principle in which they are all agreed',[9] was something with which Wellington and Peel could certainly identify. Peel, though, a clever but shy man more comfortable at a desk than on a podium, was notoriously bad at glad-handing his fellow MPs and did not much care for local campaigning. In 1834 he wrote of one trip to Blackburn:

My efforts to escape unnoticed failed, but the only inconvenience I suffered was not from a Radical, but a Conservative assemblage (mob I must not call them) headed by pensioners who insisted for a long time in dragging me for about a mile into the town preceded by an enormous flag and a band of music. I escaped this infliction, but was pursued to the inn by my friends, who of course congregated half the town in front of the inn.[10]

The one piece of campaigning he was happy to endorse was the address he delivered to his constituents in Tamworth on 18 December 1834 (and promptly circulated round the country as a 'manifesto'), in which he warned against 'a perpetual vortex of agitation' but accepted not just that the Reform Act was 'a final and irrevocable settlement of a great constitutional question' but that civil and ecclesiastical institutions should be reviewed.[11] This new political posture did not win him the 1835 election, but it was evidence of a strategic mind keen to push at the boundaries of Tory thought. Moreover, although initially suspicious of the value of the Carlton Club arrangements, following the 1835 defeat Peel brought the garrulous (and often indiscreet and foul-mouthed) Billy Holmes together with another MP, Sir Francis Bonham (described as 'rough, faithful, honest, indefatigable, the depository of a thousand secrets and the betrayer of none'[12]), to organize registration campaigns and coordinate the work of local associations that sprang up across the country. Other Conservatives saw the importance of Holmes's and Bonham's new campaigning techniques, so when even Peel was prepared to urge people to 'register, register, register', they had the makings of a Conservative party that could win an election.

This is what happened in 1841, when, with an economic recession, a huge deficit, working-class demonstrations for a six-point charter of political reform and campaigns for repeal of the corn laws providing a turbulent political background, Melbourne lost a vote on sugar duties and a vote of confidence and, at the Cabinet's insistence, called an election. The Whigs lost 73 seats; with just 271 seats to Peel's

367 in the new House of Commons, Melbourne resigned over the weekend of 28–9 August, after the debate on the queen's speech.

Peel had won an election, but he never enjoyed the wholehearted backing of his Conservative colleagues. His volte-face on Catholic emancipation still rankled, and although even Disraeli reckoned that Peel could be 'the easiest, most flexible and adroit of men' and could 'play upon the House of Commons as on an old fiddle',[13] yet there was something forced, unnatural and ultimately uncongenial about him. Wellington commented bluntly that 'I have no small talk and Peel has no manners,'[14] but Disraeli's dislike of Peel amounted to loathing. He snobbishly complained about his speech being 'marred with provincialisms',[15] and described him in action with venom:

> His flights were ponderous; he soared with the wing of the vulture rather than the plume of the eagle; and his perorations, when most elaborate, were most unwieldy. In pathos he was quite deficient; when he attempted to touch the tender passions, it was painful. His face became distorted, like that of a woman who wants to cry but cannot succeed.[16]

With opinions like these emanating from his own benches, the relationship between party and premier was an uneasy one from the start. Conservative MPs just about managed to swallow the re-introduction of income tax in 1842, but they quibbled when he cut the duty on Canadian corn in 1843. When Lord Ashley, son of the earl of Shaftesbury, tabled an amendment to Peel's Factories Act in 1844 that would limit children's and women's working hours to ten a day, ninety-five conservative MPs voted for it; and the same year, sixty-two of them voted to amend Peel's Bill to reduce the tariff on colonial sugar. In both cases Peel's MPs were forced to rescind their amendments, but it was clear that this was not the happiest of parties.

What cast the Conservatives into the melting pot, though, was the repeal of the protectionist corn laws brought in by Liverpool's administration in 1815, which banned the import of corn until such time as the price of British corn reached eighty shillings per quarter. The aim had been to protect British farmers, but the consequent hike in corn prices led to palpable public hostility. Huskisson had tried to moderate the laws in 1821 by introducing a sliding scale, but despite nine votes in the Commons on their abolition, starting in 1837 under prompting from the liberal Whig Charles Pelham Villiers, they were still on the statute book in 1841. Peel had already voted against repeal five times, and would continue to do so right up until 1845, but his heart was not in it. Villiers' one-man parliamentary crusade (he was once referred to by the Peelite poet and MP Richard Milnes as 'the solitary Robinson Crusoe sitting on the rock of Corn Law repeal'[17]) had been vindicated by the publication of a blue book delineating in bleak detail the effects of the laws on the labouring poor, and reinforced by the extremely effective Anti Corn Law League led by Richard Cobden, who was elected as MP for Stockport in the 1841 election. In response, Peel introduced a further modification to the sliding scale in 1842, but this did little to appease those clamouring that bread was too expensive, and in August 1843 Cobden's ally, the Rochdale Quaker John Bright, who had toured the country for the League, was returned in a by-election in Durham. Events then overtook politics, for after a pause in 1844, when grain yields were abundant and the campaign lost momentum, in 1845 a poor harvest meant a real shortage of bread – and in Ireland there was a grinding famine. Melbourne had been laconically non-committal on the issue, even asking his colleagues after an acrimonious 1841 Cabinet meeting:* 'By the bye, there is one thing we haven't agreed upon, which is, what we are to say. Is it to make our corn dearer or cheaper, or to make the price steady? I don't care which: but

---

* Having developed as a committee of the Privy Council (hence the fact that all Cabinet members are privy councillors), the 'inner Cabinet' or 'cabinet council' consisting of ministers alone had steadily superseded in political significance both the Privy Council itself and the 'outer' or 'Grand' Cabinet, including the monarch and royal household officials. Rather than provide counsel as individuals, ministers began to act in concert, and by the mid-nineteenth century a doctrine of collective responsibility normally applied.

we had better all be in the same story.'[18] That was then. Now, Lord John Russell, the new Whig leader in the Commons, declared his support for Cobden and Bright's campaign, and Peel was convinced that the corn laws would have to be repealed – a view he relayed to the Cabinet in late autumn while parliament was not sitting.

Party unity might have been maintained had it not been for the determined egotism or manful independence (take your pick) of a small coach-load of men. The charabanc was being driven by Edward Smith Stanley, who arrived in the Commons in 1820, aged twenty-one, as a Whig and the very wealthy heir to the 13th earl of Derby. His early life on the family estate at Knowsley with a large family, extended first by his ebullient grandfather's second marriage to an actress and then by his father's obsession with naturalism (which on his death left his son with a menagerie of 345 mammals and 1,272 birds to dispose of) made Stanley a man of lightly held loyalties, whom *The Times* nevertheless described as the only 'brilliant eldest son produced by the British peerage for a hundred years'.[19] He rose with the Whigs, becoming Chief Secretary for Ireland and Secretary for War and the Colonies, but departed the government in 1834 with a band of followers including the former premier Viscount Goderich (who had progressed to be earl of Ripon), Sir James Graham and Charles Gordon-Lennox, the 5th duke of Richmond, over Russell's plans for the Irish church, angrily comparing the Whigs to 'thimble riggers' or tricksters at a country fair. O'Connell, always a witty satirist, dubbed these third-wayers the 'Derby dilly', after Canning's anti-Jacobin poem 'The Loves of the Triangles', which trilled, 'Still down thy steep, romantic Ashbourne, glides / The Derby dilly carrying three insides'. O'Connell changed the number inside the 'Derby diligence', or coach, to six, but it is impossible to know quite how many adherents Stanley could ever keep on board, numbers varying between a dozen and seventy. At first Stanley and Graham had remained on the Whig benches, but by the time of Peel's victory in the 1841 election their conservatism was increasingly apparent, and they joined Peel's Cabinet. Graham got on well with Peel and soon became his closest political confidant, but the Prime Minister and his Colonial Secretary were about as incompatible a pair of politicians as could be imagined: Peel the managerial activist, Stanley the flashy orator. Disillusioned and feeling under-used, Stanley abandoned the Commons in 1844 and asked to be advanced to the upper house under a writ of acceleration* so as to take over the ageing Wellington's role as Leader of the House of Lords.

Stanley had a track record as a reformer. He had voted for the 1832 Reform Act and, from the Colonial Office, had driven through the abolition of slavery. In February 1828 he had even told the Commons that 'the old stubborn spirit of Toryism was at last yielding to the increased liberality of the age'.[20] But now he aligned himself with the protectionist conservatives. Like the country men who populated the government benches, he owned land (a great deal of it), and he reckoned that protection of agricultural interests in general, and defence of the corn laws in particular, had been 'our main inducement to others to give us . . . support'.[21] So in late 1845 he resigned for the second time, prompting Peel's own resignation and a brief flurry of unsuccessful government-forming by Russell, whose preference for compelling Peel 'to bear the burden' won the day.

Back as Prime Minister, Peel presented the case for repeal in the Commons on 27 January 1846, backed by Russell but with his own ranks in open revolt. Peel was especially unfortunate in having attracted the hostility of one backbench member of his own party in particular. Benjamin Disraeli had shown his fangs a year earlier when he had questioned whether Peel's government was 'a Tory Ministry',[22] and followed that barb up with a speech ending with the bold declamation that 'a Conservative Government is an organised

---

* From 1482, the eldest son and heir apparent of a peer who held several noble titles could be summoned to the Lords under one of the subsidiary titles, in this case as Baron Stanley of Bickerstaffe. The most recent example was in 1992, when Robert Gascoyne-Cecil, heir to the 6th marquess of Salisbury, was summoned as Baron Cecil of Essendon.

Hypocrisy'.[23] And on 22 January he had launched into the debate on the queen's speech with invective loaded upon sarcasm piled upon irony. 'My idea of a great statesman is of one who represents a great idea,' he started, before patronizingly drawing an oblique reference to Peel's provincial calico-manufacturer parentage: 'I do not care whether he be a manufacturer or a manufacturer's son. That is a grand – that is, indeed, a heroic – position. But I care not what may be the position of a man who never originates an idea – a watcher of the atmosphere, a man who, as he says, takes his observations, and when he finds the wind in a certain quarter, trims to it.'[24] This was the classic charge of the conviction politician against the pragmatist, the purist against the trimmer. It fitted perfectly with Disraeli's charge a year earlier that Peel had 'caught the Whigs bathing, and walked away with their clothes'.[25] But it was also nasty, disingenuous stuff. He ended with a sententious flourish. 'Above all,' he begged, 'maintain the line of demarcation between parties; for it is only by maintaining the independence of party that you can maintain the integrity of public men, and the power and influence of Parliament itself.'[26] This was a novel assertion. One passenger on the Derby dilly, Richmond, had stormed out of both Wellington's and Grey's governments over religion, and centrists like Canning and Huskisson often held the balance between administrations of different hues. Few were as keen on party delineation as Disraeli.

The struggle continued until the third reading vote in the Commons, which came on 15 May. Thanks to Whig votes Peel had a comfortable majority of ninety-eight, and on 25 June a similar victory was secured by Wellington in the Lords. But Conservatives had now got used to rebelling, and while their lordships voted for corn law repeal, Conservatives combined with Whigs, radicals and Irish MPs in the Commons to defeat the government on a completely different measure, the Irish Coercion Bill, by a margin of seventy-three. Peel resigned and, in warmly commending Cobden in his resignation speech, signalled his effective departure from the Conservative fold. His significance, however, was far from over, for the governments of the 'Liberal'* Lord John Russell (June 1846 to February 1852), the Peelite earl of Aberdeen (December 1852 to January 1855) and the conservative-minded Whig Viscount Palmerston (February 1855 to February 1858) were all either to rely on Peelite support from the likes of Gladstone or else to be brought into existence by the Peelites' refusal to do business with the Conservative leaders. The allegiance of Peelites remained essential to the parliamentary arithmetics of governments long after Peel died from injuries suffered in a fall from his horse on 2 July 1850.

A combination of the creation of an electoral machine in the Carlton Club, Disraeli's belief in party demarcations, the sense of being betrayed by Peel and the ardently held protectionist creed now shaped the new Conservative party, which turned to Stanley to lead it, even though he had told a close friend in December 1845 that his 'official life' was over. Leading the Conservatives was not an easy task, especially from the Lords. But then, there was little choice, because however much his protectionist colleagues had whooped and cheered at Disraeli's caustic jibes at Peel, the mindset of the average Conservative could just not comprehend how this flamboyantly dressed and constantly indebted Jewish scribbler came to be one of them. Useful, yes. Wonderful to listen to. Brilliant. But not quite the kind of chap who could lead the party. Lord Malmesbury thought he would do anything and act with anyone to gain office, while Stanley thought him the most powerful repellent possible to any repentant Peelites – and told him as much. 'Certain feelings exist,' he wrote, 'call them prejudices if you will, that will make many of our friends desire, in the man who is to lead them, a degree of station and influence which circumstances have not yet enabled you to acquire.'[27]

---

* Russell first used the term 'liberal' in 1839 as a portmanteau term covering the Whig grandees in the Lords and the radicals in the Commons, their central uniting principle being free trade and therefore opposition, as liberal Conservatives, to the protectionist Conservatives. Its currency steadily grew, although the first Liberal government is reckoned to be that formed by Palmerston in 1859.

Hostility to Disraeli in large measure explains one of the mysteries of nineteenth-century politics: how Stanley (or the earl of Derby as he became on his father's death in 1851) was able to dominate the Conservative party for two decades. Lugubrious and prone to bouts of depression when the parliamentary and racing seasons were over, he made little effort to woo colleagues. Wining and dining was not part of his political style – and even when he and the Countess of Derby did entertain, her company was reckoned to be 'of a dullness as depressing as a London fog'.[28] He could also be cruel. When his son turned up at Knowsley unannounced, Derby rasped: 'What the devil brings you here, Edward? Are you going to get married, or has Disraeli cut his throat?'[29] Some complained that he seemed to think that everyone should be awfully grateful that he chose to lead the party at all. And yet Derby had two things in his favour. He had an authority by virtue of his social status, his inordinate wealth and his calm sagacity that few could match; and he was not that flashy, mercurial, irritatingly brilliant fellow Disraeli. Whether the objection to Disraeli was thinly veiled anti-semitism or simple snobbery (until he bought Hughenden Manor, thereby plunging himself into even greater debt, he could hardly be thought of as a country gentleman), the reluctance of Conservatives to accept his leadership was undoubtedly there. In one sense it was fair enough. Disraeli was permanently living beyond his means. It was well known that he had found parliament a c omfortable way of escaping his creditors. And he had started political life as a radical independent. But the Conservatives could have benefited from a bit more irritable searching after office during these Derby years, when, so Derby's son reckoned, 'the Captain does not care for office, but wishes to keep things as they are, and impede "Progress"'.[30] Derby, of course, unlike Disraeli, could amply afford not to 'care for office'.

They did get into office, though, in 1852. As with each of Derby's three terms as Prime Minister, it was to be a short tenure. Lacking the support of the Peelites, the government was staffed almost entirely by newly minted privy councillors, with Disraeli as Chancellor of the

Exchequer and Leader of the Commons. In the hope of improving the parliamentary numbers Derby dissolved parliament in July, but returned with just 299 Conservatives against 315 Liberals, Whigs and radicals and 40 Peelites. When Disraeli came to the House with a second, emergency budget in December, he hoped he had been clever enough to appease his colleagues who were still clamouring for protectionist measures, but in fact he had only succeeded in riling the opposition, who complained that he had bribed the agricultural lobby by cutting the malt excise.

Then came one of those moments when personal animosity spontaneously brought about the end of a government. As was customary, Disraeli spoke last on the fourth night of the budget debate on 16 December. He presumed on having the last word and laced his speech with venomous jibes directed particularly at Graham, now a Liberal, who had attacked Disraeli earlier in the debate for not having 'learnt his business'. Disraeli accused Graham of utter 'recklessness' when he had been in office and insisted that 'if he has learnt his business, he has still to learn some other things – he has to learn that petulance is not sarcasm, and that insolence is not invective'.[31] The barbs kept coming, as he described Graham as a man 'whom I will not say I greatly respect, but rather whom I greatly regard',[32] a phrase that stuck in the gullet of many a well-bred Tory. When Disraeli sat down he expected the vote immediately, but in the midst of a fierce thunderstorm that shook the windows of the new House of Commons, Gladstone, who had also left the Conservatives, suddenly stood up to speak for the opposition. 'Gladstone's look when he rose to reply will never be forgotten by me,' wrote Derby's son, the new Lord Stanley; 'his usually calm features were livid and distorted with passion, his voice shook and those who watched him feared an outbreak incompatible with parliamentary rules.'[33] Furious at the personal attack on Graham, he was howled down time and again by the Conservatives as he launched into an attack on Disraeli, who, he said, had 'not yet learned the limits of discretion, of moderation, and of forbearance'.[34] It was a tightly argued speech, but it was its evident spontaneity that hit home. He ended with a passionate call to Tories to vote with him:

> I look back with regret upon the days when I sat nearer to many of my hon. Friends opposite than I now am ... I tell you that if you give your assent and your high authority to this most unsound and destructive principle on which the financial scheme of the Government is based – you may refuse my appeal now – you may accompany the right hon. Gentleman the Chancellor of the Exchequer into the lobby; but my belief is that the day will come when you will look back upon this vote – as its consequences sooner or later unfold themselves – you will look back upon this vote with bitter, but with late and ineffectual regret.[35]

It was the speech of one who might so easily have rejoined his old colleagues now they had effectively renounced protectionism, but had been spurred into hatred by Disraeli. The Ayes came in at 286, the Noes, 305. Disraeli's budget was defeated, and the next day Derby resigned after just ten months. Many praised Gladstone for landing the final punch; others blamed Disraeli for leading with his chin.

The Carlton was not the only political club in town. The Whigs were not far behind in forming their own club in the 1830s, Grey's son-in-law John Lambton (now earl of Durham) having argued during the 1835 election that 'the great nail to drive home is the formation and organisation of political associations in every town and village of the Empire'.[36] Others, more prosaically, wanted a club that would be, as one radical wrote, 'like the Athenaeum, a good dining club. The great object is to get the Reformers of the country to join it, so that it may be a place of meeting for them when they come to town. It is much wanted.'[37] The idea caught on, and the following year Grey's brother-in-law Edward Ellice MP (nicknamed the 'Bear' for his Canadian fur trade connections) hosted a series of meetings at his home at 14 Carlton House Terrace with the intention of creating 'a new club that should be neither exclusively Whig, like Brooks's, nor exclusively Radical . . . one in which all who professed to be Liberals might find a congenial home'.[38] As Ellice had been both Secretary at War and whip in the Whig ministries of 1830–4, he was more aware than most that there were sharp divisions in the government party between Whigs and radicals like Sir William Molesworth MP, who wrote of his own party's leadership that 'they are the miserablest brutes that God Almighty ever put guts into'.[39] There had been various attempts to bridge the gap. An approach was made to Brooks's to admit radicals. It was rejected. A Reform Association was founded by Joseph Parkes and Durham. It briefly had a headquarters, but failed to gain momentum. The radical MP Joseph Hume joined a Westminster Club and suggested changing its name to the Westminster Reform Club, but that too died. Yet Ellice's plan, to bind twenty radicals and fifteen Whigs into a new Reform Club, was to succeed; and soon it had nearly two hundred and fifty MPs, fifty peers and most of the Cabinet as members.

The emphasis on 'reform' was important. For although the Whigs, radicals and Irish reformers, who with Peelite support formed the government for just over twenty-eight years between 1830 and 1868 (to the Tories' ten) could often disagree about the pace, the nature and the necessity of future reform, and although foreign policy would often divide them, the battle over the Reform Act had seared itself into the non-Conservative mind so effectively that 'reform' remained a clarion call. There was an irony in this. Grey had boasted that his Cabinet owned more acres than any other in history, but his Reform Act enfranchised a middle class who had little in common with these wealthy Whig grandees, while the radicals, by contrast, gained a new electorate to whom they could appeal in the industrial cities. For them, reform was far from complete: they campaigned for the secret ballot, for further enfranchisement, for the abolition of more pocket boroughs and for an end to the still endemic electoral corruption.

Party unity proved just as elusive for 'reformers' as for the 'conservatives'. The Tories' corn law schism should have taught that personal animosity, poor discipline and high-handedness would undo any party. It didn't. First, Russell nearly brought down his own minority administration when in 1850, in an attempt to pander to anti-Catholic public sentiment, he penned a coruscating letter to the bishop of Durham attacking the Tractarian Oxford Movement, the tone of which alienated high church Peelites like Gladstone. Russell, the longstanding advocate of religious toleration, the man who had introduced the Sacramental Test Act 1828 that abolished the Test and Corporation Acts, who had created the new see of Manchester (and, rather than increase the number of bishops in the Lords, invented the episcopal escalator that bumps the longest-serving bishops on to the red bench) and had appointed the politically and theologically liberal Renn Dickson Hampden as bishop of Hereford, had become an anti-Catholic bigot. So when the government tried to vote down a new Bill to equalize the franchise and electorate for county and borough seats in the new session in February 1851, Russell's coalition of support collapsed. Defeated, he resigned, only to be reinstated when Derby – much to his own relief – failed to form a government.

It was not just Russell's high-handedness that undermined the unity of the non-Conservative government. Equally unsettling were the impetuosity and ambition of the Foreign Secretary, Palmerston, who summarily recognized Napoleon III's December 1851 *coup d'état* that suspended the French Assemblée Nationale. Russell sacked him for insubordination but Palmerston got his revenge in February by tabling an amendment to the government's Militia Bill, which was carried by eleven votes. Russell was again forced to resign – and this time Derby did take the helm. Palmerston blithely commented: 'I have had my tit-for-tat with John Russell; and I turned him out on Friday last.'[40]

There was also Russell's small-man prickliness (he was just five feet five inches, reputedly thanks to a premature birth). When Aberdeen formed a Whig–Peelite government in December 1852, Russell at first accepted the offer of the Foreign Office but inexplicably resigned after a matter of weeks. The next year he insisted on being Lord President of the Council, despite its being a post that had been held exclusively by peers since the time of Henry VIII; and then, after a period of rowing with Aberdeen about British failures in the Crimea, he resigned in early 1855 when a motion was tabled in the Commons demanding an investigation into the conduct of the war. His Cabinet colleagues expressed their fury with him so forcefully that Russell contemplated doing what Palmerston had done in 1852, voting out the government in which he had just sat. His disloyalty understandably disbarred him from the premiership, and the queen sent for the seventy-year-old Palmerston.

The new Prime Minister's attitude to party loyalty was no more disciplined than Russell's – as, indeed, his wife implied when she confessed that he felt that 'in England change of principle was more easily forgiven than change of party'.[41] But he was a remarkable political escapologist. When the Lords sought to censure him as Foreign Secretary in 1850 for a completely disproportionate naval expedition to avenge the seizure of the property of a Portuguese–Gibraltarian crook called 'Don' David Pacifico, he extricated himself with a masterly four-and-a-half-hour speech without notes that ended with dodgy populist nationalism: 'As the Roman, in days of old, held himself free from indignity, when he could say *Civis Romanus sum*; so also a British subject, in whatever land he may be, shall feel confident that the watchful eye and the strong arm of England will protect him against injustice and wrong.'[42] It was nonsense. Nobody genuinely believed in such lurid British dilettantism, nor that British law superseded that of every other country in the world. But his unashamed guff appealed to the patriotic public, so he survived – just as he did in July 1855, when Disraeli and a coalition of radicals and Peelites tried to oust him after a loan to Turkey, essential if it was to continue fighting in the Crimea, scraped through by three votes. And when on 3 March 1857 he lost the vote on a motion over the Second Opium War tabled by Cobden, he happily sauntered off to the polls and secured himself a resounding victory.

Most significantly, though, when Palmerston lost the Bill which would have made it a crime to plot in Britain to murder someone abroad – a response to the attempt to assassinate the French Emperor with a British-made bomb – and was consequently forced to resign in February 1858, he realized that he had to bring the whole non-Conservative family back together; so when Derby called another election, Palmerston gathered the Whigs, Liberals, radicals and Peelites in Almack's Assembly Rooms (later known as Willis's Rooms) in King Street off St James's on 6 June 1859. For once Palmerston and Russell managed to stand on the same platform without rancour, and even said they would serve under each other. Four days later Derby and Disraeli were defeated by 323 to 310 and Palmerston created a thoroughly Liberal administration in which, for the first time, the constituent parts merged. Russell was Foreign Secretary again, Gladstone was prevailed upon to return as Chancellor of the Exchequer, and the ministry even brought in two radicals, Charles Villiers in charge of the Poor Law Board and Thomas Milner Gibson as President of the Board of Trade. Despite loud moaning from several displaced Whigs, Palmerston was certain he was doing the right thing. As he explained to Lord Ernest Bruce, he had reconstructed the government on a different principle because 'to have merely brought in the administration . . . turned out in 1858 would have been trifling with Parliament and the country'.[43]

Ashley-Cooper, now the 7th earl of Shaftesbury, saw it differently. 'If Palmerston were removed,' he said, 'the whole thing would be an agglomeration . . . of molecules floating in various, and even opposite directions,'[44] and he was eventually proved right. When Palmerston died not long after winning the 1865 election, Russell (now an earl, and seventy-three years old) returned as Prime Minister on 29 October that year, his enthusiasm for further reform of parliament boosted by the victory of the anti-slavery Union in the American Civil War and the creation of the Reform League in the United Kingdom under Edmond Beales. Although Disraeli had courted controversy in his own opposition ranks with talk of reform of the House of Lords and was keen to avoid the 1832 trap that had left Tories in the electoral Antarctic, Russell knew the Conservatives would oppose his proposals;

and sure enough, when the queen's speech presented to the re-assembled parliament on 6 February included a reference to voting rights reform, the Tories duly barked in the Lords that afternoon. But Russell's real problem lay within his own party. For Palmerston had pre-ferred to gain popular support through jingoistic foreign escapades rather than parliamentary reform, and several of his junior ministers who had been sacked by Russell or disappointed in their hopes of office, including Robert Lowe, Edward Horsman and Francis Charteris, Lord Elcho, now preferred to stick with the old Palmerston line.

The two leaders of this group, Elcho and Lowe, were a curious pair. Elcho, a Peelite of 'booming, crude, unsubtle energy',[45] was president of both the London Homeopathic Hospital and the Liberty and Property Defence League; Lowe, an albino with very poor sight, advanced an argument that was remarkably similar to the Ultra line peddled by Knatchbull so many years earlier. Lowe was particularly caustic about franchise reform, telling the Commons in March 1866:

> If you want venality, if you want ignorance, if you want drunken-ness, and facility for being intimidated; or if, on the other hand, you want impulsive, unreflecting, and violent people, where do you look for them in the constituencies? Do you go to the top or to the bottom? . . . The effect [of reform] will manifestly be to add a large number of persons to our constituencies of the class from which if there is to be anything wrong going on we may naturally expect to find it. It will increase the expenses of candidates . . . you must look for more bribery and corruption than you have hitherto had.[46]

But it was the demeanour of a third leader, Horsman, that gained the group its nickname when Bright cleverly suggested that, like David hiding from Saul, he had retreated into the 'cave of Adullam'.[47] The name caught on, as thirty-five 'Adullamites' joined forces with Disraeli. On 18 June 1866 they defeated the government on the Franchise Bill, thereby forcing Russell – and their own party – out of government. Derby was back.

Despite having elevated inaction to a political art, Derby had one capacity above all others – the judgement to see when to act. This is why, despite the old Tory opposition to reform, it was a Conservative government that piloted the Second Reform Act (more properly known as the Representation of the People Act) on to the statute book. The 1865 election had added to the sense of a nation demanding reform. A string of Liberal MPs who supported the enfranchisement of the (male) working classes had won seats and combined with John Bright to mount a sustained campaign for reform. There was a mass demonstration in Trafalgar Square on 29 June 1866 calling for the Reform League's programme of male suffrage and the secret ballot, and the new Home Secretary, Spencer Walpole (who, as his name suggested, had two prime ministers among his ancestors), was forced to resign when he failed to prevent a second meeting in Hyde Park. By the turn of the year Derby was convinced that 'in some shape or another we must deal with [franchise reform], and that immediately',[48] although several others in the Cabinet which met on 15 February 1867 were furiously opposed, including Jonathan Peel (Sir Robert's not very Peelite younger brother), Henry Herbert, the 4th earl of Carnarvon, and Robert Gascoyne-Cecil, Viscount Cranborne. These last two, both in their thirties, were so incensed by the idea that they tendered their resignations before the meeting started; nevertheless, in an attempt to maintain a fragile unity the Cabinet agreed to bring forward a Bill based on a £6 franchise just ten minutes before a meeting of the parliamentary party. The compromise came under such sustained Liberal and Adullamite attack in the Commons that same day, though, that it was abandoned. Having made the judgement that 'the loss of reputation which a vacillating or subservient policy would inevitably bring'[49] was worse than the loss of three ministers, Derby returned to the fray on 2 March, putting a yet more radical proposal for household suffrage to the Cabinet. Peel, Carnarvon and Cranborne stalked out, leaving Derby, by now an ill man, to moan over his ministerial red box, 'the Tory party is ruined' – to which Disraeli sarcastically added, 'poor Tory party'.[50]

It wasn't ruined, though. Cranborne complained that 'a clear majority of votes in a clear majority of constituencies [had] been made over to those who [had] no other property but for the labour of their hands',[51] and that Derby and Disraeli had 'fully hoodwinked' their colleagues, but he did not conspire against the leadership, and the Liberals had proposed a similar measure a year earlier, so the Bill was given a Commons second reading without a division. When it came to committee, Disraeli went further, accepting amendments from radical Liberals that significantly extended the borough franchise. The strongest attack came at third reading from Lowe, who foretold 'a new era, when the bag which holds the winds will be untied, and we shall be surrounded by a perpetual whirl of change, alteration, innovation, and revolution'. He complained that whereas Britain had always adopted the principle that 'you ought to put the franchise in the hands of persons fit to exercise it', Disraeli was introducing 'the principle of numbers as against wealth and intellect . . . the principle of equality'.[52] The Bill, now in an even more radical form than Derby had initially intended, got its third reading none the less, again without division, and proceeded to the Lords, where Derby dragged himself from his sick bed to argue that it was 'a Bill at once large, extensive, and Conservative',[53] only to be condemned by Carnarvon for 'hazarding a great experiment' and 'taking a leap in the dark'.[54] Neither second nor third reading was opposed, though, and despite some amendments in the Lords and further debates about the franchise threshold, the Bill became law in August. The result was that the Totnes and Great Yarmouth patronage seats were finally abolished, thirty-five boroughs went from two members to one, Hackney and Chelsea got two seats each, the likes of Burnley, Darlington, Hartlepool and London University got their first representation, and a general election was no longer required on the death of the monarch. Most significantly, in extending the suffrage in the boroughs to all householders with twelve months' residency and to £10 lodgers, and in the counties to £5 property owners and £12 occupiers, the Act roughly doubled the electorate. Gladstone later scoffed at Disraeli, writing: 'The governing idea of the man who directed the party seemed to be not so much to consider what ought to be proposed and carried as to make sure that whatever it was it should be proposed and carried by those in power.'[55] The end result, though, was a significant achievement for a Conservative government.

It wasn't the end of the Conservatives' reforms, either. The Commons had wrested control over its own membership from the crown in 1604 and had jealously guarded that right ever since. One of the first things a newly elected parliament did was appoint committees to hear petitions to void the election of an individual member on legal grounds such as bribery, treating or 'colourable employment' (employing voters in sinecures in exchange for their votes). In theory, under the provisions of the Parliamentary Elections Act 1770, these Commons committees were quasi-judicial affairs and the members acted 'with the greatest impartiality', or so Edward Pleydell-Bouverie, the MP for Kilmarnock, who chaired a large number of them, maintained. In practice, though, an election petition was a way of perpetuating the election campaign by other means, and the outcome largely depended on the composition of the committee. Thus, between 1852 and 1868, 102 Liberals and 66 Conservatives faced petition hearings: where a Liberal faced a committee chaired by a Liberal, he was less likely to lose his seat, and a Tory facing a Tory-led committee was hardly ever dislodged. Many feared that the new franchise provisions of the 1867 Act would mean that the kind of campaigning already seen in contested county elections and boroughs with large electorates like Westminster (the ballot was still public) would be repeated all over the country, as candidates sought to bully, bribe and treat their way to Westminster. Elections were already expensive: one petition committee revealed that the Liberal candidate in Wakefield in 1859, William Leatham, had spent £3,900 and the Tory, John Charlesworth, £4,015. As long as matters of electoral malfeasance were decided on a partisan basis by the Commons itself, there was little or no brake on such corruption; so both Liberals and Conservatives worried that without some independently enforced mechanism of deterrence the costs of election would continue to rise exponentially. In 1844 there had been a proposal to cut the committee size from thirteen to three in the hope that this would curb the worst aspects of partisanship, but when the 1865 election led to fifty petitions, MPs on all sides demanded more radical change. George Sandford suggested that judges could be added as assessors to the election committees; a Bill that would have transferred jurisdiction to the Court of Queen's Bench died in the 1867 session. Eventually, in 1868, a compromise was drawn up between Disraeli and Gladstone, and the Parliamentary Elections Act handed the resolution of disputes to an election court sitting under two judges.

The Second Reform Act had one other effect: in enabling the Conservative government to survive, it handed the premiership to Disraeli when on 19 February 1868 Derby, finally succumbing to a long succession of illnesses, resigned and urged Victoria to appoint Disraeli in his place as leader of another minority Conservative administration. A little over a year later Derby died, muttering the words 'bored to the utmost powers of extinction'.[56] For all his steady sense, and despite the organizational prowess of the Carlton Club, he had been leader of the opposition for longer than any other politician in history; and, having started life a Whig, he had split one party, rescued another from schism and enabled a third to form.

The next thirteen years were to be dominated by two sharply contrasting personalities. Disraeli, who had mastered opportunism as a successful leader of the opposition (a position he would hold again for just over five years); Gladstone, an impervious, stern moralist. Disraeli, a converted Anglican sceptic who delighted in debating religion and equally detested high church ritualists and broad church rationalists ('rits' and 'rats' as he called them); Gladstone, a devout, troubled high church Anglican keen to establish the church on as sustainable a footing as possible. Both had been Chancellor of the Exchequer: Gladstone, successfully, during two long bouts (December 1852 to February 1855 and June 1859 to June 1866); Disraeli, reluctantly, during three shorter ones (February to December 1852,

February 1858 to June 1859, and July 1866 to February 1868).

Gladstone came to the premiership at the end of 1868, when Disraeli's first brief administration was snuffed out in that autumn's elections, with a whole *conciergerie* of political baggage. Macaulay had described him in 1839 as 'the rising hope of those stern unbending Tories who follow reluctantly and mutinously a leader whose experience and eloquence are indispensable to them, but whose cautious temper and moderate opinions they abhor'.[57] But his political journey had meandered. He had resigned over Peel's insistence on a substantial grant for the Catholic seminary at Maynooth in 1845, but returned later that year as Colonial Secretary and voted with Peel on the corn laws. He joined Aberdeen's government as Chancellor of the Exchequer, but having become one of Palmerston's sternest critics in opposition, refused to serve in his first administration in 1855. As he told his friend Samuel Wilberforce, the bishop of Oxford (the abolitionist's son, known as 'Soapy Sam' thanks to Disraeli's description of him as 'unctuous, oleaginous, saponaceous'), in 1857, 'I greatly felt being turned out of office, I saw great things to do. I am losing the best years of my life out of my natural service, yet I have never ceased to rejoice that I am not in office with Palmerston, when I see the tricks, the shufflings, the frauds he daily has recourse to as to his business.'[58] Gladstone had then added that he rejoiced not to sit on the Treasury bench with the viscount, but when he accepted the Exchequer in 1859 he sat alongside Palmerston for six years.

Gladstone showed little more consistency on parliamentary reform. Having voted with the Derby government for the Reform Bill that was lost on 31 March 1859 and for Sir Edward Baines's 1861 Borough Franchise Reform Bill (with five other Cabinet colleagues but to the fury and consternation of Palmerston), when a similar Bill reappeared in 1864 he voted against it, despite arguing 'that every man who is not presumably incapacitated by some consideration of personal unfitness or of political danger is morally entitled to come within the pale of the Constitution'.[59] In the debates on the 1866 Bill, he expressly argued against extending the franchise to all householders, sticking rigidly to a £7 rental qualification, as he thought anything lower would 'place the working class in a clear majority'. In Gladstone's mind doubtless there was consistency in these views. His wife, Catherine, was the daughter of a baronet, and Gladstone spent much of his time at the family home of Hawarden Castle in north Wales; this semi-aristocratic background inclined him away from universal suffrage.

The one constant in Gladstone's life was his faith, for religion of a high church hue imbued with a clear moral purpose and a dutiful desire to render public service provided his personal *raison d'être* and defined his political posture. He gave generously to charitable causes, he scourged himself for his sinfulness, he chopped down trees, he tried to rescue 'fallen' women, he read voraciously. Unhappy with what he saw as the undermining of the Church of England, he unsuccessfully filibustered the Matrimonial Causes Bill in 1857, declaring its provisions on divorce 'opposed to the law of church, the law of nature and the law of God', and he consistently tried to ensure a sustainable future for the church. To some this came across as priggishness, not least because he also had a very unnerving habit of referencing God when he performed his political volte-faces, prompting Henry Labouchere to protest that he 'did not object to the old man always having a card up his sleeve, but he did object to his insinuating that the Almighty had placed it there'.[60]

By the time he became Prime Minister, just short of his sixtieth birthday, Gladstone had executed six budgets and transformed them into major national political events. In his first four-and-a-half-hour outing in 1853 he abolished 123 tariffs and reduced 133, and in his 1860 sequel he abolished duties on 371 articles. He had sought to fuse all the different public accounts into the one dominant department of finance and brought a policy of tight money to the Treasury. He had created the post office savings banks and put his personal stamp of frugality on every aspect of public spending. As he told the people of Edinburgh in 1879, a Chancellor of the Exchequer 'is under a sacred obligation with regard to all that he consents to spend' and no Chancellor 'is worth his salt who is not ready to save what are meant by candle-ends and cheese-parings in the cause of the country'.[61]

The immediate journey to the premiership started with Gladstone's advocacy from the opposition benches in February 1868 of the abolition of compulsory church rates, a policy that bound together his fissiparous party. When Disraeli called the general election later that year the result was clear. Although Gladstone himself had lost in South Lancashire and had to pick up the seat at Greenwich, the Liberals had won a majority of 112. The stage was Gladstone's – and he used it to phenomenal effect. The secret ballot, which had been called for by the Chartists in the 1830s, was brought in via the Ballot Act 1872. Flogging was banned in the peacetime army. Local government was put on a secure footing. An Education Act brought in elementary education for all five- to twelve-year-olds in England and Wales, and a series of Acts decriminalized trade unions.

It was Ireland that was to provide the defining issue of the administration, though. When Gladstone had been told that the queen's commissioner was en route to ask him to form a government, he had been felling trees on the estate at Hawarden and paused briefly before declaring (with characteristic portentous certainty): 'My mission is to pacify Ireland.' So, against the background of Fenian violence, he brought in a pair of Irish Bills to disestablish the church (thereby removing the Irish bishops from the Lords) and reform Irish land laws. The former was carried by 100 in the Commons and survived largely unscathed in the Lords, and the latter was so watered down in Cabinet that when it arrived in parliament it was barely opposed. But by the time they introduced a third Bill to reform the Irish universities, Gladstone and his team were losing energy and had courted unpopularity with some casual examples of sharp practice and a licensing Bill that irritated all bar the teetotallers. Disraeli (who might easily have been ousted as Conservative leader by a coup plotted at Burghley House in February 1872, if anyone had been brave enough to broach the matter with him) made the point with characteristic verve at the Free Trade Hall in Manchester: 'Ministers reminded me of one of those marine landscapes not very unusual on the coasts of South America.

You behold a range of exhausted volcanoes. Not a flame flickers on a single pallid crest. But the situation is still dangerous. There are occasional earthquakes, and ever and anon the dark rumbling of the sea.'[62] One such occasional earthquake came on 11 March 1873, as the Irish Universities Bill fell by three votes and Gladstone resigned – only to find himself thrust back into office by Disraeli's refusal to run a minority administration. Forced to soldier on, Gladstone eventually dissolved parliament by writing to the queen on 21 January 1874 during the recess and without giving the Cabinet prior warning (yet another piece of sharp practice). The subsequent election delivered as clear an outcome as in 1868, but in the other direction: Disraeli had 352 seats to Gladstone's 243. Having had to content himself with second place behind a Tory brewer in Greenwich, Gladstone told his brother Robertson: 'We have been borne down in a torrent of gin and beer.'[63]

In foreign policy Disraeli often seemed to court controversy, but in domestic terms, his second term was a washout. There were occasional pieces of enlightened legislation: another Education Act; a Conspiracy and Protection of Property Act that legalized strikes and peaceful pickets; and an Artisans' Dwellings Act, which allowed local authorities to replace slum housing. But the parliament was dominated by the internal disputes occasioned by Disraeli's attitude on foreign policy. For plenty of Conservatives still worried about his flashiness. On taking office in 1866, Derby had told the Lords that 'the Conservative party . . . are the party who are the least likely to be carried away by that popular enthusiasm and those popular impulses which may hurry even a prudent Government into the adoption of courses – I might say, into the adoption of Quixotic enterprises – inimical to the welfare of the country.'[64] This was a calm, steady-as-she-goes foreign policy about as distant from the populist belligerence of Palmerston as could be imagined. But with Derby dead, Disraeli's Palmerstonian tendencies came to the fore when internal divisions in the vast Ottoman Empire began to surface and the Russians threatened war. Something bold must be done, thought Disraeli.

Britain could not stand idly by. Perhaps it should send the fleet through the Dardanelles or take Constantinople. He had a problem, though. For he had (re-)appointed as his Foreign Secretary the new (15th) earl of Derby, who held rather similar views to his father on foreign affairs. He confided as much to his diary in 1876: 'To the premier the main thing is to please and surprise the public by bold strokes and unexpected moves: he would rather run serious national risks than hear his policy called feeble or commonplace, to me the first object is to keep England out of trouble, so long as it can be done consistently with honour and good faith.'[65] This was a very different creed from that of Disraeli, who brought forward in 1876 a preposterous (but popular) Royal Titles Act, which made Queen Victoria Empress of all her dominions, including India.

The tone of affairs changed when a Bulgarian uprising that April and May was brutally repressed by the Turks. When news of this event reached London on 23 June, Disraeli's initial response, in his last appearance in the Commons (he had decided to move to the less vigorous House of Lords as the earl of Beaconsfield – pronounced, so he insisted, 'beacon' not 'beckon'), was to dismiss the talk of massacre as 'coffee house babble'. However, when witness accounts of the destruction of fifty-eight Bulgarian villages and the summary execution of 15,000 rebels were revealed, and when in September Gladstone went on the offensive with a demand that the Turks leave the Balkans 'bag and baggage', Disraeli reasserted his belief that the integrity of Turkey must be maintained at all costs as a bulwark against Russian expansionism, even while privately admitting to the marquess of Salisbury that 'had it not been for these unhappy "atrocities", we should have settled a peace very honourable to England and satisfactory to Europe, [but] now we are obliged to work from a new point of departure, and dictate to Turkey, who has forfeited all sympathy'.[66] The 'Eastern question' turned the political atmosphere poisonous. Gladstone addressed vast public meetings with an ever more aggressively personal attack on imperialism and 'Beaconsfieldism'; in return, the windows of his London house were smashed and the traditionalist Prince George, duke of Cambridge and commander-in-chief, refused to shake his hand.

In April 1877 Russia declared war on Turkey, and Disraeli was left with the prospect of Turkey's imminent collapse and his own and Britain's humiliation. This time Disraeli's official position was that Britain would remain neutral so long as Russia did not invade Constantinople or close communications routes through Suez. When Russia invaded Adrianople, Disraeli told the Cabinet on 17 December 1877 that his ultimatum had been breached and that war was inevitable (he had earlier said Britain would not 'terminate till right was done'). The Cabinet refused to back him, Derby a prominent dissenter. Disraeli first threatened resignation but then recruited another member of the Cabinet, the India Secretary, Cranborne, now the 3rd marquess of Salisbury, to his cause with a juicy piece of gossip, accurately accusing Derby's wife Mary of passing secret information to the Russian ambassador, Count Pyotr Shuvalov. This was crafty manipulation. Salisbury and Derby were pretty much of an age (born 1830 and 1826), had both studied at Eton and had succeeded to their respective titles in 1868 and 1869, but since Lady Derby was Salisbury's stepmother and had married Derby less than two years after the death of her first husband (the 2nd marquess), Salisbury suspected that she had started her affair with Derby before his father's death. Over the Christmas break, Derby complained to Salisbury that Disraeli

> believes thoroughly in 'prestige' – as all foreigners do and would think it quite sincerely in the interests of the country to spend 200 millions on a war if the result of it was to make foreign states think more highly of us a military power. These ideas are intelligible, but they are not mine nor yours, and their being sincerely held does not make them less dangerous.[67]

But by January Salisbury was fairly and squarely behind Disraeli. So much so that after Derby resigned for all of two days in January 1878, Salisbury encouraged scurrilous stories about Derby's drinking via his nephew Arthur Balfour. When Russia forced a humiliating peace on Turkey in March in the Treaty of San Stefano, Derby noted that at two successive Cabinet meetings 'Salisbury [was] by far the most eager for action: he talked of our sliding into a position of contempt: of our being humiliated' and said that 'if our ancestors had cared for the rights of other people, the British empire would not have been made'.[68] On 27 March, furious that the Cabinet had resolved to call up the reserves and seize the Turkish island of Cyprus without warrant, Derby resigned again – and this time Salisbury took his place just in time to reap the rewards of peace (including the voluntary handing of Cyprus to Britain) at the Congress of Berlin in June. Derby, meanwhile, despite finding Gladstone 'uncongenial', soon joined the Liberals.

Disraeli received a rapturous response in the music halls. One song went:

> We don't want to fight, but by Jingo if we do,
> We've got the ships, we've got the men, we've got the money too.
> We've fought the Bear before, and while we're Britons true
> The Russians shall not have Constantinople.

He had been fortunate, though, and while his next bout of 'jingoism' (the Second Afghan War) was to be initially successful, events in South Africa, where a British force was heavily defeated by the Zulus at Isandlwana on 22 January 1879, proved that imperial ambitions were not without danger. By the time Disraeli called a general election in March 1880, the economy was uppermost in most people's minds, especially in the countryside, as there had been three bad harvests; but even so, events overseas loomed large in a bitter campaign. Britain was sharply divided between two camps: those who believed in a strong nationalist foreign policy and those who thought Disraeli's jingoism immoral. As peers, neither Disraeli nor Salisbury campaigned; indeed, Salisbury took himself off to Biarritz for the duration. But Gladstone did, standing this time in yet another constituency (Gladstone was as politically peripatetic as Winston Churchill would be, each man representing five seats over the course of a long career), the normally Conservative seat of Midlothian, where the incumbent Conservative MP, William Scott, Lord Dalkeith, had the advantage of a whole pile of faggot votes,* supplied by his father the 5th duke of Buccleuch.

The result was a rout of the Tories. In virtually a mirror image of the previous election, Disraeli slipped from 352 seats to 238, the Tories' worst result since 1832, and the Liberals went from 243 to 352, the remnant being Irish home rulers. Gladstone even beat Dalkeith; and although he had startled his newly ex-Cabinet on 16 February 1874 with the news that he would 'no longer retain the leadership of the liberal party, nor resume it, unless the party had settled its difficulties',[69] he was back as Prime Minister. Beaconsfield, who thought Gladstone almost criminally insane and derided him as 'a sophistical rhetorician inebriated with the exuberance of his own verbosity', fumed from the comfort of the Lords, where he considered himself 'dead, but in the elysian fields'.[70] For a while he continued to lead the diminished Tory troops. But within a year, on 19 April 1881, he caught pneumonia and died. One of parliament's great sparring matches was over.

Disraeli was a man of talent who added colour to a rather dingy circle of aristocrats and industrialists. But there are elements of his character that are difficult to explain away. In the Commons battle with Peel over the corn laws, when Peel claimed that Disraeli had sought a ministerial post from him, he denied it. We now know that Peel had Disraeli's importunate letter asking to join the government in his pocket – but inexplicably chose not to deploy it as he sank under

---

* From 1432 only those with freehold property worth 40s had been entitled to vote, but subsequent centuries had seen this provision diluted so that the freeholder could subdivide the property many times over and thereby enfranchise tenants, allies and friends. These 'faggot' votes were abolished by the 1867 Reform Act for borough constituencies, but remained for county constituencies until the Representation of the People Act 1884.

the waves of Disraeli's contempt. To lie and get away with it is one thing. But years later Disraeli was in a similar position to Peel, and took a very different course. Robert Lowe, who notwithstanding his assault on parliamentary reform had been Gladstone's Chancellor of the Exchequer and Home Secretary, had made a rather wild claim regarding the Royal Titles Act at a dinner in East Retford, namely that 'at least two previous Ministers have entirely refused to have anything to do with such a change. More pliant persons have now been found, and I have no doubt the thing will be done.'[71] In other words, the queen had previously asked for the title and been refused it. Disraeli could easily have let the matter pass. It was hardly a matter of great consequence. But with an eye for a vindictive put-down he took no time in having Lowe humiliated, getting his friend Charles Lewis to table a motion on 2 May which ostensibly sought to establish whether successive prime ministers had broken their oath of office wherein they bound themselves not to reveal the queen's counsel, but effectively censured Lowe for taking the queen's name in vain. Disraeli added to Lowe's misery by delivering a message from the queen herself – involving a moment of pantomime in which Disraeli sought the Speaker's permission, as the rules of the House specify that one cannot cite the monarch in such a way as to influence debate. The Speaker, well aware what the Prime Minister required of him and pretending that what Disraeli was about to communicate related 'to matters of fact, and is not made to influence the judgment of the House', allowed Disraeli to proceed.[72] Disraeli then swatted Lowe. He was there to say, on behalf of her Majesty, that there was 'not the slightest foundation' in his remarks and it was all just 'calumnious gossip'. Two days later Lowe abjectly apologized, a crushed and defeated man who was never again to rise to his former oratorical heights.

Gladstone was to serve four terms as Prime Minister, handing in his final resignation at the age of eighty-four and outlasting Disraeli by seventeen years, during which the melting pot of party politics would be reheated by the issue of home rule for Ireland. New parties would again be formed; but even before the splitting off of the Liberal Unionists, the supposedly clear divide between Whig–Liberal and Tory–Conservative bestows a false degree of clarity on a politically chaotic half-century.

With massive sociological and industrial change at home, and immense challenges abroad (most notably the Crimean, Afghan and Boer wars), it was an era of political cross-dressing. Although Disraeli made the case for keeping the party demarcations clear, as often as not it was the centrists and the party switchers who led the way – the Canningites, the Peelites, the liberal conservatives. Graham, for instance, once a Whig and then a Peelite Tory, was elected as a Liberal at Carlisle in 1852 and joined the Aberdeen government later that year as First Lord of the Admiralty, the very post he had held (and resigned) under Grey. Burdett, by contrast, eschewed his radicalism in 1837, crossed the floor and subsided into wealthy Tory old age, 'the head of the un-ennobled English Aristocracy', as *The Times* put it.[73] The Liberals' 'Grand Old Man' Gladstone had also made a political journey and would describe himself as a 'liberal conservative' as late as 1870. And the 15th earl of Derby abandoned his father's (second) party and joined the Liberals, though he eventually fell out with Gladstone.

Even more importantly, there was no ineluctable process whereby Whigs became Liberals and Tories Conservatives, as both Liberals and Conservatives were far looser agglomerations than a modern political party: emulsions that could easily separate into their constituent fluids rather than solutions. And while some elements of the modern party system were now in place, party politics was by no means yet fixed as the best or only way to run the nation. Grey's son General Sir Charles Grey wrote to Derby in 1866 that he had 'no personal predilection for any party' and owned merely that if he had to choose one side of the House, 'it might very probably be yours'.[74] So too J. A. Roebuck, the independent radical MP who condemned the Whigs out of office as demagogues and in office as exclusive oligarchs, and seemed to distrust pretty well everyone, reckoned that 'there is really no difference between the two [parties], except some small rages of bigotry and intolerance that stick unwillingly to them' and hoped for the formation of 'a strong Ministerial party in England'.[75]

Even at the substratum level of fundamental political principle the two parties were shifting sands. The Whigs and radicals brought in the 1832 Reform Act and the secret ballot, but Wellington and Peel drove through Catholic emancipation, and Disraeli and Derby's Reform Act of 1867 was more significant than Grey's thirty-five years earlier. Disraeli's second administration claimed the idea of a strong-armed British foreign policy for the Conservatives, but his jingoism was on a par with that of Palmerston, the first Prime Minister of an entirely Liberal government. No one party had a monopoly of concern for the poor, either. The former miner Alexander Macdonald, who was elected MP for Stafford in 1874, said of the Conservatives in 1879 that they had 'done more for the working classes in five years than the Liberals have in fifty',[76] and Conservative MPs such as Shaftesbury, Michael Sadler and Richard Oastler campaigned on social issues that many later laissez-faire Conservatives might find abhorrent. In policy terms only free trade, the rock on which Peel foundered, provided a constantly clear party demarcation between the liberal Conservatives and the protectionist Conservatives. In one sense this was only to be expected. All MPs were still cut from the same, very expensive cloth (and the same cloth as their brothers, uncles, fathers and cousins in the Lords). They were unpaid and a political campaign was costly. It was not surprising that in an era of hung parliaments, personality and performance mattered more than policy or party, nor that the besetting sin of the Victorian parliament was the acrimony that only small distinctions can engender.

_d_ Edition. Price 1s.

CRAWFORD DIVORCE CASE

(VERBATIM REPORT.)

ILLUSTRATED WITH PORTRAITS OF

SIR CHARLES DILKE

AND OTHERS CONCERNED.

LONDON:—F. HENNING, 11, RED LION COURT, FLEET STREET, E.C.

As President of the Local Government Board from 1882 to 1885, Sir Charles Dilke was one of the Liberal party's most effective radical leaders, but any further aspirations he might have had came to an abrupt end when he was involved in the well-publicized divorce of his parliamentary colleague Donald Crawford.

3

Extravagant and Erring Spirits

IT WAS FRIDAY, 16 JULY 1886. Sir Charles Dilke, the prominent Liberal MP for Chelsea, was in the witness box. The jury had to decide whether the decree nisi granted to the dour Scottish newly elected Liberal MP for Lanarkshire North East, Donald Crawford, should be made absolute. In the original divorce hearing in February neither Crawford's wife Virginia nor Dilke, who the Crawfords maintained had seduced her, had taken the stand. The only evidence brought forward then had been some anonymous letters sent to Crawford and his account of his wife's 'confession', which included the resonant allegation that Dilke had taught her 'every French vice'. In any normal circumstance this would have been regarded as inadmissible hearsay; but the judge had both granted the divorce and implausibly declared that there was not 'the shadow of a case' against Dilke. In other words, she was guilty of adultery with him, but he was not guilty of adultery with her.

But now Dilke was in the witness box, as, under pressure from the press, especially the editor of the *Pall Mall Gazette*, W. T. Stead, he had decided to get the queen's proctor* to intervene by seeking that the

---

* The monarch's solicitor acting in probate or divorce cases.

divorce should not be allowed on the grounds that no adultery had taken place. As Dilke's day in court wore on it became clear to all that this was an act of monumental legal folly. The judge clarified that whereas in the previous trial 'it was for the petitioner [Crawford] to prove that his wife had committed adultery', on this occasion 'it is for the Queen's Proctor to prove that the respondent did not commit adultery with Sir Charles Dilke'.[1] Proving a negative is a tall order at the best of times, but in this case it was virtually impossible. As Dilke wrote in his diary, 'I [am] not a party, and – though really tried by a kind of Star Chamber – not represented, not allowed to cross-examine, not allowed to call witnesses.'[2] The counsel for the queen's proctor, Sir Walter Phillimore, did help establish a robust alibi for Dilke for at least one of the supposed encounters. But under cross-examination by Henry Matthews, himself a former MP who was soon to be back in the House as a Tory Home Secretary, Dilke looked shifty and un-convincing. He confessed he had had an affair with Virginia Crawford's mother, Mrs Eustace Smith, whose other daughter was married to Dilke's brother. Dilke's alibis were undermined by new evidence, a new set of liaisons was alleged, and he was ridiculed for providing his diary as evidence but cutting out sections. When it came to Virginia's turn, although under questioning she admitted adultery with a Captain Forster, she came across as serious, sensible and reliable. The jury took just fifteen minutes to deliberate: the queen's proctor had not proved that adultery had not taken place, the divorce should proceed and, by extension, Dilke must have lied.

In one sense this was just a personal tragedy. It is quite probable that Dilke was telling the truth, as the second case did not, properly speaking, determine his innocence or guilt. Yet the events shook his recently contracted marriage to an old friend, Mrs Pattison, and in retrospect the folly of his taking to the courts at all ranks with that of Oscar Wilde's madcap suit against the marquess of Queensberry for libel, the failure of which led to Wilde's prosecution and imprison-ment in 1895 for 'gross indecency' with men. But Dilke's disgrace was of even greater significance. For Dilke could so easily have been a radical Liberal Prime Minister. *Soigné* and well connected, he was also clever and capable. He wrote well and he knew how to run a campaign. He was courageous and principled, and was widely respected as an aficionado of the arts, a powerful oarsman and a passionate exponent of a muscular Christianity (although his political attitudes were entirely secularist).

He had a clear idea of what he thought, and was ready to act accordingly. When first elected in 1868, just days after the publication of his bestselling travel book, *Greater Britain*, he rapidly made a name for himself, helping to restore the vote to women ratepayers in municipal elections (which they had lost in 1835) and running a countrywide republican campaign against the requests for parliamentary pensions for Victoria's children. The campaign received little support in parliament and earned him the perpetual enmity of the queen, but was not to be the last of his divergences from the Victorian straight and narrow. In 1870 he travelled with the Prussian army and regularly visited France during the nine months' siege of Paris. He was back in Paris in 1874, by his own admission sent 'mad' by the death of his first wife Katherine, and by the time he returned to London for the 1875 parliamentary session he had become a teetotaller and vegetarian. After another lengthy foreign tour, he started the 1876 session with a new political friend at his side: Joseph Chamberlain, who had been mayor of Birmingham from 1873 to 1876, but now sought a larger stage for his brand of Liberal radicalism as MP for the city, and who stayed with Dilke at his home in fashionable Sloane Street. By the time of the 1880 election this was a firm and mutual political partnership and Gladstone, recognizing their talents, promoted Chamberlain as President of the Board of Trade and made Dilke under-secretary at the Foreign Office for two and half years before giving him the presidency of the Local Government Board with a seat in the Cabinet, in which capacity he took through the radical Redistribution of Seats Act 1885 which enfranchised more than half the male population.

In every respect then, Dilke was a formidable, well-supported member of the Liberal front bench with a promising career ahead of him. The timing of his discovery that Mrs Crawford had 'confessed' to her husband, on Saturday, 18 July 1885, could not have been worse. Gladstone had only recently (8 June) been defeated on an amendment to the Finance Bill and resigned (24 June), to be replaced by the marquess of Salisbury at the head of a minority Tory government. Considered the most effective radical Liberal member of the Cabinet, Dilke was in a strong enough position to think of the premiership for himself, but he knew that a scandal of this kind could put paid to any such ambition. The following Tuesday he tried to get Virginia to retract her story, but she refused. Downcast, he wrote in his diary two days later: 'It is curious that only a week ago Chn. & I agreed at his wish that I shd. be the future leader, & that only three days ago Mr G. had expressed the same wish.'[3] Dilke now judged that he might throw the hounds off the trail with a judiciously timed marriage and rapidly got in touch with Mrs Pattison, who was in India. Four days after parliament was prorogued for the summer, their engagement was announced in *The Times* of 18 August and on 3 October they married at St Luke's Chelsea with Chamberlain as best man. This show of marital harmony availed him little, though, as Crawford, whom he had appointed to the Scottish Boundary Commission in 1884 and for whom he was busy securing a parliamentary seat in the forthcoming election, pushed for a divorce, naming Dilke as the co-respondent.

As the election approached, then, with demands for Irish home rule tipping the balance in the political seesaw and an internal party battle raging between the Whiggish (and priggish) marquess of Hartington and the radical Chamberlain (who was threatening to run a 'Radical in every constituency'), one of the most effective radical Liberals was absorbed in defending his own personal position, rather than engaging with the 75-year-old Gladstone, who had long been thinking of retiring. Dilke retained his seat, narrowly, and he was numbered among the Liberals and home rule supporters who voted Salisbury out on 27 January 1886. Indeed, he and Chamberlain drafted the key amendment over breakfast at Sloane Street. But with the first divorce case imminent and the queen as hostile as ever, Dilke was left off Gladstone's list of the new government. Colleagues wrote kind notes. The new Foreign Secretary, the 5th earl of Rosebery, even thought that by 'universal consent' his job should have been Dilke's had he not had to stand aside. But as Dilke focused on the February trial, the row between Chamberlain and Gladstone festered, and on 26 March Chamberlain resigned from the new Cabinet, determined to vote against the Home Rule Bill Gladstone believed was necessary to secure the wider support of the home rule MPs led by Charles Parnell. Dilke disagreed with Chamberlain and wrote to him poignantly: 'It is a curious fact that we should without a difference have gone through the trials of the years in which we were rivals, & that the differences & the break should have come now that I have – at least in my own belief, & that of most people – ceased for ever to count in politics.'[4] When the second reading came, on 8 June, Chamberlain joined the Tories and Whiggish Liberals in defeating the Bill by thirty, but Dilke silently stuck by Gladstone. The subsequent election saw Gladstone lose 143 seats, including Dilke's at Chelsea; so by the time of the second trial eleven days later Dilke had lost his seats in the Cabinet and in parliament, he had effectively lost his closest friend, and he had seen his divided political family suffer the biggest reversal of any party since 1832. For most men that would be enough to crack their sanity or self-esteem.

Although vicious commentary was passed on Dilke's fall and the queen even tried to have him removed from the Privy Council (which was by then and is now a lifetime appointment), Dilke did accomplish a minor comeback, getting elected in 1892 for the mining constituency of the Forest of Dean and remaining its MP until his death in January 1911, by which time he had become a close friend of all the new leaders of the Labour party and secured the first legislation for a minimum wage for the 200,000 or so workers in the ready-made tailoring, chain-making, paper box-making and machine lace-making industries. There were further sadnesses. His wife died in 1904 and his son was locked up as a 'lunatic'. But for his ill-advised recourse to the law in

1886, Dilke might have united the Liberals under his own leadership, deprived Salisbury of the premiership and made the creation of the Labour party redundant. It is impossible to tell. But it is difficult not to regret the fall of a man over what his lawyer provocatively called 'indiscretions', especially when much of the now available evidence suggests that he was innocent.

The bigger point, though, is that all too often the axe of political humiliation has fallen so capriciously when it comes to sexual peccadilloes. Parliament has always had its fair share of MPs, lords and bishops who were more sexually active than a conventional monogamous marriage would allow. In the aristocratically self-confident era of the Restoration, extra-marital sexual activity was as actively pursued in semi-private as it was condemned in public (witness Samuel Pepys, who supposedly detested infidelity yet regularly engaged in it). The epitome of this rakes' world was the group of well-placed courtiers and politicians Andrew Marvell dubbed the 'merry gang', most of whom were members of one house of parliament or the other. These included George Villiers, the 2nd duke of Buckingham, whose sexual reputation seems to have done little to prevent his joining the all-important foreign affairs sub-committee of the Privy Council or playing a central role with Shaftesbury in the Exclusion crisis. John Sheffield, 3rd earl of Mulgrave, had a momentary lapse from favour when it was rumoured that he had tried to seduce the duke of York's daughter Anne, but neither his several liaisons nor his two illegitimate children stood in the way of his becoming Lord Chamberlain to James II in gratitude for his consistent support during the Exclusion crisis, and Lord Privy Seal and Lord President of the Council as one of Queen Anne's closest favourites. John Wilmot, the 2nd earl of Rochester, who inherited his title (but not much else) when just ten, and who led a life, as he put it, devoted to Cupid and Bacchus, was also a member of the gang, having enough mistresses to people a seraglio, including the talented but ugly Elizabeth Barry and 'the prettiest, but also the worst actress in the realm', Sarah Cooke. When terminally ill he told Gilbert Burnet that it seemed unreasonable to imagine that natural appetites 'were put into a man only to be restrained'.[5] Sir Charles Sedley would have agreed, as he led a similarly unconventional life, especially once he had packed his mentally unstable wife off to a convent in Ghent. On one occasion in 1663 his antics got the better of him, when he, Lord Buckhurst and (the appropriately named) Sir Thomas Ogle appeared on the balcony of the Cock Tavern in Bow Street, Covent Garden, kept by 'Oxford Kate'. According to Samuel Pepys, Sedley 'showed his nakedness – acting all the postures of lust and buggery that could be imagined, and . . . that being done, he took a glass of wine and washed his prick in it and then drank it off; and then took another and drank the King's health'.[6] This earned him raucous cheers, a minor riot and a fine of 2,000 marks in court, but it did not stop him getting elected as MP for New Romney in 1668 and in every election bar one up until his death in 1701. Nor did Henry Jermyn's membership of the gang prevent the former MP from being Lord Chamberlain and earl of St Albans. Even the accusation, recycled in Pepys's diary, that John Dolben, the bishop of Rochester, had put his hand 'into a gentleman (who now comes to bear evidence against him) his codpiece while they were sitting at table together',[7] while it might have deprived Dolben of a few nights' sleep, did not deprive him of his see, or indeed of promotion, as he was later made archbishop of York.

At this time, of course, ministerial promotion was entirely dependent on the whim of the monarch,* and it would have been beyond hypocritical for either Charles II or his brother James II to cavil at anyone's sexual mores. Charles sired at least fourteen illegitimate children, one of whom, the duke of Monmouth, was for a time the main Protestant claimant to the throne; and the 'merry gang' regularly aided and abetted Charles's own sexual exploits. James was no different, conducting well-publicized affairs with Sir Charles

* Formally speaking, ministers still are appointed by the monarch; however, with the entrenchment of the two-party state in the early nineteenth century, the monarch's freedom to choose the Prime Minister diminished, just as the Prime Minister's freedom of manoeuvre in assembling a ministry grew.

Sedley's only daughter, Catherine, with Arabella Churchill, the sister of the duke of Marlborough, with Marlborough's sister-in-law Frances Jennings and with Anne Carnegie, the countess of Southesk. The same could be said of nearly all their successors. If anything, William III's lack of a mistress made people suspicious of his male friendships, especially with Hans William Bentinck and the handsome young Arnold Joost van Keppel, both of whom William raised to earldoms.

In the eighteenth century, sexual deviation from the monogamous norm was a bar to public office only in extreme circumstances. Walpole had a string of extra-marital affairs and was widely known to be estranged from his wife, who had so many lovers of her own that people played a guessing game as to the parenthood of her son Horatio. Sir Francis Dashwood was so bold as to rebuild an old Cistercian abbey in Buckinghamshire and fit it out for orgies attended by a special order of 'knights of St Francis'. The oath of secrecy imposed on the knights clearly had some effect as his membership proved no bar to his becoming Chancellor of the Exchequer to Lord Bute or in 1766 Postmaster-General to Chatham, a post he held for fifteen years until his death in 1781.

In the nineteenth century the same continued to be true for many key political figures. Palmerston, for instance, may have married late, at the age of fifty-five, but he did not acquire his nickname of 'Lord Cupid' by chance. A regular at Almack's Club in St James's, which was renowned as the only club to admit women, Palmerston managed to conduct affairs with at least three of the club's principal patronesses: Dorothea Lieven, the extremely independent wife of the Russian ambassador; Sarah Villiers, the wealthy countess of Jersey, who was such a chatterbox that she was nicknamed 'Silence'; and, most sustainedly, the vivacious Emily Cowper (née Lamb), Melbourne's sister, who was married to the lethargic Lord Cowper. Nor was this the full extent of the wild oats Palmerston scattered throughout his twenty-seven pre-marital years in the Cabinet, for his diary's constant references to a 'fine day' or 'fine evening' suggest yet more liaisons with a string of unnamed women. Indeed, it was widely believed that he had fathered at least one of Lady Cowper's children. The earnestly religious and philanthropic Lord Shaftesbury might suggest that 'his light and jaunty manner did him great disservice in his earlier years: and . . . I could see nothing in him of the statesman, but a good deal of the dandy,'[8] and Victoria and Albert disapproved of his reputation as a roué, but these sexual dalliances did Palmerston little or no political harm. If anything, his renown endeared him to the working population – and the relationship with Emily Cowper, which eventually became a loving marriage when Lord Cowper died two days into Victoria's new reign, tied one originally Tory viscount (Palmerston) to a resolutely Whig viscount (Melbourne) in a way that would otherwise have been unthinkable.

Melbourne's own private life could easily have suffered the slings and arrows of tabloid journalism. Every age has its own fashion in human attractiveness, but William Lamb (who inherited his father's titles as Viscount Melbourne in July 1828) would have passed for handsome in pretty well any age. Tall, with cascades of thick dark hair and an intense gaze, he could command a room. The second son of an elegant Whig society charmer and (probably but not certainly) her brutish and shy husband, Peniston Lamb, sometime MP and Viscount Melbourne, Lamb was destined to lead a complex emotional life. He married Caroline Ponsonby on 3 June 1805, but it was to prove an unhappy match: their first child Augustus was, in the language of the time, 'retarded', their daughter died after just a few days and Caroline herself suffered from severe bouts of mental instability. Most notably, in July 1813 she attempted to take her own life at Lady Heathcote's ball when Lord Byron had refused her approaches, smashing a glass and trying to slash her wrists with it. Since Lamb had lost his parliamentary seat the previous year, as much through carelessness as anything, these were vagrant days in his career, estranged from his wife and politically ill-at-ease with either the Perceval or the Brougham set. Caroline's whirling decline into insanity continued, and for much of the rest of her life she was confined at Lamb's country home at Brocket, even after their formal separation in 1825. It would be particularly hypocritical of her husband to have condemned Caroline merely for her adultery, however, for he was himself twice named as co-respondent in divorce cases. In the Regency era of sexual freedom, Melbourne barely had to miss a day in parliament to deal with these legal cases, but by the end of the century either of these affairs could easily have ended Melbourne's career if a jealous lover or an indignant journalist had thought to stir up a scandal.

Even in the late Victorian era there were senior figures in government who had illicit affairs yet survived without opprobrium. Henry James,* for instance, started life as a Liberal, abandoned Gladstone over home rule and sat in Salisbury's Cabinet as Chancellor of the Duchy of Lancaster, yet refused to marry the mother of his daughter – or anyone else. Gladstone himself, for all his high Anglican sermonizing (and his attempt to talk out the Matrimonial Causes Act 1857, which brought divorce within the purview of the civil courts), would hardly count among the pure, as he regularly visited prostitutes to rescue them or lose himself and returned home to flagellate himself for courting evil; and Spencer Cavendish, the 8th duke of Devonshire, who succeeded Gladstone as Liberal leader in opposition between 1875 and 1880, kept the same mistress, Catherine Walters (albeit at a different juncture), as the future King Edward VII.

Two successive Liberal prime ministers of the early twentieth century, H. H. Asquith and David Lloyd George, were similarly casual in their marital fidelity. Again, their predilections were hardly a secret. The suffragette Ethel Smyth complained of Asquith: 'I think it disgraceful that millions of women shall be trampled underfoot because of the convictions of an old man who notoriously can't be left alone in a room with a young girl after dinner'; and Lord Lovat complained about Asquith's addiction to 'drink, bridge and holding girls' hands'.[9] Lloyd George maintained a thirty-year affair with his secretary Frances Stevenson, leaving his wife Margaret at home in north Wales even while he attended the Paris peace conference with his mistress.

---

* Not to be confused with the American-born author.

Although, much to the fury of his two children, he eventually married Frances after Margaret had died, by then he had persuaded her to have an abortion on two occasions and she had borne him a daughter, Jennifer. Twice Lloyd George sued those who threatened to cite him as co-respondent in a divorce, and he had affairs with the wives of at least three Liberal MPs. Even the magnificently haughty and judgemental George Curzon, whose wife died in 1906 soon after he returned from a spell as Viceroy of India, had a decade-long affair with the married novelist Elinor Glyn, overlapping with his time in the Cabinet from 1915.

Considering the fact that in 1869 the Prince of Wales had very nearly been cited as co-respondent in the divorce case of the Conservative MP Sir Charles Mordaunt, and that some thirty years later he was reputed to have had a box reserved at his coronation as King Edward VII for his lovers, including the actress Sarah Bernhardt and the married Alice Keppel and Mrs Hartman, it is difficult not to construe the reaction to Dilke as capricious and hypocritical, fashioned out of distaste for his politics rather than his mores. Indeed, it is a particular irony that the Harmsworth brothers who formed the backbone of the new tabloid press in the Edwardian era, owning the *Sunday Dispatch*, the *Daily Mail*, the *Daily Mirror*, *The Times*, *The Sunday Times* and the *Observer*, led far from conventional lives. The eldest, Alfred, had a son by a family maid, but did not marry her, and when he did marry had two further sons and a daughter by one mistress, Kathleen Wrohan, and conducted a second affair with his secretary, Louise Owen, and a third with the novelist Betty Van Hutten. None of this stopped him exercising phenomenal political influence, leading the British war effort in America in 1917 and becoming Viscount Northcliffe (although his lack of a legitimate heir did stop him from passing the title on). As for the second Harmsworth brother, Harold, he had a string of affairs with other women, while his wife Mary was mistress to another Harmsworth brother, St John. Yet Harold became President of the Air Council in Lloyd George's wartime government and joined the House of Lords as Viscount Rothermere, a title inherited by Esmond Harmsworth, though he was probably St John's son. Sexual infidelity, even on a grand scale, was not of itself a bar to advancement.

The same mixture of political misfortune and social hypocrisy that engulfed Dilke also trapped the Irish nationalist Charles Stewart Parnell, the third son of a large but broken family in Wicklow, who first came to parliament in 1875. Parnell was always a man of mixed political loyalties, a landowner with Tory sympathies but a nationalist scandalized by what he saw as an iniquitous and oppressive system of Irish government. He started to make his mark almost immediately as, with other Irish colleagues, he mounted a deliberate campaign of parliamentary obstruction, using every available technical manoeuvre to delay business. When Parnell managed to get the House declared inquorate late on 2 July 1877 by moving the same motion seventeen times, the Chancellor of the Exchequer Sir Stafford Northcote moved the next day that a new power be granted to the Speaker to declare a member out of order such that he be not heard again during the remainder of the debate. The motion was carried, but Parnell knew how to stretch rather than break the rules, and on 31 July the Irish members dragged out a debate that started on Tuesday afternoon at four o'clock for twenty-six hours. This 'barricade' of obstruction continued unabated throughout the next three years – years of terrible famine in Ireland – until 1880, when Northcote returned with a new idea: any member named by the Speaker for obstruction could be removed from the House for a day, and three such namings would lead to a week's suspension. When Gladstone rose to speak on 3 February 1881 another Irish member, John Dillon, was so 'named' for constantly interrupting the Prime Minister; once the House had voted to remove Dillon and he had been dragged out by the Sergeant-at-Arms, Parnell took up the baton, demanding a debate on the motion that Gladstone 'be no further heard'. As Hansard puts it, 'From this incident forward, the Business of the House proceeded under indescribable confusion.'[10] Parnell too was named and removed – as, one by one, were thirty-three more Irish MPs.

Parnell was undoubtedly accomplished. He engineered the close identification of home rule with the Irish Catholic Church, though he was himself an Anglican. He gave structure and discipline to the Home Rule League, which he renamed the Irish Parliamentary Party, and increased its seats to eighty-six at the 1885 election (but, curiously, only eighty-five in 1886). When it was alleged that he had privately supported the murder in 1882 of the Chief Secretary for Ireland, Lord Cavendish, who was married to Gladstone's niece and was younger brother of Lord Hartington, he managed to secure a commission of inquiry that proved the supposed evidence to have been forged, and returned to parliament on 1 March 1890 to be greeted by a standing ovation led by Gladstone.

Parnell was at the height of his power, then, when on 24 December 1889 Captain William O'Shea MP, for whom he had personally secured a parliamentary selection in 1886, named Parnell as the co-respondent in his divorce. In this case there was no doubting the facts. Katherine (Kitty) O'Shea had long been separated from the captain, had borne Parnell three children and had set up home with him in 1886. Nor, at first, was there any political problem, as resolutions supporting his continuing leadership of the party streamed in and even the Catholic hierarchy remained taciturn. But something changed when the divorce was granted on 15 November 1890. Parnell was re-elected leader on the twenty-fifth, but by then Gladstone had let Parnell know of his disapproval, which might be terminal for their parties' alliance. This changed things. Irish MPs demanded a new leadership election, and at noon on Monday, 1 December the first of five packed meetings was held in Committee Room 15 in the Commons, with Parnell in the chair. Tim Healy, the volatile MP for North Longford who had only backed O'Shea's nomination in 1886 out of respect for Parnell, laid into him, deriding any service he had given to the party. Parnell replied by pointing out that the ingrate owed everything to him – and survived the first day. Healy even wrote to his wife that he could not 'conceive of any other man going through such an ordeal with so much dignity'.[11] But the acrimony grew ever more sour as the days wore on. On the Tuesday, Parnell lost a technical amendment tabled by his supporter Colonel John Nolan to delay the matter by forty-four votes to twenty-nine; Healy stood up to suggest that if Parnell would stand aside temporarily, he would be the first to demand his return – and wept. On the Thursday, after a long speech by Parnell on the continuing discussions with the Liberals, Healy charged him with insincerity and the meeting collapsed into bitterness. J. J. Clancy, a former classics teacher, now MP for North County Dublin and a Parnell supporter, demanded 'away with him, away with him', to which John O'Connor, another Parnellite, sarcastically added 'crucify him', and it was only with difficulty that order was restored. When it came to the Saturday, by which time overtures to the Liberals had failed, Parnell lost control of the meeting as O'Connor and William Abraham (the Congregationalist MP for West Limerick*) jumped up to propose opposing motions. In the ensuing pandemonium another Parnell supporter, the ever-conciliatory John Redmond, shouted out: 'Who is the master of the party?' – to which Healy responded with witty venom: 'Aye, but who is the mistress of the party?' It was waspish and effective. Parnell was on the brink of assaulting him, then merely called him a 'cowardly little scoundrel' and attempted to return to the agenda as forty-four MPs stormed out to form the separate Irish National Federation.

Parnell had been masterly in his use of the chair, but finally Healy had realized that 'unless we had deposed [him] . . . he would have kept us there proposing resolutions like repeating decimals until doomsday'.[12] Parnell even had the emotional strength to jest – 'You may get another leader to succeed me, but you'll find it very hard to get a leader who takes so much killing as I' – but by the end of the day he was a broken leader, and although he received a hero's welcome in Dublin on 10 December, the remaining Parnellites, led by Redmond, were few in number and he failed to win a seat in three successive

* Not to be confused with William Abraham, known as 'Mabon', MP for the Rhondda.

by-elections. Even his marriage to Kitty on 25 June at the registry office in Steyning near Brighton could not rescue his career. That same day the Catholic hierarchy, who were now actively supporting the Irish National Federation, published a harsh condemnation. 'By his public misconduct,' they wrote, he 'has utterly disqualified himself to be . . . leader.' He died on 10 October that year, just forty-five years old, and it was not until 1900 that the Irish nationalist parties were to reunite under the single banner of the United Irish League.

Although public attitudes towards divorce and adultery began to change in the twentieth century, and there were several attempts to change the unequal provisions of the 1857 Act that allowed a man to divorce his wife on the grounds of adultery alone but a woman to divorce her husband only if she could also prove some other matrimonial offence, culminating in the Matrimonial Causes Acts of 1923 and 1937 and the Divorce Reform Act 1969, Parnell was not to be the last politician undone by marital infidelity. Indeed, social opprobrium and political disgrace attended sexual laxity long after Cole Porter's innuendo-strewn song 'Let's do it, let's fall in love' became a hit in 1928. With parliament still a largely male preserve, fears about blackmail, prostitution, venereal disease and unwanted pregnancies littered the public and parliamentary debates, especially prior to the arrival of cures for syphilis and gonorrhoea after the Second World War. Throughout, the Church of England maintained a fiercely moralistic approach, best exemplified by the archbishop of Canterbury, Cosmo Gordon Lang, who waged a particularly vicious campaign against Edward VIII's proposal to marry the twice-divorced Wallis Simpson in 1936. Dripping poison into the ears of both the Prime Minister, Stanley Baldwin, and the editor of *The Times*, Geoffrey Dawson, Lang alleged Edward was an alcoholic, mentally ill and suffering from 'symptoms of persecution-mania'. When he had finally engineered Edward's abdication it was difficult not to conclude that relations with a divorcee could end even a royal career.

Quite what circumstances merited a political resignation, though, became steadily more uncertain – and still the axe fell capriciously. In the case of John Profumo, the son of an Italian baron and diplomat, who was first elected in 1940 while serving in the army and was attacked by the Tory chief whip David Margesson for voting against the Chamberlain government in the Norway debate*with the stinging words 'you utterly contemptible little shit', it was fairly clear. On 5 June 1963 he confessed to the Commons not only to having had an affair with a model, Christine Keeler (who also counted the Russian naval attaché among her lovers), but, more importantly, to having lied about it when a Labour MP, George Wigg, had challenged him in the Commons. A subsequent inquiry found that no harm had been done to national security, but the right honourable member had lied; so he resigned as Secretary for War and as MP and devoted himself to charity.

In the case of George Jellicoe, who in 1935 inherited an earldom from his father, the renowned naval commander of the First World War, the argument for resignation was less clear. Indeed, he was particularly unfortunate. Jellicoe was a bit of a Lothario and forfeited his diplomatic career in the Foreign Office for conducting an extra-marital affair in 1958, but throughout the 1960s he successfully mixed a business career with attendance at the Lords and, despite being breathalysed and banned from driving just before the 1970 election (which would almost certainly preclude a ministerial career today), was made Lord Privy Seal and party leader in the Lords by Edward Heath. Jellicoe's downfall in 1973, in fact, came about entirely by accident. News reached the ears of the Prime Minister and of the Leader of the Commons, James Prior, that another Conservative, Lord Lambton, the far less pleasant MP for Berwick-upon-Tweed, who had disclaimed his father's peerage in 1970 in order to continue in the Commons as under-secretary for defence, frequently availed himself of the services of a London call-girl, Norma Levy. Bizarrely – indeed, by today's standards, incomprehensibly – both the *News of the World* and the *Sunday People* had refused to run the story, but the police had

* See pages 171–4 below.

investigated and uncovered some cannabis and amphetamines in Lambton's flat. On 22 May Lambton resigned as both a minister and an MP. Jellicoe was only dragged into the matter at all because the police also came across a reference in one of Norma Levy's notebooks to 'Jellicoe.' Although this was nothing to do with the earl, and in fact referred to Jellicoe Hall in north London, when Heath asked Jellicoe whether he knew anything about the affair Jellicoe blithely admitted that he had used a separate call-girl agency, Mayfair Escorts, and swiftly resigned. Throughout the redundant inquiry, which concluded that the threat to security had been minimal, Lambton was prickly, providing a string of excuses for resorting to prostitutes (the futility of being a junior minister, the row over disclaiming his title); Alan Beith, who succeeded him as MP for Berwick, recalls that he was the kind of imperious Tory who thought nothing of using a government car to drop him off at a brothel and considered it an impertinence that anyone should question him. Jellicoe, by contrast, was remarkably cheery, and even his opponents in the Lords were notably effusive in their praise of him. But then, Jellicoe could afford his bonhomie. After all, he had retained his peerage –and would go on to survive the cull of hereditary peers in 1999. Lambton's misdemeanour was marginally greater, but his loss immeasurably so.

At the time, the *Daily Express* shared the contemporary sympathy, asking: 'Can we really afford to discard men of talent, wit and patriotism because their private lives fall short of blameless perfection?' Yet the political tumbrils continued to roll throughout the ensuing decades. In 1983 Cecil Parkinson, the debonair millionaire Secretary of State for Trade and Industry in Margaret Thatcher's government, resigned in the midst of the Tory party conference in Blackpool over the news that his secretary, Sara Keays, was pregnant with his child. Mrs Thatcher had been aware of his personal problems when she re-appointed him Chairman of the Conservative party after the 1983 election, but when Sara's father began to demand that Parkinson honour his pledge to marry her, Thatcher moved Parkinson to the trade and industry brief and Parkinson came clean to the press. What finally led to his resignation, though, was Keays' distressing account of the affair, which broke mid-conference. As with Lambton and Jellicoe, many of the press were sympathetic, and in 1987 Parkinson was to return to the Cabinet, a rehabilitation that might have suggested that judgemental attitudes around politicians' sexual lives were losing their purchase. So too might the reaction in 1992 to the revelation in the *News of the World* that the married leader of the Liberal Democrats, Paddy Ashdown, had had an affair with his secretary Tricia Howard. The fact that the evidence had been stolen from Ashdown's lawyer barely troubled the *News of the World*, but Ashdown's straight-forward admission of the affair left him virtually unscathed. When the actress Antonia de Sancha revealed later that year that she had had an affair with the married National Heritage Secretary, David Mellor, he remained in office, and it was only when the press reported that he had received two free holidays from overseas that he was forced to resign.

But then, in 1993, John Major launched his ill-fated 'back to basics' campaign at the Conservative party conference. Major never mentioned sexual morality, calling only for 'a country united around those old common-sense British values that should never have been pushed aside'. Yet the gentle suggestion that a Conservative govern-ment would embody 'traditional values' invited people to judge whether ministers practised what they preached. In other words, the sin was not sex, but hypocrisy; and it did not go unpunished. One by one the press unveiled Steven Norris, the transport minister, who had five mistresses; Tim Yeo, the married minister for the environment and the countryside, who had fathered a child by a Tory councillor, Julia Stent; the unmarried PPS Richard Spring, who had enjoyed a threesome; the married backbencher David Ashby, who had shared a bed in France with another man for reasons of economy; and Gary Waller, a bachelor backbencher, who had fathered a child by a mistress. The fact that Major himself, an uncensorious Prime Minister, had had an affair with Edwina Currie makes his adoption of the 'back to basics' campaign inexplicably crass.

Subsequent 'revelations' of infidelity have had to work hard to make themselves newsworthy. Robin Cook took a fair kicking from his former wife when his affair with his Commons secretary was revealed, but was highly respected as both Foreign Secretary and Leader of the House until his early death. John Prescott apologized for sleeping with his secretary and continued in government until Tony Blair resigned as Prime Minister, shaken in office but not stirred from it. MPs' sex lives still get covered in the press, but nobody seriously expects an adulterer to resign any longer. Perhaps a more fastidious era will return.

It was not just divorce, adultery and heterosexual promiscuity that could deal a blow to a political career, though. Sodomy (as opposed to homosexuality per se) had been a crime for centuries before Victoria came to the throne. In 1540 one of Thomas Cromwell's protégés, Walter Hungerford, was attainted for treason and executed on the basis of a charge sheet that included offences under the new Buggery Act of 1533 which had made sodomy a capital offence (as it was to remain in England until 1861). Nearly a hundred years later, in May 1631, Mervyn Truchet, the 2nd earl of Castlehaven (in the Irish peerage) and Baron Audley (in the English peerage), was beheaded for sodomy with two of his male servants, and in December 1640 John Atherton, the bishop of Waterford and Lismore, was hanged alongside his steward, lover and accuser John Childe. In all three cases the allegations were as much political and religious as they were criminal, but from at least the sixteenth century rumours about the sexual interests of politicians and courtiers were a key weapon in the political arsenal, and although prosecutions were rare, prominent political figures such as George Villiers, the 1st duke of Buckingham, and Francis Bacon faced a steady drone of scurrilous yet often well-founded accusations.

The same was true throughout the eighteenth century. John, Lord Hervey, the son of the Tory earl of Bristol, sat as MP for Bury St Edmunds for eight years from 1725 and was then accelerated into the House of Lords as a Whig supporter of Walpole. Hervey was effeminate, vain and bisexual. Despite being married and producing eight children, he had a longstanding affair with Henry Fox's brother Stephen, with whom he travelled abroad and frequently lived. He had other affairs, both with men – possibly including Frederick, the Prince of Wales, and the 24-year-old Italian intellectual Francesco Algarotti – and with women. His physical frailty (possibly due to epilepsy), his strangely bland diet, his tendency to cover his face in white powder so as to hide a scar: all these were fair game for his political opponents. So the arch-Tory poet Alexander Pope satirized him as a 'fop at the toilet' who 'now trips a lady and now struts a lord' and William Pulteney reckoned him 'such a nice Composition of the two Sexes, that it is difficult to distinguish which is more predominant'[13] – a gibe that led to a duel in which Hervey was nearly killed. Yet notwithstanding these barbs, he spent nearly thirteen years as Vice-Chamberlain and Lord Privy Seal, managed to persuade Walpole to make his lover Fox earl of Ilchester, and when he died in 1743 left his friend, fellow privy councillor and quite probably lover Thomas Winnington MP a large legacy. Another member of the Holland House group, Sir Robert Walpole's son Horace, who was a particular fan of Winnington's, was probably homosexual and certainly had a crush on his schoolfriend and travelling companion, the duke of Newcastle's young nephew and heir Henry Pelham-Clinton, earl of Lincoln. Such a liaison between the scions of two premiership families might have attracted the attention of opponents, had not the principals protected themselves by their reticence: for Lincoln, who was reputedly the handsomest and best-endowed man in England, largely eschewed politics and Walpole largely kept himself celibate.

One MP who was not attracted to celibacy was the only son of a wealthy sugar planter in Jamaica, William Beckford, who followed his father into parliament in 1784 as MP for Wells. Having inherited his father's very extensive estates in 1781 and married sensibly (if not wealthily), Beckford might have expected to prosper politically. There was talk of his receiving a peerage. But then Alexander Wedderburn, Lord Loughborough, the recently appointed Lord Justice of the

Common Pleas, intercepted love letters between Beckford and Loughborough's new wife's nephew, William 'Kitty' Courtenay. Fearing prosecution when Loughborough gave these to the press, Beckford fled the country. He nevertheless retained his seat, re-electing himself in his pocket borough of Hindon in 1790 and, once Loughborough had died, serving another fourteen years as MP. Beckford's political impact was minimal as he devoted his energies to writing (his best-known novel is *Vathek*), setting up a harem of young men, creating the most extensive art collection in Europe and building the vast Gothic masterpiece Fonthill Abbey; he died in 1844 aged eighty-four, having managed the transition from wealthy, scandalous roué to rebellious, impoverished eccentric. As he put it: 'Politics was not my mission. I was not destined to lead in politics and was too stiff-necked to be a follower.'[14]

Several prominent parliamentarians were caught up in the inexplicably growing public concern about homosexuality in the early years of the nineteenth century. In 1808 it was reported that George Townshend, the recently married earl of Leicester, had fled to France (where the penal code of 1792 made no reference to homosexuality), having been accused by his wife of having had sex with his Italian secretary. Leicester sued for libel and the judge found in his favour on the grounds that papers should not publish rumours with impunity. Even so, Leicester's father, the Marquess Townshend, disinherited him and he lived out his life in exile near Genoa. Next to go was Sir Eyre Coote, who succeeded to his more famous uncle and namesake's vast estates in England and Ireland and had a mixed career, being captured by the Americans at Yorktown in 1781, sitting as an MP in the Irish parliament from 1790 to 1800 and then serving as Governor-General in Jamaica before being elected to the UK parliament in 1810. In 1816 he was cashiered from the army when it was revealed that the previous year he had paid fourteen-year-old boys at Christ's Hospital school for several sessions of mutual flogging. He managed to avoid a criminal conviction by volunteering £1,000 to the school's coffers and narrowly escaped being expelled from the Commons. He chose not to stand again in 1818.

Each decade produced new cases. In 1826 two MPs faced charges of propositioning other men. In the radical Henry Bennet's case the alleged misdemeanour had occurred in Spa in 1824, and in Richard Heber's two young men maintained he had made sexual advances to them at the Athenaeum. Both Bennet and Heber were forced to relinquish their seats at that year's general election, and it was said that Heber died 'without a friend to close his eyes, and ... broken-hearted'.[15] Seven years later the wealthy MP Charles Baring Wall was acquitted of indecently assaulting a policeman in Harley Street and served another twenty years as an MP, acting as a generous host to much of London society, whereas one of his regular dinner companions, William Bankes, the MP for Dorset, who was similarly acquitted that same year of importuning a guardsman in the public toilets near St Margaret's Westminster (the duke of Wellington appeared as a character witness for him), had to flee the country in 1840 when he was caught with another soldier in Green Park.

Even more scandalously, in 1870 another Pelham-Clinton, Lord Arthur, son of the 5th duke of Newcastle and former MP for Newark, was charged with 'conspiring and inciting persons to commit an unnatural offence' along with two transvestites, his housemate Ernest Boulton and Frederick Park, also known as Fanny and Stella. Whether Lord Arthur died of scarlet fever, took his own life or disappeared into exile, no more was seen of him after he was subpoenaed, and only Boulton and Park faced trial. Surprisingly, they were acquitted as the prosecution failed to prove either that buggery had taken place or that cross-dressing was illegal. Less fortunate was the unmarried Whig MP Edward Protheroe, who in 1846 brought charges of extortion against his valet who had accused him of homosexual practices. The judge sided with Protheroe, but a year later he faced another set of allegations and he decided to stand down.

Applied to any of these cases, the concept of 'homosexuality' is an anachronism. None of these men considered themselves as such, and the law dealt with buggery rather than homosexuality or transvestism. But such was the censoriousness of the Victorian era that new legislation made the legal environment even harsher. The driving force behind the complete criminalization of homosexuality in 1885 was one of the least pleasant MPs to have taken his place on the green benches. For Henry Labouchere was not just a hypocrite who, despite being a pronounced agnostic, called himself the 'Christian candidate' in the 1880 election in Northampton, so as to differentiate himself from the other candidate, the atheist Charles Bradlaugh; he was also a nasty anti-semite who ran a sustained campaign against 'Hebrew barons' and 'Jewish cowardice' in the scurrilous and outrageously mis-named periodical *Truth*, into which he poured some of the considerable fortune he had inherited from his rather nicer uncle, also called Henry. In 1885, seemingly out of the blue and late at night, Labouchere tabled an amendment to the Criminal Law Amendment Bill to penalize 'gross indecency', a term so euphemistically vague that it was used for eight decades by the police, judges and juries to criminalize any sexual conduct between men, even if there was no evidence that sexual intercourse had actually taken place.

Whether the Labouchere legislation begat the homophobic censoriousness of the late nineteenth and twentieth centuries or vice versa it is difficult to know. Certainly fear of discovery was an extremely potent force in the late Victorian era. When Henry Fitzroy, the earl of Euston and son and heir to the duke of Grafton, was accused in 1889 of visiting a male brothel at 19 Cleveland Street and of availing himself of one of the 'telegraph boys', he sued for libel, and won, but when Lord Arthur Somerset, the third son of the duke of Beaufort and a member of the royal household, was also about to be arrested for his association with Cleveland Street, he was tipped off and allowed to flee the country. Labouchere was furious. He ran the story in *Truth*, accused the Prime Minister, Salisbury, of conspiring with Somerset, and was removed from the House of Commons when he said that he did not believe the Prime Minister's account of events. Labouchere's campaign bore further lamentable fruit in 1894, when Francis Douglas, Viscount Drumlanrig, the eldest son of the atheist 9th marquess of Queensberry and brother of Oscar Wilde's lover Lord

Alfred Douglas ('Bosie'), was found dead of a gunshot wound. Queensberry blamed 'snob queers like [the Prime Minister the earl of] Rosebery' for corrupting and killing his son, as Rosebery had appointed Drumlanrig as his private secretary and secured him a peerage, and Drumlanrig's nephew, the 11th marquess, later maintained that his uncle had taken his own life over allegations of a sexual relationship with Rosebery. It is impossible to know how much truth there is in this, but Bosie thought that the real reason behind the Liberal government's prosecution of Oscar Wilde was an attempt to conceal the fact that 'the Liberal Party contain[s] a large number of men whom I have already called the salt of the earth' (i.e. homosexuals) and that the Home Secretary, Asquith, had been told by Rosebery that 'unless a second trial was instituted and Mr Wilde convicted, the Liberal Party would be out of power'.[16] In other words, Rosebery, whose wealthy Jewish wife had recently died, was pursuing Wilde through the courts to deflect attention from his own affair with another Douglas.

Certainly, if the rumours about Rosebery were true, he was not alone in the upper echelons of the Liberal party at the turn of the twentieth century, as the only son of his fiercest opponent for the premiership in 1894, Lewis Harcourt, was also renowned, in private, for his propensity to pursue much younger men. It is impossible to piece together a full psychosexual history for such a figure, but having lost his mother in childbirth Lewis enjoyed a phenomenally (some would say unnaturally) close relationship with his irascible father Sir William, who was a tempestuous Home Secretary and then Chancellor of the Exchequer to Gladstone. The thirteen-year-old Lewis was best man at his father's second wedding, and even accompanied the happy couple on their honeymoon. Right up until Sir William's death in 1904 he devoted his whole energy to his father's career as his private secretary, running a particularly vindictive (and hence unsuccessful) campaign for the leadership of the party for him against Rosebery when Gladstone stepped down in 1894. Not long before Sir William's death Lewis, or 'Loulou' as he was universally known, was returned unopposed as Liberal MP for Rossendale, just in time to join the

Liberal ranks (now led by Campbell-Bannerman) as they came to power in December 1905. It was to be the start of a starlit career. First Commissioner for Works in 1905, promoted to the Cabinet the following year, Colonial Secretary in 1910 and back to his first post in the Asquith coalition in 1915, he enjoyed more than a decade as a minister before being granted the old family viscountcy in 1917.

Many disliked his conspiratorial air. Sir Charles Hobhouse, who sat in the Cabinet with Loulou for four years, described him as 'subtle, secretive, adroit, and not very reliable or *au fond* courageous'.[17] Yet he was a more than competent administrator, he was close to Asquith and he held some firm beliefs, opposing rearmament (and women's suffrage) and founding the London Museum. He also seemed to have a happy family life, marrying the wealthy American heiress May Burns, who brought him a son and three daughters as well as an extravagant mansion house in Brook Street, Mayfair (which is now the Savile Club), to add to the family estate at Nuneham Courtenay. However, one of Loulou's close friends, Regy Brett, MP for Penryn and Falmouth from 1880 to 1885 before succeeding his father as Viscount Esher in 1899, knew of darker habits. Esher was immensely well connected, enjoying the close confidence of Edward VII, of Balfour and of Lord Hartington, to whom he was private secretary, but despite regular offers of posts, his political career extended no further than being Permanent Secretary to the Board of Works while Loulou was First Commissioner and chairing a War Office Reconstitution Committee in 1903. Esher's preference for remaining behind the scenes may well have been founded on a desire to protect his own privacy, as he not only lusted after a string of young men, but had a lengthy incestuous affair with his own son Maurice. Esher was also well aware of Lewis Harcourt's predatory inclinations, as Loulou not only made a pass at Maurice on a visit to Eton but also seduced Esher's 25-year-old daughter Dorothy, who was so upset by the whole affair that she was put off men for the rest of her life and wrote that 'it is so tiresome that Loulou is such an old roué. He is as bad with boys as with girls . . . he is simply a sex maniac. It isn't that he is in love. It is just ungovernable

Sex desire for both sexes.'[18] Esher's own comment on the matter was less than scandalized: 'Curious in a Cabinet Minister, because so risky!'[19] Yet what is most curious, not to say extraordinary, is that the long queue of young men (and, if Dorothy is to be believed, girls), many of them well under any age of consent, never broke the story until another young Etonian (he was just twelve) called Edward James complained to his mother about Loulou's advances on a family visit to Nuneham Courtenay – and his mother went to the police. Within days, Loulou was found dead at home in Brook Street, on 24 February 1922, aged fifty-nine, having swallowed a whole draught of Bromidia. Scandalously, Loulou was too well connected for his paedophile predilections to gain currency, so the coroner dismissed the theory that he might have taken his own life as 'grotesque', maintaining that there was no reason for suicide. Since the twelve-year-old went on to be a very successful art collector who made no bones about his own homosexuality and Esher had to recover his collection of paedophile pornography from Loulou's house after his death, we can be fairly certain that Loulou got away with blue murder, thanks to the arrant hypocrisy of an age that exercised its venom with capricious energy on some but turned a culpably blind eye on others.

Things were little different a decade later, for when it was rumoured in 1931 that William Lygon, the handsome 7th earl of Beauchamp, former Governor of New South Wales (1899–1901), First Commissioner of Works (1910–14) and Lord President of the Council (twice: 1910 and 1914–15), as well as leader of the Liberals in the House of Lords from 1924, was travelling in Australia with his male lover Robert Bernays, not only did Beauchamp's brother-in-law Hugh Grosvenor, the thrice-divorced and virulently anti-semitic 2nd duke of Westminster, demand that Beauchamp leave the country, but King George V, perhaps unaware that his own son Prince George, the duke of Kent, was bisexual, declared: 'I thought men like that shot themselves.' Beauchamp evaded the law by his resignation and long-term exile in Italy (and was immortalized as Lord Marchmain in *Brideshead Revisited*), but the social stigma was so total that he was, in the words

Evelyn Waugh put into Anthony Blanche's mouth, 'the last, historic, authentic case of someone being hounded out of society'.[20] The fact that Westminster, a right-wing Tory, pursued Beauchamp as much out of a desire to destroy the Liberal party as out of any real moral consideration (just as Queensberry pursued 'that cur and Jew friend Liar Rosebery'[21]) merely adds vindictiveness to self-righteousness in his list of personal failings.

While some evaded the law by fleeing the country, a number of MPs and peers were caught in its talons well into the twentieth century. Sir Paul Latham, for instance, was impeccably conservative. He was an Eton- and Oxford-educated baronet, the wealthy married heir to a fortune from Courtaulds, the owner of Herstmonceux Castle, and the Conservative victor, aged just twenty-six, in the Scarborough and Whitby by-election of 1931. When war came he promptly volunteered for the Royal Artillery. But Latham also enjoyed attending the 'pink sink' bar beneath the Ritz. When an incriminating letter to him from a young gunner in his own regiment was intercepted in 1941, he attempted to kill himself by driving an army motorbike into a tree. Convicted in a court martial of 'improper behaviour' with three gunners and a civilian and of attempted suicide, he was cashiered from the army and dispatched to prison for two years. So too William Field, the talented Labour MP for Paddington North, was prosecuted in 1953 when a policeman became suspicious of his activities in a West End toilet. Field's initial response to his arrest, saying he was a 'university graduate' and pleading guilty, did not help, indeed rather undermined his later plea of not guilty. Convicted of a breach of the peace and fined £15, he appealed; when he lost his case (in which he was represented, for free, by the former Tory MP John Maude) he departed the political scene. And again, when Ian Harvey, the Tory MP for Harrow East and parliamentary under-secretary at the Foreign Office, slipped away from a dinner into St James's Park in November 1958 and was found in the bushes with a guardsman, he was initially charged with gross indecency and a breach of the park rules. The former charge was dropped and the men were merely fined £5 each, but Harvey found himself under a deluge of obloquy and resigned both his ministerial post and his seat. By a quirk of history, Field's mother had been housekeeper to Harvey's grandfather for years.

That the cases of Field and Harvey – and that of Edward Douglas-Scott-Montagu, Lord Montagu of Beaulieu, the youngest peer in the Lords, who was found guilty in 1954 of 'conspiracy to incite certain male persons to commit serious offences with male persons' – came to court at all was largely due to a decision by the Home Secretary David Maxwell Fyfe to run a campaign to 'rid England of this plague'. Montagu got twelve months in prison and his associates eighteen each; but, a seat in the Lords being a more durable berth in an hour of need than a seat in the Commons, he was able to return to the upper house, was chairman (in a more enlightened age) of English Heritage from 1984 to 1992, and even managed to survive the cull of hereditary peers in 1999.

Others succeeded in concealing their sexuality. Sir Philip Sassoon's biographer Peter Stansky concludes that he could find no certain evidence of his sexual activities with another man (although he admits the possibility of some affection for a fellow army officer called Jack), but Sassoon, who was private secretary to Earl Haig in the First World War, the MP for Hythe from 1912 till his death in 1939, PPS to Lloyd George, under-secretary for Aviation, First Minister for Works and the most exuberant society host in England, with a host of homosexual guests, certainly took issue with the allegations made by Noel Pemberton-Billing MP that the war was being lost because Germany was blackmailing 47,000 members of the ruling class for being 'perverts'. Sassoon wrote:

> All attention is diverted from the Battle of the Aisne to the Battle of the Anus . . . I always liked it when the Sultan came over & was given a ball and was asked by the Master of Ceremonies how he had enjoyed himself & what he thought of the English beauties replied 'Lady Dudley est exquise & Lady Granville est ravissante et Lady de Grey est une femme parfaite – mais pour le vrai plaisir donnez-moi Lord Downe.'[22]

Likewise James Agg-Gardner sat for four spells and thirty-nine years as Conservative MP for Cheltenham between 1874 and 1928. Although the oft-repeated charge that he only ever made two speeches in the Commons is untrue, he was an infrequent speaker – and he was as quiet about his sexuality as he was about politics. The peak of his career came with his chairmanship of the Commons Kitchen Committee, but his quietness gained him a knighthood, a privy councillorship and the nickname 'Minister of the Interior'. One of his Conservative successors at Cheltenham, Charles Irving, was also gay (and also head of the renamed Commons Catering Committee), but he too kept his head down and received a knighthood before stepping down after eighteen years in 1992. In private, Irving was gossipy and jovial. He was wealthy and could be cautiously flamboyant, driving a white Cadillac with white leather upholstery, and he delighted in sending Mrs Thatcher a bouquet of fresh flowers every day. He even paid the hospital expenses of the far more exuberantly gay left-wing Labour MP for Bootle, Allan Roberts, when he was injured being flogged naked in a dungeon in Berlin – a newspaper account of which his local party simply refused to believe. Irving always took the liberal line in votes on social issues. But in public the most personally revealing he dared to be was in reply to an attempted intervention by Dame Elaine Kellett-Bowman, when they took opposite sides on the death penalty: 'If you were the only girl in the world, And I were the only boy,' he trilled, pausing before 'I would not give way to you.'[23] As Matthew Parris wrote, Irving was 'discreet silence made flesh',[24] a description that could also have been applied to George Thomas, a Methodist preacher and MP from 1945 to 1983, who paid blackmailers hundreds of pounds to avoid exposure and thereby enabled himself to rise to become Welsh Secretary and Speaker.

Equally fortunate, but much less discreet, was the communist *Daily Express* journalist turned Labour MP Tom Driberg, who was remarkably acquitted of 'gross indecency' with two strangers in 1935 and managed to talk his way out of being arrested by an Edinburgh policeman who caught him fellating a Norwegian sailor in 1943. The posthumous publication of Driberg's memoirs laid bare a life of constant assignations and rough anonymous sex (including a claim that he had given Nye Bevan a blow job), but despite what amounted to wilful recklessness he was never hauled over the coals in the press and ended his days a peer of the realm. As one of Labour's best-known politicians with a strong following in the media, Driberg might have expected a job in Attlee's 1945 government; but, possibly fearing a scandal, Attlee refused to appoint him. He dealt similarly with Oliver Baldwin, who sat for Dudley during the MacDonald Labour government of 1929–31 on the opposite benches from his father Stanley and returned to the Commons as MP for Paisley after serving in the Intelligence Corps in the war. Baldwin's sexuality almost certainly put paid to his rising any further than parliamentary secretary to the Secretary for War, but when his father died in 1947 he became the 2nd earl and Attlee packed him off to the Leeward Islands as Governor. He too survived without major scandal – although the islanders were disconcerted that he brought his lover John Boyle with him.

On the other side of the House, Bob Boothby had affairs with Harold Macmillan's wife and a string of male lovers, and attended orgies organized by the notorious Kray twins. Colonel Jack Macnamara (whose research assistant was Guy Burgess) made regular visits to homosexual sex parties and clubs in Paris and Berlin with members of the Hitler Youth in the 1930s. These associations did not, however, stop him from courageously commanding the 1st Irish Rifles in the Second World War, with whom he was killed by a German mortar in Italy. Similarly, the Liberal National MP for Bristol North from 1931 to 1945 and junior minister from 1937 to 1940, Robert Bernays, was not only close to Lord Beauchamp, but confessed in his diary that what he really 'want[ed] in a woman is that kind of mental affinity which I get from someone like HN' as 'he is very fond of me as I am of him'.[25] The HN in question was the National Labour MP for Leicester West, Harold Nicolson, whose own diaries and his son Nigel's book *Portrait of a Marriage* make clear his bisexuality. Boothby, Macnamara, Bernays, Nicolson, Macmillan (who Derek Jarman maintained visited a gay sauna in Jermyn Street) and the baby of the House, Ronald Cartland (who shared a flat with Bernays and visited Sassoon and Latham) all became determined opponents of appeasement in the late 1930s, and although both Nicolson and Bernays married, Chamberlain's oft-repeated reference to the anti-appeasement group as the 'glamour boys' may owe something to their sexual reputation. Like Macnamara, Cartland and Bernays served in the war and died on active service in 1940 and 1945; all three are commemorated in the Commons Chamber. There were others: Nancy Astor's son by her first marriage, Bobby Shaw, was cashiered out of the army for having sex with another officer; Napier Sturt, the 3rd Baron Alington, known as 'Naps', shared men, women and copious quantities of drugs with Tallulah Bankhead and Noel Coward, and, having fought as a captain in the First World War, died of pneumonia as a staff officer in Cairo in September 1940; and Henry 'Chips' Channon's marriage to the daughter of the 2nd earl of Iveagh ended in divorce after the Second World War when he took up with a landscape designer and a series of male lovers, including the playwright Terence Rattigan.

By the 1960s social attitudes had changed significantly, but the law had not, which left many homosexual law-makers in the hideous position of having to lie about their sexuality. Arthur Gore, the 8th earl of Arran, whose elder brother had committed suicide out of despair about his own sexuality, made three brave attempts in the Lords to decriminalize homosexuality; one of his private member's Bills was even supported by the archbishops of York and Canterbury. However, with the former Lord Chancellor, the virulently homophobic earl of Kilmuir, opposing him and the government refusing to give the Bill time in the Commons, it ran into the buffers in 1965 – as did his second Bill introduced in February 1966 and another introduced by the gay Conservative MP Humphrey Berkeley just before the election in which he lost his seat. So it was not until the new Labour Home Secretary, Roy Jenkins, made clear in 1967 that the government would give time to a new Bill introduced by the flamboyant but straight Labour MP Leo Abse that change became possible. Despite opposition from the likes of Captain Walter Elliot MP, who declaimed that the measure would 'corrupt and poison' the 'national blood-stream', the Bill sailed through the Commons with easy majorities and through the Lords without amendment. On 27 July it received royal assent and homosexuality was partially decriminalized. The Labouchere offence of 'gross indecency' remained, as incorporated in the Sexual Offences Act 1956, but sex in private between two consenting men over twenty-one was legal.

Even after this, several MPs still fell foul of the law. A jury was unable to come to a verdict on whether Keith Hampson, the married PPS to Michael Heseltine, had indecently assaulted a police officer during a male strip show in the Gay Theatre in Berwick Street in 1984. When the Attorney-General decided that a fair retrial was impossible, a not guilty verdict was entered and he remained a respectable Tory MP until 1997. Harvey Proctor, a Tory with right-wing views on immigration, was relentlessly pursued in 1986 first by the press and then by the Serious Crimes Squad of the Metropolitan Police over allegations of spanking male prostitutes who were under twenty-one. Pleading guilty to 'gross indecency' in the midst of the 1987 general election campaign, he was fined £1,450 and stepped down from his Billericay seat. Alan Amos, Tory MP for Hexham, was caught with a young man on Hampstead Heath and cautioned by the police just before the 1992 general election in which he lost his seat, and in 1994 the *News of the World* published a photograph of another Conservative, Michael Brown, on holiday in Barbados with a twenty-year-old man. Brown lost his Cleethorpes seat in the 1997 election.

Several more years were to pass before an MP could be openly homosexual. Martin Stevens, the Tory MP for Fulham from 1979 to his early death seven years later aged just fifty-six, was gay and a member of the Tory Campaign for Homosexual Equality, but occupied that curious world where everyone knew, but nobody wrote about it. Matthew Parris attempted to out himself late one night in a debate, but failed; so the honours for the first openly gay MP go to Chris Smith, the Labour member for Islington South, whose coming out during a political rally in Rugby in 1984 did not prevent him from retaining his marginal seat or joining Tony Blair's Cabinet as Secretary of State for Culture, Media and Sport from 1997 to 2001. Then, in a series of measures from 1994 onwards, the law changed even more fundamentally. The age of consent was equalized, gays were allowed to serve in the police, the Foreign Office and the military, the law on sexual offences was changed, gay couples were allowed to adopt, homophobic discrimination in employment or the provision of services was outlawed, and civil partnerships and same-sex marriage were instituted. Over these years a string of MPs have either been elected as openly gay or come out as such once elected, and even peers have come out. In a few cases the press tried to create a fuss. Peter Mandelson had his private life spread over the pages of the *News of the World* at the start of the 1987 general election campaign when he was the Labour party's Director of Communications, and was then re-outed by Matthew Parris on *Newsnight*. Similarly Nick Brown, the Labour chief whip and Agriculture Secretary, was forced out by the *News of the World* in 1998, and when the gay former Catholic priest and Scottish Office minister David Cairns died of acute pancreatitis in 2011, the archbishop of Glasgow, Philip Tartaglia, incorrectly suggested that it had something to do with his sexuality. Still, try as the press might to stir up distaste about Greg Barker, Crispin Blunt and Daniel Kawczynski all being married when they voluntarily came out, the public has respected their honesty, and although some MPs prefer to keep their sexuality private, the likes of Stephen Gilbert, Stephen Williams, Stuart Andrew, Eric Ollerenshaw, Conor Burns, Margot James, Mike Freer, Iain Stewart, Nigel Evans, Gordon Marsden, Steve Reed, Ben Bradshaw and Stephen Twigg have all flourished as openly gay MPs, and Alan Duncan, Clive Betts, Angela Eagle and Nick Herbert have entered into civil partnerships (as did the author in 2010).

For many people, especially those of a religious disposition, these developments, and the dissipation of public judgementalism around matters sexual, is not progress; if anything, it is a sign of the moral decline of the nation. But the twentieth century has seen remarkably few such figures in the House of Commons. Even Ian Paisley, the Democratic Unionist MP for North Antrim, who campaigned to Save Ulster from Sodomy in 1977, rarely spoke on such matters in the Commons; and the lesson of Iris Robinson, MP for Strangford, who compared homosexuals to murderers and told the Commons that 'there can be no viler act, apart from homosexuality and sodomy, than sexually abusing innocent children',[26] while engaging in an extra-marital affair with a nineteen-year-old man, is well taken by most MPs. In the nineteenth century it might have made sense to uphold in public a moral code to which you could not privately adhere. But with religious conviction in remorseless decline, the greatest fear for a modern MP is not eternal damnation but the charge of hypocrisy; and the media have taken up the vacant seat of judgement with enthusiasm. Nobody has expressed this self-righteousness better than the journalist who initially befriended Charles Dilke, but then hounded him through the pages of the *Pall Mall Gazette*, W. T. Stead. 'The simple faith of our forefathers in the All-Seeing Eye of God has departed from the man in the street,' he told a Royal Commission on divorce. 'Our modern substitute for him is the press. Gag the press under whatever pretexts of prudish propriety you please, and you destroy the last remaining pillory by which it is possible to impose some restraint on the lawless lust of man.'[27] Appointing yourself as a replacement for God is an act of phenomenal arrogance, but in the even more prurient modern age, with recording devices, mobile phones and digital cameras making detection even easier, public attitudes towards what would once have been considered sexual misdemeanours have changed. Judgementalism and prurience, always incompatible bed-companions, are finally parting company – not least because the combination has led to such hypocrisy in the past.

One further instance makes the point. Ian Maitland was the 15th earl of Lauderdale and sat as a Scottish representative peer from 1931 to 1945. In November 1943 the police caught him having sex in a Soho alleyway with a kitchen porter called Robert Willson, whom he had picked up at the cab shelter near the public toilets on Leicester Square. Both men were arrested and spent the night in the cells, during which Lauderdale explained that his son had been killed in action, that he was drunk and that he didn't know what was happening. Above all, he wanted to stress: 'I am happily married and I hate this sort of thing, boys and buggery, you know.'[28] Considering that Sir Paul Latham had been cashiered out of the army and sent to prison for two years for a far lesser 'crime' in 1941, Lauderdale might have expected a quick conviction and a harsh sentence; but when the case went to court his wife and a friend, Major-General John Beith (the author Ian Hay), gave witness that he was perfectly 'normal' and the judge deferentially instructed the jury that they should 'give all weight possible' to this evidence – thanks to which Lauderdale was acquitted. It is difficult to see how the porter could have committed an offence if the other party, the earl, had not committed it with him. Yet such was the hypocrisy of the age that no merciful act of voluntary judicial blindness was afforded Willson, who was sent down for nine months for the nebulous offence of 'importuning for an immoral purpose'.

Such hypocrisies abounded throughout the twentieth century, during which the caprice of history enabled an angry spouse, a vengeful political opponent or a newspaper vendetta to topple some of the most important and talented political figures of the age, while many others whose deviation from the monogamous heterosexual norm was every bit as marked were left untroubled. The obese Liberal MP for Rochdale, Cyril Smith, for instance, was feted in his lifetime, but we now know that he committed heinous crimes in the form of systematic sexual abuse of children, pursued over many years. Many, of course, argue that politicians should set an example of sexual continence; many go further, and maintain that heterosexual marital fidelity is the foundation of the family and of society. Even so, recent evidence suggests that voters care less about parliamentarians' sex lives than tabloid writers presume, making it far less likely that the likes of Dilke, Parnell and Beauchamp will ever be hounded out again.

AWFUL SCENE OF GLOOM AND DEJECTION, WHEN THE MINISTRY HEARD OF THE LORDS' DECISION TO REFER THE BUDGET TO THE COUNTRY.

The dispute over the Liberal budget of 1909, which sought to fund the introduction of national insurance and pensions through higher taxation, pitted the Liberals and Labour in the Commons against the massive inbuilt Conservative majority in the Lords. By forcing two general elections in 1910 on the matter, the Lords and the diehard Conservatives played into the hands of Asquith, Lloyd George and Churchill, who are seen here rejoicing.

4

The End of Aristocracy

WHEN ROBERT ARTHUR TALBOT Gascoyne-Cecil, the 3rd marquess of Salisbury, was summoned to Balmoral (which he hated) in June 1885 to be asked to form a government, he travelled third class on the train so as to avoid the press. It must have been something of an ordeal. For fortune had smiled on him. He had been born at Hatfield House, the palatial home of the family since James I had granted it to the first earl of Salisbury in 1607 in exchange for the Cecils' house Theobalds. Admittedly Lord Robert was but a second son, so after a hideous few years of being bullied at Eton he had to supplement a mere £400 annual allowance from his grudging father by writing splenetic articles for Tory periodicals, but his parentage afforded him plenty of other benefits, including an honorary fourth-class degree in mathematics at Oxford; a fellowship at All Souls' College, Oxford; and in 1853, aged twenty-three, the pocket borough seat of Stamford. Robert was never close to his father, who so objected to his marriage to the less than aristocratic Georgina Alderson that he refused to attend the wedding, but when the congenital condition that had left the eldest son and heir James with severely impaired sight and hearing brought him to an early grave in 1865, Robert inherited the courtesy title of Viscount Cranborne and, on his father's death three years later, the marquessate and a seat in the Lords. The timing was impeccable, as the 1867 Reform Act had abolished his Commons seat.

The good fortune continued. Despite writing vitriolic attacks in the press on Disraeli and his own Tory party, he was Secretary of State for India under Derby in 1866–7 and under Disraeli in 1874–8, and Foreign Secretary between 1878 and 1880. He was fortunate too when Disraeli died, for although Sir Stafford Northcote might more readily have sprung to mind as Disraeli's likely successor, there was no one other than Salisbury – notwithstanding his resignation in 1867 – who could plausibly lead the Conservatives in the Lords, where they had more chance of overturning Gladstone's government than in the lower house. A joint leadership of Salisbury and Northcote lasted for a while, but with younger bloods like Randolph Churchill, John Gorst and Henry Wolff making the running as a 'Fourth Party' against the Liberal government, Northcote looked increasingly out of his depth and became sidelined. Salisbury was soon undisputed Conservative leader.

But Salisbury's greatest piece of good fortune came in the shape of Gladstone's Irish policy. The number of Irish home rule MPs had grown from forty-six in 1874 to sixty-three in 1880 and under Parnell's leadership they had become increasingly assertive. Then the Fenian dynamite campaign that had seen bombs go off at the Carlton Club and the home of the Conservative MP Sir Watkin Williams-Wynn came to the Palace of Westminster on Saturday 24 January 1885, when devices exploded in the Chamber and in Westminster Hall. At the time, the minds of the Conservative and Liberal leaders were focused on two new parliamentary reform Bills (ending the multi-member seats, redistributing the seats and increasing the franchise) that were hammered out between Dilke and Salisbury, but as soon as these were passed into law in May 1885 the home rulers proved their capacity to make trouble by trooping into the lobbies with the Conservatives to oppose Gladstone's Customs and Inland Revenue Bill, which was lost on 8 June by twelve votes. Gladstone resigned and Salisbury became Prime Minister of a very unstable minority government pending an election.

Gladstone's reaction was to concede to the Irish. It was manifestly the rational thing to do. Even disregarding the rights and wrongs of the home rulers' desire for at least a return to the Grattan dispensation of the 1780s endowing the Irish parliament with limited legislative authority, even ignoring the moral imperative of self-determination and even leaving to one side the folly of further repression, Gladstone knew that if he wanted to deliver his wider programme he needed the willing support of Parnell. The parliamentary arithmetic was rammed home to Gladstone by the results of the 1885 election. He had a comfortable lead over the Tories, 335 to 249, but if Parnell's MPs, who numbered eighty-five in Ireland and one extra in Liverpool, were to combine with the Conservatives, he could not afford a single Liberal abstention.[1] At first Gladstone toyed with a bipartisan solution and approached Salisbury's nephew Arthur Balfour, but then, having quietly resolved at Hawarden that the Act of Union had been a 'gigantic, though excusable mistake' and that there was no ethical alternative to home rule, he authorized his son Herbert to fly his 'Hawarden Kite' via a letter to *The Times* on 17 December 1885, declaring: 'Nothing could induce me to countenance separation, but if five-sixths of the Irish people wish to have a Parliament in Dublin, for the management of their own local affairs, I say, in the name of justice, and wisdom, let them have it.' It was enough for Parnell. When the Birmingham MP Jesse Collings introduced an amendment to the Conservative government's speech from the throne on 26 January 1886 (calling for a Smallholdings Amendment Act), Parnell voted with Gladstone to oust Salisbury and two days later the Conservative Leader in the Commons, Michael Hicks Beach, told the House that the ministry had resigned.

Thus far, Gladstone had calculated quite correctly; but there was a lot that he had not factored in. There had been discontent in the Liberal ranks for several years, the disastrous decision to send Gordon to his death in Khartoum had inspired public fury, and seventy Liberals had voted for or abstained on the key budget vote in 1885. Moreover, Gladstone was straddling two very different parties. For every Joseph Chamberlain or Charles Dilke, looking to the newly enfranchised working classes for support, there was a George Goschen, disturbed by the very idea of municipal or state intervention, and a Spencer Cavendish (the marquess of Hartington or 'Harty-tarty' to his friends), worried about the threat to the landed interest. So when it came to Collings's amendment, Chamberlain eagerly supported his Birmingham friend, but Hartington, Goschen and eighteen Liberals voted with the Conservatives. Gladstone might have written this off as a freak vote on the specific issue of smallholdings, but he would have been wiser to spot the growing trend within his party, which had clearly been exacerbated by his bringing forward such a dramatic change in party policy on Ireland while parliament was dissolved and without alerting his colleagues. After all, Hartington and Goschen had at least voted with Gladstone the previous year. Now they thought Gladstone was engaged in an act of high-handed folly. But Gladstone remained immovable. Having formed his Cabinet (without Hartington or Goschen), in the spring of 1886 he brought forward a twin-set of Irish Bills and immediately faced resignations from the Cabinet by Joseph Chamberlain and George Trevelyan.

This was manna from heaven for Salisbury. For the marquess's instinctive and inherited dislike of democracy could now be given free rein in the interests of his party. His views were hardly enlightened. As he told a National Union conference in May: '[what] is called self-government, but is really government by the majority – works admirably when it is confided to people of Teutonic race, [but] you will find that it does not work so well when people of other races are called upon to join it'.[2] Since he had started this part of his speech with the words that 'you would not confide free representative institutions to the Hottentots', it was pretty clear that he thought the Irish unfit for democracy. Liberals would repeat the offensive phrase time and again. Yet Salisbury had a point – a thin, specious point, but a point none the less. For in his view home rule undermined a basic principle. As he put it: 'We are bound by motives, not only of expediency, not only of legal principle, but by motives of honour, to protect the minority.' This was another part of the equation that

Gladstone had not factored in, for although Parnell called the proposals a 'final settlement', the Protestant community of Ulster were resolutely opposed to what they presumed would be tyranny by the Catholic majority; so as the Bill started its passage there were riots in Belfast (where Catholics represented just 29 per cent of the population) and the Orange Order began its steady climb to political ascendancy.

In unambiguously opposing home rule, Salisbury was dressing partisan advantage up as high principle, but in the process he managed to seize a strategically vital parcel of political high ground for the Conservatives, transforming them into *the* party of the Union. Others scrambled to join him. On 14 April 1886 Hartington and Goschen joined Salisbury on the stage of Her Majesty's Theatre to condemn home rule, and when Gladstone's first Bill came to its second reading on 8 June, ninety-three Liberals voted with 250 Conservatives against Gladstone and Parnell's 313.[3] The Bill having been lost, Gladstone persuaded his Cabinet to seek a new mandate in a general election, despite the fact that a significant tranche of his own party had already decided they would stand as Liberal Unionists under an electoral pact with the Conservative chief whip. The 1886 Conservative campaign, by contrast, was united and vigorous. Lord Randolph Churchill told Unionists in Ulster that they might have to go beyond the lines of 'what we are accustomed to look upon as constitutional action' and announced that 'Ulster will fight; Ulster will be right'. It was a scurrilous rallying cry that was to fester in the Irish body politic for decades, followed up by the slogan 'Home Rule is Rome Rule', but it did the trick in 1886. The Gladstonian Liberals were trounced at the polls, Salisbury picked up an extra sixty-four seats and, with the Liberal Unionists securing seventy-seven, the Conservatives and Unionists could count on a majority of 112 against home rule. A formal coalition of the two parties was on offer, but not yet accepted, and Salisbury formed a Conservative administration.

Gladstone's Irish mission was a gift that was to keep on giving. For when he came out of the next election, in 1892, with the largest number of seats but not a majority, and brought forward another Government of Ireland Bill, which managed to struggle slowly through eighty-two lengthy sittings to its laborious third reading in the Commons on 1 September 1893, Salisbury was easily able to defeat it in the Lords (419 votes to 41) and ride roughshod over the rest of the government's legislative programme. Gladstone had frankly confessed to his diary in 1892 that 'for the condition (*now*) of my senses, I am no longer fit for public life: yet bidden to walk in it. "Lead thou me on." '[4] Finally, aged eighty-four, he decided to hand over the reins to his Foreign Secretary Archibald Primrose, the 5th earl of Rosebery, and while he surveyed his 556th Cabinet meeting on 1 March 1894 without so much as a flicker of sentiment, his ministers sat around him weeping. Four years later, on May 1898, the Grand Old Man (or 'God's Only Mistake', as Salisbury and Northcote dubbed him) died at Hawarden, to be granted a state funeral and a proud place in Westminster Abbey.

Salisbury continued to reap the benefits of Gladstone's policy long after the Liberal leader's death, wooing Liberal Unionists assiduously. When Rosebery's government lost a motion on the army estimates on 21 June 1895 to cut the salary of popular Secretary for War, Sir Henry Campbell-Bannerman, by £100 in retribution for the troops' lack of cordite in the First Boer War, even though it was a tight vote on a very low turnout (just 132 to 125), Rosebery tendered his resignation and Salisbury formed not a Conservative but a Unionist coalition government before calling an election. Four leading Liberal Unionists joined the Cabinet. Two of them had direct interests in Ireland: Hartington's younger brother had been murdered by Irish nationalists in 1882 and Henry Petty-Fitzmaurice, the 5th marquess of Lansdowne, had extensive Irish estates. But for the others, and many more Liberal Unionists, their real discontent lay with the general direction of the party. Goschen, a merchant banker, was one such. Looking at his record it is difficult to see how he ever found himself in the Liberal party at all, let alone in both Russell's and Gladstone's Cabinets. True, free trade was still a Liberal, not a Conservative, mantra and he preferred a laissez-faire, market-driven economic policy. Even his heightened patriotism, perhaps the result of being the son of a naturalized German, was just about Liberal in a Palmerstonian way. But Goschen opposed the extension of the franchise in case new voters started campaigning for 'social benefits'; he declared the Irish home rulers 'steeped in treason';[5] and he held that: 'Liberty is the power to possess as much as you please or as little as you please, to work, to get forward, to rise in the scale of life, if you can. Equality is against all that, and says every man must be exactly the same as his neighbour.'[6] None of this was mainstream Liberalism by 1886, so it should have been no surprise when Goschen stood as a Liberal Unionist and resigned from the Reform Club. What did come as a shock, though, for Goschen, was losing his seat in 1886 and then losing again by just eleven votes in a Liverpool by-election on 26 January 1887. When Lord Randolph Churchill spectacularly resigned as Chancellor of the Exchequer and Leader of the House on 20 December 1886 (ostensibly over a battle with W. H. Smith over the defence estimates, possibly as a result of tertiary syphilis and certainly in a fit of exaggerated self-importance), Salisbury deftly offered the post to Goschen.

The fourth Liberal Unionist to join the coalition Cabinet was Joseph Chamberlain, 'Radical Joe', who had arrived in the Commons aged thirty-nine with the self-confidence and bravura afforded by a successful business career topped by a spell as mayor of Birmingham. He had brought the local water board in Birmingham into public hands, he had launched a national campaign for better universal education, he had built swimming pools, libraries and schools, he had torn down slums. The Commons often resents such figures, but Chamberlain's career blossomed. He received his first promotion as President of the Board of Trade in 1880, and having in the 1885 campaign taken to the road with his own 'Radical Programme' out of exasperation with the languid Whigs such as Hartington he was again rewarded by Gladstone, this time with the post of President of the Local Government Board. Although he resigned over home rule in

1886, he originally refused to join Salisbury's love-in with Hartington at Her Majesty's that April; but when Hartington summoned a meeting a month later, Chamberlain became a founding member of the Liberal Unionist Association.

Although Salisbury's political fortunes were as favourable as his birthright, and although he went on to win the 1900 election, he proved to be a half-hearted, mildly depressive Prime Minister whose administration left remarkably little to show for itself apart from dubious military success in South Africa. Despite a large majority in the Commons and dominance in the Lords, the legislative programme was threadbare – most of Chamberlain's radical ideas (for pensions and workers' compensation) were either watered down or ruled out by his Conservative colleagues – and some of the measures the government did bring forward were defeated. A thoroughly Anglican Education Bill was assaulted with a thousand amendments and when, after five full days of debate, just thirteen words of the first clause had been agreed, it was withdrawn. Salisbury himself was a large part of the problem. Excepting Derby, whose peerage was older, he was by far the most patrician of premiers, outranking the only other hereditary marquess to hold the post, Rockingham, and the relatively recently created dukedoms of Grafton and Portland, and his background was reflected in his choice of ministers. Russell had got away with the fact that his 1846 Cabinet had reflected his own aristocratic lineage, including two cousins, a cousin-in-law and his father-in-law, but as the relative authority of the Lords declined Gladstone was criticized in both 1880 and 1892 for including too many peers in his Cabinet, and the criticism intensified when Rosebery took over in 1894. Rosebery himself was hardly a man of the people – he had inherited his titles and estates from his grandfather at the age of twenty-one and married a Rothschild heiress, he owned a town palace in Belgrave Square, three other houses and a yacht, and his horses had won the Derby three times – and his appointment of John Wodehouse, the earl of Kimberley, as Foreign Secretary meant that the government's two most senior ministers were in the Lords.

Salisbury, though, took patrician clannishness to new heights. His first Cabinet, in 1886, included just four MPs (one of whom was his own nephew, Arthur Balfour, and another the son of the earl of Stanhope), and those of 1895 and 1900 were put together from ten peers and three representatives of the old landed gentry class, Walter Long, St John Brodrick (the heir to the 8th Viscount Midleton) and Henry Chaplin. Thereafter, far from dissipating, Salisbury's nepotism got worse. In 1900 he appointed Balfour Leader of the Commons, another Salisbury nephew, Gerald Balfour, as President of the Board of Trade, his son-in-law the earl of Selborne as First Lord of the Admiralty and his son, Viscount Cranborne, as under-secretary at the Foreign Office. When Balfour seamlessly succeeded his uncle as Prime Minister and Leader of the Conservatives in 1903 the patrician knot was pulled even tighter. In addition to the two brothers Balfour and their cousin Selborne, the Cabinet included father and son Joseph and Austen Chamberlain, a duke, two marquesses, two earls, three barons, a baronet, the son of a duke and the son of a viscount. In 1898 the Tory MP George Bartley had bemoaned the fact that all honours, emoluments and places are reserved for 'the friends and relatives of the favourite few', but under Balfour things were even worse than before.

By the start of the twentieth century, such an aristocratic cadre of ministers looked anachronistic. Society had been changing – and parliament with it. Some of the old landed class that still peppered the Commons noticed their number dwindling. Walter Long lamented that the 1880 parliament was the last to include the 'country gentlemen's party', and the 1885 election saw a swathe cut through the gentry in Ireland, in Scotland and in Wales. In 1888 Henry Chaplin looked contemptuously at the Conservative front bench when Goschen proposed a tax on horses and groaned that 'there was not a single man amongst them who knows a horse from a cow'.[7] The following year Salisbury moaned that 'we live no longer, alas, in Pitt's time; the aristocracy governed then . . . Now democracy is on top'.[8] In 1900 he added: 'I expect the House of Commons will be mainly filled by tradesmen trying to secrete gentility.'[9] They were right. There were men of a new complexion in the House – even, on occasion, in the government. The millionaire W. H. Smith, who had made his money in his father's newsagent business, had arrived in parliament in 1868 as a Conservative and Disraeli had quickly given him a job as Financial Secretary and then First Lord of the Admiralty. So too Richard Cross, the son of a well-to-do but definitely middle-class Lancashire lawyer, became Home Secretary in 1874 thanks to his friendship with the younger Derby. Cross was very much the legislative star of Disraeli's 1874 government, winning working-class plaudits with a Licensing Act that lengthened the drinking day and a Factory Act that shortened the working day; as the latter measure also made Saturday a non-working day, he could be credited with the invention of the weekend. To this he added the Artisans' Dwelling Act and changes to the law of contract that made striking no longer a conspiracy. Disraeli was delighted, writing that this last measure alone 'will gain and retain for the Tories the lasting affection of the working classes'.[10] By the mid-1880s Smith and Cross formed the mainstay of the Conservative government in the Commons, much to the derision of Lord Randolph Churchill, the third son of the 7th duke of Marlborough, who haughtily called them 'Marshall and Snelgrove' in reference to the department store on Oxford Street. But they were not alone. In 1891 Balfour suggested to his uncle that he should make W. L. Jackson, who ran a tanning business in Leeds, the new Postmaster-General because he 'has great tact and judgment – middle class tact and judgment I admit, but good of their kind . . . he is that *rara avis*, a successful manufacturer who is fit for something besides manufacturing'.[11]

Nor was it just the people who were changing. Pocket boroughs were disappearing, either abolished by Act of parliament or dismantled by the wider franchise. The landed gentry could no longer presume on the loyalty of the local electorate. Despite the fact that his father was 4th Baron Scarsdale and Kedleston Hall in Derbyshire had been the family seat since the twelfth century, George Curzon lost at South Derbyshire in 1885 and had to find a new berth at Southport.

Henry Chaplin, who owned large tracts of Lincolnshire, and his younger brother Edward could rely on local deference to return them both for Lincolnshire seats through the 1880s, but in 1906 Henry lost his Sleaford seat and ended up sitting for suburban Wimbledon.

Part of the reason for the decline in aristocratic dominance of parliament lay with the aristocrats themselves. Many of them disliked modern politics and the kind of people with whom it compelled them to associate. Many loathed the nasty business of electioneering, or, as Viscount Cranborne termed it in writing to Curzon in 1885, 'the disgusting work in which we are engaged'.[12] Lord Ernest Hamilton, the youngest son of the duke of Abercorn, three of whose brothers were also Conservative MPs, hated representing Tyrone North from 1885 to 1892, complaining that 'nobody wanted me except as a voter in divisions'.[13] The trend would continue, with the gentry slowly feeling themselves eased out by a modern world. As Lord Grey of Fallodon, who had been Liberal Foreign Secretary for eleven years between 1905 and 1916, put it in 1921, 'as to politics, I am not the sort of person that is wanted now . . . Lloyd George is the modern type, suited to an age of telephones and moving pictures and modern journalism.'[14] He had a point. Curzon was later made Viceroy of India and Foreign Secretary, but when he remained Lord President of the Council under Lloyd George in 1924, the marquess of Crewe described him as 'like a Rolls Royce car, with a highly competent driver, kept to take an occasional parcel to the station'.[15] Since Lloyd George found his effortless superiority irksome and Curzon complained that the Prime Minister treated him as 'a valet, almost a drudge, and he has no regard for the conveniences or civilities of official life,'[16] it is difficult to see why Lloyd George bothered.

The decline of the landed MPs was marked but not exactly precipitous. At the start of the First World War the Commons still included the heirs to the duke of Atholl, the marquesses of Lansdowne, Londonderry and Zetland, the earl of Dartmouth and Viscount Halifax, and long into the twentieth century it received the scions of noble families, including the three sons of the 16th earl of Derby and both sons of the 17th, and the future 10th duke of Devonshire, 7th and 8th marquesses of Londonderry, and the 27th and 28th earls of Crawford and Balcarres. But by 1918 there were just twenty-two Conservative MPs who were related to peers; and some thought the new parliament full of 'hard-faced men, who looked as if they had done well out of the war'.[17] This was no longer a place for titled families, as the eccentric and eventually alcoholic and fascist 8th marquess of Londonderry, who was an MP for Down from 1931 to 1945, admitted. 'I deplore the existence of politicians,' he said, 'and regard it all as a rare waste of time.'[18]

Even the House of Lords was changing. The historical rationale behind the Lords' individual writs of summons had related to their tenancy of the land, and although royal favourites and national treasures had been bumped up into the Lords, many had continued to come from within the landed classes or had acquired land. But as time passed, money, fame or political favour came to matter more than territory: between 1880 and 1939 seventy-four non-landed millionaires joined the Lords, compared to just thirteen in the previous seven decades. Even Salisbury succumbed to the fashion, telling Victoria in 1891 that it was 'very desirable to give the feeling that the house of lords contained something besides rich men and politicians',[19] and persuading her to give peerages to the Quaker surgeon and inventor of antiseptics Sir Joseph Lister, and to the artist and president of the Royal Academy Sir Frederic Leighton (whose peerage was to last just a single day; he died the day after it was created and, being unmarried and possibly homosexual, he sired no children). The mandarins of the civil service began to get a look-in, too, with Sir Thomas Erskine May becoming Lord Farnborough in 1886 after fifteen years as clerk to the House of Commons and Sir Arthur Godley becoming Lord Kilbracken in 1909 after twenty-six years as permanent under-secretary at the India Office.

The main thrust, though, was to ennoble the wealthy, Gladstone explicitly urging the queen in 1869 to 'connect the House of Lords ... with the great representatives of the commerce of the country'.[20] Disraeli had started the process, with the promotion of two baronets, the heir to the Irish brewing fortune, Sir Arthur Guinness, and the snobbish Welsh owner of the world's largest ironworks at Dowlais, Sir Ivor Guest, respectively as Baron Ardilaun and Baron Wimborne. Guinness's younger brother also got a peerage, as baron, viscount and then earl of Iveagh, and another brewer, Michael Bass, became Lord Burton. Dudley Marjoribanks, an innocuous Liberal MP for Berwick-upon-Tweed from 1853, inherited Coutts banking money from his father, made even more of it in brewing and duly became Lord Tweedmouth in 1881; Thomas Brassey, son of a wealthy railway contractor, became a baron in 1886 and an earl in 1911; Henry Eaton, son of a silk broker, became Lord Cheylesmore in 1887; Samuel Cunliffe Lister, who made his money in Bradford's wool trade, became Lord Masham in 1891; the banker Sydney Stern became Baron Wandsworth in 1895; and the ship-owner and chairman of Cunard, John Burns, became Lord Inverclyde in 1897. This was not a development that was greeted with unanimous approval. The *Saturday Review*, for instance, snootily objected in 1905 to 'this policy of adulterating the peerage with mere wealth',[21] and Curzon averred in 1911 that the hereditary principle had 'saved this country from the danger of plutocracy or an upper class of professional politicians'.[22]

The trend was just as manifest among the lords spiritual. You only had to look at the packed House of Lords gathered on 4 December 1902 to debate the government's controversial Education Bill to see how they had changed. The bench of bishops, which had been placed on the government side of the new Chamber,* was full of prelates in

* Unlike the House of Commons, the Lords were originally supposed to sit in order of precedence according to an Act of 1539, on three sides of a square around the Woolsack and clerks' tables, but by the late eighteenth century this was more honoured in the breach than in the observance and like-minded peers often sat together. Voting was by acclamation (shouting 'content' or 'not content'), unless the presiding officer's ruling was challenged, when a division would be counted, for which, up until 1675, the contents stood and the not contents remained seated. Increasingly thereafter the contents moved below the bar of the House and the not contents remained seated to be counted by a teller. For judicial decisions the Lords voted by roll call in their places or, very occasionally, by secret ballot. The new chamber provided government, episcopal, opposition and cross-bench seats, and separate voting lobbies for the 'contents' and the 'not contents'.

their now traditional parliamentary attire of flowing lawn sleeves, rochet and chimere. The archbishop of Canterbury, Frederick Temple, rose to speak early in the debate. He had just celebrated his eightieth birthday a week earlier and was unwell – indeed, many were surprised that he turned up at all. When he collapsed in the middle of his speech – as recorded in a painting by Sydney Hall, published in the *Graphic* a week later – it was a new breed of bishops that rushed forward to support him. As the former headmaster at Rugby School, Temple was a keen educationalist. So were several of his colleagues. George Ridding (Southwell) had been headmaster at Winchester. Edward Talbot (Rochester) had been the first warden of Keble College, Oxford and with his wife had founded Lady Margaret Hall. John Wordsworth (Salisbury) had taught at Wellington and been professor of Holy Scripture at Oxford. Francis Jayne (Chester) had been principal at St David's College Lampeter. There were a couple of episcopal scions of old families. Alwyn Compton at Ely was son of the 2nd marquess of Northampton; Edward Talbot's grandfathers were the 2nd earl Talbot and Lord Wharncliffe, and his father-in-law was the 4th Baron Lyttelton. But for the most part these were the sons of clergy, not lords. Indeed, the bishop of Winchester, Randall Davidson, was the son of a prosperous Scottish grain merchant, the archbishop of Canterbury was but the son of a colonial administrator, and his counterpart at York, William McLagan, was the son of a Scottish physician. These were not prince-bishops, but professional clergymen.

The reasons for the change were clear, and the bishops had only themselves to blame. Scandals over aristocratic prelates simultaneously harvesting the incomes of several church posts and doling out sinecures to their relatives had made their graces seem rather less than spiritual. Many, too, had adopted a rather casual attitude towards their dioceses. The palace at Wells, for instance, was only very rarely inhabited by its bishop, as John Wynne (1727–43) largely lived in his family estate in Flintshire, while Edward Willes (1743–73) and Charles Moss (1774–1802) lived in London, George Law (1824–45) in Banwell and Richard Bagot (1845–54) in Brighton. The vast archiepiscopal palaces of Lambeth, Canterbury, Bishopthorpe in Yorkshire and Addington in Croydon, and the bishops' residences of Auckland Castle, Fulham Palace, Hartlebury Castle, Wolvesley Palace and Farnham Castle seemed increasingly inappropriate. The incumbents got rich on their episcopal stipends, too, with most earning £5,000 a year in 1866, the same as the Prime Minister and roughly equivalent to half a million pounds in today's values, and the wealthier diocesan bishops receiving £14,000.

By the mid-nineteenth century there was real resentment at this grand old style, exacerbated by scandal. One such incident, fictionalized by Anthony Trollope in *The Warden*, makes the point. St Cross Hospital in Winchester had been founded in the twelfth century to assist the poor, but in the 1840s it became clear that many of its assets were being used to feather the already very downy nest of Francis North, the 6th earl of Guilford, who in addition to being the rector of the joint parish of Old Alresford, Medstead and New Alresford and of St Mary's, Southampton, held a prebend's stall at Winchester Cathedral and the wardenship of St Cross, all four posts being gifts of his father, Brownlow North, the bishop of Winchester and half-brother to the Prime Minister. In total, Guilford's income came to some £7,000 p.a., nearly £3,000 of it from St Cross alone. When this came to light, parliament condemned the practice and the courts deprived the warden of all bar £250 a year. Understandably the public fumed at the nepotism, greed and sense of episcopal entitlement. It was clear that the church needed to change, and bishops like Edward Denison at Salisbury from 1837 to 1854 and Samuel Wilberforce at Oxford (1845–69) began to see anew their duty as pastors rather than princes. By the turn of the twentieth century even patrician bishops like Charles Gore, brother of the 4th earl of Arran, took their pastoral duties seriously. Indeed, as bishop of Worcester, Birmingham and Oxford, Gore became a prominent supporter of the Christian Social Union, preaching the dignity of labour, condemning sweatshops and supporting the rights of women.

Moreover, just as the growth of Manchester and Leeds had led to demands for new Commons constituencies, so too there were calls for new dioceses. At first the church insisted that all bishops must be members of the House of Lords from the moment of their first appointment, but the Whigs and Liberals refused to countenance an increase above the historic number of twenty-six.* So, in order to create Ripon diocese, Gloucester and Bristol were united, and it was proposed that two Welsh sees, Bangor and St Asaph, be united to allow for the creation of Manchester. In the end Lord John Russell's government came up with the idea of an 'episcopal elevator' whereby the twenty-six longest-serving bishops would sit in the Lords, and a string of new dioceses were created: Manchester (1847), Carlisle (1856), St Albans (1877), Truro (also 1877), Liverpool (1880), Newcastle (1882), Southwell (1884), Wakefield (1888) and Birmingham (1905). From their inauguration it was clear that these were jobs, not sinecures, to be filled by professional theologians, academics and pastors, not minor aristocrats.

The Liberal party had been no more immune to change than Tories, peers and bishops. In the 1860s nearly half of all Liberal MPs had been landowners, but by 1914 just 6 per cent could claim such a background. Instead, there were lawyers in large numbers and a smattering of teachers and social workers. More than half the Liberal MPs elected in 1895 were nonconformists. More and more were individuals who had already made their own money and served on a county council or a board of guardians. Indeed, the split over Irish home rule had decanted a fair proportion of the old Whig aristocracy into the new skin of the Liberal Unionists, and Gladstone and Rosebery had both assiduously courted new money in an attempt to bolster their feeble numbers in the Lords. They too had their company directors and their wealthy professionals in both houses – and in 1899, following the resignation as leader first of Rosebery in 1895 and then of Sir William Harcourt (who took particular pride in the fact that his family

* Ireland was entitled to send four bishops in rotation from 1801 until 1869.

included an archbishop of York, a brace of dukes and a marquess), they acquired in Sir Henry Campbell-Bannerman their first leader of wealthy but definitely non-patrician, non-landowning stock.

'CB' was not the immediate choice. Some thought of Gladstone's sidekick John Morley, but he declined, as did the former Home Secretary H. H. Asquith, who preferred to ride out the years in opposition making money at the Bar. But Campbell-Bannerman had been Chief Secretary for Ireland and Secretary for War, and was wealthy enough to take on the task of leader of the opposition, which remained unpaid until 1937. He approached the 1900 election with trepidation, as the Second Boer War had separated the Liberal Party into its constituent parts again. Some hated the imperialist pretensions of British foreign policy that it exposed, while others – the political heirs to Palmerston – celebrated it. When a hastily convened autumn session of parliament started with a debate on an amendment to the speech from the throne decrying the war, the majority of the Liberal front bench abstained on 14 October 1899, but many Liberal MPs, including Augustine Birrell, John Morley, Charles Dilke, Sir William Harcourt and David Lloyd George, voted for the amendment, while Sir Edward Grey and Richard Haldane voted for the war. When a further opportunity came a few days later in the shape of a vote of supply, Campbell-Bannerman and Asquith voted with the government, but Lloyd George stayed in the diminished, mostly Irish nationalist, ranks of the anti-war brigade. By 6 February 1900 the balance of opinion in the party had moved somewhat, and a fresh amendment to the new session's speech from the throne, insisting that the war was unjust and unnecessary, gained the support of the Liberal front bench and 139 votes to the government's 352; but by the summer the divisions were on show again. Rosebery formed a Liberal Imperialist Council, and in a vote in July on a motion tabled by the pro-Boer anti-imperialist Liberal Sir Wilfrid Lawson, forty-one Liberal MPs voted with the Unionist government, twenty-nine voted with Lawson and the majority abstained. The voters' relief when the war started to go Britain's way with the lifting of the sieges of Ladysmith and Mafeking, followed by the British annexation of the Transvaal in October, was ably encouraged by Chamberlain's stout jingoism and paved the way for his clever, opportunistic timing of a 'khaki' election between 26 September and 24 October. When the results came in, the Unionists had 402 seats to the Liberals' 189.

The war was not to play entirely into the Unionists' hands, though. As it wore on over a further two years, more people began to condemn its conduct. Asquith furiously denounced the use of concentration camps and Campbell-Bannerman damned them as 'barbarism'. And then in 1902 and 1903 the Liberals had a bit of good fortune, when the Unionists did a number of things that could have been designed to unite their opponents. First was a new attempt in 1902 at a thoroughly Anglican Education Bill, which tore at the Liberal nonconformist heartstrings. Then in July that year Salisbury handed the premiership to his nephew Balfour, giving rise to angry charges of nepotism – and, it is widely believed, the phrase 'Bob's your uncle'.* Balfour, whose place in history Lloyd George casually dismissed as 'no more than the scent of perfume on a pocket handkerchief',[23] proved to be a vacillating premier with little personal warmth or physical energy (he did, however, prove to be a rather better Foreign Secretary under the very man who also typed him 'less a man than a mannerism' and at best 'an honest man without convictions'[24]).

Even more helpful for the Liberals was the Unionists' decision to tear themselves apart all over again over protectionism, when Chamberlain, as Colonial Secretary, started to militate for tariff reform or 'imperial preference' in a speech in Birmingham on 15 May 1903. The idea might have looked good on paper. After all, in an echo of the old arguments about the North American colonies in 1765, the war had to be paid for, and if foreign rather than imperial importers could be made to pay for it through higher duties, then surely the working man would be happy? As with many populist moves, though, it was soon to prove a millstone round the Conservatives' collective neck (as

---

* It is difficult to be certain, but in Latin *nepos* means 'nephew', and the marquess's Christian name was Robert.

many of the Liberal Unionists like Goschen and Hartington knew). It was easy to argue that food prices would rise, that the Liberal loaf would be bigger than the Unionist loaf, and that while landowning dukes and marquesses might benefit, the working man would not. However much Radical Joe Chamberlain toured the country drumming up support, tariff reform was to prove profoundly unpopular with everyone other than diehard protectionists. It helped unite the Liberals, for whom free trade had been the *sine qua non* of economic policy. It precipitated important Cabinet resignations, including those of Chamberlain (to campaign *for* tariff reform), the Chancellor of the Exchequer Charles Ritchie, the India Secretary Lord George Hamilton and the old (and deaf) Liberal Unionist leader Hartington, now duke of Devonshire (all three to fight *against* it). It pitted the Free Food League against the Tariff Reform League; it prompted Randolph's young son Winston Churchill, the Unionist MP for Oldham, to cross the floor; and it lost by-elections for the Unionists: five in 1903, seven in 1904 and seven again the following year. To top it all, the one issue that divided the Liberals in 1900, the Boer War, suddenly resurfaced to divide their opponents when Chamberlain decided to allow indentured Chinese workers to be imported into South Africa to extract gold as fast as possible from the imperial mines. Some called it slavery; others objected that these were jobs that could easily be done by British workers. Either way, it meant that the Boer War had lost its khaki sting by 1905.

Most importantly, by the end of 1905 Balfour's government had the stale air of the nineteenth century about it. The Irish Secretary, George Wyndham, had resigned in March, the Viceroy of India, George Curzon, stormed off in August, and when the Conservatives gathered for their conference in November Balfour failed to win a key vote on a motion tabled by Chamberlain. So, even though he had not lost a vote of confidence in parliament, Balfour resigned on 1 December 1905, bizarrely handing Campbell-Bannerman the right to form a Cabinet and decide on the date of an election. The Unionists must have expected defeat; but the scale of it was stunning. The Liberal chief whip, Herbert Gladstone, had done an electoral deal with the new Labour Representation Council, so whereas 153 Unionists were returned unopposed in 1900 and many had won thanks to a divided Liberal/Labour vote, this time just five Unionists were unopposed and in many cases either Liberal or Labour stood aside in favour of the other. Campbell-Bannerman won 400 seats, and in addition could normally rely on 83 Irish nationalists and a new phalanx of 29 LRC MPs. By contrast, the Conservatives had just 133 MPs and their Liberal Unionist colleagues 24.*

The social composition of the government was transformed. For every Cecil there was now a man of business. Lawyers from modest backgrounds crowded the Cabinet, with Asquith as Chancellor of the Exchequer, Augustine Birrell at the Board of Education, Richard Haldane as Secretary for War and the son of a schoolteacher, David Lloyd George, as President of the Board of Trade. There was a journalist, John Morley, and an academic in the shape of James Bryce, the former Regius professor of civil law at Oxford. There was even a Methodist, Henry Fowler (another lawyer), and a representative of the working class, John Burns, a teetotaller veteran of the London dock strike of 1889 and son of a washerwoman.

With such a mix, such a Commons majority and such a head of steam, Campbell-Bannerman's team ran at legislation with quixotic energy. Their only problem was the Lords, where, far from having a majority, at best they could count on only eighty-five supporters in a very bloated house of 602 peers. Education was one of the first issues to be addressed, as Birrell introduced a Bill in April 1906 to repeal the 1902 provisions, place all denominational schools under local authority control and curtail religious indoctrination. It foundered in the Lords, wrecked by amendments. In like manner a Licensing Bill, put forward in retaliation for another Unionist measure, was refused a second reading in the Lords on 27 November 1908 by 272 to 96. Lord

* Including the Speaker there were now 670 MPs. The number of seats continued to rise, peaking at 707 between 1918 and 1922, and falling back to 615 with the creation of the Irish Free State, when Northern Ireland retained 13.

The contest in Bedford in the general election of 1830 was tight. The sitting Whig member, William Whitbread, topped the poll, but Captain Frederick Polhill beat the duke of Bedford's son, Lord John Russell, by a single vote. Tensions ran high at the next election in December 1832, seen here, with 1,572 able to vote after the Reform Act had been passed. Polhill stood as a Conservative but, despite spending some £14,000, lost to another Whig, Samuel Crawley, by just three votes.

The campaign for parliamentary reform was often portrayed in violent terms, and real violence was never far away. The radical baronet Sir Francis Burdett (**above left**) tries to pull down the twin pillars of 'corrupt representation' and 'unlawful privilege' while trampling on Speaker Abbott's warrant for his arrest of 1810. Two years later his opponent, the Prime Minister Spencer Perceval (**above right**), arrived in the lobby of the House of Commons, where a disgruntled former employee of the East India Company, John Bellingham, shot him dead at point-blank range.

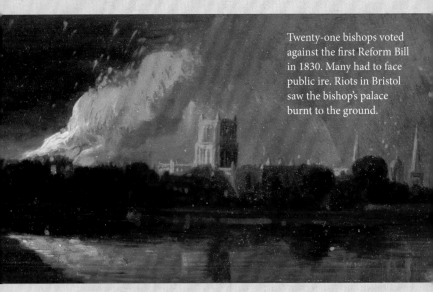

Twenty-one bishops voted against the first Reform Bill in 1830. Many had to face public ire. Riots in Bristol saw the bishop's palace burnt to the ground.

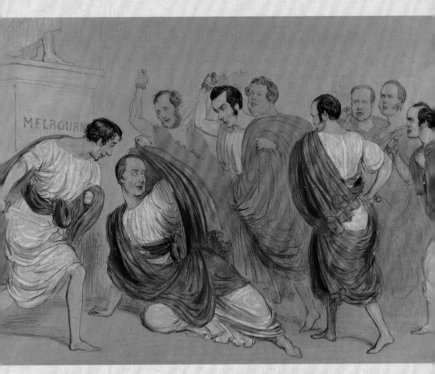

Above: Sir Robert Peel had long upheld the corn laws, but when he was eventually persuaded to repeal them in 1846, outraged fellow Conservatives united with Whigs to oust him as Prime Minister. Here the Conservative protectionists Benjamin Disraeli and Lord George Bentinck strike the first blows, and Peel falls at the feet of his predecessor Viscount Melbourne.

Right: Prior to 1850 Acts of parliament were inscribed on parchment rolls. The Reform Act of 1832 secured its passage through the Lords thanks only to the last-minute intervention of the king, but for all the controversy that surrounded it, it gave the vote only to an extra 250,000 men.

Above left: Nineteenth-century campaigns were fought in robust terms on party political grounds, as in this Whig broadside from Southampton in 1832.

Above right: Although the atheist Charles Bradlaugh was expelled from parliament four times for refusing to swear the oath, he was re-elected every time; finally, in 1886, he was allowed to affirm the oath.

By the mid-nineteenth century the Cabinet (as shown here in 1867 under the 14th earl of Derby) operated under a rule of collective responsibility.

Above: On 24 January 1885 the Fenian bombing campaign produced explosions in the Chamber of the Commons and in Westminster Hall.

Below: The aristocratic Cecil family provided bishops, ministers and MPs for centuries, from the reign of Elizabeth I up to the twentieth century.

Above: W. E. Gladstone, Lord Randolph Churchill and John Bright are among the MPs shown here in the Members' Lobby of the House of Commons in 1886.

MICHAEL DAVITT

Left: The question of whether Ireland should have home rule inspired many rowdy scenes in the Commons. On 3 February 1831 'indescribable confusion' led to thirty-four Irish MPs being excluded, including Charles Parnell.

ARTHUR:—
"THAT'S
RIGHT JOE,
CUT THE FOREIGNERS DOWN, THEY'RE ALWAYS OBSTRUCTING THE EMPIRE'S PROGRESS."

Above: In 1903 Joseph Chamberlain's campaign for tariff reform and Empire preference split Arthur Balfour's Conservative and Unionist Party between free traders and protectionists.

Left: Lloyd George said that his 1909 budget aimed to 'wage implacable warfare against poverty and squalidness', but his immediate battle was with the Conservative-dominated House of Lords.

Clockwise from top left: Although many politicians strayed from the monogamous heterosexual norm, only a few suffered scandal. **Viscount Palmerston's** many affairs – he is here satirised as Cupid – did not prevent him from becoming Prime Minister. The Liberal leader in the Lords, **Lord Beauchamp**, here dressed as Governor of New South Wales, was hounded out of his job, out of society and out of the country when it was rumoured that he was homosexual in 1931; yet **Jack Macnamara** sat as the Conservative MP for Chelmsford from 1935 until his death in active service in 1945, despite being an active homosexual. **Lord Lambton** was forced to resign as a minister and as an MP in 1973 over allegations of associating with a call-girl.

Fitzmaurice joked that at least with such a great number of mourners the Bill was to get 'a first class funeral',[25] but the ensuing series of rebuffs was no laughing matter. A similar fate met the Plural Voting Bill, which aimed to end the right to vote not just where one lived but wherever one had a residence, an Irish Councils Bill and another Education Bill in 1908. Rosebery's words to Queen Victoria in 1894 were proving foresighted: 'When the Conservative Party is in power there is no House of Lords; it takes whatever the Conservative Government brings it from the House of Commons without question or dispute; but the moment a Liberal Government is formed, this harmless body assumes an active life, and its activity is entirely exercised in opposition to the government.'[26]

The one policy that really caught the attention of the public was the introduction of old age pensions in Asquith's 1908 budget. Germany had introduced them in 1889 and ten other countries had followed suit, but despite sustained campaigning by the likes of George Barnes MP, the Scottish founder of the National Committee of Organised Labour for Old Age Pensions, it was not until the Old Age Pensions Act came into force in January 1909 that the elderly could draw a non-contributory pension in Britain – and even then it was a deliberately miserly means-tested amount, 5s a week or 7s 6d for a married couple, so that scrimping and saving would not be discouraged. By the time of the budget, Campbell-Bannerman had retired (on 1 April) after a series of heart attacks, so that when Asquith rose to the dispatch box on 7 May he did so as Prime Minister. In an inspired piece of personnel management, he had just handed the Treasury to Lloyd George and the Board of Trade to the 'rat' Winston Churchill, who Charles Hobhouse, the Chancellor of the Duchy of Lancaster, maintained was really nothing other than a spoilt child – but 'endowed by some chance with the brain of a genius'.[27] It was to be a brilliant, sparky, unreliable, opportunistic, roguish pairing.

Despite these energetic achievements, the Liberal government had sailed into the doldrums in early 1909, whereupon Lloyd George blew fresh wind into their sails with a breathtaking first budget. The new old age pensions, a new child allowance, new roads, a national system of labour exchanges and the construction of much-needed warships were to be paid for by two new higher rates of income tax, increased death duties, stamp duties on share transactions, increased duties on beer, spirits and tobacco, new petrol duties, a road fund licence and new land taxes. Thus the rich would be made to pay for the advancement of the poor. Lloyd George took four and a half hours to deliver his budget speech on 29 April; Austen Chamberlain, son of Radical Joe, thought he looked exhausted before he began and 'half-way through he was dead-beat'. At one point Balfour even leant across the dispatch box and suggested the Chancellor take a break, so the House adjourned for half an hour. But despite his nerves Lloyd George ended with aplomb, explaining why he had to raise so much money in peace-time, calling it 'a War Budget. It is for raising money to wage implacable warfare against poverty and squalidness.'[28]

He might as well have said, 'let battle commence', as he must have known that his 'war budget' would be met with apoplexy in the Lords. There had been battles between the two chambers before. Queen Anne had boosted the ranks of Tory peers to secure the passage of the Treaty of Utrecht, and the tussle over the Reform Act in 1832 had only been resolved by the intervention of the monarch. These skirmishes had brought an unwritten convention into play, articulated by Peel back in 1832: 'The House of Lords, to avoid the consequences of collision, declined acting upon that which was notoriously the deliberate judge-ment and conviction of a majority.'[29] In other words, once a matter had been put to the test in an election, the Lords would not interfere. Salisbury too accepted that the Lords should give way, but 'only when the judgement of the nation has been challenged at the polls and decidedly expressed', an eventuality he thought 'so rarely applicable as practically to place little fetter upon our independence'.[30]

There had been proposals in the air for reform of the upper house for some time, and when the government's earlier Bills were un-ceremoniously shredded by the Lords it had pushed through a resolution in the Commons in 1907 that 'the power of the other House should be so restricted by law as to secure that within the limits of a single Parliament the final decision of the Commons must prevail', winning the vote by a healthy 432 to 147 (one hundred members having previously supported Labour's amendment to abolish the Lords). Churchill had damned the House of Lords in the debate as 'one-sided, hereditary, unpurged, unrepresentative, irresponsible, absentee'.[31] The financial prerogative of the Commons, though, its exclusive competence in matters of finance, was a much older principle, and the government had won the Old Age Pensions Act by insisting that it was a 'Money Bill' that was therefore not subject to the Lords. So, even though Balfour complained that the 1909 Finance Bill was 'vindictive, inequitable, based on no principle and injurious to the productive capacity of the country',[32] Sir Edward Carson thought it meant 'the beginning of the end of all rights of property', the Tory leader in the Lords, Lansdowne, fumed that it was 'a monument of reckless and improvident finance', and Rosebery thought it 'inquisitorial, tyrannical and Socialistic',[33] the government can initially have had no idea that the Lords would seek to kill off the 'people's budget'.

There might have been some inkling of trouble brewing, however, when the Bill was subjected to a total of seventy-two days of debate in the Commons, including regular all-night sittings and 554 divisions (compared to 544 for the whole of the two-year session of 2010–12) throughout the summer and up until 4 November, when the majority for third reading was even larger than it had been for the second, 379 to 149. By now Churchill reckoned that if the Unionists were to sink the Bill, 'it would give the Government a great tactical advantage';[34] but although Henry Somerset, the 9th duke of Beaufort, said he wanted to see Churchill and Lloyd George in the middle of twenty couple of dog hounds, Henry Manners, the 8th duke of Rutland, called them 'piratical tatterdemalions', and several other hard-pressed aristocrats complained that if they had to cut corners they would be forced to lay off a valet or two, it was unclear precisely how the Lords would deal with it until 10 November, when Lansdowne gave notice that he would move a reasoned amendment to the effect that the Lords should not give its consent to the Bill 'until it [had] been submitted to the judgment of the country'. If it were carried the Bill would fall. This was folly. Plenty of wise heads in the Unionist ranks knew it, too. They forecast a general election, a Liberal victory, a new Bill and new laws to restrict the powers of the Lords.

For most Bills the government spokesman would speak first, but when the Lords debate started on 22 November the leader of the House, Robert Crewe-Milnes, the earl of Crewe (Rosebery's son-in-law), formally moved second reading and pointedly refused to speak out of disdain for the idea of the Lords breaching the financial prerogative of the Commons. So Lansdowne spoke first instead and, thick with a cold, discoursed at length as much on the powers of the Lords as on the subject of the Bill, even praying in aid Oliver Cromwell's creation of his own house of lords so as to protect 'the people of England against "an omnipotent House of Commons – the horridest arbitrariness that ever existed in the world"'.[35] He derided the government's arguments that financial privilege should apply, as they themselves had referred to the budget as having 'far-reaching political and social results'; he attacked the proposed death duties as 'naturally odious' and the land duties as 'predatory taxation'. He ended with a constitutional point: 'My Lords, depend upon it that by rejecting this Bill . . . you will say that it is a Bill to which you have no right to give your indispensable consent until you have been assured by the people of the country that they desire it to pass into law.'[36] It was self-serving nonsense.

The debate lasted six days, and the vast majority of speakers supported Lansdowne. Despite the formal courtesies observed in the Lords, there was a simmering fractiousness throughout. The Conservative church historian and archaeologist Forrest Browne, the bishop of Bristol, ostentatiously backed up Lansdowne's line about forcing the government to consult the people, as did many of the Conservative peers, but the under-secretary for war Auberon Herbert, the 9th Baron Lucas, directly charged those who had adopted a 'democratic attitude' of doing so dishonestly. There were steady, deliberately understated but unmistakable attacks on Lloyd George and Churchill; the duke of Marlborough accused the government of 'party vindictiveness' and called Crewe 'a self-constituted mute at the obsequies of the British Constitution'.[37] Just a few backed the government. Bishop Gore thought the budget was 'only one more instance of the gradual growth towards a more proper distribution of the constantly-increasing burdens of public expenditure',[38] and Donald MacKay, the Dutch-born Liberal 11th Lord Reay, counselled against rejection with the warning 'that oligarchies are seldom destroyed and more frequently commit suicide'.[39] Bishop Percival also spoke in favour, arguing that

> you may send this Budget to the country; but . . . my belief is that the answer will come back to your Lordships in very plain English, and I fear it may come in some form which you may regret. The answer will come, I think, something like this – 'Never again, never again, in this country shall the fundamental liberties of the people be endangered by any privileged class.'[40]

Rosebery grandly announced that he despised the Bill and the only concession he would make to his son-in-law's injunctions was that he would abstain, as 'he was not willing to link the fortunes of the second chamber with opposition to the Budget';[41] but, speaking on 29 November, John Morley (now a viscount) argued that although some might see the previous days of debate as a great stage play, the truth was that when everyone trooped home, 'we shall all know in our hearts that the note has sounded for a very angry and perhaps prolonged battle'.[42] He was right. The vote the next day was decisive. The Bill was lost by 350 to 75, evidence that Balfour could not have restrained his noble troops even if he had wanted to.

The following Tuesday Asquith went to the Commons and announced a dissolution and a general election to be held in the second half of January. The campaign was not a particularly exciting one, as the issues were already well rehearsed, and the result only moderated the *status quo ante*. The Unionists made 116 gains and on 273 were within spitting distance of the Liberals on 275, but since Asquith could rely on the Irish nationalists and Labour members, the government had an effective majority of 124. Lansdowne's 'democratic attitude' could now be put to the test; but Asquith still faced a massive Conservative majority in the second chamber and was uncertain what to do if the Lords rejected the Bill again. Building a Liberal majority in the Lords would require at least 300 new peers, and Edward VII's private secretary let Asquith's secretary know that the king thought he would not be justified in making additional peers to secure the Commons' will until after a *second* election. This left Asquith in the unenviable position of having to pretend there had been no discussions about new creations – so as not to embarrass the king politically – while driving through measures to reform the Lords, which he could only possibly achieve if he could dangle in front of their eyes the threat of swamping the House with three to four hundred of his own supporters committed to reform.

The Cabinet was united, though, and resolved at least to get resolutions through the Commons that indicated the desire to limit the power of the second chamber. The mood was highly charged in the lower house on 14 April, when three resolutions were put: namely, that the Lords could not amend or reject a Money Bill, that Bills that had been carried three times in the Commons could become law without the Lords' agreement, and that parliaments be curtailed from seven to five years. Asquith first tried to tell the House what the government intended to do should the Lords continue in their opposition. Unionists howled him down and the Prime Minister was prevented from speaking until later in the evening, when he laid out that

> if we do not find ourselves in a position to ensure that statutory
> effect shall be given to that policy in this Parliament, we shall then

either resign our offices or recommend the dissolution of Parliament. Let me add this, that in no case will we recommend a dissolution except under such conditions as will secure that in the new Parliament the judgment of the people as expressed at the elections will be carried into law.[43]

It was as close as he could get to threatening new creations.

Then, on 6 May 1910, Edward VII died; and, out of deference to the inexperienced new king, George V, Asquith felt bound to seek a consensus with the Unionists and set up cross-party talks on Lords reform. The negotiations were doomed from the start, but when they finally collapsed in November Asquith went to Sandringham to request a new dissolution for an election before Christmas on the express understanding that if the same situation pertained in the new parliament the king would create the necessary peers for 'an adequate majority'. George V baulked, but the political facts of life were clear: without the guarantees he sought, Asquith would resign and Balfour would be unable to form a government. So George reluctantly acquiesced and a second election was held in the run-up to Christmas 1910. The result was remarkably similar, with few seats changing hands. Balfour quietly let the king know that there was no alternative government that could be formed and that he expected the king could not really refuse a request for peers if it were made – and Asquith presented a new Parliament Bill codifying the provisions of the previous year's resolutions.

The Unionists had certainly not yet given up when the Commons second reading started on 27 February 1911. All pretences of a 'democratic attitude' were now gone, and Balfour made as robust a defence of the hereditary principle as one would expect from a member of the Hotel Cecil: 'I say it is folly for us as practical men simply to lay down the proposition that we have nothing to do with the hereditary principle . . . it is in conformity with the general feeling of mankind over the greater parts of the earth. Let it be our servant, let it be no longer our master.'[44] Everyone cheered this last point,

Liberals with enthusiastic sarcasm, but when Balfour went on to accuse ministers of imposing measures on the country 'by fraud', the Liberals were so incensed that once the Speaker had ruled that one could refer to a whole party but not to an individual in such terms, they shouted out one after another that 'the Tory Party are frauds'. For all the sound and fury, Asquith's Commons majority was assured; second reading went through by 368 to 243 and after ten days in committee third reading was carried by 362 to 241 on 15 May.

So far, so easy. But then came the Lords, where second reading started on 23 May. Lansdowne's tactic this time was to allow second reading but slice the Bill to pieces in committee, and the government lost every vote on an amendment bar one (which even Lansdowne considered too extreme). With both sides approaching the endgame, on 14 July, the day after report stage was concluded, Asquith wrote to the king that the Lords' amendments were 'destructive of [the Bill's] principle and purpose' and that his strong advice was that the crown must exercise its prerogative 'so as to get rid of the deadlock'.[45] On the eighteenth, Lloyd George told Balfour and Lansdowne directly what their plan was, and two days later in the Lords the Unionist front bench sat on their hands, allowing third reading of the amended Bill to go through without division. The next stage would be consideration of the Lords' amendments in the Commons. On the twenty-first, the Unionists held two meetings. The Shadow Cabinet meeting at 11.30 a.m. divided thirteen to eight in favour of a new policy of moderation. An hour earlier a separate meeting at Grosvenor House, the London home of the duke of Westminster, had come to a very different decision.

The climax came on Monday, 24 July. Asquith rose to give the government's response to the Lords' amendments, but in the quaint words of Hansard 'was immediately assailed with Opposition cries of "Traitor"'.[46] The barracking went on for the best part of half an hour with the Prime Minister unable to make himself heard. Unionists shouted and screamed, they made pointless points of order, they hurled abuse, they twitted him that some of the very men he had given peerages to had voted against him, they accused him of doing a dodgy deal with Redmond and the Irish, and even when he managed to get a couple of sentences out they kept up the volley of interruptions. As the LRC member Will Crooks pointed out, many a man had been certified insane for less. There were further speeches from Balfour (who was heard in silence) and a rather emotional Foreign Secretary, Sir Edward Grey,[47] but when F. E. Smith, who had mercilessly heckled Asquith, rose to speak the brouhaha lasted for five minutes and the Speaker decided that the 'grave disorder' required the suspension of the House.

The Unionist bellowing had been directed at Asquith, but the row that prompted the Speaker to act was an internal Unionist one. For at the previous Friday's meeting at Grosvenor House, Lord Willoughby de Broke had gathered a group of eighty 'ditchers', all of whom were prepared to fight to the last, including F. E. Smith and the elderly former Lord Chancellor, Hardinge Giffard, the earl of Halsbury (who wildly screamed in a meeting of Unionist peers: 'I will divide even if I am alone'[48]).

With the battle between 'ditchers' and 'hedgers' raging around him, Balfour then tabled motions in both the Lords and the Commons censuring the request for additional peers. It was another mistake. Balfour's speech in support of the motion on 7 August left him open to accusations of insulting the king, referring to George as 'a sovereign who had only just come to the throne, and who, from the very nature of the case, had not and could not have behind him that long personal experience of public office which some of his great predecessors had'.[49] The Glasgow MP Alexander MacCallum Scott shouted out that this was to censure the king, not Asquith – and from a distance the king agreed. Even Salisbury, who was busy hosting a dinner for 120 ditcher peers on the eighth, would have agreed that insulting the king was a rather queer way of proceeding if one wanted to be his Prime Minister.

On Wednesday 9 August, the hottest day on record, the Lords met at 4.30 p.m. to debate the Commons amendments. Tempers had not improved. Morley called a specious point made by Salisbury 'juvenile'.

Archbishop Lang urged the 'ditchers' to back down, but since he had originally voted with the government his argument carried little weight. The bishop of Winchester reckoned that even if the Bill were killed off there would be a resurrection within a week. Lord Ribblesdale, whose wife was half-sister to Margot Asquith and who was hobbled by a broken leg, thought it time 'to beat a dignified, but determined retreat'.[50] Accusations of treachery within Unionist ranks simmered under the surface as Halsbury, who had been extremely busy conspiring against the policy of moderation, denied the allegation made in a 'vile journal' by a 'degraded journalist' that he had been intriguing and added the archaic word 'forsooth!' for effect. Salisbury, too, asserted: 'Whether we will be in a majority or a minority none can tell; but this is certain – that in the annals of this year it will go down to history that a certain number of your Lordships were as good as their word and voted according to their opinions.'[51] He was backed up by Willoughby de Broke, who made only too clear his disdainful view of the democratic mandate: 'You may claim majorities if you like in favour of the Parliament Bill at a dozen General Elections, but that will not alter my view.'[52] So the debate continued. The royal palace was watching carefully and, realizing that the strongest argument being advanced by the diehards was that the government was bluffing about the possible creation of peers, told Crewe the next morning that he could make a definitive statement that the king would indeed proceed to create peers in sufficient numbers if the Bill were defeated. So on 10 August, in the midst of a largely unprepared speech, Morley read out the pre-arranged words: 'If the Bill should be defeated to-night His Majesty would assent to a creation of Peers sufficient in number to guard against any possible combination of the different Parties in opposition by which the Parliament Bill might again be exposed a second time to defeat.'[53]

The Conservative leadership knew that the game was up, even if their diehard colleagues were still looking for a ditch to die in, so when it came to the key vote they abstained. Thirty-seven Unionists even voted with the government – and were hissed for it when they next attended the Carlton Club. As for the lords spiritual, both archbishops and eleven bishops voted with the government; only the bishops of Bangor and Worcester voted with the diehards.[54] Given the front-bench Unionist abstentions, the result was tight, just seventeen votes in it; but the government had won, by 131 to 114.

One of those who had organized the diehard group of Unionists and had hectored Asquith most viciously – and whose behaviour was described by Asquith's daughter Violet as 'like mad baboons' – was Lord Hugh Cecil, the fifth son of the (by then late) 3rd marquess of Salisbury. A clever man, who had (according to his biographer) read all of Macaulay's essays by the age of seven, he was none the less a potent symbol of the dying aristocracy. His manner could be acerbic at the best of times. He thanked one hostess for her 'charming if parsimonious hospitality' and told another that 'the conversation was surprisingly well sustained and the dishes various and sufficient'.[55] With his etiolated form (he was over six feet tall yet weighed just seven stone), his high-pitched voice, his stooped shoulders and his habit of plucking at his ill-kempt jacket, he struck a strange figure in the Commons, to which he was elected in 1895 and 1900 and where he and a group of allies known as the 'Hughligans' mounted a robust assault on tariff reform. Having lost his seat in Greenwich in 1906, he returned, unopposed, in 1910 as the MP for Oxford University, just in time to do battle over the powers of the Lords. Lord Hugh admitted that he would have preferred the House of Commons of the eighteenth and nineteenth centuries, 'with its oratorical figures, its vehement and even violent debates, its impression of the grandeur of historic controversy',[56] and his contribution to the discourse of his own time did seem strangely anachronistic as he became more and more shrill in the debate on the Lords' amendments on 8 August 1911, screaming at Asquith and caustically damning his own leader with faint praise. He charged the government with using the royal prerogative 'for party convenience'. He said he would gladly see the Prime Minister 'punished by the criminal law'. He thought the government and Prime Minister had been 'guilty of high treason'.[57]

Hugh's high-blown rhetoric was matched by that of his elder brother, James, the 4th marquess, who after hosting an eve-of-vote dinner for 120 diehard peers at his spacious London home in Arlington Street snootily threatened the Lords that 'if it comes to creating peers, two can play at that game', and derided the archbishop of Canterbury's call for courageous restraint: 'I hoped that we should have been spared an appeal to courage, but the Most Reverend Prelate could not avoid it.'[58] James was to go on to serve in the Cabinet from 1922 to 1929 (with a brief respite during the Labour government of 1924), but neither he nor his other younger brother Lord Robert Cecil MP, who was a minister between 1915 and 1919 and again between 1923 and 1927, and president of the League of Nations Union from 1923 to 1945 (for which he received the Nobel Peace Prize in 1937), was truly suited for twentieth-century politics. James wrote in 1911 that 'politics are beastly' and Robert (elevated as Viscount Cecil of Chelwood in 1923) said of himself that he was 'quite unfitted for political life, because I have a resigning habit of mind',[59] and complained that Baldwin's second Cabinet of 1924–9, in which both he and James (and the two brothers Austen and Neville Chamberlain) sat, had too many 'middle class monsters' and 'pure party politicians'.[60]

True, there were people who still espoused views similar to those of the Cecils. As late as 1934 the ill-educated, eccentric, xenophobic and reactionary landowner Lord Redesdale, David Freeman-Mitford, proclaimed that 'generally speaking a man who had spent all his life in politics and public affairs was more likely to have a son capable of following his footsteps . . . than a man who had never paid any particular attention to either'.[61] For him the hereditary principle was a core aspect of the British way of life. Yet in the initial Lords debate on the 1909 budget, even the 4th marquess of Salisbury had resorted to an appeal to democracy, declaring with chutzpah that his sole reason for insisting that the hereditary house reject the will of the elected house was his belief that 'the considered judgment of the people is essential to the working of our Constitution'. He ended: 'To that considered judgment we appeal; to our masters, my Lords; yes and [the Government's] masters too, and by that judgment we will abide.'[62] When even the patrician's patrician declared for the authority of the people, the old order was sure to fade away.

Many MPs and peers fought in the two world wars and several lost their lives on active service. Sir Frederick Cawley, MP for Prestwich and then a peer, lost all three of his sons: Harold, MP for Heywood, John, and Oswald, his father's successor as MP for Prestwich. This is Harold's grave in Gallipoli. Because MPs' correspondence was not censored, his letters to his father helped reveal the many mistakes in the Dardanelles campaign. Personal tragedy also touched many senior members of the government: Arthur Henderson and Herbert Asquith each lost a son and Andrew Bonar Law lost two.

5

Two Houses at War

On 12 February 1793, just weeks after the execution of the French King Louis XVI, William Pitt the Younger told the Commons in a seemingly interminable speech that France had to all intents and purposes declared war on Britain. His immediate assumption was that 'whatever difference of opinion might formerly have existed', there would now be 'one unanimous sentiment and voice expressed', as when war was declared 'it remained only to be considered whether we should meet it with a firm determination'.[1] He was to be disappointed in his appeal for unanimity, as Fox promptly tabled an amendment. It was lost, but the point had been made that war did not of itself automatically obtain parliament's unanimous quiescence.

Just over a century later, H. H. Asquith was still running a minority Liberal government when the Foreign Secretary, Sir Edward Grey, made a similar statement to the Commons on Monday, 3 August 1914, outlining why Britain was joining the war that had already been declared between Germany and the Austro-Hungarian Empire on the one hand and Serbia, France and Russia on the other. On this occasion the responses of the party leaders made it clear that the government would enjoy overwhelming majority support, as first the relatively inexperienced new leader of the Conservative party, the Scotsman

Andrew Bonar Law, declared Unionist backing for the war and then John Redmond, for the Irish Parliamentary Party, gave his assent.

Redmond had an ulterior motive. Asquith had twice driven the Government of Ireland Act through the Commons, in 1912 and 1913, only to see it fail by large margins in the Lords, but under the provisions of the 1911 Parliament Act he had only to do so once more for home rule to pass into law. Ulster, led ably by the Dubliner lawyer turned Ulster Unionist MP Sir Edward Carson, had reacted to this prospect with fury and had attracted the ostentatious support of Bonar Law, who had declared in July 1912 at a mass meeting at Blenheim Palace that the loyalists 'would be justified in resisting by all means, including force'.[2] In May 1914 the Bill had received its third Commons third reading; under pressure, Asquith had tabled his own compromise to allow for the temporary segregation of Protestant Ulster; and in July a special conference convened by the king to broker an agreement ended in failure. So when Redmond spoke on 3 August all was still to play for. That he so clearly backed Asquith made it that much easier for the Prime Minister to table a Suspensory Bill that allowed the king to give royal assent to the Government of Ireland Act in September 1914, but meant that neither it nor the Welsh Church Act (which, in disestablishing the church in Wales, would also take the four Welsh bishops out of the Lords) could be implemented until 18 September 1915 at the earliest. Redmond would never see home rule, as he died in 1918; but by backing the British war he secured an uneasy, partial and delayed Irish autonomy and paved the way for the creation of the Irish Free State in 1922.

By John's side was his younger brother, Willie, who had already been an MP for more than thirty years. Having fought what he called 'the battle for self-government for Ireland [and] lain in Kilmainham prison with Parnell', Willie became an active recruiting sergeant and told the crowds in Cork that November: 'Old as I am, and grey as are my hairs, I will say "Don't go, but come with me"'.[3] Good as his word, three months later, aged fifty-three, Willie joined the Royal Irish Regiment; and although the harsh repression of the Easter Rising in

1916 revolted him, he spoke in the Commons of his hope that one day he would be able to say to Canadians and Australians: 'Our country, just as yours, has self-government within the Empire.'[4] The Redmond brothers were to have one further, highly significant, role in the eventual creation of the Irish Free State. Having led his troops over the top at Messines Ridge on the morning of 7 June 1917, Willie was shot and died that afternoon. The subsequent by-election was won by the Sinn Féin leader, Éamon de Valera.

On 3 August 1914, then, of the party leaders only Labour's Ramsay MacDonald disagreed with Asquith and Grey, arguing that the Foreign Secretary had not proved that either Britain or Belgium was in danger. If he were to do so, MacDonald said, 'we will vote him what money he wants. Yes, and we will go further. We will offer him ourselves if the country is in danger'; but in the absence of that proof, the only reason for Britain's involvement could be that same appeal to honour that had led Britain into the Crimean War and made it rush to South Africa. Labour saw things differently. 'Whatever may happen,' he ended, 'whatever may be said about us, whatever attacks may be made upon us, we will . . . [say] that this country ought to have remained neutral, because in the deepest parts of our hearts we believe that that was right and that that alone was consistent with the honour of the country and the traditions of the party that are now in office.'[5] MacDonald (who soon resigned as Labour leader when his party disagreed with him) was not quite alone. Later that day the wealthy ex-Eton and Balliol Liberal MP Philip Morrell (who enjoyed a very open marriage with Lady Ottoline, immortalized by D. H. Lawrence in *Women in Love*) urged further efforts for peace. So too Josiah Wedgwood, who would later receive the DSO for his action in the Dardanelles, took issue with Grey's 'jingo' speech, warning 'that this is not going to be one of the dear old-fashioned wars of the eighteenth century over again'.[6] Two Quaker Liberals, Edmund Harvey and Arnold Rowntree, made it clear that they 'would have nothing to do with this war'.[7] One member, Joseph King, referred to rumours that a member of the Cabinet was threatening to resign. He was howled down, but he was right. At the Cabinet that morning four members had tendered their resignations. Two, the Attorney-General Sir John Simon and the First Commissioner of Works, Earl Beauchamp, were prevailed upon to recant, but John Morley, now seventy-five but still Lord President of the Council, whom Campbell-Bannerman had often derided as 'that old-maidish Priscilla' for his frequent threats of resignation,[8] followed through on his threat this time, and took John Burns with him.

In the three mini-debates that day just one backbench member, Sir Arthur Markham, spoke in support of Grey, but it was clear that the overwhelming majority of the Commons and the Lords enthusiastically backed a war that they thought would be over by Christmas. The next day Asquith told the House that he had issued an ultimatum to Germany, on the fifth he announced that 'since eleven o'clock last night a state of war has existed between Germany and ourselves',[9] and on the sixth the Commons approved a grant of £100 million for the war without a single vote or voice in opposition. So began a nine-month period of unparalleled Liberal–Unionist front-bench cooperation, including a pact that by-elections would go uncontested.

Cross-party cooperation is not remarkable in itself, but in 1914 it swaddled all debate in the Commons into silence, even though both main party leaders had real difficulties keeping their respective backbench colleagues under control. Asquith had a committed band of refuseniks who harked back to the Boer War, and Bonar Law, who had only become Unionist leader as the compromise candidate, had his erstwhile rivals, Joe Chamberlain's son Austen and Walter Long, agitating for tariff reform or stirring up discontent as part of the new Unionist Business Committee of backbench MPs, as noted by the Conservative whip William Bridgeman in December 1914: 'The rank and file became very restless, partly because they were always haunted with the idea that the leaders of both parties were meeting in secret and giving away the party on Home Rule.'[10] This Unionist malaise led Bonar Law to his sole act of non-cooperation, when he staged a mass walkout of the Unionist MPs over the Suspensory Bill on

15 September, a dramatic flounce that Asquith dismissed as 'a lot of prosaic & for the most part middle-aged gentlemen trying to look like early French revolutionists in the Tennis Court',[11] and that merely succeeded in irritating the very people it was designed to impress, Unionist backbenchers, who took part only reluctantly.

Despite all this rustling in the undergrowth, little dissent came out into the open. Even when the government suffered its first major setback in the shape of the disastrous Dardanelles campaign, which the First Lord of the Admiralty, Winston Churchill, had promoted as an ambitious means of seizing Constantinople and securing a sea route through to Russia, the Commons merely sucked in its collective cheeks. Gallipoli was to become a byword for tragic military failure, and as the campaign festered into another bout of stinking overheated trench warfare the temperamental Jacky Fisher, who had always opposed the venture, resigned as First Sea Lord on Saturday, 15 May. This could and should have led to a major parliamentary row. After all, Unionists were, albeit sotto voce, demanding both Churchill's removal and a new, unfettered, more Conservative approach to managing the war. But the government took action without any reference to parliament: on the Monday after Fisher's resignation Asquith and Bonar Law concocted a plan for a wartime coalition, which would keep the key posts in Liberal hands, but would appease the tacit Unionist diehard majority by demoting Churchill to the Duchy of Lancaster and by bringing Carson, Long and Austen Chamberlain into the government.

That afternoon the industrialist Conservative MP Sir Richard Cooper complained that the government was preventing MPs from raising real concerns about the provision of munitions to the Western Front, while the former journalist turned Liberal MP for Kirkcaldy, Sir Henry Dalziel, having called for a government 'of national representatives, including opponents as well as friends',[12] was told by George Radford, the Liberal MP for Islington East, that a coalition government would have little support in the House. One man, Asquith's ally Frederick Handel Booth, did predict that 'a united Ministry – call it what you will – is coming, and will come before very long',[13] but the senior minister in the Chamber, the Liberal chief whip John Gulland, lamely ended the debate with the promise that he would 'convey to the Prime Minister the very varied views which have been expressed by hon. Members'.[14]

On Wednesday, 19 May, with the two-week Whitsun adjournment fast approaching, Asquith made a brief statement to the Commons confirming the speculation about a coalition and was immediately summoned to a disgruntled meeting of Liberal MPs, at which, according to the Glasgow MP Alexander MacCallum Scott, he 'spoke with deep feeling – his voice husky and his face twitching. He looked old and worried. He flung himself on our mercy,'[15] suggesting darkly that there were matters of grave national importance that he could not now divulge to his colleagues. Soon the meeting was in tears and Asquith received a hearty standing ovation. The negotiations continued during the recess, and by the time the Commons returned on 3 June, much of the new government had been appointed, with twelve Liberals, eight Unionists and one Labour member in the Cabinet, but the job was still far from complete. Despite determined efforts by Lloyd George and Churchill to oust him, the supposedly non-aligned Horatio, Lord Kitchener was still at the War Office, Lloyd George moved to the new Ministry of Munitions, Bonar Law took the Colonial Office and Balfour the Admiralty, and the new Labour leader Arthur Henderson took over the Board of Education. Although Liberals kept both the Home Office and the Treasury, Curzon, Long and Austen Chamberlain all entered the government, respectively as Lord Privy Seal, Education Secretary and India Secretary. Still no formal announcement was made to parliament, nor was a debate even mooted, while emergency legislation was swept through both houses in two days by the new Home Secretary, suspending the by-election requirement for ministers who were accepting Cabinet posts. Finally, on 9 June, a string of junior posts was filled and the coalition was complete. The last Liberal Cabinet had resigned, to be replaced by the first all-party coalition government. Charles Hobhouse, the gossipy outgoing Paymaster-General, declared it was 'the end of the Liberal Party as we have known it'.[16] Charles Trevelyan went further: 'All Liberalism will be abandoned and we shall live under conscription and martial law.'[17] Even more notable, though, was the fact that the whole reconstruction of the government had happened, in the thick of war, without a single reference to parliament. Politics had gone underground.

Binding the most vociferous Unionists into the new government was a stroke of genius, and even though military ineptitude and political vacillation at the War Office produced yet more casualties and more sultry backbench discontent through the rest of 1915, it was not until the early days of 1916 that parliamentary discontent spilled out into the open. Yet again the problem came from within Unionist ranks. For some time it had been clear that voluntary recruitment would not provide sufficient troops for the bloodthirsty war. Embarrassed by or furious with further military failings in the Balkans, Carson had resigned as Attorney-General in October and started arguing, via a new Unionist War Committee, for a more 'total' approach to war, which he believed required opening up an economic front against Germany and introducing conscription. This last issue had sharply divided the Cabinet, where just two Liberals – Lloyd George and Churchill – supported the idea and just one Unionist, Balfour, opposed it, while the Labour party contrived to adopt two mutually contradictory positions at the same time, against the proposed Military Service Bill, but in favour of assisting 'the Government as far as possible in the successful prosecution of the war'.[18] The government's halfway house Bill, which brought in conscription for unmarried men only, had a rocky passage through the Commons on 5 and 6 January 1916, with Labour and twenty-seven Liberals consistently opposing it, but by February it was clear that even this measure would not suffice, and although there was little evidence that the army could actually recruit any faster, Carson's Unionist War Committee, which incorporated virtually every backbench Unionist MP not on active military service, cried out for general conscription, a policy that was anathema to all Labour and many Liberal backbenchers.

Yet again the coalition Cabinet was torn. Arthur Henderson threatened resignation and Lloyd George, who was getting more and more frustrated by Kitchener's ineptitude, Asquith's inanition and his Liberal colleagues' refusal to grasp the seriousness of the situation, spotted an opportunity to resign over a matter of principle. Try as he might throughout April to get Cabinet backing for general conscription, Lloyd George failed to persuade either his Liberal colleagues in the Cabinet or even the pro-conscriptionists Bonar Law and Austen Chamberlain to push it through, Chamberlain privately acknowledging: 'I think my own party in the House quite unreasonable.'[19] So the government took another compromise Bill to a secret session* of the Commons on 25 and 26 April, which was itself a major departure from the norm and sparked a furious response from Carson (whom Lloyd George thought so contrary that he would oppose any government, including one that his own party supported). From the unpublishable reaction of the Commons it was clear that the government had little choice over conscription but to capitulate, and on 2 May the Cabinet came forth with a new Bill conscripting all men aged 18 to 41, subject only to minor exemptions. For the first time the Unionist ranks had stamped their hallmark on the war.

Immediately thereafter, however, parliament returned to its

---

* According to a Commons rule dating from 1705, if a member shouted 'I spy strangers' the House could immediately decide to meet in secret, requiring all observers to leave. So frequently had it done so between 1768 and 1774 that the parliament was dubbed 'the Unreported'. It had done so again in 1810 (controversially) over the Walcheren expedition. Following this two-day debate in 1916, secret sessions became a fixed part of wartime parliaments, being used on seven occasions in the First World War and thirty-seven in the Second. The galleries were cleared, no record of the debate was kept other than a formal notice prepared by the Speaker, and it was considered a serious breach of parliamentary privilege to reveal what had been said. The Commons agreed to lift the secrecy about the Second World War sessions on 19 December 1945, thereby exceptionally enabling Churchill to publish his secret session speeches, for which he received more than $50,000 in royalties.

default position of quiescent support for the government, which sauntered relatively unhappily through the rest of the year while the war continued its remorseless attrition. Neither house was exempt from the blood-letting. Although a few fought tooth and nail to prevent their family members from being exposed to danger (as Catherine Bailey proves happened in the case of the 9th duke of Rutland[20]), by January 1915 139 Unionist MPs and 41 Liberals had enlisted, some continuing old Territorial careers, others joining up for the first time. And steadily the roll call of dead and wounded MPs and peers grew. One family's experience will suffice to make the point. The bespectacled barrister Harold Cawley, Liberal MP for Heywood, was the second son of the wealthy cotton merchant and MP Frederick Cawley. Having joined the No. 2 Volunteer Battalion of the Manchester Regiment in 1904, Harold had been drafted as aide-de-camp to Major-General William Douglas, who was commanding the 42nd East Lancashire Division in 1914. In September he sailed with the Manchesters for Egypt and arrived in Gallipoli in May 1915. His younger brother John, who had been a regular in the 20th Hussars, had died in the retreat from Mons just days before Harold had left England in 1914, and on 4–5 June 1915 four of Harold's schoolfriends from Rugby were killed in the attack on Krithia, but he was frustrated by a headquarters job, writing: 'I have always felt rather a brute skulking behind in comparative safety while my friends are being killed.' So, despite misgivings about the whole Gallipoli campaign, which he expressed in a forthright letter to his father, he demanded to be drafted to the front – just as Brigadier-General Thomas Pakenham, the 5th earl of Longford (who told his officers at Suvla, 'Don't bother ducking, the men don't like it and it doesn't do any good'), was killed on 21 August 1915. The same fate befell Captain Cawley on 23 September 1915. Because both father and son were MPs their correspondence was covered by parliamentary privilege and could not be suppressed, which enabled the father to campaign on the military's manifest failures. It was not the end of the Cawleys' pain, as Harold's younger brother Oswald, who took his father's seat of Prestwich in

January 1918 on Frederick's becoming a peer, also expressly sought out the front line, joining the 10th King's Shropshire Light Infantry as a captain. In their attempt to advance north of the Lys canal near Merville on 22 August 1918 he was shot in the arm; after having his wound dressed, he went back to the fray and was shot again, this time fatally in the jaw. By the time the ceasefire was called, Lord Cawley, who had campaigned so assiduously for a better-run war, and had joined Lloyd George's Cabinet as Chancellor of the Duchy of Lancaster, had lost all three of his sons.

They were just a tiny part of the phenomenal losses sustained. The 2nd Highland Light Infantry, for instance, left Britain with 30 officers and 977 soldiers; of those thousand and more men, just thirty were still standing by the end of the first battle of Ypres on 16 November 1914. Nearly 20,000 British troops were killed and another 37,470 injured at the Somme on 1 July 1916, most of them in the first thirty minutes of the failed offensive. By November 1916, 400,000 imperial forces (and roughly the same number of Germans) had been lost at the Somme; Arras would go on to take another 159,000 casualties in thirty-nine days, Passchendaele another 250,000. In all, there would be 886,939 British military deaths, and another 1.7 million were wounded.

It is astonishing that so little of this made it on to the floor of the House of Commons. Yes, there were occasional backbench forays. The May conscription crisis had happened against the background of the failed Aubers Ridge exploit, in which a peer and his half-brother had died, so it was argued, for lack of shells. The Unionist War Committee and its Liberal counterpart demanded a more effective war effort, and some MPs took pot shots at the Government. The left-leaning Liberal MP for Sowerby, John Higham, vituperatively attacked the War Office's many failures in 1915 with a demand that 'it is necessary to take two or three of the principal offenders and hang them in front of that great building in Whitehall, and leave them hanging there as an example and a warning to all who serve in that Department'.[21] And when the government yet again attempted hastening home rule for Ireland, so many Tory diehards seemed intent on finding a ditch to die in that the Unionist whips worried that just 60 per cent of their MPs would continue to support Bonar Law, and Lord Willoughby de Broke angrily told a colleague in the Lords that 'we ought to smash the Coalition', which he thought 'an entrenchment for every pernicious & "democratic" fallacy'.[22]

Thus far this was a minority view, mostly restricted to private correspondence, as few wanted to play Delilah and tempt Asquith or Bonar Law to bring the whole coalition edifice crashing down. But then came the 'Nigeria' debate on 8 November 1916, which pitted a significant number of Unionists who were in favour of selling the German oil-palm businesses captured in West Africa exclusively to British interests, against their own leader, Bonar Law, who, after being rowdily accused of talking nonsense by Carson, pleaded with his Unionist colleagues that he was 'sorry, very sorry to be so at variance' with them.[23] In all, 117 MPs voted for the protectionist motion that night. This gave a perfect opportunity to Lloyd George, who had taken over the War Office after Kitchener's death when his ship, HMS *Hampshire*, sank in June en route for Russia. Bonar Law clearly needed to calm his backbench critics, but was too weak to assume the premiership himself; so the two men drew up a plan for reinvigorating the seriously inadequate war effort by creating a small group within the Cabinet charged with the conduct of the war, this group to be led by Lloyd George. Whether the intention was to oust Asquith, who was mourning the death in combat of his son Raymond on 15 September, we will never know, but the plan was presented to Asquith merely as a memorandum on how better to seize the initiative in the war, and at first he accepted it, before making the proviso that the group report daily to him. When, however, *The Times* reported that Lloyd George would effectively be taking over the government, Asquith angrily rejected the proposal, prompting Lloyd George's resignation.

Asquith knew that it was one thing to lose a figure like Morley at the start of the war, quite another to lose such a key figure as Lloyd George at this crucial stage, especially when Lloyd George could count on the support of the Conservative leader: his departure would do irreparable damage to public confidence in Asquith's government. Effectively, the Prime Minister had lost an unannounced vote of no confidence – and on 5 December 1916 he resigned, hoping that everyone would come to their senses and reinstate him. The following day he compounded his bluff-calling by declaring that he would not serve under Bonar Law, who urged the king to ask Lloyd George to form a government. On 7 December, as Asquith took the core of the Liberal party off to the opposition benches, Lloyd George became Prime Minister, at the head of a new, smaller coalition War Cabinet, with Bonar Law as Chancellor of the Exchequer and Leader of the Commons and Labour's Arthur Henderson as minister without portfolio. Significant posts were again found for all Bonar Law's potential challengers for the Unionist leadership, and although the new balance in the wider Cabinet was overwhelmingly Unionist (thirteen out of twenty-three, including a Cecil, a Stanley and a Derby), enough of the Liberals were bought off for Lloyd George to fear little from those loyal to Asquith, who, understandably exhausted and demoralized, took to his bed.

This whole palace coup happened entirely without recourse to parliament. On 12 December both Lloyd George and Asquith were ill in bed, and although the new government was announced on the fourteenth, parliament was prorogued in January – and even when it reassembled on 7 February, it was Bonar Law who led the debate on the king's speech for the government. Lloyd George did not address the House until 23 February, a full seventy-nine days into his premiership. Indeed, for much of the rest of the war Lloyd George was able to ignore parliament. When military and naval fortunes were at their worst, in early 1917, the only pressure, for a secret session, came from Churchill; and when the subsequent debate, held on 10 May, was over Lloyd George and Churchill congratulated each other behind the Speaker's chair. There was a brief skirmish with Conservative backbenchers over the 1917 Corn Production Act's provisions for a minimum wage, and when the government came forward with a Representation of the

People Bill that would give all men over twenty-one and women over thirty the vote, restrict plural voting, redistribute seats and introduce a single voting day, there was the usual lengthy partisan brouhaha, but second reading was carried in the Commons by 329 to 40 on 23 May 1917 and third reading was carried on 7 December. In the shuttling between houses, both the Commons vote (by a majority of one) in favour of the alternative vote and the Lords' preference for proportional representation were overturned, and the Act made it on to the statute book without either brand of electoral reform.

There were other occasions when the government was dragged into the parliamentary weeds. The publication of the Mesopotamia Commission's Report, or more importantly the minority report by one of the Commission's members, Josiah Wedgwood, with his fierce attack on the Viceroy of India as 'a calamity for England', led to Austen Chamberlain's resignation as India Secretary in July 1917 and, thanks to the ensuing mini-shuffle, the political resurrection (as Minister of Munitions) of Churchill, who had spent four months after resigning from the government in 1915 commanding the 6th Battalion of the Royal Scots Fusiliers on the Western Front.

Some MPs complained at the government's insouciance. In April 1917 Sir Charles Henry told the Commons that 'for some time it has become apparent that the control of Parliament is being undermined, that the Executive and the permanent officials have assumed the power which, if not checked, threatens to become a menace to our Parliamentary life ... Members of Parliament are no longer able to exercise the function which the electorate rely upon them to do.'[24] Others agreed. Asquith's chief whip Godfrey Collins tabled a motion in July 1917 calling for a special Commons committee to examine government expenditure and complained that 'the increasing use of the Press by the Government [had] reduced the power of this House',[25] and in the same debate Tudor Walters vented his frustration that: 'When the House of Commons raises any particular question on which it feels strongly, and asks that something definite should be done, somebody immediately representing the Government gets up and offers something which is entirely different.'[26] Bonar Law conceded that as long as the Commons was not seeking to determine policy he was content to allow a body to consider expenditure *after* it had been spent, so a new committee was set up, with six sub-committees, chaired by the former Cabinet minister, Herbert Samuel, but its effect on the executive was minimal.*

Asquith had wisely taken a self-imposed oath of silence on departing office, so when in February 1918 Lloyd George dismissed the Chief of the Imperial General Staff, Field Marshal Sir William Robertson, Asquith counselled colleagues against a parliamentary division as it would 'give the Gov. an easy victory if not a triumph'.[27] It was not until May 1918 that parliamentary debate so much as scratched the paintwork of the government, as neither its Tory nor its Asquithian opponents thought they would win the inevitable election that would follow the ousting of the Prime Minister. When the challenge came, on 9 May 1918, it was in the shape of a motion calling for a select committee to enquire into allegations made by Major-General Sir Frederick Maurice (following his removal as Director of Military Operations) that both Lloyd George and Bonar Law had lied to parliament about troop numbers on the Western Front. It was Asquith's motion, but he proved unequal to the task of slaying two leaders with one sword. His speech was meticulous, pedantic and cautious, lacking the brio that others, especially Lloyd George, could bring to a big occasion. He even failed to make the central charge, betraying his hesitation and getting riled by impatient government supporters. Lloyd George, by contrast, delivered his response with panache, attacking Maurice, demolishing his supposed evidence and ending with a powerful, if shameless plea:

* It was under Lloyd George's wartime administration that the outline of the modern Cabinet system, with a committee structure served by a Cabinet Office of civil servants, took shape, although the Cabinet itself was not recognized in statute until 1937, and the maximum number of Cabinet ministers (21, excluding the Lord Chancellor) was not laid down until the Ministerial and Other Salaries Act 1975.

These controversies are distracting, they are paralysing, they are rending, and I beg that they should come to an end. It is difficult enough for Ministers to do their work in this War . . . I really beg and implore, for our common country, the fate of which is in the balance now and in the next few weeks, that there should be an end of this sniping.[28]

Lloyd George had the numbers – just 106 voted with Asquith against 293 – but he must have been pained to see former Cabinet colleagues vote against him. It was a clear sign of a disconsolate and split Liberal party; but it also proved that the Unionists could still do more damage than the Asquith rump.

There were disagreements within the coalition. The one-time iron moulder Arthur Henderson, always more a manager than a tub-thumping leader, had acted as the chief contact between the government and organized labour, but when he returned from a visit to Russia in August 1917, his Cabinet colleagues kept him waiting outside the room while they discussed his suggestion that the Labour party participate in an international socialist conference in Stockholm. They decided against, which was bad enough, but the manifest rudeness infuriated him into resignation, whereupon his place was taken by the former general secretary of the Amalgamated Society of Engineers, the mild-mannered Scottish MP George Barnes, while Henderson dedicated his time to party organization and preparations for a general election.

As for the war, at the start of 1918 victory was far from certain. The Bolshevik November Revolution had led to Russia's opening peace negotiations with Germany in December; when these were concluded in the treaty of Brest-Litovsk in March 1918, Germany was able to transfer its efforts hurriedly and successfully from the Eastern to the Western Front. Five major assaults were launched on the Allies. Germany had swift victories and got within thirty-seven miles of Paris, and there was a fear that even though the United States had joined the war, American resources would not come into play soon enough. But when the Allies decisively won the battle of Amiens in August and pushed forward in what was termed the Great Offensive, the Germans crumbled. At the start of October 1918 they sent a message to the American President Woodrow Wilson, seeking an armistice; on 3 November the German navy mutinied at Kiel, just as Austria-Hungary concluded its own armistice; and starting on 7 November an armistice with Germany was hammered out in the forest of Compiègne in the private railway carriage of the Supreme Commander of the Allied armies, France's Marshal Ferdinand Foch. On the ninth Kaiser Wilhelm abdicated, and at 5 a.m. on 11 November Germany capitulated. That afternoon Lloyd George announced the terms of the armistice in the House of Commons, there was a very short debate, and at 3.17 the whole House of Commons trooped off to St Margaret's Westminster for a service of thanksgiving. The war was over.

Lloyd George had a sentimental streak, but he took no time in capitalizing politically on the moment. Within twenty-four hours he had called the general election that was now more than three years overdue and would be fought under the provisions of the new Representation of the People Act with an increased electorate of 21.7 million. There was one problem, though. He was, to all intents, partyless. For some time he had considered forming a new party in his own likeness, 'national' in tone, committed to the state's protection of the common man, but since these vaguely mooted ideas had come to nothing the only option open to him, if he wanted to remain Prime Minister, was to lead an electoral pact for a peacetime 'National' government. Despite the fact that the Conservatives could reliably expect to make significant gains in the Commons, Bonar Law was equally attracted to such a pact as it brought with it the 'man who won the war'. So, on 20 November, the two leaders wrote letters of endorsement to coalition Liberal and Conservative candidates. Asquith, who had a vague hope of returning the free-standing Liberals at full strength, sarcastically branded the letters as 'coupons', but when the results came in it was clear that the trick had worked. Although Lloyd

George's own coalition Liberals retained just 127 seats, and Bonar Law had 332 (and could rely on 47 Conservatives who refused a coalition 'coupon'), Asquith's Liberals were a paltry band of 37, and both Asquith and MacDonald lost their seats.

Moreover, the vicious suppression of the Easter Rising in Ireland had wrought its own political devastation as Irish voters switched their allegiance to Éamon de Valera's Sinn Féin, which went from no seats in 1910 to 73 in 1918, all but obliterating Redmond's old party. Twenty-seven of de Valera's MPs then gathered in Dublin in January 1919, calling themselves the Dáil Éireann (without de Valera himself, until he escaped from prison in England). After a hard-fought war of independence, the declaration of an Irish Republic and the setting up of a separate Northern Ireland parliament, a deal was eventually reached with Lloyd George in 1921 that brought the Irish Free State into existence on 6 December 1922. Initially this incorporated the whole of Ireland, but the treaty allowed the six counties of Northern Ireland to secede from the other twenty-six, which they did two days later. The bicameral Northern Ireland parliament continued to sit until it was dissolved in March 1972 and direct rule was instituted. The Irish Free State, governed by a bicameral parliament of Dáil and Seanad, but still under the formal rule of the 'king in Ireland' and his representative the Governor-General, continued in existence until 1937, when de Valera drafted a new constitution, which was narrowly carried in a referendum, thereby creating the new independent state of Eire.

Labour, led in 1918 by William Adamson, also gained significantly in the share of the vote; the party now had 57 seats and could rely on a handful more left-wing and working-class MPs. In total the Commons had 707 seats, so the combined Conservatives could have just managed a majority without Lloyd George, and since the Sinn Féin members immediately removed themselves from parliament, Conservatives could easily have seized matters into their own hands. But history allows moments of grace, and the whole point of the Conservative and Unionist party since home rule and the Boer War had been its undying fatalistic patriotism. Country above party, total war by all and any means, and the bond of Union were its essence. Salisbury and Curzon might think Lloyd George 'a dirty little rogue',[29] the mayor of Birmingham, Neville Chamberlain, might opine that '*all* Unionists [did] not regard with pleasure the notion of permanently enrolling under [his] standard',[30] and Walter Long might fret that Lloyd George was 'really determined to split our Party as his own is split',[31] but Bonar Law knew that removing the Prime Minister would have looked like gross and ungentlemanly ingratitude. The Conservatives would maintain their long-term independence, but Lloyd George was to be kept on, under sufferance, at least until he betrayed his feet of clay.

Parliament was irrelevant to the First World War, but the same could not be said of the Second, which began to steal upon the Commons the moment Neville Chamberlain entered Downing Street in 1937 on the back of Stanley Baldwin's unforced retirement, inheriting the Conservative-led National government with 430 seats, a majority of 245, Labour as the official opposition (led by Clement Attlee) and the Liberals split three ways between the Liberal Nationals led by Sir John Simon, the Liberals led by Sir Herbert Samuel and the Lloyd George extended family enclave. In keeping with the liveliness he had exhibited as Health Minister and Chancellor of the Exchequer, Chamberlain approached the new job with a sense of verve that had been completely lacking from the avuncular Baldwin. Workers were guaranteed two weeks' paid holiday, slums were cleared, the school leaving age was increased – all policies that Neville's father Joe might have approved.

As for foreign policy, though, the whole point of the government was the prevention of war with Germany. Active British disarmament – the policy ever since Churchill had been Secretary for War between 1919 and 1921 – was tentatively abandoned in favour of appeasement couched as pragmatic diplomacy, with new ships, tanks and planes very much a last resort. Under Baldwin, Mussolini had been allowed to invade Abyssinia in 1935 with impunity, and when Hitler's

Wehrmacht marched into Austria on 12 March 1938, Chamberlain told the Commons two days later that 'nothing could have arrested this action by Germany unless we and others with us had been prepared to use force to prevent it',[32] a course of action he was clearly not prepared to contemplate. Churchill, by now sixty-three and a much-derided self-appointed prophet on the Conservative back benches, warned that Europe was facing a 'programme of aggression, nicely calculated and timed, unfolding stage by stage',[33] but he was ignored. When Hitler demanded in the early autumn that the Sudetenland in Czechoslovakia be ceded to Germany as it had a majority German population, Chamberlain met with the Führer at Berchtesgaden on 15 September and two weeks later in Munich signed an agreement (others called it the 'Munich diktat' or 'Betrayal') with Hitler, Mussolini and the French Prime Minister, Édouard Daladier, acceding to his demand. The following day Chamberlain proffered Hitler a miserable peace treaty between the UK and Germany, which the Führer signed. On returning, exhausted, to London, Chamberlain deliriously waved the flimsy piece of paper for the cameras as evidence of 'peace for our time.'* And the public cheered.

Chamberlain doubtless expected a grateful parliament to applaud him to its neo-Gothic rafters – but the standing ovation he received from the Conservative benches was not unanimous. When Anthony Eden had resigned as Foreign Secretary in February over appeasement of Mussolini, 168 MPs had voted in his support, including the now 75-year-old Lloyd George, and before Chamberlain could speak on 3 October 1938 he had to listen to a long personal statement from Alfred Duff Cooper, who had just resigned as First Lord of the Admiralty, decrying the 'rape of Austria' and condemning the Munich Agreement as peace with dishonour. Cooper, Eden, Churchill and the

---

* Chamberlain's words were 'peace for our time', perhaps a reference to Disraeli's words on returning from the Congress of Berlin, although Disraeli said, possibly quoting the Book of Common Prayer, that he had returned with 'peace in our time', a phrase often inaccurately attributed to Chamberlain. *Peace in our Time* was also the title of a Noel Coward play set in the war.

National Labour MP Harold Nicolson pointedly refused to stand for Chamberlain and the atmosphere was unsettled. Both Attlee, speaking for the Labour party, and Sir Archibald Sinclair for the Liberals were far from convinced by Chamberlain's statement, and Hugh Dalton ended his speech by quoting R. H. Tawney: 'The ambition to be eaten last, which inspires our present policy, is intelligible but futile. We shall (if we remain edible) be eaten all the same, nor shall we be consulted as to the date of the ceremony.'[34] Labour was edging towards an acceptance that the defeat of Fascism was more important than pacifism, and in any case nurtured a profound enmity towards Chamberlain, who had preached the free market at them as Chancellor of the Exchequer in the arch-traitor MacDonald's government while Attlee advocated a national health service and secondary education for all.

Chamberlain's reception in the country was as unsettled as that in the Commons. Quintin Hogg narrowly won the Oxford by-election on 27 October for the Conservatives over an Independent Progressive anti-appeasement candidate, Sandy Lindsay, the Master of Balliol, who had Liberal and Labour support; but then the Bridgwater by-election on 17 November 1938 went the other way, with the Progressive candidate, the broadcaster Vernon Bartlett, defeating the Conservative Patrick Heathcoat-Amory; and on 21 December Katharine Stewart-Murray, the duchess of Atholl, was defeated when she resigned her seat expressly in order to stand again in opposition to the Munich deal. When it came to the North Cornwall by-election on 22 July 1939, Labour withdrew in favour of the Liberal, Tom Horabin, who comfortably defeated the Tory on a clear anti-appeasement platform; on the twenty-seventh Glenvil Hall doubled the Labour majority in Colne Valley, and on 1 August William Jackson seized the Brecon and Radnor seat from the National government for Labour with a majority of 1,636.

The long-anticipated crunch came in the summer of 1939 as Britain and France desperately tried to form an alliance with the Soviet Union and the threat of a German invasion of Poland loomed large. Remarkably, on 2 August Chamberlain moved that parliament adjourn until 2 October. He convincingly lost the argument as Sinclair pointed to the clear evidence that Germany was building up an invasion force on the Polish border and Arthur Greenwood demanded: 'Are the Poles to be let down in the next two months? Is Danzig to be sacrificed? Is the pass to be sold in the Far East? Are any betrayals of this kind to take place during the Recess without public discussion?'[35] A young Tory, Ronald Cartland, caustically accused Chamberlain of having 'ideas of dictatorship' and cited a constituent who thought him a 'friend of Hitler'.[36] Harold Macmillan, Duncan Sandys and Churchill weighed in too, urging Chamberlain to think again and 'make himself the true leader of the nation as a whole'.[37]

Chamberlain may have lost the argument, but he won the vote, by almost two to one – only to have to summon the Commons back on the twenty-fourth, after Germany announced an unexpected non-aggression treaty with Russia, to hear a new statement and pass emergency powers legislation. This time both Greenwood and Sinclair backed the government's slightly tougher line. A week later, on 1 September 1939, Germany invaded Poland, and that day in the Commons Chamberlain moved the necessary financial package preliminary to war. Even now his words were hesitant and reluctant. He started with an apology, 'I do not propose to say many words tonight,' and ended on a downbeat conditional: 'If out of the struggle we again re-establish in the world the rules of good faith and the renunciation of force, why then, even the sacrifices that will be entailed upon us will find their fullest justification.'[38] In other words, even now Chamberlain was not quite prepared to go to war. The sullen, anxious House was not impressed. Appeasers saw their plan in tatters. Those who had argued against appeasement demanded greater clarity. So, just when Chamberlain might have expected unambiguous support, his apparent ruefulness was met by the stony faces of the supremely unimpressed. As Labour's deputy leader Arthur Greenwood stood up to reply for the opposition, the exasperated one-time journalist Leo Amery shouted out: 'Speak for England!' Greenwood tried his best. 'The die is cast,' he said; the act of aggression had already taken place, so Labour 'shall, at whatever cost, in the interests of the liberty of the world in the future, use all our resources to defend ourselves and others against aggression'.[39] Still the Prime Minister prevaricated. The next day Chamberlain returned to tell the House that if Germany were to withdraw from Poland, Britain 'would be willing to regard the position as being the same as it was before';[40] and it was not until 3 September that he broadcast the news that he had issued an ultimatum to Germany that it should undertake to leave Poland, but that no 'such undertaking has been received, and that consequently this country is at war with Germany'. His words to the House yet again betrayed his complete sense of (self-obsessed) failure:

> This is a sad day for all of us, and to none is it sadder than to me. Everything that I have worked for, everything that I have hoped for, everything that I have believed in during my public life, has crashed into ruins. There is only one thing left for me to do; that is, to devote what strength and powers I have to forwarding the victory of the cause for which we have to sacrifice so much. I cannot tell what part I may be allowed to play myself; I trust I may live to see the day when Hitlerism has been destroyed and a liberated Europe has been re-established.[41]

Notwithstanding this tone of defeat, Chamberlain's natural tenacity resurfaced in his next decision, to reshape the government by bringing some of his key detractors into a new nine-strong Cabinet. While two-thirds of the incumbent ministers stayed in place, Churchill was given the Admiralty – despite the Conservative leadership's loathing of him – and Eden returned as Dominions Secretary; Labour was offered a seat at the table, but turned it down. It was enough. Chamberlain found himself more popular than ever during the early stages of the 'phoney war', and although Greenwood told him that 'neither you nor I nor anyone else will be able to hold the House of Commons',[42] Chamberlain was easily able to survive the dismissal of Leslie Hore-Belisha as War Secretary in January 1940, an April mini-shuffle and the rejection of the Labour MP Herbert Morrison's calls for a Minister for Economic Coordination. Indeed, those who despaired at Chamberlain's lack of pugnacious zeal for the war were dismayed by his domination of the Commons. As Churchill's ally Brendan Bracken put it: 'The House of Commons was no good, the Tory Party were yes-men of Chamberlain. 170 had their election expenses paid by Tory Central Office and 100 hoped for jobs.'[43]

Chamberlain's fortunes, though, lay not in his own hands but in Hitler's. A sense of disquiet had been gently simmering in the All-Party Parliamentary Action Group set up by the Liberal MP Clement Davies and in the marquess of Salisbury's 'Watching Committee', both aimed at instilling a sense of urgency into the prosecution of the war. Churchill had been spotted in the Commons smoking room with the Liberal leader Sinclair and with Labour's A. V. Alexander. When Britain signally failed to prevent Hitler's invasion of Norway, that disquiet spilled over. There were all kinds of dark rumours. Harold Nicolson thought it would mean the return of Lloyd George and wrote in his diary on 30 April that 'the whips are putting it about that it is all the fault of Winston who has made another forlorn failure'.[44] Two days later came worse news: the British had been ignominiously forced into evacuating from Norway. Playing for time, Chamberlain delayed a Commons debate on the Norway campaign until the following week, but by then the Watching Committee were arguing for a new coalition including Labour, who had already declared that they would never serve under Chamberlain.

Once again a Commons debate changed the course of the war. Chamberlain's first mistake was to make it a two-day debate, which meant that the opposition could judge the mood of the House on the first day before deciding how to play its hand on the second. It also meant that the natural deference a Prime Minister enjoyed when he spoke on the first afternoon could all too easily be forgotten by the second evening. True, Churchill would be summing up for Chamberlain's government at the end of the two days, but the danger was that he would outshine his master. In fact, the battle had probably been lost by then. When Chamberlain rose to his feet at 3.48 p.m. on 7 May there were such constant interruptions that the Speaker repeatedly had to shut Labour colleagues up, but even when the Prime Minister was listened to in silence there was confusion over a new role that he had given Churchill. Then Attlee meticulously laid out the charge sheet, recalling Chamberlain's failed judgement over Czechoslovakia and Poland, and citing an article in *The Times* that called the government's ministers 'failures or men who need a rest'. Although Labour did not decide until the following morning to push to a vote, nobody could have missed his caustic point: 'In a life-and-death struggle we cannot afford to have our destinies in the hands of failures or men who need a rest.'[45] As the day rambled fractiously on, it was clear that even attempts to help Chamberlain were failing miserably. When Brigadier-General Sir Henry Croft urged the House to 'sink our animosities and encourage the Government, instead of indulging in carping criticism day by day', he almost certainly swayed minds in exactly the opposite direction with his injunction: 'If you are convinced that you can find a better man then put him there.'[46] It was little wonder that the next speaker, (Colonel) Josiah Wedgwood, accused Croft of 'facile optimism'. Just after seven o'clock Sir Roger Keyes hove into view, kitted out in the full uniform of Admiral of the Fleet, and delivered a broadside on the ineptitude of the naval command; and then Leo Amery gave a speech of unexpected and uncomfortable ferocity which punctured Chamberlain's authority by its sheer asperity. Amery later wrote of the occasion: 'I found myself going on to an increasing crescendo of applause.* So evident was the whole feeling on our side, as well as on the opposition, ready for a change that I cast prudence to the winds and ended full out with my Cromwellian injunction to the Government to go in God's name.'[47] His peroration hurt, calling Chamberlain's men 'old, decayed serving

---

* Clapping is expressly forbidden in the rules of the House, although Michael Martin was applauded as he was dragged to the Speaker's chair in 2000 and both Betty Boothroyd and Tony Blair were applauded on their last appearances. Amery's 'applause' was a running chorus of 'hear, hear'.

men', and ending on a rising cadence: 'This is what Cromwell said to the Long Parliament when he thought it was no longer fit to conduct the affairs of the nation: "You have sat too long here for any good you have been doing. Depart, I say, and let us have done with you. In the name of God, go."'[48] From then on it was clear there would be a vote and that, although it was technically on the question 'that this House do now adjourn', it was a vote of confidence.

The next day's proceedings started with the former errand boy, conscientious objector and leader of the London County Council Herbert Morrison, who deliberately riled Chamberlain, accusing him of lacking in self-confidence and demanding that Britain 'be led by Ministers who will command the respect of the population and whose lead the population will be happy and proud to follow'.[49] It worked. Chamberlain was not meant to speak again, but Dalton reckoned he jumped up, 'showing his teeth like a rat in a corner', to say:

> I do not seek to evade criticism, but I say this to my friends in the House – and I have friends in the House. No Government can prosecute a war efficiently unless it has public and Parliamentary support. I accept the challenge. I welcome it indeed. At least we shall see who is with us and who is against us, and I call on my friends to support us in the Lobby to-night.[50]

It was impromptu; and it was forlorn. So, as Sir Stafford Cripps ridiculed the government's response as a demand 'that the Mad Hatter's tea party should have another session',[51] and Duff Cooper charged that if his colleagues should be beguiled by Chamberlain they would be 'unworthy to represent their fellow countrymen',[52] the All-Party Group met and one hundred MPs determined to vote against the government. Lloyd George added his two-penn'orth as well, cleverly undermining Churchill's speech by urging him not to act as an air-raid shelter for Chamberlain. The final two contributions, from co-conspirators A. V. Alexander and Churchill himself, sealed Chamberlain's fate. Alexander derided the Prime Minister's appeal as one to put 'personal friendship and personalities before the question of really winning the war',[53] and Churchill delivered a peroration that gave ostensible support to Chamberlain while hinting at what might be with another man at the helm: 'Let pre-war feuds die; let personal quarrels be forgotten, and let us keep our hatreds for the common enemy. Let party interest be ignored, let all our energies be harnessed, let the whole ability and forces of the nation be hurled into the struggle, and let all the strong horses be pulling on the collar.'[54] Chamberlain won by 281 to 200, but his opponents knew instantly that in falling so far short of the usual 200 majority the result was not good enough to stabilize the government. Wedgwood and Macmillan were shouted down as they started to sing 'Rule Britannia', while the PPS Chips Channon noted that 'Neville appeared bowled over by the ominous figures, and was the first to rise'.[55] Chamberlain's wife looked on, disconsolate, from the gallery.

Thirty-three Conservative MPs had voted against their 'friend', along with sixteen officers in military or naval uniform; a further sixty Tories abstained. When Chamberlain reached out to the rebels at ten o'clock the next morning and even offered Labour a formal coalition just as they prepared to go to Bournemouth for their party conference, he was met with a flat refusal from Labour and a demand that Sir John Simon and Sir Samuel Hoare be sacked. That afternoon he met with the Foreign Secretary, Halifax, Churchill and the chief whip, David Margesson. There are many contradictory accounts of this meeting; even Churchill contradicted himself as he told and retold the story with the sharp edges of his ambition smoothed out. But some things are clear. All three thought that an all-party coalition was vital and knew that Labour would not serve under Chamberlain, who was prepared to serve under either Churchill or Halifax (but had a private preference for Halifax). It also seems that Halifax, whether out of gentlemanly self-deprecation, or out of respect for the constitution or for Churchill, or just because he was fed up with his irritable bowel, ruled himself out of the premiership on the grounds that he was a peer. There was not a little irony in this, as Halifax had opposed an earlier Bill to allow a peer to disclaim his peerage, but it cannot have been the whole story as advice had already been given that a noble Prime Minister and an emergency Disclaiming Bill were constitution-ally possible. Either way, the end result was the same: with Halifax ruled out, should a final appeal by Chamberlain be rejected, it had to be Churchill. The next day Attlee and Greenwood consulted their colleagues in Bournemouth and phoned in their answer. An hour later Chamberlain resigned as Prime Minister and Churchill was summoned to form a new National government, just as the Germans invaded the Netherlands and Belgium.

The aura of heroism that eventually attended Churchill was notably absent in the early days of the new government. The Tory MP Rab Butler's view was not uncommon, namely that 'the good clean tradition of English politics' had been sold to a 'half-breed American', the 'greatest adventurer of modern political history';[56] even Churchill's new assistant private secretary, Jock Colville, thought it 'a terrible risk'.[57] Conservatives were still angry. So when Chamberlain, who remained leader of the Conservatives and might have become Leader of the House, had Attlee not vetoed it, arrived in the Commons as Lord President of the Council on 13 May, 'MPs lost their heads; they shouted; they waved their Order Papers, and his reception was a regular ovation'.[58] By contrast, Churchill was heard in sullen silence when he told the House what he had told his new ministers: 'I have nothing to offer but blood, toil, tears and sweat.'[59] The sultry antagonism did not end there. Labour might still fume that Chamberlain and the other 'guilty men' had any post at all, but snobbery, anger and partisan envy all ensured a fractious parliamentary reception for Churchill, even as the British Expeditionary Force was evacuated at Dunkirk and when the threat of invasion was at its height. His speech on 4 June reduced some Labour members to tears: 'We shall fight on the beaches, we shall fight on the landing grounds, we shall fight in the fields and in the streets, we shall fight in the hills. We shall never surrender.'[60] But Conservatives remained unmoved, both then and when he declared two weeks later that the 'Battle of France' was over and the 'Battle of

Britain' would now begin. Then Churchill ended with the first of his great war-by-rhetoric flourishes:

> If we fail then the whole world, including the United States, and all that we have known and cared for, will sink into the abyss of a new dark age made more sinister, and perhaps more prolonged, by the lights of a perverted science. Let us therefore brace ourselves to our duty and so bear ourselves that if the British Commonwealth and Empire lasts for a thousand years men will still say, 'This was their finest hour.'[61]

His words soared, but still it was just Labour, the Liberals and his few Tory allies who cheered him, while Butler thought: 'All we have to do is pull the string of the toy dog of the 1922 Committee and make it bark. After a few staccato utterances it becomes clear that the Government depends upon the Tory squires for its majority.'[62] Many in the party thought the situation dangerous enough to warn that Labour colleagues should not try to push Chamberlain out lest he become a centre of disaffection, to which Dalton's answer was: 'Leave him where he is, as a decaying hostage.'[63] The bigger issue of how to get Tories to love Winston was partially resolved when Chamberlain and the Conservative whips stage-managed a mass waving of order papers for him on 4 July and Channon noted: 'Winston suddenly wept.'[64] The spell was broken, and each successive Commons appearance thereafter brought greater garlands. On 23 July Channon thought him 'at the very top of his form and the House is completely with him',[65] and a week later Dalton reckoned that Churchill led the House 'unquestioned and ascendant'.[66] The Chamberlain issue also soon resolved itself, as the former premier left work in July for an operation for bowel cancer and only briefly returned to work in September. He thought the chance 'of further political activity, and even a possibility of another premiership after the war, [had] gone',[67] and he was right. He resigned on 22 September and on 9 November, at home, he died. Churchill could now become Conservative leader, and finally it felt as if, 'after eight months of vaguely wondering what the war was about, the people suddenly knew what they had got to do . . . It was like the awakening of a giant.'[68]

With all three main parties in the government there was a danger that parliament would again become an irrelevance. Indeed, Churchill used the power of patronage deliberately to ensure he had as free a hand as possible. Every persuadable shade of opinion was included. Half of Chamberlain's old Cabinet stayed. Halifax remained Foreign Secretary with another Chamberlainite, Rab Butler, as his under-secretary, but elsewhere each department had a mixed party leadership. Labour took rich pickings with Attlee as Lord Privy Seal, Greenwood as minister without portfolio and, from outside parliament, Ernest Bevin, the bullish General Secretary of the Transport and General Workers' Union, who was found a seat and co-opted as Minister of Labour.

The same skilful and extensive use of patronage was evident outside the Cabinet. In February 1941 Churchill created an additional twenty-two ministers and gave them all parliamentary private secretaries, who although unpaid were expected to vote with the government and remain silent. He even extended his power of patronage by passing the Disqualification of Members (Temporary Provisions) Act 1941, which suspended the stipulation in the Act of Settlement that still disqualified anyone appointed to a non-ministerial office of profit under the crown from remaining an MP. Even though it seems this was in practice occasionally circumvented – in August 1939 Jack Lawson, a Labour member, had been made Deputy Regional Commissioner for the North Eastern Region on the understanding that he would not have to resign – under the new Act Churchill was allowed up to twenty-five such appointments every year. He used this new power to make Malcolm MacDonald High Commissioner in Canada, a Liberal National MP, Major J. S. Dodd, tank production adviser to the Ministry of Supply, and the Conservative MP Sir Isidore Salmon (appropriately enough) catering adviser to the War Office; it also enabled him to send the two difficult knights, Sir Stafford Cripps and Sir Samuel Hoare, as ambassadors to Russia and Spain respectively. All these men had two salaries. The Tory MP for Evesham, Sir Rupert de la Bere, complained that such power corrupts, but for Churchill it was merely what total war demanded.

All this activity left but a small band of MPs who either, like Sydney Silverman, Rhys Davies and Jimmy Maxton's pacifist Independent Labour Party group, opposed the 'imperialist war' or, like Aneurin Bevan, thought that ministers expected MPs to 'listen, like the Reichstag, to a long speech by the Prime Minister and say "Amen", and then go home'.[69] For them, holding the government to account through parliament was an act of patriotism. It was a lonely furrow. Others taunted them. Patrick Donner, the right-wing MP for Basingstoke who briefly flirted with Oswald Mosley's Fascist party and enlisted in the RAF, wrote in his mean-spirited autobiography that 'leading Socialists, such as the late Aneurin Bevan, though of fighting age, so managed things that they never fought in either war. To be a "squalid nuisance" was, for Bevan, apparently enough.'[70]

For many MPs and peers, parliamentary scrutiny was not enough. By January 1940 eighty-five National government MPs had joined the forces, and in total 162 MPs joined the services at some point in the war. The overwhelming preponderance of them, 136, were Conservatives, a fact that several Tories ascribed to either cowardice or inadequate patriotism on behalf of the other parties, although fourteen Labour MPs, six National government members and two each from the Liberal, Commonwealth and Independent parties signed up. To be fair, the median age of a Labour MP at the last election in 1935 was fifty-four, five years older than for the Tories, and 53 per cent of Tory MPs had then been under fifty as opposed to just 29 per cent of Labour MPs, but the figures are so stark that it is difficult not to conclude that the same difference in attitudes to 'total war' as had surfaced in the First World War over conscription affected the relative numbers enlisting. Not that all military service was very military. Many served at home in Britain, and when the 39-year-old David Maxwell Fyfe, later a prosecutor at Nuremberg and a Conservative Home

Secretary and Lord Chancellor, enlisted in the Territorial Army he served exclusively in the Judge Advocate General's Department.

Not every MP was a hero. When the Tory MP Alec Cunningham-Reid returned from a Blitz-time trip with his mother and children to Canada he came to blows in the Chamber with a colleague, Oliver Locker-Lampson, who accused him of cowardice. Duff Cooper attracted criticism for evacuating his children abroad, and several pointed to the hypocrisy of Crawford Greene inveighing against Labour 'cowards' when he himself had moved out of London to the countryside. Of an altogether different order were the cases of Sir Oswald Mosley and Archibald Ramsay. Mosley had originally been a Conservative MP, and had crossed the floor to Labour before founding the New Party in 1931 and turning to Fascism. From 23 May 1940 until 1943 he and his second wife (and former mistress) Diana, the daughter of the equally right-wing 2nd Lord Redesdale, were interned in Holloway, and they spent the rest of the war under house arrest. The Scotsman Ramsay (imaginatively nicknamed 'Jock') had fought in the First World War and had married the widow of Ninian Crichton-Stuart MP, but having been elected as a Conservative MP in 1931 he developed ever more right-wing views, supporting Franco in the Spanish Civil War and Hitler on Sudeten independence. A member of the far-right Nordic League, in May 1939 he set up the Right Club, whose declared aim was to wrest control of the Conservative party from its reliance on 'Jew money' and whose crest carried the letters 'PJ' for 'Perish Judah'. When war came he drafted a hideous anti-semitic poem to the tune of 'Land of Hope and Glory' in the Commons library, he campaigned for a peace with Hitler, and on 20 March 1940 he used parliamentary privilege to publicize the wave-length of a Nazi-sympathizing radio station. Since Mosley had lost his seat in 1931, Ramsay was to be the only MP interned under Defence Regulation 18B, and he remained in Brixton from 23 May 1940 until 26 September 1944, when he returned to the Commons in time to move the reinstatement of the 1275 Statute of Jewry before he was turfed out by the voters in 1945.

Although many were determined to do their bit, sustained military service was a double-edged sword for an MP. True, when Thomas Galbraith offered to resign his seat if his local party in Glasgow Pollock thought he should, they said his naval duties should come first, and when J. R. Robinson missed the July 1941 AGM of the Blackpool Conservative Association but strode in at the end in his RAF bomber jacket he was given a standing ovation. But increasingly local parties and associations complained at their MPs' absences and at their second military salaries, and when politics got darker in 1941, the whips demanded that several MPs resign their commissions. Twenty did so.

The war also came very directly to parliament on fourteen occasions, three of them particularly serious. On 26 September 1940 a bomb fell in Old Palace Yard, lifting the statue of Richard the Lionheart off its plinth and bending his sword. On 8 December another bomb struck the old cloisters of St Stephen's Chapel, and on Saturday and Sunday 10 and 11 May 1941 incendiary bombs rained down on the Palace, setting fire to the roofs of both the Commons and Westminster Hall. A swift decision was made to save the older building and overnight the Victorian Commons Chamber was burnt to a cinder, while along the corridor the Lords sustained a direct, unexploded hit. It being the weekend, no peers or MPs were present, but the resident superintendent Captain E. H. L. Elliott and three others were killed. Thenceforth, with both chambers out of action, the Commons and Lords sat temporarily two hundred yards away in Church House. Once the Lords had been patched up, the Commons secretly decided to move back to the Palace at the end of June and squatted in their lordships' chamber, while the Lords sat in the much smaller Robing Room; this arrangement was to last until 1950, when a much more workaday Commons Chamber, with furniture gifted by the countries of the Empire, was completed within the shell of the old Chamber under the direction of Sir Giles Gilbert Scott. The only mark of war to remain, at Churchill's request, was to be the arch between the Members' Lobby and the Chamber, which was reconstructed out of the pock-marked stones that had borne the blast of the explosion.

Stanmore Library

Memorial shields for the nineteen MPs who had died in the First World War and the twenty-three killed in the Second were added later.* Many noted that the first MP to die in active service was Major Ronald Cartland, who fell on the retreat to Dunkirk on 30 May 1940, aged thirty-three. His acerbic attack on Chamberlain in the Commons just ten months earlier had included the words: 'We are in a situation that within a month we may be going to fight – and we may be going to die.'[71]

Days before MPs and peers were evicted by incendiaries, the Commons Chamber had seen a querulous two-day debate, on 6 and 7 May 1941, which was couched by the government as a motion of confidence in its war policy. (The precise motion approved the policy of His Majesty's Government in sending help to Greece and declared the House's confidence that the war would be pursued 'with the utmost vigour'.) Prior to the debate Channon had reckoned that 'on all sides, one hears increasing criticism of Churchill. He is undergoing a noticeable slump in popularity and many of his enemies, long silenced by his personal popularity are once more vocal.'[72] Even Lloyd George made a direct attack on both Eden and Churchill. Nevertheless, just five MPs voted or acted as tellers against the government. With 447 'Ayes' the government was more than safe, but with rude attacks like that of Maurice Petherick ('We want a panzer and not a pansy Government'[73]) it was clearly shaken, 'and both Anthony and Winston know it'.[74]

Notwithstanding Churchill's powers of articulation, his ability to hold the Commons largely depended on the success or failure of the war. In June, after the failure of his Operation Battleaxe to lift the siege of Tobruk, Field Marshal Archibald Wavell was sacked; and the next day Hitler attacked Russia. The gloom lifted somewhat with the relief of Tobruk on 27 November and the entry of America into the war after the attack on Pearl Harbor in December, but with two major British ships, the *Prince of Wales* and *Repulse*, sunk by the Japanese off the

* A campaign by the author has led to three additional shields being commissioned for Dr John Esmonde, Tom Kettle and Asquith's former PPS, Charles Lyell, who were inexplicably omitted.

coast of Malaya on 10 December, Churchill left parliament in a sour mood as he visited Roosevelt over Christmas. Ever one to enjoy a bit of intrigue, Channon noted in January 1942 that 'the ineffectual whips are in a frenzy and a first class crisis, no doubt chuckled on by the Germans, is upon us'.[75] Even the chairman of the Conservatives' backbench 1922 Committee, Alexander Erskine Hill, reckoned that there was little point in Churchill just making another wonderful speech; what the government was in desperate need of was a reshuffle. Churchill obliged, offering Sir Stafford Cripps, who had recently returned from Moscow with garlands in his hair (and an Astrakhan hat on his head) as the man who had brought Russia into the alliance, the Ministry of Supply. Such was Cripps's self-confidence and Churchill's insecurity that, while the junior education minister James Chuter Ede reckoned 'parliament is given over to intrigue',[76] Cripps held out for a better offer, and when a new War Cabinet was announced on 19 February, he found himself Lord Privy Seal and Leader of the Commons, number three in the government hierarchy after Attlee, who was made Deputy Prime Minister. For the best part of six months there was talk of Cripps unseating Churchill. His austere abstemiousness (partly the result of a medical condition) was just about as different from Churchill's well-known sybaritic tendencies as one could imagine. He could claim to have been vindicated in his calls during the 1930s for a united front of Russia, France and Britain against Hitler, and his expulsion from the Labour Party on the eve of war gave him an aura of stand-alone rectitude. Meanwhile, Churchill's problems continued. In March the 1922 Committee forced the government to back down on its plans for fuel rationing, on 21 June Tobruk fell to the Germans, and four days later Tom Driberg won the Maldon by-election as a 'critical friend' of Churchill, with the emphasis on the 'critical'.

Against this background another two-day debate on 1 and 2 July 1942 could easily have seen a serious challenge to the government. The motion, tabled by the tall, calm, monocled Scottish MP for Kidderminster, Sir John Wardlaw-Milne, spoke directly to widespread concern by declaring 'no confidence in the central direction of the war'.

Wardlaw-Milne started well enough, with an analysis of the recent military setbacks, and his argument that the Prime Minister had too much to do as both military supremo and director of the home front chimed with some people. But then he digressed, suggesting that the duke of Gloucester should be appointed Commander-in-Chief of the British army. He made clear that this would merely be in a decorative capacity and that he should not have any 'administrative duties',[77] but the rest of his speech was heard in quizzical embarrassment as the duke was generally reckoned to be by far the least impressive member of the royal family. Churchill must have breathed a sigh of relief. The seconder of the motion was Admiral Sir Roger Keyes, who had helped deliver the fatal blow to Chamberlain in the Norway debate in 1940. But he too flunked it. The motion criticized the central direction of the war. If it were carried, the Prime Minister would undoubtedly have to resign. Yet Keyes made it clear that he thought it would be 'a deplorable disaster' if Churchill were to go.[78] After this, although the second day of debate saw Nye Bevan land several palpable hits with his charges that 'the Prime Minister wins debate after debate and loses battle after battle' and that 'he fights debates like a war and the war like a debate',[79] and Lloyd George referred to 'blunders' and incompetence, the vote was never really in doubt. Just twenty-five supported the motion. In Churchill's lobby there were 475. Walter Elliot pointed out that this was the largest number that the Opposition had been able to muster against Pitt in the darkest moments of the Napoleonic Wars.

Despite the strength of the government vote, the summer was full of talk of a successor to Churchill, with Cripps at the top of the list. He had been on manoeuvres, wining and dining MPs (or rather sitting with them while they ate, as he enjoyed a very meagre vegetarian diet), and although he was still party-less, the Labour MP Ivor Thomas reckoned that events would 'bring Cripps to the top'. Yet Cripps's skill as a courtroom and platform speaker availed him little in the Commons, and on 8 September 1942 he blew his chance. A large number of MPs had left the Chamber for lunch and Cripps complained to the House: 'I do not think that we can conduct our proceedings here with the dignity and the weight with which we should conduct them unless Members are prepared to pay greater attention to their duties in this House.'[80] This was innocuous enough, and probably fair, but when Cripps laboured the point several MPs took umbrage. Dalton called the speech a 'priggish sermon' and reckoned that Cripps was 'rapidly losing all that is left of his "mystique"',[81] the 1922 Committee complained to the chief whip, and Chuter Ede reckoned that he had no right to upbraid other MPs on their dining habits when he himself lunched 'on two nuts and half a carrot'. Within weeks Cripps was drafting a resignation letter to Churchill, who, as the political situation was transformed by Montgomery's victory at El Alamein, reshuffled him to the Ministry of Aircraft Production.

Churchill also came under challenge from the Lords, his policy of aerial bombardment of Germany attracting a particularly sharp attack from one of the most articulate members of the upper house, George Bell, the bishop of Chichester. Several bishops had taken a view on the matter early in the war, including Mervyn Haigh of Coventry, who had unambiguously supported the requirements of total war even after the 1,400 casualties in the German bombardment of his city and its destruction of the cathedral. 'If we are not prepared for that,' he argued, 'we should have done better not to have begun resisting Nazi aggression by force.'[82] Arthur Headlam, the bishop of Gloucester, argued that although terror bombing of *civilian* populations was illegal under the Hague Convention, since the government was only directly attacking *military* targets it was in the right. But, he added, 'it would be quite legitimate for us to give notice to Germany, that if they treat any other city in this country as they have treated Coventry we should hold ourselves justified in destroying a German city'.[83] It was a very similar argument to that advanced by the archbishop of Canterbury, Cosmo Gordon Lang, who told Convocation on 27 May 1941: 'It is one thing to bomb military objectives to cripple the industries on which the prosecution of the war depends and, alas! in so doing it may be impossible to avoid inflicting loss and suffering on many civilians. It is a very different thing to adopt the infliction of this loss and suffering as deliberate policy.'[84] The naivety (or wilful blindness) of this position was breathtaking, as the government was already engaged in direct and indiscriminate aerial attacks on the civilian population, a point Bell made to his fellow bishops in Convocation, only to be shouted down by Bishop Cyril Garbett of Winchester. Bell temporarily retired quietly from the field, but the bombardment campaign became more sustained with the appointment in February 1942 of Arthur Harris to Bomber Command. His rationale was brutally simple: 'You destroy a factory and they rebuild it. In six weeks they are in operation again. I kill all their workmen and it takes twenty one years to provide new ones.'[85] It was a policy of ferocious totality, and as the RAF went all-out to destroy Lübeck, Rostock, Cologne, Bremen, Hamburg and Dresden some 593,000 civilians lost their lives, along with 55,573 British airmen. In the new year of 1944 Bell felt he could no longer keep silent and on 9 February he forced a debate in the House of Lords, declaring that Hitler was 'a barbarian' but that 'the policy is obliteration, openly acknowledged. That is not a justifiable act of war.' He continued: 'To justify methods inhumane in themselves by arguments of expediency smacks of the Nazi philosophy that Might is Right.'[86] The debate did not affect the government's policy one iota, as the Colonial Secretary Viscount Cranborne made abundantly clear, but the matter nagged away at Lang's successor in 1942, William Temple, whose death on 26 October 1944 led to a vacancy that should have gone to Bell. An irritated Churchill appointed Geoffrey Fisher instead, and Bell was not even allowed to replace him at London. It is one of the few cases of Churchill's vindictiveness.

It was not just the conduct of the war that exercised parliament in these years. Just before the start of the First World War Josiah Wedgwood, who later joined the Labour party, had told the Commons that 'when it comes, you will see something far more important than a European War – you will see a revolution,'[87] and Churchill told schoolboys at Harrow in December 1940 that 'the advantages and privileges that have hitherto been enjoyed by the few shall be far more widely shared by the many'.[88] Yet the 'equality of sacrifice' so often preached in the First World War still seemed a distant pipe-dream and, as military fortunes in the Second improved, Labour ministers began to argue for the very post-war revolution that had been promised but never delivered. They had helpful allies. William Temple, son of the former archbishop of Canterbury, resigned as a member of the Labour party when he became bishop of Manchester in 1921, but as archbishop first of York and then, from 1942, of Canterbury, he advocated a socially responsible version of Christianity which chimed with Labour values. His Malvern Conference of 200 Anglican clergy and laity in January 1941, which addressed 'the life of the church and the order of society', and his 1942 best-seller *Christianity and the Social Order* laid the ethical foundations for the kind of state-guaranteed social welfare system advocated by William Beveridge (who was briefly a wartime MP) in his ground-breaking report published at the end of the year, promising an end to the five 'Giant Evils' of squalor, ignorance, want, idleness and disease. Temple not only coined the term 'the welfare state', in contradistinction to the Nazi 'security state', but welcomed Beveridge's report, calling it 'the first time anyone had set out to embody the whole spirit of the Christian ethic in an Act of Parliament'.[89] At the same time a new party, Common Wealth, was founded by the playwright and social commentator J. B. Priestley, who made a series of well-received *Postscript* radio broadcasts preaching socialism, and by Sir Richard Acland, the Liberal MP who donated his extensive Devon estates to the National Trust as a sign of the shared ownership principles of Common Wealth. A series of religiously inspired MPs of radical, even revolutionary views were elected in by-elections: first the *Daily Express* columnist Tom Driberg, elected as an Independent at Maldon on 25 June 1942, and then three Common Wealth members: the RAF pilot John Loveseed in Eddisbury in April 1943; Hugh Lawson at Skipton in January 1944; and in April 1945 in Chelmsford Wing Commander Ernest Millington, who fought under the slogan 'this is a fight between Christ and Churchill'.

Parliament's role in pressing for action on these matters was crucial, for Churchill showed little interest in them and purposely dragged his heels. This palpable lack of any sense of urgency infuriated Labour MPs, fifty of whom voted against the government's pension policy in July 1942. Their anger found a clarion voice in Bevan, who lambasted Conservatives in the House on 12 November 1942 for being 'well-meaning and smooth-tongued decoys' and making 'agreeable speeches, in ambiguous terms, about a new world' while really defending the status quo. As he put it: 'The British Army are not fighting for the old world.'[90] As the months passed, the Labour view hardened, and although when the Beveridge Report was debated over three days on 16–18 February 1943 an amendment tabled by Jim Griffiths and Manny Shinwell calling for immediate implementation of the report's findings was lost, by 338 to 121, 97 Labour MPs (including Greenwood) and David and Megan Lloyd George voted for the amendment. By now it was clear that whatever Attlee and Morrison might think about the idea of a post-war National govern-ment akin to that of 1918, the parliamentary Labour party was going to plough its own furrow.

As late as September 1943 Dalton still felt that 'it would be total lunacy to fight an election, if it could be avoided, against the present Prime Minister while the laurels of victory were on his head';[91] but as the war wore on the party political divide grew wider. Butler took through the Education Bill in late 1943 (to the exaggerated indiffer-ence of most Tory MPs), but even he thought that Beveridge was 'a sinister old man, who wishes to give away a great deal of other people's money'.[92] Churchill's vulnerability was confirmed in elegant style by the West Derbyshire by-election of February 1944. The seat had survived as a pocket for the dukes of Devonshire, and when the sitting tenant, the duke's brother-in-law Henry Hunloke, 'retired' (he was actually forced out over an affair with a married woman) the coalition agreement should have allowed the Conservative candidate, the duke's son the marquess of Hartington, a clear run. Instead, Charlie White resigned from the Labour party expressly to stand as an Independent and overturned a 5,000 majority to win by 4,500. So

Churchill *could* lose; and in October 1944 he admitted that it would be a mistake to prolong the government's tenure beyond the end of the war with Germany.

On 30 April 1945, the day after the surrender of his commanding officer in Italy, Hitler took his own life. A week later, on 7 May, General Alfred Jodl surrendered on behalf of the German Supreme Command, and Churchill declared Victory in Europe in the Commons the next day before both houses went off to St Margaret's for a service of thanksgiving. Now the debate about whether and when to break up the coalition and hold the election became urgent. After a fortnight of negotiations, Labour decided against continuing in the coalition at conference in Blackpool, and on the twenty-third Churchill resigned to form a 'caretaker' administration. Five days later he hosted a reception for the retiring Labour ministers at which, 'with tears visibly running down his cheeks', he told them history would recognize what they had achieved: 'The light will shine on every helmet.'[93] On 15 June the parliament that had lasted for nine years, five months and twenty days was prorogued.

The election itself was held on Thursday 5 July (Thursdays having become standard since 1935) but, owing to the time taken to collect and count the votes of service personnel serving overseas, the results were not known for the best part of three weeks. Despite a calamitously misjudged broadcast by Churchill, in which he suggested that a 'Socialist government' would have to 'fall back on some sort of Gestapo' to get its policies through and that a 'free parliament is odious to the Socialist doctrinaire',[94] Attlee, who riposted that Churchill 'wanted the electors to understand how great was the difference between Winston Churchill, the great leader in war of a united nation, and Mr Churchill, the party Leader of the Conservatives',[95] believed that Churchill would win a narrow majority. Attlee was massively, self-deprecatingly wrong. Labour secured nearly two million more votes than the Conservatives and galloped home with 393 seats to Churchill's meagre 213. It was the least anticipated election outcome of modern political history.

*

Churchill had been at his most sentimental when he explained the Allied victory in the Commons before the election. 'The golden circle of the Crown' had been at its heart, he reckoned, as 'the wisdom of our ancestors' had led Britain to an envied and enviable situation. 'We have the strongest Parliament in the world. We have the oldest, the most famous, the most secure and the most serviceable monarchy in the world.'[96] It was precisely the kind of orotund, self-congratulatory stuff and nonsense that warmed the cockles of parliamentary hearts but left most of the public cold.

Churchill's heel-dragging and campaigning missteps meant that he spectacularly failed where Lloyd George had succeeded, yet posterity has been much kinder to him. There was a queue of detractors waiting to condemn Lloyd George. Keynes did so in scintillating style, accusing him of 'cunning, remorselessness [and] love of power', of being 'rooted in nothing' and 'a vampire and medium in one'.[97] Opponents cited the allegations of insider trading in Marconi shares following the grant of a government contract in 1913 and the sale of honours, his son Richard viciously attacked him as a serial philanderer, and many Liberals would echo what Michael Foot recalls was the standard complaint in the home of his Liberal MP father, namely 'that he had broken the once so-powerful Liberal Party; that he had thrown open the gates to triumphant, gloating Toryism; [and] that the deed had been done in pursuit of raw, personal ambition'.[98] Yet Lloyd George provided the drive and energy vital to turning around Britain's fortunes in the First World War. On occasion his direct intervention rescued Britain from disaster, most notably in completely restructuring the war effort to produce ships and munitions in 1915 and in forcing the navy to adopt the convoy system that outwitted the German submarines. Moreover, the list of his peacetime achievements is almost unparalleled: extending the vote to all men and most women, introducing national insurance and old age pensions, raising the school leaving age. Even in Ireland he achieved peace of a bloody, mutilated sort by persuading Sinn Féin, who had left the Commons to form themselves as the Dáil Éireann, to accept the creation of the Irish

Free State and the segregation of Ulster with its own parliament. He got plenty of things wrong. Riddled with guilt about the harsh and vindictive anti-German reparations and border provisions of the Versailles peace treaty (which he had negotiated) and eager for a renegotiated settlement, he visited Hitler at Berchtesgaden in 1936 and declared him 'the greatest living German'.[99] When war came again he was old and tired and had the air of defeat about him. Yet he helped dispatch Chamberlain in the Norway debate and was even offered the embassy in Washington by Churchill. His wife Margaret died in 1941 and two years later, much to his daughter Megan's distress, he married his long-term mistress Frances Stevenson. In the autumn of 1944 they moved to Ty Newydd, a remote homestead in the hills near Llanystumdwy, where he learned of his elevation to the Lords as an earl in the 1945 New Year honours. He was never to be introduced to the Lords, though, as he died of cancer on 26 March, to be buried under a great boulder with no inscription by the River Dwyfor.

Churchill, by contrast, has flourished in the annals (partly thanks to his own greater talent as a writer, deployed in a series of historical tomes). Yet, for all the differences of their respective upbringings on a farm and in Blenheim Palace, Lloyd George and Churchill were very similar. Churchill too was a keen opportunist of a pragmatic temperament. His occasional prejudices (for instance, against the Russians) and his drive, spontaneity and confidence in his own judgement (as in the Gallipoli campaign) nearly undid him. His linguistic fluency bound the nation and lifted the spirit (although it frequently strayed into romantic exaggeration). When the Second World War came, the sense that his anti-appeasement cries from the wilderness had been vindicated gave him a presidential air above and beyond politics. As with Lloyd George, his very irrepressibility and incorrigibility simultaneously infuriated and endeared him to those outside his political party.

In 1951 Churchill would return to parliament as a Conservative Prime Minister, but his strengths were not those of a peacetime leader. While his Housing Minister Harold Macmillan built 200,000 houses (the main achievement of the administration), he concentrated on foreign affairs, sending troops to put down rebellions in Kenya and in Malaya. He had the first of a series of strokes in 1949, but when another came in June 1953 he was incapacitated for several months and in April 1955 he retired as Prime Minister. Despite his frailty he stood for parliament again in 1959 and was, like Lloyd George, Father of the House for five years (Lloyd George managed fifteen). Unlike the Welshman, he refused a peerage, but when he died on Sunday, 24 January 1965, aged 90, he was accorded a three-day lying-in-state in Westminster Hall and a state funeral.

Parliament had been entirely irrelevant to the First World War. It had determined neither its leadership nor its conduct. Key moments had passed without reference to either Commons or Lords. By contrast, despite sitting for fewer (and shorter) days in the Second World War than in the First – roughly 120 a year compared to 145 – parliament unseated Neville Chamberlain, threatened Churchill, ended Cripps's sojourn in the sun, challenged Churchill's war methods, ensured that the Labour party would leave the government before the end of the war with a policy of support for Beveridge, and laid the ground for Churchill's electoral defeat.

Moreover, in at least one respect, the two wars did change parliament. The 1701 Act of Settlement stipulated that anyone holding an office of profit under the crown was disqualified from membership of the Commons, and the 1707 Regency Act had allowed office-holders to be members so long as they won a by-election subsequent to their ministerial appointment. Between 1868 and 1913 there had been 278 such by-elections, and eight new ministers had failed to get re-elected. A tradition had grown up that any minister appointed immediately after a general election would be given a free run in the subsequent by-election, but that when a minister was appointed mid-term the by-election would be fiercely contested. Prime ministers were consequently understandably reluctant to appoint anyone in a less than impeccably safe seat; but even such precautions did not always work.

PARLIAMENT: THE BIOGRAPHY

When Balfour appointed the Conservative MP for ultra-safe Brighton, Gerald Loder, as a whip in 1905 he lost and was never to return. By the start of the First World War this rule was a major irritant. In 1911 the Liberal Andrew Anderson lost his by-election when he was appointed Solicitor-General for Scotland (having already fought two general elections the previous year) and in 1914 the Liberal Charles Masterman lost his seat of South West Bethnal Green in the by-election following his appointment as Chancellor of the Duchy of Lancaster, and failed again at Ipswich in May. Considering the fact that both major parties had suffered from the rule, it is surprising that there was so little interest in abolishing it, but many thought it an important gauge of public opinion and there would have been little sympathy for Winston Churchill's grandiose views expressed to his fiancée when he lost his ministerial by-election in 1908: 'It is an awful hindrance to anyone in my position to be always forced to fight for his life and always having to make his opinions on national politics conform to local exigencies.'[100]

In time of war, though, that argument carried more force, especially since the coalition formed in 1915 of necessity involved the appointment of several new ministers mid-term. So, with the approval of the opposition front bench, Sir John Simon introduced a Re-election of Ministers Bill to end ministerial by-elections for the duration of the war. The back benches greeted the proposal with scorn, and under attack Simon backed down, amending the measure to cover just the two months necessary for the creation of the coalition. The process was repeated a year later when Asquith appointed Edwin Montagu and F. E. Smith, and again for the creation of the Lloyd George coalition. Since both a general election and local elections had been delayed by statute during the war there was a logic to this, but when Churchill was reappointed to government in July 1917, with Conservative hostility ringing in Lloyd George's ears, a by-election went ahead and Churchill had to defend himself against a pacifist, Edwin Scrymgeour. Churchill won, but the irritation factor led Lloyd George and Bonar Law to introduce a new Re-election of Ministers

Bill as one of their first measures after the war in February 1919, aimed at preventing another string of ministerial by-elections. Bonar Law had hoped to get the legislation through in a single day, but the Commons was far from convinced, and the measure foundered. Two defeats, of the Conservative Minister for Agriculture, Lieutenant-Colonel Sir Arthur Griffith-Boscawen, in the Dudley by-election of 1921 and of the Welsh-speaking coalition Liberal, the new junior whip Arthur Lewis, in Pontypridd in 1922, proved that the rule could still be a major inconvenience, and although Baldwin managed to win several tight ministerial by-elections, in 1926 his stand-alone Conservative government assisted the backbencher Christopher Clayton in bringing a private member's Bill to abolish ministerial by-elections altogether. There was a minor Tory rebellion, but it was carried by 143 votes to 74. As *The Times* put it, 'Queen Anne is dead.'[101]

In large measure this altered attitude towards prime ministerial patronage was the result of the wartime determination that everything be subjugated to the war effort. That same spirit also enabled Lloyd George to increase the number of ministers from sixty-two in Asquith's peacetime administration to eighty-five, a number that barely diminished once the war was over. From this high water mark of prime ministerial patronage the tide was never to recede. Churchill went even further in extending the parliamentary tentacles of government during the Second World War by adding yet more ministers and appointing MPs as ambassadors and departmental advisers, so that by 1950 there were sixty-eight MPs in paid government posts and twenty-seven PPSs. Thereafter, although two Acts of 1975 limited the number of ministers in either house to 109 and the number of MPs in paid jobs to 95, by 1999 the total number of MPs in posts that required them to support the government in a division was 129: nearly a fifth of the Commons.[102]

In our 'finest hour' we surrendered parliament into the hands of the executive – and thus far nobody has ever thought to ask for it back.

**Don't Keir-Hardie,
M.P. for 'Am.**

*For centuries parliament had been reserved, with but a few
exceptions, for wealthy scions of the nobility. Late Victorian
changes in the franchise and the failure of the Liberal party
to meet working-class political aspirations enabled men like
James Keir Hardie, who had started work as a child in the
shipyards and mines of Lanarkshire, to consider standing
for parliament. First elected for West Ham South in 1892,
Hardie was much satirized for refusing to wear the
conventional Victorian parliamentary attire of frock coat
and top hat.*

6

The Dignity of Labour

AT ELEVEN O'CLOCK ON THE cold morning of Saturday, 28 May 1898 the grey-haired, ruddy-cheeked Henry Broadhurst, whose girth matched his name, stood among the mourners as Big Ben tolled and the muffled bells of the Abbey rang out for the start of Gladstone's brief funeral procession from Westminster Hall. Although Broadhurst, now aged fifty-eight, had been an MP for sixteen years and had even been a junior minister under Gladstone, he felt curiously out of place. After all, unlike Gladstone's pallbearers, who included the Prince of Wales and his brother the duke of York, Broadhurst had no title. He had been born the youngest of twelve children in 1840 and had followed his father in his nomadic career as a journeyman stonemason, in which capacity he had worked on the new clock tower at Westminster in the late 1850s. It had been hard work 'roughing-out' the blocks of stone in the middle of winter. As he later put it in his memoirs: 'At times the bitter blast would numb my hands until it was impossible to hold a chisel. My very bones would be penetrated with its icy edge until I felt as if clothed in a garment of lace.'[1] As Gladstone's funeral cortège set off, he recalled,

my eye involuntarily sought the clock tower, on whose tall flanks I had worked, chilled to the bone, nearly thirty years before; and my memory recalled one bitter cold, wet day in the winter of 1858–59 when, almost barefoot, I had crossed the Palace Yard . . . The contrast was almost overwhelming: then unknown and penniless; today in a place of honour, the sorrowing colleague of the greatest Englishman of the century.[2]

He was not alone in his amazement that a working man, dressed in clothes made by his wife Eliza and subsisting on just his £150 salary as secretary of the parliamentary committee of the Trades Union Congress, should have become an MP. Yet his passage from stone-mason's bench to Treasury bench was not unique. There had been a few working-class MPs in earlier eras. Thomas Cromwell was the son of a brewer, blacksmith and fuller. Thomas Brereton, a Liverpool MP between 1724 and 1756, was 'the son of an ordinary fellow who kept an ale-house in Chester',[3] Robert Mackreth, who sat in the Commons from 1774 to 1802, was a coffee-house waiter who married the proprietor's daughter, and Joseph Pitt, the son of a Gloucestershire carpenter, used to hold men's horses for a penny before he was taken up by the local attorney and became MP for Cricklade from 1812 to 1831. Yet all these men had risen in business or in the law long before they entered parliament. By contrast, the three Labour Representation League candidates who stood for election in 1874 under the Liberal banner were working men: Thomas Burt, who had gone down the mines at the age of ten as a trapper and pony driver, at Morpeth; Alexander MacDonald, who had started as a miner aged nine, at Stafford; and Broadhurst in High Wycombe. Burt and MacDonald were elected and in 1880 Broadhurst joined them in the Commons.

This advent of the working man was not always a smooth process. Police had to be called to break up fights outside the Liberal selection meeting in Birmingham Bordesley when Broadhurst was chosen as candidate in 1885, and there was much snobbery about the fact that he and several of the other Lib-Lab MPs did not include the silk top hat that was *de rigueur* in the Chamber as part of their workaday attire but preferred to turn up at the House in a mere bowler or flat hat. Yet when the two new redistribution and representation Acts of 1884–5 came into force in the latter year, a chunk of the working class was enfranchised and many of the old double-member seats (including Broadhurst's seat in Stoke) were carved up, creating singleton seats where a working-class majority required the Liberal Party to adopt working men if it wanted to win. MacDonald died in 1881, but in 1885 Broadhurst and Burt were joined by eleven other working-class MPs standing as Liberals. Miners were returned in Rhondda (William Abraham), in Mid Durham (William Crawford), in Wansbeck (Charles Fenwick), in Normanton (Ben Pickard) and in Houghton-le-Spring (John Wilson). Other trades were represented: Joseph Leicester was a glassmaker; Joseph Arch was the founder of the National Agricultural Labourers' Union; John Charles Durant was a printer, George Howell a building labourer and Randal Cremer a journeyman carpenter whose father had abandoned the family in poverty before his birth. The number of these Lib-Lab MPs continued to grow. In 1892 there were twelve, in 1906 there were eighteen, by 1910 there were fifteen miners alone in the Commons and four years later there were four gas-workers. Some have been exceptionally rude about these men. One scholar has said that 'with the exception of one or two individuals, they were all colourless, unobtrusive figures' and that 'they proved completely inadequate to any role in the House'.[4] Yet both Broadhurst and Burt served as junior ministers and notched up twenty-six and forty-four years respectively as MPs. Moreover, several had a more important extra-parliamentary role. Abraham (whose bardic name was Mabon) was the undisputed leader of the Welsh miners, who could still a crowd by starting up the Welsh National anthem, and Arch appeared almost messianic when he led what Marx termed the great agricultural 'awakening' of 1872. But both men ended their careers weighed down by respectability: Mabon joined the boards of several companies, moved away from the Rhondda to a smart house near the coast and even did adverts for tobacco and tomato sauce. By the time of his retirement as MP due to ill-health in 1920 radicals in the Rhondda had been calling for him to 'move on or move out' for a decade.[5] As for Arch, he barely uttered a word in the Commons in his last six years and retired with a pension from his Liberal colleagues in 1900, by which time a common refrain was heard among his former followers:

> *Joseph Arch he stole a march,*
> *Upon a spotted cow.*
> *He scampered off to Parliament,*
> *But where is Joseph now?*

*

It was one thing to have working men in parliament. It was quite another, though, to have *socialist* workers in the House. After all, the Lib-Lab MPs were, to a man, respectable applicants to the managerial class. They might have started at the coalface but they had progressed to be checkweighmen, clerks or full-time union officials. They went to chapel and to evening classes and avoided pubs and music halls. They were content to supplement the Liberal ranks and sit alongside industrialists, landowners and bankers. Yet by the time they were taking their seats the ideas of Marx and Engels had reached the drawing rooms and chapter houses of England, and many socialists openly dismissed the idea of merely promoting working-class candidates per se. Stewart Headlam, for instance, a prominent East End vicar and leader of one Christian Socialist group, the Guild of St Matthew, refused 'to vote for a man simply because he is a carpenter and will try to improve carpenters' wages'.[6] If real emancipation was to come, then what was needed was a fusion of socialism with labour representation. Some still hoped this new movement could be housed within the Liberal party, but a sense of disillusionment began to fester in trade union committee rooms during strikes by the gas-workers, the London dockers and stevedores, the match-girls and the Manningham Mills textile workers between 1888 and 1890, which not only proved that union militancy paid better dividends than deference to the Liberal party, but helped launch figures like the dockers' champions Ben Tillett and Will Crooks on a national scene. Admittedly Tillett, who had started his working life on a building site aged eight and worked as a fisherman, an apprentice bootmaker and a sailor in the Royal Navy, stood repeatedly for parliament in 1892, 1895, 1900 and 1910, but it was not until 1917 that he was to find a place on the green benches as MP for Salford North, while Crooks, the son of a seamstress and a disabled ship's stoker, who had seen the Poplar workhouse from the inside, became mayor of Poplar before being elected MP for Woolwich in 1903. Both were established public figures long before they were MPs.

The first self-declared socialist to get elected, though, was no proletarian. R. C. Cunninghame Graham not only had an admiral and a Spanish noblewoman as his maternal grandparents, but his father's family stretched back to the eighteenth century Radical Scottish MP Robert Graham, on whose extensive estates he was brought up. Nobody could have been more different from the Lib-Lab MPs. Cunninghame Graham managed to fit in running an Argentinian cattle ranch (which earned him the nickname 'Don Roberto'), working as a fencing instructor in Mexico, travelling in Africa dressed as a sheikh and prospecting for gold in Spain before his father's death in 1883, when he returned to Britain and began associating with the likes of William Morris and George Bernard Shaw. In 1885 he stood in North West Lanarkshire as a Liberal with socialist backing, but it was not until the following year that he won the seat on a platform that included not only the usual Liberal pledges (disestablishment and Irish home rule) but also demands for the abolition of the House of Lords, extensive nationalization and home rule for Scotland. From day one his adventuring past shone through in the Commons. In a frequently hilarious first speech he excoriated Liberals as 'crutch-and-toothpick gentlemen', equated Randolph Churchill to 'the froth on the licensed victualler's beer' and condemned 'that society in which one man worked and another enjoyed the fruit'.[7]

It did not take long for him to get into trouble. He was thrown out of the House for complaining that the Lords dared to 'dictate' to the Commons in 1886, again in 1888 for accusing a minister of a 'dishonourable trick' by refusing to discuss the nail- and chain-makers' strike in Cradley Heath, and a third time in 1892 for attacking the shareholders in 'swindling companies' and shouting at Sir John Lubbock, who was bellowing out a demand that he be named, 'Oh, leave me alone; I do not care a damn.' It was clear to him that he was suspended from the Commons 'for standing up for socialism'.[8]

By 1892, though, he was far from alone. The trade unions were now almost as multitudinous as the old City livery guilds, the Social Democratic Foundation had been founded in 1881 and the Fabian Society had followed it three years later. This was hardly a harmonious band of troubadours. While Henry Hyndman's SDF dreamed of a sturdy Marxist revolution and the trade unions struggled for better working conditions, Beatrice and Sidney Webb were solely intent on influencing the Liberal party. But there was a further dimension. As early as 1852 George Robinson, the second son of the Prime Minister Viscount Goderich, had been elected for Hull, having recently written a Christian Socialist tract in which he claimed 'that every man . . . has a claim to a share in the government of his country' and that 'we can no longer blink the questions which are being asked of us on every hand; we must take some part in the coming struggle'.[9] He was unseated on petition when his agent suspiciously disappeared, but he soon found another seat and succeeded his father as earl of Ripon in 1859. His career was to include four years as a junior minister and eleven in Liberal Cabinets. (He even managed to stumble, aged seventy-eight, into the 1905 Cabinet as Lord Privy Seal.) In the 1850s he associated with the small group of Christian Socialists led by the academic theologian F. D. Maurice and the young lawyer Thomas Hughes (later a Liberal MP and author of *Tom Brown's Schooldays*). By the turn of the century Christian Socialism had entered the mainstream. James Fraser, the mountainous red-headed second bishop of Manchester, whom Gladstone had plucked out of parochial obscurity in 1870, and who had earned himself the soubriquet 'citizen bishop' by adopting every social(ist) cause going, died in 1886, but two years later the Lambeth Conference of bishops, including all twenty-six lords spiritual, condemned 'excessive inequality in the distribution of this world's goods' and even urged clergy to show 'how much of what is good and true in socialism is to be found in the precepts of Christ'.[10] In 1889 three future bishops, Brooke Fosse Westcott, Charles Gore and Edward Talbot, together with the Liberal MPs Charles Dilke and H. J. Tennant, formed the Christian Social Union. Theirs was a simple message: 'The socialistic movement is based upon a great demand for justice in human life . . . The indictment of our present social organization is indeed overwhelming. And with the indictment Christianity ought to have the profoundest sympathy. It is substantially the indictment of the prophets.'[11]

Prophets were not in short supply; quite the reverse. As the 1890s began there was a chaotic plethora of left-leaning political organizations, and with elected school boards and town councils being supplemented by the incorporation of more town councils and the creation of county councils in 1889 there were more opportunities for socialists to get elected. Then came the 1892 general election. In 1888 one of Cunninghame Graham's friends, the Scotsman James Keir Hardie, had stood at the neighbouring West Lanarkshire by-election as an Independent Labour candidate and had come a rather dismal third, which had prompted the two men to form a Scottish Labour party, including two radical Liberal MPs, the barrister Charles Conybeare and the leader of the Highland Land League, Dr Gavin Clark, as allied members. It was under this banner that Cunninghame Graham stood in Glasgow Camlachie in 1892. He did just as badly as Hardie had done in 1888, but three other union-backed working-class allies were elected as 'Independent Labour' candidates in England: Hardie himself at West Ham South, John Burns at Battersea and Havelock Wilson in Middlesbrough. Hardie had rejected offers of safe Liberal seats in Scotland, and now he had won thanks to the Liberal candidate dying, but he immediately set about replicating the Scottish Labour party for the rest of the country, calling a meeting at the Labour Institute in Bradford the following January. Some thought the new grouping might be called the Socialist party. Indeed, the *Bradford Observer* of 14 January 1893 noted that 'the large number of socialists among them was apparent from the large proportion of wideawakes, red ties, and shirts with flannel collars', but when Ben Tillett was cheered at the meeting for declaiming that if it were to be called the Socialist party 'he would repudiate it', the 120 attendees opted for the 'Independent Labour party' and for Hardie as its chairman.

If Cunninghame Graham was all Latin braggadocio, Hardie carried his prophetic mantle in the new parliament with Celtic pride. His arrival has been cast into legend. He was variously described as wearing a peaked cap, a soft cap, a blue scotch cap and (which is more likely) a deerstalker. None of these, nor his checked trousers, were the parliamentary fashion of the day, which dictated a black frock coat, striped trousers and silk top hat. True, a lone trumpeter played the 'Marseillaise' as he arrived, but there was no East End mob and no red flag. He voted with Gladstone on 11 August 1892 to oust Salisbury, but his first attempted intervention, an amendment to Salisbury's queen's speech, came to nothing as he failed to understand the forms of the House, and when he repeated the move by trying to amend Gladstone's queen's speech on 7 February 1893 not even Burns supported him – although 109 opportunistic Tories did. Hardie was bold. He criticized the Commons on 14 July 1893 for spending a whole day congratulating the duke and duchess of York on their new baby when a woman had been found starved to death the day beforehand and the Prince of Wales earned £60,000 a year from slum property; but when he tried to slash the pension being awarded to the former Speaker Arthur Wellesley Peel from £4,000 to £1,000, he failed to find a single colleague to act as a teller.

Hardie might be a rather solitary figure inside the House, but outside his party attracted another Scotsman, Ramsay MacDonald, who had failed to get selected as the Liberal candidate in Southampton and now announced that 'the Liberal Party has done its work' and that 'Socialism is to inspire the progressive forces of the twentieth century as Individualism inspired those of the nineteenth'.[12] Others joined too, most notably a disabled evangelical Methodist from the West Riding, Philip Snowden. Nevertheless, the 1892 election was to prove a false dawn, as not a single ILP candidate won a seat in the 1895 election and there was a real danger that, just as Cunninghame Graham's career had ended after one term, so might Hardie's. Conscious that disunity in socialist ranks was hindering progress, under the direction of Hardie the TUC decided in autumn 1899 to summon a two-day meeting of the whole plethora of socialist and labour organizations on 27 and 28 February 1900 to consider creating 'a distinct Labour group in Parliament, who shall have their own whips, and agree upon their policy, which must embrace a readiness to cooperate with any party which for the time being may be engaged in promoting legislation in the direct interests of Labour'.[13] The only sitting MP present at the meeting was John Burns, but the conference belonged to Hardie and MacDonald. When Hardie moved the original motion and the SDF resoundingly failed in its attempt to get the conference to adopt a clear socialist policy and left, Hardie became chairman and MacDonald secretary of the resulting Labour Representation Committee, which put forward fifteen standalone Labour candidates in the Boer War 'khaki' election later that year. Yet again the results were disappointing. MacDonald failed to get in alongside Broadhurst in Leicester and even Hardie, having lost at Preston, only squeaked in thanks to a virtually unsolicited last-minute offer from the miners in Merthyr Tydfil, which polled after Preston. Hardie's sole companion as LRC MP was the less than socialist general secretary of the Amalgamated Society of Railway Servants, Richard Bell.

Since Bell was effectively another Lib-Lab MP (and would later stand as a Liberal), Hardie was yet again a sole trader. It was a role in which he felt comfortable. He liked to raise a rabble, he actively enjoyed a row and would often strike out on his own. He was rough at the edges, a great hewer of political coal who would forget a grudge as fast as he would start an altercation. A committed member of the Evangelical Union, he saw politics as an extension of his lay preaching and his gospel embraced the temperance movement as heartily as it advocated standalone socialism and militant feminism. These were not very parliamentary attributes. Burns caricatured him as 'the leader who never won a strike, organised a union, governed a parish or passed a Bill, Barren Cumnock in the Duchy of Doctrinaire',[14] and Hardie himself said of his time in parliament: 'I feel like a bird with its wings clipped.'[15]

MacDonald, the secretary of the LRC, was a very different style of man. He was all sartorial smoothness, a born pacifier and coalition-builder, a natural parliamentary performer, an only child who would nurse a slight until it festered. They had things in common. Although Hardie was born the son of a ship's carpenter and a domestic servant in Glasgow, both had been brought up in Lanarkshire, where, as *John Bull* savagely pointed out in an attempt to sully MacDonald's First World War pacifism, MacDonald was born 'the illegitimate son of a Scotch servant girl'. Both men knew poverty, too, but Hardie's was the tougher start in life, as he started work at the age of seven and went down the mines at ten while MacDonald stayed at school until fifteen. Moreover, MacDonald married the daughter of a well-to-do professor of chemistry, Margaret Gladstone, who brought with her a healthy private income, on the back of which they could afford a smart flat in Lincoln's Inn Fields, while Hardie had to rely on the kindness of benevolent strangers for a roof over his head in London.

As the new Conservative and Unionist dominated parliament opened in 1900, Hardie had some allies to whom he might have looked: Lib-Lab MPs such as William Abraham from the nearby constituency of Rhondda and radical Liberals such as Charles Dilke. But it was a legal decision of the House of Lords in the case of the Taff Vale Railway Company in 1901, to the effect that the Amalgamated Society of Railway Servants was responsible for the costs incurred by the company following its strike (to the exorbitant, bankrupting tune of £23,000 plus costs), that galvanized the trade unions. Suddenly it was clear that the only way to secure their future was through legislative reform; and that required sympathetic, labour-minded, union-sponsored MPs. Trade-union affiliation to the LRC rose from

350,000 to 850,000 in two years and the LRC started to win by-elections. First David Shackleton, a cotton worker from the age of nine, was elected unopposed at Clitheroe in 1902. Then Will Crooks was elected at Woolwich in 1903 when the Liberals gave him a free run against the Conservatives. And even more surprisingly, on 24 July 1903 Arthur Henderson won the Barnard Castle by-election under the LRC banner by just forty-seven votes against both a Liberal and a Conservative candidate.

As the next general election approached, MacDonald, though not yet elected himself, came into his own as a natural coalition builder, capitalizing on the manifest Liberal fear of another 1900-style split in the non-Unionist vote by offering the Liberal chief whip Herbert Gladstone (no relation to MacDonald's wife, but son of the Grand Old Man) an electoral pact by which the LRC and the Liberals would not stand against each other in some fifty seats. It was to bring spectacular results. The Liberals won a convincing majority in 1906 that could have left Labour a small irrelevance on the opposition benches below the gangway. But Labour won twenty-nine seats, twenty-four of them unopposed by Liberals, and when one union-sponsored Lib-Lab MP (John Jenkins of the Associated Shipwrights, the member for Chatham) decided to join the new grouping in the Commons, they numbered thirty. This was a big enough group to demand the reversal of the Taff Vale judgment, and when the Miners' Federation affiliated to Labour in 1908 and the TUC resolved that all union-sponsored MPs should take the Labour whip, not the Liberal, the Lib-Lab miner MPs crossed the floor. Labour's support for Asquith in the battles with the Lords became even more important after the 1910 elections, which saw twelve of the former Lib-Lab mining MPs elected as Labour, while just three remained as Liberals. Labour was beginning to look like a national party.

When Broadhurst arrived in parliament he had one great advantage: the financial support of the trade unions, who paid him his election expenses (which after the Corrupt Practices Prevention Acts of 1854 and 1883 were not as ruinous as formerly but still put parliament beyond the financial reach of a working man) and a salary. Not all the new MPs enjoyed that luxury. For Hardie, who earned his living as a lecturer paid piecemeal, every day parliament sat was an added expense. And in 1909 the salaries given to Labour MPs by trade unions were declared illegal. So when Asquith sought Labour support in 1911 the party had one main condition. Charles James Fox had called for MPs to be paid in 1780, so had the People's Charter of 1838, and so had the National Democratic League and the Metropolitan Radical Federation, whose campaigns led to the Commons debating the idea in 1870, 1888, 1892, 1893, 1895 and 1903. Finally, over two centuries since an MP had last been paid a parliamentary salary,* Labour demanded the introduction of a parliamentary wage for all non-ministerial MPs, which Lloyd George justified in ringing terms in the Commons:

> When we offer £400 a year as payment of Members of Parliament it is not a recognition of the magnitude of the service, it is not a remuneration, it is not a recompense, it is not even a salary. It is just an allowance, and I think the minimum allowance, to enable men to come here, men who would render incalculable service to the State, and whom it is an incalculable loss to the State not to have here, but who cannot be here because their means do not allow it. It is purely an allowance to enable us to open the door to great and honourable public service to these men, for whom this country will be all the richer, all the greater, and all the stronger for the unknown vicissitudes which it has to face by having there to aid us by their counsel, by their courage, and by their resource.[16]

The vote was far from unanimous – 265 to 173 – with the Conservatives and Unionists in vigorous opposition on the historically inaccurate grounds that 'hitherto the reward which has been

---

* The poet Andrew Marvell, whose borough insisted on paying him.

considered sufficient has been the dignity and honour of the position'.[17] Thereafter, the salary for non-ministerial MPs rose steadily over the years (apart from in 1931 when it was cut); in 1957 ministers were allowed a proportion of it in addition to their ministerial salaries (and all of it in 1996), and allowances were introduced for secretarial staff, for travel and for office accommodation. Many argue that this turned the job of MP into a profession, but it also meant MPs were less concerned about the length of parliamentary sessions or earning a living outside the House. For the Labour party in 1911 it meant trade union money could go towards the election of far more Labour candidates.

Three developments now contributed to the unsteady parliamentary rise of Labour that saw the party form governments in 1924 and 1929. The first was the role Labour and the trade unions played in the First World War as recruiting sergeants, munitions labourers and government ministers, with Henderson ensuring that the pacifism of Hardie and MacDonald did not detract from the public perception of a patriotic national party that knew how to do its duty.

Second was the unravelling of the coalition government. Conservative MPs had long been unhappy with Lloyd George and keen to break the coalition, but it was only when Bonar Law sided with Conservative backbenchers at a meeting at the Carlton Club on 19 October 1922 (hence the Conservatives' backbench '1922' Committee) against the party's leader, Austen Chamberlain, that Lloyd George and Chamberlain were ousted and Bonar Law became Prime Minister of a standalone Conservative government. In the subsequent general election on 15 November the Conservatives won a comfortable majority of seventy-seven and looked set for a five-year stint in office, but in May 1923 Bonar Law was diagnosed with incurable throat cancer and resigned. His replacement, the laconic and inexperienced Chancellor of the Exchequer Stanley Baldwin, had a series of problems to face – a party split over war reparations, a burdensome American debt and growing unemployment – and took a much less confrontational attitude to Labour than other Tories (Neville

Chamberlain, for instance, told Baldwin of Labour that 'intellectually, with a few exceptions, they are dirt'[18]). In search of a populist measure that might rally the ambivalent support of his Tory colleagues, Baldwin returned to the old Tory hymn book in October 1923 and declared his support for tariff reform. Since the 1923 election had featured a prominent commitment that a Conservative government would *not* adopt protectionist measures, Baldwin found himself on the defensive. On 15 November MacDonald, who had only just returned to the Commons in the general election and the Labour leadership a week later, tabled a no-confidence motion in the Commons and although Baldwin won it, the next day he decided to call an early general election for 6 December. The shock result was a delicately hung parliament with the Conservatives on 258, Asquith's disgruntled Liberals on 158 and Labour on 191. Baldwin waited to be voted out by the Commons, and on 21 January 1924 the Liberals combined with Labour in voting to amend the loyal address by 328 votes to 256. It was the last time a government was ejected after, rather than by, an election.

The third factor in Labour's favour now came to the fore: its own immense adaptability. From the outset the new party was something of a magpie, a determined purloiner of other people's ideas – and of other parties' personnel. Even before the war wealthy figures from resolutely Tory backgrounds were recruited, including the Etonian Hugh Dalton and the Haileyburian Clement Attlee. Even some declared Tories joined Labour. Arthur Strauss was a Liberal Unionist and then a Conservative MP before standing as an 'Independent Labour' candidate in 1918; his son George (known as G. R. Strauss) was a Labour MP for forty-six years. So too, after a career building railways in South Africa, William Royce had stood twice in 1910 as the Conservative candidate in Spalding, but in 1918 he stood for Labour and remained a Labour MP until his death of a heart attack on a London bus in June 1924; and John Strachey (Evelyn John St Loe Strachey, to give him his full name), the Etonian son of the editor of the *Spectator*, joined Labour in 1923 and was elected in 1929.

It was not enough to have Labourites in the Commons. A Labour government needed peers as well. So, in addition to promoting Labour men like the Royal Engineer and unsuccessful parliamentary candidate Christopher Thomson and the former Liberal MP Captain Sydney Arnold to the Lords, Labour recruited from the nobility. Herbrand Sackville, the 9th Earl de le Warr, joined the Labour party when he came of age, the first hereditary peer to do so; George Hay, the 28-year-old 14th earl of Kinnoull, soon joined him; William Hare, the 5th earl of Listowel, took the Labour whip despite having a younger brother, John, who sat in Conservative governments; Frederic Thesiger, who had been made Viscount Chelmsford for his service as a Conservative Viceroy of India, accepted the Admiralty in the Labour government of 1924 on the understanding that he would not have to attend political Cabinet meetings; and the High Court judge John Sankey was made a baron expressly so as to be the Labour Lord Chancellor in 1929. Perhaps the most remarkable scalp, though, was that of Charles Cripps, who alongside a lucrative legal career was a Conservative and Unionist MP, but was made Baron Parmoor by the Liberals in 1910 and joined the Labour party in time to take his seat in the Labour Cabinet of 1924 alongside his brother-in-law Sidney Webb. This conversion paid double dividends, for Parmoor's barrister son Stafford was drafted into MacDonald's second government as Solicitor-General (and made his maiden speech from the Treasury bench).

There were Liberals as well in MacDonald's first government, which he managed to form on 22 January 1924. A typical instance was Sir Charles Trevelyan. He came of good Liberal stock. His great-uncle was the historian Thomas Babington Macaulay, his maternal grandfather was a Liberal MP and his father Sir George sat in the Cabinet under Gladstone and Rosebery. Sir Charles was a wealthy landowner and was elected Liberal MP for Elland in 1898, serving as parliamentary secretary to the Board of Education from 1908 to 1914. Everything about Trevelyan, including the 11,000-acre estate at Wallington Hall which he left to the National Trust in his will, reeked of old-school Gladstonian Liberalism and *noblesse oblige*. Beatrice Webb certainly approved, describing him as 'a man who has every endowment – social position, wealth, intelligence, an independent outlook, good looks, good manners'.[19] But in 1918 he stood for the ILP in Elland (and lost), four years later he tried again at Newcastle Central and was elected, and in 1924 he was to be one of the reassuring though not particularly effective mainstays of MacDonald's administration as President of the Board of Education.

Although MacDonald told the Commons on 12 February 1924 that 'coalitions are detestable, are dishonest',[20] with three former leaders of the parliamentary Labour party (J. R. Clynes, Adamson, Henderson), a textile worker (Tom Shaw), two miners (Stephen Walsh and Vernon Hartshorn), a brace of Fabians (Sidney Webb and Lord Olivier), a string of ILP-ers (Philip Snowden, Fred Jowett and Jimmy Thomas), two Tories and four Liberals, MacDonald's 1924 Cabinet looked remarkably like a magpie coalition. Despite the ten working-class Cabinet ministers, this was a safe, nation-embracing Labour government.

In later years the myth of right-wing betrayal would be so potent that it was to dominate internal Labour debates well into the 1990s, but the fourth factor that enabled Labour to form governments in 1924 and 1929 was its sheer moderation. Sure, the parliamentary numbers necessitated it. After all, the Conservatives had 258 seats and the Liberals 158. It was also true that although in later years he would project his own guilt on to those around him, MacDonald's personal style was to conciliate. But within the wider movement too there was a hopeful air of compromise. Jennie Lee found it utterly infuriating, complaining that when she tried to rouse the 'solid rows of decent, well-intentioned, unpretentious Labour back-benchers' from inertia 'they reacted like a load of wet cement'.[21] Yet even the most ardently left-wing voices in the Labour party bought the cautious line in 1924. As the briefly communist MP W. J. Brown acknowledged,

> there would be a permanent difference in point of view between Government on the one hand and the Trade Union on the other:

and that difference in point of view did not arise from any wickedness on the part of the political side, or on the part of the industrial side, but arose from the fact that the Trade Unions had different functions to follow than the functions of Government.[22]

Against this background the communist revolution in Russia gave Labour a headache. On the one hand there was a clear appetite in some quarters for a Marxist political party. In 1918–19 there was talk of the Communist Party of Great Britain affiliating to the ILP and of Labour affiliating to the Communist International, and although both ideas were rejected in 1921, individual communist MPs subsisted within Labour. The first such was Cecil Malone, a native of Yorkshire who was a lieutenant-colonel in the army, commanded HMS *Ben-my-Chree* and served as air attaché at the British Embassy in Paris. Elected as a National Liberal for Leyton East in 1918, he joined the British Socialist party, which soon merged into the Communist party, and was arrested for his inflammatory comments at the Albert Hall on 7 November 1920 when he asked: 'What are a few Churchills or a few Curzons on lampposts compared to the massacre of thousands of human beings?'[23] After six months in prison he lost his seat in 1922 and joined Labour, becoming MP for Northampton in the by-election of 9 January 1928. Later evidence shows that Malone was almost certainly a spy, passing information to the Japanese. Two other communist MPs elected in 1922, Walton Newbold and Shapurji Saklatvala, were rather more conventional Marxists.

Despite Labour's decision to prove its moderation by keeping communism at arm's length, opponents of socialism seized every opportunity to link Labour to Lenin. There was plenty of ammunition. When a group of Glasgow Labour MPs accused the Tory MP Sir Frederick Banbury of being a murderer for supporting a proposal to cut child welfare, they were all suspended from the House. The Labour leadership was appalled at such parliamentary ruffianism and abstained, but half the parliamentary Labour party voted against the suspension, a feat they repeated when Malone was suspended. The subsequent PLP meeting agreed that such exhibitions of radical temperament were counterproductive as 'when a Labour government arrives it will be greatly hampered if, in the meantime, Parliamentary Government has been destroyed',[24] and Snowden asserted: 'We must show the country that we [are] not under the domination of the wild men.'[25]

As might be expected of a minority government supported by less than a third of MPs, it was the Commons that brought the 1924 government down. The first danger came in the shape of an Asquith motion censuring the government's treaty with Russia. This MacDonald met with cold indifference and a general rant about Liberal inconstancy. But then came an attack from the Tories on the question of whether the Attorney-General, Sir Patrick Hastings, was right to withdraw a mooted prosecution against the editor of the *Workers' Weekly*, John Campbell, for incitement to mutiny. It was true that Hastings had consulted the Cabinet, though not that he had been leant on by the Prime Minister; but when asked about it in the Commons on 30 September, MacDonald stepped well beyond the bounds of truth by claiming that he 'was not consulted regarding either the institution or the subsequent withdrawal of these proceedings'.[26] With a leaked Cabinet minute to hand, both Baldwin and Asquith scented blood, and on 8 October the Tories tabled a motion of censure and the Liberals an amendment to set up a select committee to investigate the matter. MacDonald started the day by apologizing to the House for implying 'that [he] had no cognisance of what was going on'.[27] Normally such an admission would be enough to assuage a sensitive House, but in this instance the apology barely met the barefaced nature of the lie, so Austen Chamberlain and Sir John Simon pushed on aggressively, implying that MacDonald had both misled the House and done so intentionally. It was clear that everyone was now treating the matter as a confidence motion, and when MacDonald continued to seem evasive the Conservatives abandoned their motion and voted with the Liberal amendment. MacDonald lost by 364 to 198 and resigned.

When the general election came, the 'wild men' did for MacDonald. On Saturday, 25 October, just four days before the poll, the *Daily Mail* ran the ludicrous headline 'Civil War plot by Socialists: Moscow Order to our Reds', and beneath it referred to a missive, supposedly from Grigori Zinoviev, the president of the Communist International, demanding the launch of a mass class war in Britain. Not only was this 'Zinoviev letter' forged, but the evidence to back it up was fabricated by MI5, and the Conservative party had a direct hand in both paying £10,000 for its acquisition and leaking it to the press through the MP for Hitchin, Guy Kindersley. Two letters in the Bodleian Library at Oxford show that the other go-between, former MI5 agent and City businessman Donald Im Thurn, thought 'there is no doubt whatever that the letter smashed the Communists, split the Labour Party, ruined the Liberals, upset any chances of revolution and made the failure of the general strike a foregone conclusion and established the Conservative Party on a basis of solidity which has never existed before', and that 'Kindersley and [he] should be given the recognition previously promised at the earliest convenient moment, say in the Birthday Honours'.[28] These letters, written in 1928 to MI5's Major Joseph Ball (who ran secret operatives within the Labour party on behalf of the Conservatives throughout the 1920s and 1930s, admitted to the Conservative anti-appeasement MP Ronald Tree that he was tapping his phone and tried to smear Churchill out of loyalty to Chamberlain in the 1930s), were denounced as forgeries by Ball, and it is possible that some Conservatives honestly believed they were doing the nation a service by placing such inflammatory material before the public. But Bonar Law and Baldwin's private secretary, J. C. C. Davidson, who became chairman of the party in 1926, appointed Ball as Director of the Conservative Research Department in 1930 largely on the basis of his 'experience . . . in the seamy side of life and the handling of crooks',[29] Ball's papers include an account of meetings with agent 'X' and requests for secret payments and a forged passport in Argentina, and Ball, Davidson and Baldwin met with Kindersley in 1928 to persuade him not to recount what had happened in 1924. It is incontrovertible that the Conservative high command was engaged in extremely sharp practice; and it paid dividends. As Davidson put it: 'I have no doubt that we would have got in in 1924, but we would have had a smaller majority . . . you will always find that it is when the country is scared of wild-cat schemes and wants safety that it turns to the Conservative Party.'[30] Such was the suspicion about Labour's links with communism that although Labour increased its vote by nearly a million, enough voters gave the allegation credence to sink the Labour government. The result was a massive 412-seat victory for Baldwin, with Labour down to 151 and the Liberals trailing on 118. When the new Commons assembled to debate the king's speech on 9 December, MacDonald was reduced to jesting that since the Conservatives had secured more than 400 seats with 7,500,000 votes and Labour 151 with 5,500,000, a Labour MP was worth twice as much as a Conservative and that the new Prime Minister would have to watch out for under-employed colleagues of a 'restive, changeable and somewhat conspiring disposition'.[31] Stanley Baldwin merely smiled on benignly.

On 2 July 1929 Frank Russell, the 2nd Earl Russell, who had recently been appointed parliamentary secretary in the Department of Transport (and had something of a reputation, having been tried by his peers and imprisoned for bigamy in 1901), led the Lords debate on the next Labour government's king's speech, which had been delivered that morning. The House looked rather askance at such an innovation. Normally these debates would be started by the youngest government backbencher, rather than a minister, but as the seconder, the Earl de la Warr put it, 'the Government are not in the possession of a Back Bench'.[32] Indeed, Labour had so few to choose from in the Lords that even the 84-year-old Lord Muir Mackenzie had been pressed into service as a government whip. Parmoor wound up the debate for the government as Lord President of the Council and virtually begged the opposition parties, who far outnumbered Labour in the Lords, 'to make our Constitution work, and work fairly well, in spite of the great disabilities under which the Labour Party suffer in this House'.[33] It was to prove a vain request, if only because it was addressed to the wrong quarter, for things were not that much easier in the Commons. Since 1924 MacDonald had adroitly swerved his way through the twin perils of trade union militancy in the shape of the failed General Strike of 1926 and renewed Liberal vigour under their new (old) leader Lloyd George, and had come to power after the election on 30 May with 288 seats to the Tories' 260. But it was not a majority government by a long stretch, as the Liberals held 59 seats, and although MacDonald offered to legislate for the alternative vote in an Electoral Reform Bill in exchange for Lloyd George's support (in striking parallel to the coalition deal in 2010), his Labour colleagues baulked at the idea of the fully proportional system the Liberals demanded, so the government had to live from hand to mouth. Moreover, within the party there was a considerable divergence of views on how to tackle the key issue on which Labour had fought the election: rising unemployment. The Cabinet was again a coalition, with Henderson demanding the Foreign Office, Snowden preaching deficit reduction orthodoxy at the Treasury, and the General Secretary of the National Union of Railwaymen, Jimmy Thomas, supposedly leading the economic fight. Within four months the exceptional nature of that economic battle was to become abundantly clear. On Thursday, 24 October 1929 the New York Stock Exchange suffered an 11 per cent fall. The following Monday saw a further 13 per cent fall and Tuesday another of 12 per cent. In less than a week the Wall Street Crash had stripped $30 billion from shares. Thomas jested in the Commons on 29 October that he 'always [took] the easiest way of getting out of a difficulty',[34] but when he gave details of a £42 million programme of public works to boost employment a week later his plans were attacked by Lloyd George as 'puny, pusillanimous and unintelligent' and by Colonel Wilfrid Ashley for the Tories as 'an orgy of expenditure'.[35]

The first inkling of major *internal* trouble came in January 1930 when the prosperous, debonair and impatient baronet, the MP for Smethwick and Chancellor of the Duchy of Lancaster, Sir Oswald

Mosley, presented a memorandum to the Cabinet on how to respond to the economic crisis, demanding a £200 million road-building programme to be financed by borrowing. When both the Cabinet and the parliamentary Labour party rejected his ideas (the latter by 29 to 210) he resigned as a minister and the opposition pounced, turning a debate on unemployment into a censure motion, which the government survived only narrowly on 28 May by 270 to 241, with Lloyd George abstaining. Throughout 1930 Labour haemorrhaged support in by-elections, and when it came to the party conference in Llandudno in October, with unemployment running at 2,725,000, MacDonald faced both a militant ILP group led by the Glaswegian Jimmy Maxton, and a contingent loyal to Mosley, whom conference elected to the national executive.

Mosley's membership of the party did not last long, though. In February 1931, exasperated by MacDonald's and Snowden's economic orthodoxy, Mosley launched the New Party, taking his wife Cynthia, John Strachey, William Brown, Robert Forgan and Oliver Baldwin with him to the opposition benches, reducing yet further Labour's diminishing lead over the Tories' 260. In debate after debate MacDonald and Snowden were berated and belittled by a growing band of erstwhile allies including Mosley, Maxton and Lloyd George, all of whom now supported a programme of public works financed by borrowing.

MacDonald must have breathed a sigh of relief when parliament adjourned on 31 July for the long summer break that had now become usual, due to last until 20 October. Any such relief was short-lived, though, as in early August the economic situation took a significant turn for the worse and the Cabinet was forced to consider swingeing cuts in expenditure to meet a projected deficit of £120 million. Top of the list was a proposal to cut unemployment benefit, which the TUC told the Cabinet on 20 August they would not countenance. Even so, three days later the Cabinet met and agreed the cuts by a narrow margin of twelve to nine. Such a close vote persuaded MacDonald that he had effectively lost the confidence of his government, so the next day he tendered his resignation (and that of his Labour colleagues) to the king, possibly expecting George V to ask the Conservative leader Stanley Baldwin to form a new administration. But with Baldwin out of town and Lloyd George ill, George asked Sir Herbert Samuel for his view. When the not exactly disinterested temporary Liberal leader recommended a new three-party National government, the king asked MacDonald to lead it.

All this had happened without any reference to parliament, or to the Labour party. Indeed, David Kirkwood, the Scottish engineers' leader, reckoned that MacDonald might have taken far more of the Labour party with him had he bothered to meet with them. Instead he sent the public school educated Lord Chancellor, John Sankey, who 'made a poor show, talking to us like a benevolent old gentleman who carries peppermints in his pocket to give to the poor workers'.[36] Lauchlan MacNeill Weir MP shared the sense of angry betrayal, charging MacDonald that 'without a word of consultation with his Cabinet colleagues, without even informing them of his intention to set up a National Government with himself as Prime Minister he proceeded to carry out his long-thought-out plan'.[37]

All the anger and hurt came to a peak when the Commons reconvened on Tuesday, 8 September 1931. The House was rowdy. Labour MPs, all bar thirteen of them, were suddenly on the opposition benches, their places taken by Conservatives and Liberals. Baldwin was now Lord President of the Council, and the very man who had advised the king to retain MacDonald, Samuel, was Home Secretary. Another former Conservative minister, Sir Samuel Hoare, was in charge of the India Office, the much-derided former Foreign Secretary Austen Chamberlain was at the Admiralty and the most vituperative of Labour-haters, his half-brother Neville, was Minister of Health. The first skirmish came over the mean-spirited enforced resignations of the two Labour Deputy Speakers, Sir Robert Young and Herbert Dunnico, and their replacement by MacDonald's sole nominee, the Conservative Sir Dennis Herbert. Labour tempers, already frayed at this wholesale clearout, were further inflamed by the exceptional message from the king that MacDonald had arranged to be read out, stating that the 'present condition of the National finances . . . calls for the imposition of additional taxation and the effecting of economies in public expenditure'.[38] So even before the debate on the financial situation began MacDonald had ranged the monarch, the chair, the Tories and the Liberals against his former friends, who were now led by Arthur Henderson. Even as the new Liberal Foreign Secretary, the seventy-year-old Rufus Isaacs, marquess of Reading,* defended the creation of the new government in the House of Lords, Henderson piled on the sarcasm. Henderson's quiet fury shines through the tidied-up language of Hansard. How could this new government consider itself a 'National' government when it did not include the largest party in the House? He looked long and hard into MacDonald's eyes and said: 'Never once did he look into the faces of those who made it possible for him to be Prime Minister. I venture to say that that is absolutely without precedence in the whole history of Parliament.'[39] Asquith might have demurred, but while A. V. Alexander hoped that the debate might be had without 'bitterness or rancour', Churchill, languishing in the wilderness, quipped: 'I felt as if I were listening to a family quarrel, to a bitter dispute which was going to break up a happy home.'[40]

At first MacDonald hoped to return to the Labour fold (and asserted ever afterwards that he would never join the Tories), but with the Conservatives worrying about what a delayed election might deliver once unpopular decisions had been taken, the government hastily went to the polls on 14 October. The campaign was nasty, as fratricide tends to be. Snowden was sharp and vindictive, attacking Labour's economic programme: 'This is not Socialism. It is Bolshevism run mad,' he said. There were rumours that were Labour to win there would be a run on the banks and all post office savings would be lost. Even the bishop of London, Arthur Winnington-Ingram, piled in, denouncing Labour with episcopal gravitas. Labour was not just

---

* Isaac was the first practising Jew to join the Cabinet. Samuel was also Jewish and kept a kosher household, but had abandoned his religious faith at university.

trounced; it had the living daylights punched out of it. In 1929 there had been just 99 straight two-way contests. This time there were 449. Labour got two million fewer votes, 225 fewer MPs. Among the remaining 52 Labour MPs, just one member of the Cabinet survived: George Lansbury, who became leader. Down in the boiler room of the government only a few junior ministers survived: the Solicitor-General, Cripps; the Chancellor of the Duchy of Lancaster, Clement Attlee; and the parliamentary secretary to the Ministry for Labour, Jack Lawson.

The party blamed MacDonald, of course. He had sold out. When he moaned on the hustings in his constituency in Seaham about his own finances, someone piped up: 'Lord Londonderry and them'll see you all right,' and when he tried to argue that 'your own leaders didn't give you all they promised', one person wistfully pointed out 'you were our leader' and another shouted: 'You're a traitor!'[41] That was to be the tenor of the debate for his remaining years in power. Lansbury, who was now in his sixties but often seemed considerably older, told the new House when it convened that 'it is a Government that has won office by chicanery and fraud, by the abuse of broadcasting, and by raising a panic for which each Member of it knew there was not the least justification'.[42] But Labour's attack would have been more justly directed at the parliamentary system. After all, it might seem a nice distinction to make, but the government was formed by the Prime Minister, not by the party. So if the monarch asked someone to form a government and he found more allies outside his own party than within it, then the government was his to take. The Labour party having always been more emotionally driven than either of its main opponents, the events of 1929–31 have often been recounted in terms of personal betrayal, hypocrisy and perfidy. But the truth is that, blasted by the fierce winds of international economic depression like a lonely huddle of figures on an icy heath, the government disintegrated; MacDonald, Snowden, Sankey and Jimmy Thomas were just the last men standing as the Labour party collapsed into its original constituent parts.

*

When the Commons gathered after the election in November 1931, Lansbury, looking more Edwardian than Georgian with his benevolent eyes, his grey muttonchops and his balding pate, had compared the recent election to that of 1918 when MacDonald had been 'chased out of his seat' by Lloyd George's khaki 'coupon' campaign. Fourteen years later the feeling was rather different as Clement Attlee, the most diffident and opaque of British politicians, rose to the despatch box on 15 August 1945 as the first prime minister of a majority Labour government. Two weeks earlier Churchill had been greeted by Tory MPs with a sentimental rendition of 'For he's a jolly good fellow' and Labour MPs had retaliated with 'The Red Flag'. At that point Attlee had been in Potsdam and the House of Commons had sat in the Lords Chamber, but for the first state opening of parliament after the war the House of Lords had insisted on using their own Chamber, the Robing Room that they had occupied since the bombing of the Commons being too small for the higher than usual attendance. It made for an odd day: MPs met at eleven in the morning in St Stephen's Hall, were summoned by Black Rod to hear the king's speech in the Lords, trooped back to St Stephen's, where they adjourned till four o'clock and then returned to the Lords Chamber, where Attlee announced peace with Japan and led both houses off to St Margaret's Church for a service of thanksgiving. Labour politicians sang the hymn 'O God our help in ages past' particularly lustily, as Attlee enjoyed a magnificent majority of 146.[43] Ranged behind him and spilling across the red benches was a new breed of Labour MPs. After the steady decline of the previous decade-long parliament there were 327 new members, and more than two-thirds of Attlee's colleagues were taking their places for the first time. The PLP was not as proletarian as before, either: Attlee prided himself on the fact that he had appointed twenty-eight public school boys as ministers. As the former teacher and new Home Secretary James Chuter Ede noted, 'The new Party is a great change from the old. It teems with bright, vivacious servicemen. The superannuated Trade Union official seems hardly to be noticeable in the ranks.'[44] One of the new members, Jim Callaghan, who had travelled back from active service specifically to stand in Cardiff, noted: 'To me it was a new world and I was enthralled.'[45]

The Labour rank and file might have been fresh-faced neophytes, but the officer class was long in the tooth. Attlee had been an MP for twenty-three years, party leader for ten, a Cabinet minister for six and deputy Prime Minister for four. Thanks to a prosperous upbringing as the son of a successful solicitor, he had a private income, and after studying for the law at Oxford found his vocation in social work in the East End of London. Attlee was above all things a 'parliamentary' leader. Had Britain adopted a presidential system, he would almost certainly not have become Labour leader, for he was neither gregarious nor charismatic, he published no great works of socialist theory and he formed no band of loyal followers. If Labour had needed a presidential candidate, another more rumbustious figure might have led the party from outside parliament, but in the British parliamentary system the cataclysm of 1931 gave Attlee a chance to prove his steady-as-she-goes competence. Attlee was not without steel. Like many an adept committee chairman, he knew how to get what he wanted; so when Lansbury was ill in 1934 Attlee stepped into his shoes, and when the elder man was forced out of the party leadership just before the 1935 general election Attlee was not only appointed interim leader but had a distinct advantage in the post-election leadership contest over Herbert Morrison and Arthur Greenwood in that he had kept his Commons seat in the 1931 rout. When the war came Attlee played Labour's hand astutely, assisting in the removal of the appeasers (despite having fought tooth and nail against rearmament earlier in the 1930s) and using his place in the shadow of Churchill's rhetoric to forge a parliament-led programme for change. Churchill might quip that 'an empty taxi arrived at 10 Downing Street, and when the door was opened, Attlee got out', and others would complain that he had no small talk, but with the war over people had less need for (and less time for) exuberant egotism, and Attlee's quiet domesticity and managerialism had its appeal.

Attlee was not the only politically weathered member of his Cabinet. His senior team had also proved their competence. The Chancellor, Hugh Dalton (educated at Eton and King's College Cambridge), who like Attlee had fought with distinction in the First World War, had been an MP since 1924 (apart from the common Labour hiatus from 1931 to 1935) and had served in two economic portfolios under Churchill. Herbert Morrison, the rather rougher and more ambitious new Lord President of the Council, had suffered two interruptions to his Commons career, but he had led the London Labour Party and the London County Council, and been Minister for Transport under MacDonald in 1929–31 and Home Secretary throughout Churchill's war premiership. Cripps, the President of the Board of Trade, had been expelled from the party on the eve of war for advocating a united front with the communists against fascism and had only just returned to the fold at the 1945 election, but he too had executive experience as former Solicitor-General, ambassador to Russia, Lord Privy Seal and Minister for Aircraft Production. As for the self-made, straight-talking Ernest Bevin, though he had been co-opted into the Commons as recently as 1940 to serve as Minister of Labour, he had by then spent nineteen tough years as secretary of the Transport and General Workers' Union. It was a government almost over-endowed with experience, with a trunk-full of policies and manifesto commitments at hand and a determined air about it. Moreover, just as Thomas Cromwell had opted for religious reformation by parliamentary statute, so Labour had resolved to bring in its brand of socialism by parliamentary means.

From the outset that meant driving legislation through, as became clear in the very first salvoes fired when the Commons returned to its temporary home in the Lords for the debate on the king's speech on 16 August. Churchill, suffering from one of his regular bouts of depression, began his response to the long list of Bills that had been announced in the king's speech the day before with a long discourse on foreign policy, but soon resorted to winding up Labour MPs: 'The production of new wealth is far more beneficial, and on an incomparably larger scale, than class and party fights about the liquidation of old wealth. We must try to share blessings and not miseries,' he stated, before ending in solipsistic mood:

> When we look back on all the perils through which we have passed and at the mighty foes we have laid low and all the dark and deadly designs we have frustrated, why should we fear for our future? We have come safely through the worst. 'Home is the sailor, home from sea, And the hunter home from the hill.'[46]

It all felt rather *passé*, but Attlee responded with an elegant and extensive eulogy to the wartime leader recumbent on the opposition benches, commending him for the energy with which he had suffused every element of government. Thus far Attlee was consensual, but he ended with a bit of chairman's steel. He asked not for leniency, but at least for understanding: 'To win through this critical period in our history will require, I think, the continuance of something of the spirit which won the war, a spirit which did not allow private or sectional interests to obscure the common interests of us all and the love which we all have for our native land and for our people.'[47]

Attlee had in mind the House of Lords, where Labour still had no majority. Indeed, the figures were severely stacked against him. In an upper house of 800, the Conservatives had a majority of roughly four to one over all other parties and Labour had just sixteen members – what Christopher, Viscount Addison, the Leader of the Lords, described as 'a tiny atoll in the vast ocean of Tory reaction'.[48] Samuel, now a Liberal viscount, wisely noted that 'the parliamentary situation might become very delicate and difficult unless handled with much discretion'.[49] 'Delicate' was an understatement. The Lords could scupper every single Labour Bill just as readily as they had Liberal measures at the end of the nineteenth century; and as the parliament wore on this power would grow exponentially, the 1911 Parliament Act having granted the Lords a two-year delaying power, potentially rendering a popularly elected government moribund for almost half its term. Indeed, this seemed a distinct possibility, for the Tory leader in the Lords, Viscount Cranborne – 'Bobbety' to friends and family – yet another Cecil, who would become the 5th marquess of Salisbury in 1947 and had been propelled from the Commons into the Lords under a writ of acceleration in 1941, had already made clear that his party was unhappy about the nationalization proposals in the king's speech.

Under different leadership, Labour might have inveighed against the unelected house or even sought to abolish it. But Attlee found another way. First, rather than limiting his power of patronage he extended it, creating eighty new peers (all of them hereditary, though until the lawyer William Mackenzie was made Baron Amultree in 1929 Labour peerages were all granted to men without male issue) to make some slight impression on the balance of the numbers. Then Cranborne and Addison, who was Attlee's closest ally in the Cabinet, agreed a new convention that any government Bill that had been clearly adumbrated in a party manifesto would not be sunk at either second or third reading in the Lords. As so often in parliamentary history, this 'Salisbury convention' (or, more accurately, 'Cranborne–Addison convention') only came into existence thanks to the personal experiences of those involved. Addison was now seventy-six and had started his parliamentary career as a Liberal, serving in Lloyd George's governments during and after the First World War, most notably as Minister for Health. Prompted to join Labour when Lloyd George had cancelled a housing programme to which he was committed, since then he had served briefly under MacDonald in 1930–1 and had led the small band of Labour peers since his elevation as a baron and then viscount in 1937. Most significantly, he had been a Liberal MP during the 1910–11 standoff between the two houses over the 'people's budget'. Cranborne, though twenty-four years younger than his counterpart, also had baggage. His father and his uncles had been leading figures on the losing side in 1911, and he had been Leader of the Lords for three years alongside Labour ministers in the wartime coalition. His uncle Robert, who had received the Nobel Peace Prize for his championing of the League of Nations and now sat in the Lords as Viscount Cecil of Chelwood, even took the Labour whip throughout the 1945–50 parliament. So when Cranborne and Addison framed an unwritten part of the constitutional settlement they were doing so not as arch-opponents but as settled occupants of the same piece of political turf. Both believed in a second chamber and neither rejected the hereditary principle, but both accepted that the will of the people, as pronounced in a general election, had to have the final decision. As Cranborne put it, he intended 'to make it our broad guiding rule that what had been on the Labour Party programme at the preceding General Election should be regarded as having been approved by the British people'.[50]

This self-denying ordinance worked well for three years, but in 1948 it came unstuck when Labour sought to nationalize the iron and steel industry. This measure had been directly referred to in Labour's manifesto, but in moving rejection of second reading of the Bill on 27 January Cranborne (now the marquess of Salisbury) insisted on the Lords' right to refer the matter back to the electorate. Faced with an insurmountable obstacle, Addison withdrew the Bill before the vote but resolved to change the rules of engagement, and by May had drawn up a plan to curtail the Lords' suspensory power from three sessions over two years to two sessions over one. Their lordships cared no more for the resultant Parliament Bill than their predecessors had done for its counterpart in 1911, but the government still had just enough time to use the earlier measure to push through the new one, which was taken through the Commons in three sessions (including a specially created short session from 14 September to 25 October 1948) and was on the statute book in 1949 in time for the new Iron and Steel Bill.

The senior members of the 1945 government were determined to secure their lasting legacy through a very heavy parliamentary programme. As Attlee put it: 'We had not been elected to try and patch up an old system but to make something new.'[51] So immediately after the king's speech they tabled a motion granting total precedence to government business, thereby denying anyone other than a government minister the right to see their legislative ideas debated. Herbert Morrison, who spoke to the motion as Lord President of the Council, offered the excuse that much parliamentary time was already 'mortgaged' or devoted to set pieces such as debates on government estimates, but his real reason was that the administration had an extensive programme of legislation and was determined to use its large majority to get it enacted. Jean Mann, the newly elected member for Coatbridge, reckoned that Labour MPs were told to 'avoid private members' bills, to keep quiet and vote the government's legislation through.'[52]

There was certainly a lot of it. In the first session, which ran from May 1945 to 6 November 1946, the government brought in 83 statutes, including Acts nationalizing the Bank of England and the coal industry, repealing the Conservatives' Trade Disputes Act of 1927, creating the National Health Service, introducing child, maternity and widows' benefits, increasing sickness and unemployment benefits, providing for new towns, regulating borrowing and reforming the police. The following sessions kept up the pace, with 55 new Acts in 1946–7, 68 the next year and a whopping 106 in 1948–9. In one sense the advance of the state was of a piece with R. A. Butler's Education Act of 1944, which was carried with bipartisan support (albeit somewhat reluctantly on the Conservative side). But much of the programme was deeply controversial. The first session of the parliament saw 294 divisions in the Commons, the next year there were 383 and across the six Labour years as a whole they averaged 250 per session (as opposed to just 200 divisions a year under the Conservatives between 1951 and 1964). When Aneurin Bevan, the fluent socialist–hedonist MP for Ebbw Vale, brought forward his National Health Service Bill incorporating all the voluntary hospitals plus the general practitioners, the shadow health minister, Richard Law, opposed it with a highly personal attack on the minister for being both inexperienced and 'disingenuous', and the Conservatives tabled an objection to its second reading on the third day of debate on 2 May 1946. So confident was Labour of the enduring value (and likely popularity) of the Bill that in winding up the debate as Lord Privy Seal Arthur Greenwood almost begged the Conservatives to vote against the measure. They did, but it got its second reading by 359 to 172 and by December it was on the statute book. Other Bills had a similarly tough time. Indeed, when the government's Criminal Justice Bill was amended in the Commons in April 1948 to suspend the death penalty for five years, by a tight un-whipped vote of 245 to 222 (in which Attlee voted to keep capital punishment), and their lordships overturned the amendment by 181 to 28, the government replaced Sydney Silverman's offending clause with a suspension of the death penalty in certain cases so as to save the Bill. Yet in the course of five years the government also national-ized civil aviation, cable and wireless, electricity, gas, the railways, and iron and steel; they created a national childcare service, legislated for independence for India and Burma, and abolished the workhouse and penal servitude. There was even some more parliamentary reform. The university seats and the two-member seats in the Commons were abolished along with plural voting,[53] while postal voting was intro-duced and it was made illegal to drive someone to the polls in a car (which was felt to give an unfair advantage to the car-owning classes).

The most remarkable facet of these six years was the discipline on the Labour benches. There were rebellions, but almost too few to mention. In the first session there were just ten, the most serious of which arose over an amendment to the National Insurance Bill tabled by the ubiquitous Sydney Silverman, which was supported on 23 May 1946 by thirty-two Labour MPs, including Barbara Castle and Jennie Lee. Three years later Cripps's 1949 budget came under strong attack from several Labour members, including the General and Municipal Workers' Union official and MP Mark Hewitson,[54] who threatened a fight against the Labour government by unionists 'as we have fought in the past against Tories and Tory employers'.[55] As the parliament wore on, dissent surfaced over foreign affairs too. In April 1948 D. N. Pritt, who had sat as an Independent Labour MP since his expulsion from the party in 1940 for supporting communist Russia against Finland, was joined by the communist-sympathizing barrister MP John Platts-Mills, expelled for declaring his support for the Italian communist-allied Socialist party; and the following May three of the six Labour MPs who voted against the North Atlantic Treaty, Konni Zilliacus, Leslie Solley and Lester Hutchinson, teamed up with them in a loosely affiliated Labour Independent Group. But while some might have taken the view that so large a majority justified some laxity, the Labour leadership were tough disciplinarians, and when 170 Labour MPs signed up to a motion criticizing the government's old age pension policy, Morrison delivered a stern lecture. His judgement was proved sound, for all the members of the Labour Independent Group lost their seats in the 1950 election. Independence, it seemed, was no guarantee of popularity with voters.

In the heat of the third reading debate on the Trade Disputes and Trades Unions Bill on 2 April 1946, the abundantly serious Attorney-General Sir Hartley Shawcross engaged in a favourite Labour pastime – teasing Churchill. The former Prime Minister had dared Labour to submit the issue of repeal of the 1927 trade union laws 'to the verdict of the people' and then, when the verdict was in, he had rejected it. He was, in short, like Humpty-Dumpty, who told Alice that a word means 'just what I want it to mean, neither more nor less'. Warming to his theme, Shawcross continued with his analogy. In the Lewis Carroll book, Alice had suggested that the question is whether you can make a word mean different things. 'Not so,' said Humpty-Dumpty, 'the question is which is to be the master. That's all. We are the masters at the moment, and not only at the moment but for a very long time to come.'[56] Considering the rather garbled nature of his analogy, it is highly debatable whether Shawcross intended his words to sound so defiantly triumphalist. He was, after all, one of the least partisan members of the government; of all the chief prosecutors at Nuremberg he was the least prone to grandstanding, and he would later resign from the Commons out of sheer boredom with party politics and become a cross-bench peer. Yet Labour cheered him in the Chamber, and when Patrick Gordon-Walker was elected as the new MP for Smethwick following the death in a car crash of Alfred Dobbs the day after the 1945 election, he was expressing a widely shared feeling when he declared: 'I think we're going to be in for 20 years of power ahead of us.'[57]

But sheer physical deterioration among Attlee's senior team soon meant that the government was running on empty. Key members of the Cabinet were far from young, having been born in 1869 (Addison), 1881 (Bevin), 1883 (Attlee), 1887 (Dalton), 1888 (Morrison) and 1889 (Cripps). Several suffered poor health. Addison had two major bouts of illness and died in 1951. Bevin suffered from angina, arteriosclerosis, sinusitis and high blood pressure. He drank, smoked and worked too much, took no exercise, and had to resort to a regimen of pill-popping for his heart. Cripps, meanwhile, also a strenuous worker, barely ate at all, owing in part to a medical condition deriving from the First World War and in part to a faddish attitude to diet and medicine. Dalton, who was estranged from his wife and had a fondness for articulate younger men, suffered from a string of psychosomatic ailments, including boils. Nor, for that matter, were these men full of the milk of human kindness towards one another. Indeed, they were adept mutual haters. Morrison and Bevin so disliked one another that Attlee made Bevin rather than Dalton Foreign Secretary partly to keep him out of Morrison's way. Cripps so despaired at Attlee's lack of political flair that he tried to stage a palace coup in 1947 – a coup that failed thanks to Attlee's astute decision to give Cripps a new job. And when Cripps and Bevin travelled together to America to negotiate the devaluation of the pound, they barely spoke to one another during the lengthy crossing.

Keeping up with the constant busy-ness of government is always tough, but for an administration in a hurry to drive through a large parliamentary programme the grind of Cabinet committees, Bill committees, legislative committees and votes in the Commons, in addition to the quotidian management of each minister's department, was intense. The figures make the point. In the 1945–6 session the Commons regularly sat five days a week, starting at 2.15 p.m. and finishing past midnight on twenty-three nights. The Finance Bill could be particularly gruelling. That year it took 20 hours and 29 minutes in continuous sitting through the night on 24 June 1946, and in June 1951 the Commons sat past midnight on the Tuesday, Wednesday and Thursday 5–7 June, then for a full 31 hours and 46 minutes the following Monday, completely losing the Tuesday; they continued on the Wednesday until three minutes past midnight, and then did so again on Monday the 18th (till 12.06 a.m.) and Tuesday 19th (till 4.13 a.m.). Nobody can doubt that such hours took their toll on ministers.

Just as debilitating, though, was the financial overhang of war, which soon re-opened the division between the party's constituent parts. The problem was not directly of Labour's making. In 1941 Franklin D. Roosevelt's US government had committed itself to providing substantial assistance in kind to the wartime Allied powers and had delivered $31.4 billion worth of material to the UK on the understanding that, if not destroyed in the conflict, it would be returned. This 'Lend-Lease' arrangement came to an end in 1945, and repayment began just as Britain secured a fifty-year loan of $4.4 billion from the United States to pay for Britain's ongoing war-related overseas commitments. The loan was neither as large nor as generous as Attlee had hoped; it included $650 million to pay for Lend-Lease, and came with tough conditions and a 2% interest rate.*

By the time Cripps became Chancellor of the Exchequer in 1947 (upon the resignation of Dalton, who had inadvertently let slip some of the details of the budget to a journalist before it was announced to the Commons), it was clear that there was a steadily widening chasm in the public finances, which were being stretched equally by commitments abroad, by the new welfare state payments and by the growing demands of the NHS. On one side in this debate stood Cripps, Morrison and the former civil servant Hugh Gaitskell, who, having

* The loan was only finally paid off in 2006.

been elected for the first time in 1945, was made Minister for Fuel and Power in 1947. All three men advocated paying off the American loan, redressing the balance of payments by restricting imports, holding down inflation through voluntary wage restraint, and severe budgetary trimming; then, with the balance of payments worsening, in September 1949 Cripps agreed to devalue the pound from $4.03 to $2.80, and both current and capital expenditure were slashed. To some, this planned austerity was just sound economics. But to Bevan, whose NHS budget had already trebled, it smelt of danger, especially when Morrison proposed a series of charges for NHS services. Ever a good hater, Bevan had inveighed against the Tories on the day that the NHS Act came into force, saying that 'no amount of cajolery, and no attempts at ethical or social seduction, can eradicate from my heart a deep burning hatred for the Tory Party . . . So far as I am concerned they are lower than vermin.'[58] That last phrase had earned him harsh Tory attacks, but he could muster the same venom, when required, for his party colleagues, especially any who dared to suggest limits on the unfettered budget of his NHS, which he publicly declared 'sacrosanct'.

Then came the general election, held a few months earlier than required in January 1950, and with it a Cabinet truce, or at least a ceasefire. The fall in the Labour share of the countrywide vote, at 46.1 per cent compared to the Tories' 43.5 per cent, was small, but Labour lost seventy-eight seats and Attlee was left with a majority of just six. The pressure on the senior members of the government, and the need for government unity, became all the more intense – as did the pressure on the public finances. Reappointed as Chancellor despite being ill, Cripps, who had spent much of the 1930s in such close co-operation with Bevan that they had been expelled from the party together in 1939, now insisted that if his old ally would not accept NHS charges he would have to accept a ceiling on the NHS budget. Bevan fumed inwardly, but he could hardly complain at Cripps's 1950 budget, which increased house building, cut income tax for low earners, and boosted the cash available for health and education. It was to be Cripps's last hurrah; thereafter his health rapidly deteriorated, and in October 1950 he resigned both the chancellor-ship and his seat and went off to a Swiss sanatorium to die.

Then came a series of disappointments for Bevan. He might just have hoped to succeed Cripps, but Attlee appointed the far drier, less mercurial Hugh Gaitskell (whom Bevan would later describe as a 'desiccated calculating machine') as Chancellor and in January re-shuffled Bevan out of harm's way to the Ministry of Labour, just as Bevin was carted off to hospital with pneumonia. Then, in March 1951, Attlee moved Bevin to the less onerous post of Lord Privy Seal and gave the Foreign Office not to Bevan but to Morrison, just as Gaitskell was preparing a budget. Against the background of the expensive new war in Korea and with Bevan no longer the responsible minister, Gaitskell made a new attempt to introduce NHS charges – and this time the Cabinet backed him. At the end of a long budget speech he told the House on 10 April that the Government had decided 'to introduce a modest charge in respect of some dental work and optical services'.[59] Four days later Ernest Bevin died. Bevan had promised during a hustings meeting in Bermondsey that he would not be 'a member of a government which impose[d] charges on the patient', so, under pressure from Jennie Lee and Michael Foot to offer himself for the leadership of the Labour left, on 23 April he resigned, taking the President of the Board of Trade, Harold Wilson, and the parliamentary secretary to the Ministry of Supply, John Freeman, with him. His resignation speech was full of caustic remarks about Gaitskell having united the City, pleased the Conservatives and distressed the Labour party, but it was also a pitch for the future: 'We have gone a long way – a very long way – against great difficulties. Do not let us change direction now. Let us make it clear, quite clear, to the rest of the world that we stand where we stood, that we are not going to allow ourselves to be diverted from our path by the exigencies of the immediate situation.'[60]

One wag, the long-term backbench MP for Orpington Sir Waldron Smithers, who was severally described as 'an extreme Tory out of a vanished age' and 'not insensitive to the consoling effect of alcohol'[61] (and who constantly demanded the setting up of a McCarthy-style Committee of Un-British Activities), promptly taunted Labour that since it was now in such evident disarray it must surely be the duty of the government to announce the date of the general election. In fact he did not have long to wait, as later that year, partly so as to accommodate a royal tour of the Commonwealth in 1952 which it was thought could not be undertaken while the government had such a slender majority, lest the government fall and the monarch be needed to appoint a new prime minister, Attlee had parliament recalled on 4 October 1951 during Labour's annual party conference expressly in order to prorogue it. Such a deferential acceptance of the role of the monarch was typical of the Victorian social conformist in Attlee, but it was political folly. The polls predicted a healthy victory for Churchill, but despite the sense of ennui and exhaustion Labour won 48.8 per cent of the vote, a smidgen ahead of the Tories. It was to be Labour's largest ever share of the vote, but the proportion was not matched in terms of seats, as Labour stacked up larger majorities in fewer constituencies. So Attlee returned to Westminster with just 295 MPs while Churchill, with 321, had a majority of sixteen – and was back in Number Ten, Prime Minister again at the age of seventy-six.

When Keir Hardie died in 1915 Sidney Webb wrote that 'he has not an enemy in the world',[62] and Sylvia Pankhurst simply described him as 'the greatest human being of our time'.[63] At an emotional funeral at the Maryhill crematorium in Glasgow the minister strangely made no mention of Hardie's socialism, but a year later Ramsay MacDonald gave the eulogy at the first anniversary memorial service at St Andrew's Hall and, wrapping himself in his old friend's cloak, described him as a 'great boulder of whinstone, telling of the freshness of the hills' and recalled that when Hardie returned to the Commons after the outbreak of war 'he was a crushed man, and sitting in the sun on the Terrace . . . he seemed to be looking out on a blank desolation'.[64] As MacDonald ended with the words 'such a man of rugged being and massive soul, of imperturbable courage and of mystic insight was the man who founded the ILP',[65] loud applause echoed round the hall. It was all rather different for MacDonald himself, who died on board a cruise liner bound for Latin America on 9 November 1937. Having been brought back to Liverpool on the HMS *Apollo*, his body was taken thence to Hampstead, from where the cortège set off on 27 November, the coffin draped in the Union flag, for a funeral service in Westminster Abbey conducted by the archbishop of Canterbury, Cosmo Gordon Lang. It was a state affair, with Baldwin, Neville Chamberlain and the Speaker (Edward FitzRoy) among the pall-bearers. Attlee could hardly refuse to help carry the first Labour Prime Minister to his rest, even though he complained bitterly in his own autobiography that his predecessor was prone to 'vanity and snobbery' and had perpetrated 'the greatest betrayal in the political history of this country'.[66] Large crowds gathered for the final obsequies in Lossiemouth, where MacDonald's ashes were laid alongside those of his wife Margaret. He was, all arguments aside, a Prime Minister.

Attlee's own funeral was a quiet affair at the Temple Church near the Inns of Court on 11 October 1967, but at his memorial service in Westminster Abbey on 7 November another Labour Prime Minister, Harold Wilson, read the lesson and the congregation sang Attlee's chosen hymns, Bunyan's 'Who would true valour see' and 'I vow to thee my country'. In his later days his reputation had faltered, partly thanks to his determination to remain as party leader for four years after losing the 1951 election until he could guarantee the succession to Gaitskell. Commentators on the right, such as Correlli Barnett, criticized his government as one under which the dream of a New Jerusalem 'turned to a dank reality of a segregated, subliterate, unskilled, unhealthy and institutionalised proletariat hanging on the nipple of state materialism'.[67] Yet those on the left saw new betrayals of the socialist utopia in every consensual act between 1945 and 1951. *The Times*'s obituary of 9 October 1967 typed him merely 'a successful if not a great Prime Minister', but the irony is that he would probably have been quite happy with that. He was fortunate. A public school boy with a small private income (very little of which was left at his death), he led a party of workers founded on the backs of miners, match-girls and journeying stonemasons; he was lucky to survive the 1931 election rout (by 551 votes) and lucky that his mild-mannered, laconic style perfectly suited a Cabinet of titanic personalities; but his ability to drive through change places him among the greatest of prime ministers.

In bringing working men to parliament, Labour had made MPs working men. It had further neutered the House of Lords, and it had tried to build by parliamentary statute the New Jerusalem of which they sang so lustily. In return, parliament had framed Labour – as a party of constitutional conformity, evolutionary centrism and social respectability.

THE GRAPHIC

AN ILLUSTRATED WEEKLY NEWSPAPER

No. 1,234—Vol. XLVIII.
Registered as a Newspaper.

SATURDAY, JULY 22, 1893

WITH EXTRA SUPPLEMENT
A Party Angling

Price Sixpence
By Post 6½d.

THE DEBATE IN THE HOUSE OF COMMONS ON THE HOME RULE BILL: AN APPRECIATIVE AUDIENCE IN THE LADIES' GALLERY

DRAWN FROM LIFE BY PAUL RENOUARD

Although women had long played a significant political role in public life outside parliament, their attendance in Westminster was limited to observing proceedings from above. At first they were allowed in the galleries of the Chapel of St Stephen's, then they were restricted to watching through a ventilator in a room above the Chamber, and when the new Chamber was built in 1850 a special Ladies' Gallery was added, keeping them well hidden behind a lattice. It was 1919 before a woman first stood on the floor of the Commons.

7

A Woman in the House

ON MONDAY, 1 DECEMBER 1919 two women journalists presented themselves at the reporters' gallery in the Commons for a special occasion. Four days earlier Nancy Astor had been elected MP for her husband Waldorf's former seat of Plymouth Sutton, vacated on his succeeding his father as viscount, and such was the air of excitement about the first woman taking her seat that the Chamber was full, the Strangers' Gallery was packed with women and, since Nancy was a Virginian, even the American ambassador had turned up. Just before four o'clock she appeared at the bar of the House, accompanied by her two sponsors, the Prime Minister Lloyd George and his Conservative predecessor Balfour. Dressed in a simple black skirt and jacket with a white blouse, a Tudor-style tricorn hat and a white gardenia in her buttonhole, she marched the mandatory five steps towards the mace, paused, took another five steps and bowed before taking the oath and signing on. Lloyd George later complained that Nancy had talked all the way, but his secretary and lover, Frances Stevenson, had a lump in her throat as she watched 'the first time that a woman had set foot upon that floor to represent the people'.[1] Another woman, the wife of a miners' leader, thought the sight thrilled her very soul, but worried that the grumpy faces on so many of the 'stodgy old politicians' did not portend well. 'It meant to me that the battle is not fully won.'[2] She was right. When Nancy had arrived at Paddington, a less than impressed man in the crowd shouted out: 'I didn't vote for you' – and received a trademark Astor retort 'Thank heaven for that.'[3] It was the same in the Commons. Old Sir Henry Craik was 'livid' about her election, Neville Chamberlain fretted about the 'melancholy news' and Churchill refused to speak to her for two years – and when he did, he explained that he had tried to freeze her out as when she arrived it felt as if a woman had entered his bathroom and he had nothing to protect himself with but a sponge. The misogyny continued for many years. When she suggested to the Conservative Speaker, Edward FitzRoy, that he must often wish he were dead when he listened to the bores in the House, he replied: 'On the contrary, I often wish you were.'[4] Even the *Manchester Guardian* was haughty in its condescension, pronouncing: 'Not that Lady Astor is likely to contribute anything very important to the collective wisdom of the House, though she has a shrewd wit and a woman's readiness.'[5]

Women had been actively involved in the country's political life for many centuries. According to the antiquary Sir Henry Spelman MP, who published a vast array of early documents in 1639, King Wightred of Kent invited abbesses to his council meeting in Beconceld in 694 and five of them, Mildred, Etheldride, Æte, Wilnoda and Herehwida, signed its decrees.[6] Another antiquary, Sir Henry Savile, citing a part-forged older chronicle by Ingulf, the abbot of Croyland, who died in 1109, claimed in 1596 that when Æthelwulf, king of Wessex, held a council of nobles at Winchester in 855 a new law was witnessed not just by the usual cast of bishops, barons and abbots, but by abbesses as well.[7] This is all part of parliamentary prehistory, but two antiquarian MPs from the Long Parliament, John Selden and Bulstrode Whitelocke, maintained that both Henry III and Edward I had summoned the four abbesses of Shaftesbury, Barking, St Mary of Winchester and Wilton to parliament,[8] and in 1361 Edward III is known to have summoned the dowager countesses Mary of Norfolk, Eleanor of Ormond, Philippa of March, Agnes of Pembroke, Matilda of Oxford and Katherine of Atholl, plus Anne le Despenser, Joana Fitz-Walter and Margaret de Roos, 'colloquium habere et tractatum': to hold a debate and make a treaty.[9] That does not, of course, amount to a summons to a parliament. Far from it. But it is demonstrably the case that in early English society notable women were considered worth consulting.

The wives of senior political figures had always wielded considerable power. Individual women such as Georgiana, duchess of Devonshire, had taken a rollicking part in campaigns, even speaking for candidates on the hustings. Together, the wives and daughters of peers could be a formidable force. Witness the events of 1738, when the House of Lords decided that they wanted to bar the peeresses from the gallery. According to Lady Mary Wortley Montagu 'a tribe of dames', led by Lady Huntingdon and the duchesses of Queensberry and of Ancaster, decided to try to force their way in. The Lord Chancellor locked the doors, but the women stood there for eight hours, 'every now and then playing volleys of thumps, kicks and raps against the door, with so much violence that the speakers in the house were scarce heard'. When that failed, the duchesses suggested half an hour of complete silence, which tricked the Lords into opening the doors, whereupon 'they all rushed in, pushed aside their competitors and placed themselves in the front rows of the gallery'.[10]

There were even instances of noblewomen exercising the vote. The seventeenth-century MP William Prynne, citing documents that are now lost, said in his *Brevia Parliamentia Rediviva* that 'some ladies' were annual suitors as freeholders in the county court of Yorkshire, where the knights of the shire were elected, as the indenture from 1412 was signed by Lucy, countess of Kent, and in 1415 another was signed by Margaret, the widow of Sir Henry Vavasour.[11] Often the nomination rights in rotten boroughs would fall to women. So, for instance, when Roger Copley died in 1549 he left the manor of Gatton and the right to nominate its two parliamentary burgesses to his widow Elizabeth, and in each of the six elections until her own death in 1559 she was the sole elector, on two occasions appointing her son Thomas. As a

Catholic, Thomas subsequently fled the country and died, whereupon the nomination reverted to his widow, Catherine. When it was discovered that she was involved in the Babington plot to overthrow Queen Elizabeth, Sir Francis Walsingham wrote to friends in Surrey that 'my lords of the council do understand that Mistress Copley hath the nomination of the two burgesses for the town of Gatton', and since 'it is not thought convenient, for that she is known to be evil affected, that she should bear any sway in the choice of the said burgesses',[12] he wrested control of the seats from her and gave it to Lord Burghley. Clearly Catherine's Catholicism was a far more important disqualification than her gender.

No such considerations complicated the situation in the case of the election of burgesses for Aylesbury in 1572, when Dorothy, the widow of Sir John Packington, wrote that she was appointing Thomas Lichfield and George Burden.[13] Lyme Regis even seems to have explicitly included the widows of free burgesses as electors, and three women are listed as burgesses for the town in 1577: Elizabeth, the daughter of Thomas Hyatt, Cuspina Bowden, widow, and Alicia Toller, widow. So too Cicely, the countess of Rutland, was directly involved in backing Humphrey Tufton against the eventual victor, Thomas Culpeper, as MP for Chippenham in 1614; and when Edward Montagu, the 3rd earl of Sandwich, was pronounced mentally incapable his wife the Countess Elizabeth, who, as daughter of the 2nd earl of Rochester, was a pronounced Jacobite Tory, battled with his Whig trustees for control of the Huntingdonshire seats and managed to get Anthony Hammond elected for the county in 1695 and for the borough in 1702, and William Naylor elected for the county in 1702.

All of which goes to show that prior to the nineteenth century women were not automatically excluded from the electoral process for parliament. Moreover, women were also allowed to vote in parochial, municipal and local elections – when the idea was contested in 1739 a court decided that not only could a woman elect a sexton, she could be appointed one – and throughout the nineteenth century women served as churchwardens (an elected parish post) even though in 1877

the Attorney-General, Sir John Holker, erroneously told the Commons
that such a thing was impossible.

It was highly ironic, then, that the Whig reformers' campaign for
electoral and local government reform, which culminated in the
Reform Act of 1832 and the Municipal Corporations Act of 1835,
suddenly disenfranchised women in elections for parliament and the
178 new municipal authorities, as both acts referred expressly to 'male
persons' voting. Thirty-four years later the word 'male' was removed
from the Municipal Franchise Act in relation to local authority
elections without a word of opposition and women ratepayers
returned to voting – but a court case two years later deprived married
women of the vote on the bizarre grounds that they had no legal entity
in themselves. It was not until 1888 that women were allowed to
vote in the new county and all borough councils, and not until 1907
that they could stand for election to them.

None of this prevented women from taking an active part in
extra-parliamentary politics – and many a campaign would bring
women to the very doors of the Chamber. Take Josephine Butler, for
instance. To polite society she might have been just the wife of George
Butler, a canon at Winchester Cathedral and principal of Liverpool
College, but to MPs she was a regular presence in the lobby of the
Commons from 1869 to 1886, campaigning on the Contagious
Diseases Acts, the protection of prostitutes, the age of consent and the
education of women. Such access to parliament was not uncommon.
By the time Nancy Astor arrived to take her seat, women had been
allowed both on the palace precincts and into the galleries of the
Chamber itself (which were occupied by both MPs and members of
the public) for more than two centuries. The first record of an illicit
female presence dates from 1675, when the Speaker thought he saw
some ladies in the gallery and tried to have them evicted but let the
matter drop when Sir Thomas Littleton craftily suggested that he
might have been misled by the gentlemen's 'fine sleeves'. The first
officially sanctioned female presence seems to have occurred when
Archibald Grant MP was being arraigned on 5 May 1732 for a massive

fraud that had left the Charitable Corporation insolvent to the tune of £450,000. Since a large number of women had been particularly affected, Speaker Onslow allowed women into the gallery to hear Grant declare his innocence with tears in his eyes, and witness his prompt expulsion. For the next fifty years women regularly attended at debates. Indeed, there was some consternation on 25 January 1743, as the MP John Campbell recounted to his son: 'On Monday, some gentlewomen in our gallery not being able to hold their water, let it run on Mr Dodington, and a Scots member who sat under. The first had a white duffel frock spoilt, the latter almost blinded.'[14]

Such attendance in the gallery, though, had always been on sufferance, as the Commons had protected its right to clear the Chamber of non-members when it saw fit ever since 1575, and in 1705 the exclusion of strangers was written into standing orders. The rule was only to be implemented on request, which meant that when an individual member wished to demand a secret *in camera* session (as happened regularly) he would simply declare that he could 'spy strangers' and the gallery would be cleared.* On one such occasion in 1774 when Timothy Caswall sought the clearance of the gallery he requested that 'the Ladies be excepted', but Speaker Sir Fletcher Norton none the less enforced the rule in its entirety; and when Charles James Fox stood up to move his controversial motion on 2 February 1778 against the American war following the surrender at Saratoga, such was the commotion that Captain George Johnstone demanded not just that the House be emptied of male strangers but that the sixty or so women present, including the Speaker's wife, be forced to leave as well. As John Hatsell, the chief clerk, recorded: 'This produced a violent foment for a long time; the ladies showing great reluctance to comply with the orders of the House; so that by their perseverance business was interrupted for nearly two hours.'[15]

The House was so angry about this unseemly kerfuffle that although there are occasional references to women's attendance

* See page 156 above.

thereafter, they were effectively barred from the galleries, regular access being confined to the curious space between the false ceiling that Wren had installed and the original Gothic roof, from which they could peruse sittings down below through the ventilator. The novelist Maria Edgeworth described her experience of this limited view in 1822:

> In the middle of the garrett is what seemed like a sentry box of deal boards and old chairs placed around it: on these we got and stood and peeped over the top of the boards. Saw the large chandelier with lights blazing, immediately below . . . no eye could see the Speaker or his chair – only his feet; his voice and terrible 'ORDER' was soon heard. We could see part of the treasury bench and opposition in their places – the tops of their heads, profiles and gestures perfectly.[16]

When Barry came to build the new Chamber after the fire of 1834, the principle that women had to be screened off was designed into the new arrangements: lady visitors were corralled behind a lattice grille in a separate gallery, and it was from here that the wives of successive prime ministers maintained a discreet surveillance of proceedings. This constraint did not stop women from sampling the other pleasures of the new building; tea on the terrace became such a society fixture that in 1893 the Speaker felt he had to rope off part of the terrace for men, and the practice of allowing women to peek through a tiny window in the Chamber door was so popular that it was banned after seven in the evening. The Irish MP James McGoan found the very concept of the grille 'a disgrace to the House' that reminded him of the stage-box in the Cairo Theatre 'where the ladies of the Khedive's harem are screened off from the profane view';[17] yet when Herbert Gladstone proposed getting rid of it in 1894 there was opposition from the women themselves, who liked the fact that whenever it was decided to clear the House of strangers they were left undisturbed, the women's gallery not now being considered part of the Chamber.

*

The explicit battle for women's suffrage had started in the late eighteenth century, with the publication of Mary Wollstonecraft's *Vindication of the Rights of Woman* in 1792. In 1848, while still reeling from the attacks on his support for Jewish emancipation, Disraeli had pointed out that

> in a country governed by a woman – where you allow women to form part of the other estates of the realm – Peeresses in their own right, for example – where you allow a woman not only to hold land, but to be a lady of the manor and hold legal courts – where a woman by law may be churchwarden – I do not see . . . on what reasons, if you come to right, she has not a right to vote.[18]

His was a lonely voice at the time, and though he subsequently voted for women's suffrage on four occasions while in opposition, when he came to be Prime Minister he refused to include it in his Representation of the People Bill. This prompted John Stuart Mill to table an amendment on 20 May 1867, thereby forcing the first Commons debate specifically on the subject. Mill argued that women's suffrage would not upset the balance of power between the classes and that while 'the ordinary occupations of most women are, and are likely to remain, principally domestic', he was certain that 'the notion that these occupations are incompatible with the keenest interest in national affairs, and in all the great interests of humanity, is as utterly futile as the apprehension, once sincerely entertained, that artisans would desert their workshops and their factories if they were taught to read'.[19] He little expected to win the debate that day and only had 72 colleagues with him in the division lobby, up against 196. Disraeli abstained. Mill none the less predicted eventual victory and was infuriated when the Court of Common Pleas ruled that the vote cast in a by-election that year by a shop-owner called Lily Maxwell, who had been incorrectly entered on the register of voters, was illegal. From this point on it felt like a steady war of parliamentary attrition. On 4 May 1870 the radical Liberal Jacob Bright (father of the more famous

John) managed to get a majority of 33 for a Bill (one of five attempts), but a week later it was rejected in committee and for each of the next seven attempts either there was a majority against women – of between 35 and 87 – or the Bill was simply talked into the buffers. And so it dragged on. Year after year successive private members tabled Bills. In 1878 and 1886 it was the Liberal Unionist Leonard Courtney, in 1890 it was the Conservative Robert Dimsdale, in 1892 it was another Conservative, the solicitor and ship-owner Sir Albert Rollit, in 1894 it was Charles Dilke and in 1897 an ebulliently named Unionist, Faithfull Begg, even managed a majority of 71 for a second reading (on one of his four attempts).

Local campaign groups had flourished for some time, but when this last attempt was abandoned before it got into committee, the charismatic suffragist Millicent Fawcett, wife of the radical Liberal MP Henry, launched the National Union of Women's Suffrage Societies, and 'Votes for Women' became one of the dominant themes of the new Edwardian era. Some of Fawcett's supporters were understandably in far more of a hurry, though, than the NUWSS's 'steady as she goes' strategy would allow for, and in 1903 Emmeline Pankhurst and her fiery, wilful daughter Christabel launched the more militant Woman's Social and Political Union, whose members became known as the 'suffragettes'. Meanwhile, the parliamentary attempts continued. On 16 March 1904 the Liberal Sir Charles McLaren (Jacob Bright's grandson) got a majority of 114 for a supportive Commons resolution and in February 1905 the recently elected Liberal by-election victor John Slack tabled a new Bill which was deliberately filibustered into oblivion by Henry Labouchere (junior) on 12 May and by Sir Frederick Banbury on 2 June. Day after day for month after month suffragist petitions were presented to the Commons. On 28 February 1908 the Liberal MP Henry York Stanger got the best majority yet, 179, for yet another second reading, but his Bill suffered the same fate as a Conciliation Bill* presented in 1910 by the

---

* So called because of its moderate proposal that just one million women be enfranchised.

Labour MP David Shackleton, and another from the Liberal Unionist Sir George Kemp in 1911. None got any further than second reading; the most Asquith, Churchill and Loulou Harcourt would concede was the promise of a government Bill to allow for universal male suffrage which others could, should they so wish, amend to include women.

By now patience had been stretched to breaking point and the suffragette (as opposed to suffragist) campaign was becoming militant. On 28 October 1908 a large banner was unfurled from the Ladies' Gallery and two suffragettes chained themselves to the grille shouting 'votes for women'; another suffragette stormed into the Chamber itself and shouted out slogans; a year later Marjory Hume chained herself to the statue of Viscount Falkland in St Stephen's Hall, and was detached from him only at the cost of his right spur (not his sword, as is often stated; this was broken when the statue was installed); and in 1911 Emily Wilding Davison locked herself in a cupboard in the Undercroft Chapel overnight so as to be counted as resident in the Palace of Westminster in that year's census. Bishops and archbishops were picketed. With every new delay tempers frayed further. Some of the violence seemed pointless. Stones wrapped in messages were thrown at the Prime Minister's car. The grandstand at Hurst Park racecourse was burnt down, as was Lloyd George's house – even though he was a supporter of women's suffrage – and Velázquez' painting *The Rokeby Venus* was slashed with an axe by Mary Richardson. Many of the suffragettes who were imprisoned, including Marion Dunlop, Grace Roe, Kitty Marion, Mary Leigh and Laura Ainsworth (and one man, the Labour MP Frederick Pethwick Lawrence), went on extended hunger strikes, and soon the horrific stories of their being brutally force-fed began to gain them added public sympathy.

The temperature continued to rise as the government managed to find time to drive through a series of Bills to deal with the suffragette violence but none to legislate for women's votes. When a third Conciliation Bill was introduced in 1912 by James Agg-Gardner and was lost by 208 to 222, with just enough government ministers voting against it to make a difference,[20] the WSPU went on the offensive against Asquith (who had finally voted in favour). As the government dealt ever more aggressively with the hunger strikers, one MP of two years' standing who was particularly close to the Pankhursts, George Lansbury, lost his temper with Asquith on 25 June 1912* and stormed up the Chamber from his seat below the gangway shouting: 'You are beneath contempt. You call yourself a gentleman and you forcibly feed and murder women in this fashion. You ought to be driven out of office.' As MPs heckled and the Speaker tried to restore order, Lansbury continued: 'You will go down to history as the man who tortured innocent women.'[21] Finally prevailed upon to return to his seat, he continued his tirade until the Speaker demanded that he leave the Chamber. Still he went on, and only after a fifth demand from the Speaker did he depart. His anger by no means abated, and in October he vacated his seat solely so as to fight a by-election on the issue. It was as valiant an effort in its way as that of Emily Davison, who at the following year's Derby tried to unfurl an NUWSS banner in front of the king's horse as the field galloped towards her, only to be trampled to death; but though not fatal it was just as futile, as Lansbury lost and was out of parliament for a decade. His colleague Philip Snowden then made an attempt to amend the Irish Home Rule Bill to include women, but that too was defeated in November by 173 votes, and when Asquith's promised Franchise Bill appeared but made no progress it felt as if the cause was lost. To cap it all, aware that the force-feeding of suffragettes was hardly helping its case, the government brought in the Prisoners (Temporary Discharge for Ill Health) Act to allow suffragettes to be released when they were virtually at death's door and be re-imprisoned when they recovered – a measure that came to be sarcastically referred to as the 'cat and mouse' law.

Then came the war. The WSPU immediately suspended its militant campaign, but with women playing key roles on the home front, notably in munitions manufacture, objections to female

* Not the 26th as often stated.

suffrage looked even more anachronistic. In 1916 the government agreed to set up a Speaker's conference on parliamentary reform under Speaker James Lowther, who was an opponent of women's suffrage but none the less included two of the NUWSS's closest allies, John Simon and Willoughby Dickinson – and replaced four Conservatives, who foolishly resigned over the radical direction of the conference, with reformers. The conference ended up with a vote fifteen to six in favour of women's suffrage, but twelve to eight against full equality, and a recommendation that only older women – especially mothers – be given the vote. This was still not the end of the matter, as a hundred Conservative MPs signed up to a campaign against any such legislation, and although the arch-Tory president of the Local Government Board Walter Long was persuaded to support this limited reform for fear of a more radical option, when Lloyd George replaced Asquith as Prime Minister he brought into the Cabinet two opponents of reform, Lord Curzon and Lord Milner. The Cabinet finally agreed to support legislation on 26 March 1917 only on the condition that there would be no whip on the women's franchise clause. When a Commons motion was debated two days later, while there was a large majority for reform (343 to 64, including tellers), and Bonar Law and 78 other Conservatives voted in favour, every opponent was a Conservative. When the resultant Representation of the People Bill, which was primarily aimed at introducing universal male suffrage, was presented as a House rather than a Government Bill, it included two provisos in its women's franchise clause: that in order to be entitled to vote, women had to be over thirty and either local government electors or married to local government electors. Yet when this far from perfect 'women's clause' was carried in the Commons by an even larger majority (385 to 55) on 19 June it was difficult to understand quite what the fuss had been all about. Even Curzon remained silent when the measure came to the Lords, and it was passed into law by 134 to 71. Henceforth some 8,400,000 women would be allowed to vote.

The one point that everyone had forgotten to raise was whether women were now entitled to sit as MPs, a question which was resolved only when the Parliament (Qualification of Women) Act was tabled by Herbert Samuel, adopted by the government and passed in double-quick time in November 1918,[22] once the dissolution of parliament had already been agreed. Consisting of just twenty-seven words,[23] it is the United Kingdom's shortest statute.

For some extraordinary reason the immediate issue that wound the men up on the arrival of Nancy Astor in December 1919 was the question of whether she would wear a hat to speak in the Commons. The issue was the supposedly long-standing custom of the House that a man sat in the Chamber with his hat on, but spoke 'uncovered' – except when making a point of order during a division, when the member should retain his top hat and speak seated (a tradition that lasted into the twenty-first century). What with hatpins and veils, this was not so simple for a woman. In actual fact the men (and their fascinated colleagues in the press) were talking nonsense. It had certainly been the case that men had worn hats in the Chamber since the sixteenth century, with fashions changing through successive generations, but the various pictures and engravings of parliament rarely show more than a dozen MPs wearing hats of any kind. Leaving aside the artistic licence that may have led Karl Anton Hickel to portray Pitt, Fox and Addington hatless, there is just one painting (that of Speaker Onslow and Prime Minister Walpole) that shows every MP wearing a hat – in this case a cocked hat atop a periwig. That MPs *had* to speak 'uncovered' is certainly true, but the tradition that MPs had to wear hats may be no more than another Victorian affectation dressed up as tradition. In any case, what hat-wearing there was declined further when the new parliament opened in 1852, ministers and whips deciding to leave their hats in their new offices and – apart from the Financial Secretary to the Treasury and the Chancellor of the Exchequer – to sit and speak bareheaded. In 1856 the principal doorkeeper of the Commons maintained that 'most of the members sit covered',[24] but even he admitted that Disraeli never wore his hat in the House.

There was a deal of fashion snobbery. When the republican Irish nationalist John Martin arrived in 1871 he refused to wear a hat 'with a crown' and insisted on a 'slouch hat', to which Speaker Denison so objected that he preferred he sit in the Commons un-hatted; and when another Irish member wore a straw hat during a Home Rule Bill debate in the summer of 1893 the Attorney-General Sir Charles Russell told him: 'You're a damned ass; go and eat that straw hat of yours.'[25] The big change came with the 1906 parliament, as many of the influx of first-time MPs left their hats downstairs in the cloakroom.

Since Austen Chamberlain, like most nineteenth- and twentieth-century Chancellors before him (apart from Bonar Law in the First World War), continued to insist on wearing a top hat in the Chamber, when Lady Astor walked past the Treasury bench towards the Speaker after signing the roll, he was not sure whether to tip his topper to her, as he would do if they had met in the street. Only seven years later, though, the longstanding lobby journalist* Michael MacDonagh noted that the 'House of Commons has become almost entirely bare-headed',[26] as just about the only male MP to wear a hat was the Father of the House, T. P. O'Connor. Some suggested that since women were now granted licence to keep their hats on when speaking in the Commons, convention had been thrown to the winds and it was there-fore the arrival of women that had killed off parliamentary hat-wearing, but in fact proportionately more women (three out of the eight) than men still wore hats in 1926, and men's hats had been in decline for fifty years before Lady Astor's arrival.

The women had to put up with much more than hypocritical nonsense about their attire. From the outset the men behaved like naughty boarding-school children with matron, teasing the early women MPs with deliberate suggestiveness. Take Sir John Rees, who

---

* Journalists who worked full-time on reporting both parliamentary proceed-ings and wider political stories had a gallery of their own in each House and enjoyed privileged access to the lobby. In 1852 the Commons press gallery accommodated just over 30 people. By the Second World War it could hold 69, and when the new Chamber was built after the bombing, the press demanded, and got, 95 seats and extensive new facilities.

knew that as a well-known abstentionist Lady Astor would be making her maiden speech after him in a debate about alcohol licensing. Staring directly at her, he ended his speech: 'I do not doubt that a rod is in pickle for me when I sit down, but I will accept the chastisement with resignation and am indeed ready to kiss the rod.'[27] Astor bested him, replying that Rees had gone 'a bit too far. However, I will consider his proposal if I can convert him.'[28] Often, though, the male members would guffaw at the women as if they were too simple to be aware of any double entendre. Thus, during questions about the falling birth rate, Lady Astor asked one minister whether he was 'aware that in Italy Mussolini coupled with the Pope has been unable to redress the birth rate?'[29] Considering her capacity for tart rejoinders, she would have known precisely what she was doing, but the men sniggered, as they did when Eleanor Rathbone, the equally sharp independent MP for Combined English Universities, said: 'We have ante-natal treatment and we have post-natal treatment: but we still have these appalling figures.'[30] And so it went on, as Dame Irene Ward, the unmarried Tory Tyneside MP, was to find when she said: 'Many of us are good at poking our own Ministers. It is much easier to poke Ministers on one's own side than it is to poke hon. Members on the other side,'[31] and, when complaining about the delay in providing new uniforms for women members of the armed forces, asked a defence minister how long he was going 'to hold up the skirts of the Wrens for the convenience of the sailors?'[32] The men delighted in what they saw as absent-minded gaffes, apparently unaware of the women's sly humour. And since Labour had used the slogan 'Labour stands for no sex in politics' in the 1918 election, it was a bit rich to laugh at Lady Astor when she said: 'I am not standing before you as a sex candidate.'[33]

The truth was that, although women repeatedly denied it in public, the Commons was stuffed with resentful, patronizing misogynists. A classic instance was that of Oliver Lyttelton, later Viscount Chandos, Churchill's wartime President of the Board of Trade, who grandly opined 'that during my fourteen years in the House of Commons [1940–54] there was not an effective lady parliamentarian'.[34] Considering that two of the most striking parliamentary performers of the century, Jennie Lee and Barbara Castle, were MPs during that time, this was a fatuous claim. He had plenty of fellows, though. On 20 March 1962 Charles Doughty, the Conservative MP for Surrey East, opined that it would be a problem if a jury consisted mostly of women as 'women are undoubtedly rather more emotional than men'. He did at least have the grace to tell Judith Hart that he meant 'no disrespect to any Honourable Lady in the House',[35] but his condescending insincerity was clear for all to see.

The one refuge the women had was their own company – indeed, it was rather rudely enforced on them by the physical practicalities of the House. The men had the smoking room, ministerial offices, toilets aplenty and even bathing facilities. For the ten women in 1928 there was just a dressing room with 'a wash-stand, a tin basin, a jug of cold water, and a bucket',[36] attached to a tiny room overlooking the terrace that had originally been allotted to Nancy Astor. The press enviously described it as wafted by the breezes from the Thames, but the women called it 'the tomb'. Uninviting as it sounds, it was their only bolt-hole, as the rest of parliament was very much a male preserve with bars and restaurants where men caroused, and where women were no more welcome than at any of the gentlemen's clubs in Pall Mall. From the outset Nancy Astor restricted herself to the Chamber and 'the tomb', as did others, but when Ellen Wilkinson arrived in 1924, she drew gasps from some of the men by venturing unaccompanied into the members' dining room. These cramped circumstances threw the early women MPs together and they provided mutual support to one another across the party divide, occasionally even cooperating in cross-party political campaigns, as when Wilkinson, Rathbone and the duchess of Atholl travelled together to Spain in April 1937 and came back equally determined opponents of British non-intervention. That is not to say that the women MPs adopted identical positions: Nancy Astor's suggestion of a women's caucus was robustly rejected by Labour women MPs. Even within a party the women quite naturally took their own views. Ellen Wilkinson, for instance, argued at the 1928

Labour Women's Conference that since birth control affected all classes, it was not a matter for Labour, whereas both Dorothy Jewson and Dr Edith Summerskill braved the wrath of the churches to campaign for family planning advice – and respectively lost their seats at the subsequent elections in 1924 and 1935. Moreover, there were several electoral contests between women. Islington East was held by Ethel Bentham for Labour from 1929 until her death in 1931, when she was replaced by Leah Manning, but when it came to the general election that same year the Conservatives' Thelma Cazalet, who had come third in the by-election with just 7,182 votes, saw her vote rise by more than 20,000 and won with a landslide majority of 14,110. Another Conservative woman, Irene Ward, beat Margaret Bondfield in Wallsend in 1931, while Cannock was represented by both Sarah Ward for the Conservatives from 1931 to 1935 and Jennie Lee for Labour from 1945 to 1970; and when Nancy Astor retired in Plymouth Sutton in 1945, it was another woman, Lucy Middleton, who won the seat.

Some of the men were alarmed by the idea of confrontations between two women in the Chamber. As Jean Mann, a Scottish MP for fourteen years from 1945, put it, it was commonplace for two men to attack one another, but if she were ever to confront one of the Tory women, the men would whisper: 'My dear, if you ever become a mother, please can I have one of the kittens?'[37] But when Margaret Bondfield became the first woman to enter the Cabinet, as Minister of Labour in 1929, it became inevitable that there would be direct confrontations, and over the years there were several high-volume rows between women members. During the 1940s and 1950s Edith Summerskill was frequently attacked by female opponents when she was Minister of Food, Priscilla Grant and Jean Mann were regularly pitted against each other, and several of the Labour women MPs took particular exception to the former factory welfare officer turned Conservative Under-Secretary at the Ministry of Pensions, Edith Pitt. Jean Mann called Pitt a coward for not allowing her to intervene in a debate (and had to withdraw the remark), and Bessie Braddock pounced on her attempt to quell demands for an increase in

PARLIAMENT: THE BIOGRAPHY

retirement pensions with the numbers – 'there are, at present, 4,600,000 of them and by the end of 1958 that figure will have gone up to about 5,200,000' – by bellowing across the chamber: 'Aye, if the Government have not starved them all to death by then.'[38] The Deputy Speaker tried to calm things down, but the two women carried on haranguing each other all the way to 'the tomb' until Viscountess Davidson intervened to bring peace.

Such clashes as these terrified many of the men, who would jest that they had come to parliament to avoid women rather than listen to them, and who feared more than anything else confronting a woman in debate lest they appear domineering – or be roundly defeated. The women had no such qualms, as Jennie Lee made clear from her very first outing. She was the youngest MP and a woman, but that did not stop her from lambasting Churchill's budget for its 'cant, corruption and incompetence' in her maiden speech. Churchill was impressed.

In view of all this, it is unsurprising that the number of women members increased only very slowly. Between 1918 and 1928, when the vote was extended to all women over twenty-one, just eleven were elected (the first of whom, Countess Markiewitz, as a Sinn Féin member never took her seat). On the Conservative and Liberal benches, several women entered parliament to replace their husbands in one way or another. Thus Nancy's first female colleague was the Liberal Margaret Wintringham, who won the Louth by-election caused by her husband's death in June 1920. Likewise in 1922, when Hilton Philipson's election as National Liberal MP for Berwick-upon-Tweed was overturned on petition owing to fraud by his agent, his wife, a famous music-hall actress called Mabel Russell, won the seat and held it (as a Conservative) until 1929, when she decided to return to the stage. So too the talented Katherine Stewart-Murray was MP for fifteen years from 1923 for West Perth and Kinross, the successor seat to that which her husband the 8th duke of Atholl represented up until his elevation to the Lords. This new way of keeping a seat in the family was practised twice in succession in the case of Gwendolen Guinness, the countess of Iveagh, who herself took over her husband's seat of Southend on his succeeding his father as earl, then retired in 1935 and rather charmingly handed the seat over to her son-in-law Henry 'Chips' Channon. It was a pattern that was to continue for decades. When the Labour Cabinet minister Noel Buxton joined the Lords in 1930, his wife Lucy took over his North Norfolk seat, just as Joan Davidson (who was Baron Northchurch in her own right but, solely because of her gender, was not thereby entitled to take a seat in the Lords) did when her husband was made a viscount in Baldwin's resignation honours in 1937; that same year Keir Hardie's brother George died and his Glasgow Springburn seat was taken by his former shop-girl wife Agnes. The Second World War brought two more such instances of widows taking up their husbands' seats: Beatrice Rathbone took over Bodmin after her husband John was killed in the Battle of Britain in December 1940, and Violet Bathurst, Lady Apsley, who was confined to a wheelchair following a hunting accident, became MP for Bristol Central in 1943 on the death in action of her husband. The tradition continued well into the late twentieth century: Llin Golding (1986–2001), Irene Adams (1990–2005) and, after a three-year gap, Ann Cryer (1997–2010) all followed their husbands into the Commons. On two early occasions women even engaged in a holding operation for their husbands. Hilda Runciman, the daughter of a Liberal MP, was elected for St Ives in a by-election in 1928 and the following year ceded the seat to her husband Walter, Asquith's former President of the Boards of Education and of Trade. Walter managed to secure himself another spell at the Board of Trade and a viscount's coronet, but when Hilda tried again in her own right, she lost the nearby seat of Tavistock by just 152 votes. Similarly, when Ben Spoor, the Labour MP for Bishop Auckland, died in late 1928, Hugh Dalton had already been selected as the Labour candidate; but since he was the sitting member for the marginal seat of Peckham, his wife Ruth ran in the by-election on 7 February and kept the seat warm for him for ninety-two days, a record for parliamentary brevity equalled only by the SNP's Margo MacDonald in 1974.

It would be wrong to dismiss these women as 'also-rans', not least because both halves in each of these marriages clearly thought of politics as a shared endeavour and several of the women had highly effective parliamentary careers. None the less, in that first decade of women in parliament a striking difference opened up between the married and unmarried women MPs largely along party lines. Most of the Conservative and Liberal women MPs of these years were wealthy, titled and married (and five of the seven had children), whereas not one of the four Labour women was married and three of them had worked prior to their election, one as a teacher, one as a trade union official and one as both. Politics was their life. Susan Lawrence, for instance, the chain-smoking daughter of a wealthy London solicitor, had started political life as a Conservative member of the London County Council but, prompted by her fury at the treatment of the LCC's cleaners, she had joined the Fabians and the Labour Party in 1912 and, having become a Labour alderman in Poplar in 1919, stood in a by-election in Camberwell North West on 31 March 1920 as part of a deliberate Labour campaign to capitalize on the voting power of newly enfranchised women. The very next day Margaret Bondfield, the diminutive shop worker turned trade union activist, who had exposed the horrific working conditions of girls in the major West End stores as effectively as Annie Besant had done in a previous generation for the match-girls at Bryant and May, and had become the first female member of the TUC General Council from 1918, stood in the Northampton by-election occasioned by a coalition Liberal MP's appointment as a minister. Both women were unsuccessful in 1920 and again in 1922, and Lawrence was imprisoned for several months as one of the Poplar councillors who had mounted a 'rates rebellion' against the unjust imposition of rates on their deprived borough in 1921, but resilience paid off for them both in 1923. Not only were both elected, Lawrence for East Ham North and Bondfield for Northampton, but Bondfield was immediately made a parliamentary secretary at the Ministry of Labour and Lawrence a parliamentary private secretary at the Board of Education. The government, the parliament and their seats lasted a mere nine months, but both were returned in by-elections in 1926, Lawrence again representing East Ham North and Bondfield, Wallsend. In 1929 Ramsay MacDonald made Bondfield Minister of Labour (and thereby the first woman Cabinet member and privy councillor) and Lawrence a parliamentary secretary in the Department of Health. These were not backroom appointments. Indeed, Bondfield found herself at the heart of the Labour schism in 1931, when she and Lawrence lost their seats. Since Bondfield had declared her sympathy for MacDonald but remained in the Labour Party, she not only failed to get re-elected as an MP but lost her seat on the TUC as well.

Nobody would ever have thought to question a male MP's marital status, but these early Labour women, who had sacrificed much to get to parliament, faced subtle criticism even from their own side. Clement Attlee recounted that when Lawrence was out of parliament she felt terribly exiled from her 'happy home',[39] as if she was a little unhinged, and Beatrice Webb classified herself as a member of 'the old order of irreproachable female celibates'.[40] But Bondfield was explicit in her autobiography about the decision she had made: 'I concentrated on my job. This concentration was undisturbed by love affairs . . . I had no vocation for wifehood or motherhood, but an urge to serve the Union – an urge which developed into "a sense of oneness with our kind". I had "the dear love of comrades".[41] Though she had criticized the campaign for votes as the 'hobby of disappointed old maids whom no-one had wanted to marry',[42] she herself never married. As for how they presented themselves, Lawrence was reputed to be so indifferent to her personal appearance that she sent round several stores for inexpensive dresses and when they were presented to her barely looked up from her papers before pointing to one with her pencil. This was a rather different attitude from Vera Woodhouse, the wife of Lord Terrington, who told the *Daily Express* when standing for Wycombe in 1923 that 'If I am elected to Westminster I intend to wear my best clothes. I shall put on my ospreys and my fur coat and my pearls.' She inexplicably sued the paper for libel, only to be told that she had not suffered 'a farthing's worth of damage'. Despite losing her legal battle, she won the seat in December 1923 and had nine months as a be-pearled Liberal MP.

Attitude to personal attire was just one of the ways in which this group of women pioneers were far from homogeneous. Three of the four Labour women from the first decade were graduates, for instance, whereas only one out of the seven Conservative and Liberal women had been to university – a difference that was to be repeated between 1929 and 1944, when just two out of thirteen Conservative women MPs were graduates compared to eight out of their twelve Labour counterparts. The first Conservative women tended to come from relatively similar social backgrounds, though not all so elevated as the duchess and two viscountesses among them; by contrast, the nine Labour women elected in 1929 were a thoroughly eclectic bunch. Susan Lawrence was returned for the third time in a row, and the four-foot-something Mancunian redhead Ellen Wilkinson, who had briefly been a founding member of the British Communist Party and hung a portrait of Lenin over her bed for inspiration, for the second. Alongside them were the 68-year-old longstanding suffragette and GP Ethel Bentham, the immeasurably posh Edith Picton-Turbervill of Ewenny Priory and the even wealthier recent Conservative convert Lady Cynthia Mosley. Another longstanding NUWSS supporter, Mary Hamilton – a former university lecturer who had been forced to resign her post when she married a colleague – won Blackburn at the age of forty-seven and became PPS to Clement Attlee. By contrast, the sparky Jennie Lee was just thirty-one and schooled in the mining towns of Fife; with little more than a large Gladstone bag to her name, she had to rely on the hospitality of Sir Charles Trevelyan when she first arrived in London until she could find a tiny studio flat in Dean Street in Soho. Several of the early women MPs had strong religious beliefs, Picton-Turbervill as an Anglican who believed in a 'Christ-centred' faith, Bentham as a Quaker, Bondfield as a Congregationalist, Astor as a Christian Scientist. Picton-Turbervill was also perfectly prepared to issue a challenge to those who thought close friendships between women unnatural or unwholesome, declaring in her autobiography that a loving friendship between women could be 'as deep, as beautiful, and as exhilarating as any human relationship'.[43]

What impact did these early women MPs have? Many became effective ministers, including the duchess of Atholl, who was a bright parliamentary secretary to the Board of Education for five years, and Jennie Lee, the first Secretary of State for the Arts, who created the Open University. The Conservative Florence Horsbrugh was such a successful parliamentary secretary to the Minister of Health in 1939 that when the Tory candidate in Moss Side died during the 1950 election she was parachuted in for the by-election, won it, and remained the constituency's MP until she died in 1959. Likewise Priscilla Grant, elected in 1946 as a very glamorous 31-year-old widow, suffered quiet wolf-whistles when she took her seat and in 1948 married the impossibly handsome son of the author of *The Thirty Nine Steps*, Johnnie Buchan, 2nd Lord Tweedsmuir, but none of this stopped her becoming parliamentary under-secretary (as an MP) and a minister of state in two departments (in the Lords) in Ted Heath's government. Often, these women brought issues to public attention that men had long ignored: witness Rathbone's early speech on female circumcision in Kenya, or Manning's campaign for the victims of the Spanish Civil War. On occasion they won specific legislative battles. Astor, whose speeches could wander rather disturbingly from the point and whose politics veered towards casual anti-semitism and Nazism in the 1930s, none the less got the drinking age raised to eighteen. Eleanor Rathbone's long campaign for family allowances paid directly to women, begun in 1918, finally bore fruit in 1945. Despite sitting for just two years, Picton-Turbervill ensured that pregnant women could no longer be sentenced to death or executed, Mabel Philipson steered through the registration of nursing homes in 1927, and Priscilla Grant and her husband jointly engineered the Protection of Birds Act 1954.

In 1923 Astor whimsically reflected that 'pioneers may be picturesque figures, but they are often rather lonely ones',[44] and it was true that women could often feel depressed by the sheer slog of sitting in a male-dominated House. Sometimes an external calm masked an internal maelstrom. The *Herald* might applaud a Barbara Castle appearance – 'A woman in a white frock coat stood undaunted for 20 minutes in the House of Commons last night against the concerted attempts of 200 Tory men MPs to shout and laugh her down'[45] – but according to Leah Manning, Castle had a miserable time in the early days of the 1945 parliament as 'her very success as a young member aroused jealousy ... [and] more than once I found the girl ... vulnerable and in tears in the Lady Members' room'.[46] And there were personal tragedies. Bentham died after just two years in parliament and Marion Phillips succumbed to stomach cancer in 1932. The Conservative Mavis Tate was elected in 1931 for Willesden West and in 1935 for Frome, and gained a reputation as a fiery speaker, albeit in a cut-glass accent. Her mental health, though, suffered and after a breakdown in 1940 she was permanently destabilized by both a searing visit to Buchenwald at the end of the war and by losing her seat. The Pathé footage of her very smartly attired visit to the death camp is all the more disturbing because it was by gas that she killed herself in 1947. And for all Ellen Wilkinson's success as education minister in the 1945 Cabinet, her emotional life was unhappy. Never married, she had a couple of affairs, with the Labour MP John Jagger and with Herbert Morrison, who was estranged from his wife but reluctant to divorce her. Probably out of frustration with Morrison, Wilkinson took an overdose of barbiturates in February 1947. Morrison, ashamed or frightened, did not even attend her funeral.

If Nancy Astor's arrival had heralded a new era in parliament's history, the event itself was echoed on 21 October 1958, when the first women took their places in the upper house. For the one issue that had perturbed some members of both houses about the fast-tracked Parliament (Qualification of Women) Act had been the fact that it applied only to the Commons. Indeed, an amendment to extend it to the Lords tabled by Viscount Haldane had been defeated in a poorly attended House of Lords by thirty-three votes to fourteen on

15 November 1918. Anomalies in the ramshackle British constitutional settlement have never raised much concern, and if it had not been for the very determined campaign of one woman, this recondite niche in parliament's history might never have been spring-cleaned. But Margaret Mackworth was an exceptional woman, endowed with a powerful self-confidence by her doting father, D. A. Thomas, who had inherited his father's businesses, including his collieries, in the Rhondda in 1880 before he had even finished his university degree. Despite growing up in the Welsh-speaking chapel-going valleys of south Wales, 'D.A.' had little time for religion and soon made a prosperous and unconventional business career before being elected as a Liberal MP for Merthyr Tydfil in 1888. By all rights as a coal-owner he might have expected to lose his seat when the Lib-Lab MPs started appearing, but in the pit strike of 1898 he backed the miners in a successful bid to keep his own mines open, and he not only consistently topped the poll in Merthyr all the way through to 1910 but spent a whole decade in the two-man seat alongside Keir Hardie. That year of 1910, though, went badly for Thomas. It began well, with victory in the more marginal seat of Cardiff in the January election; but then came the strike at his Ely Pit in Penygraig, when his attempts to break the strike were followed by the violence of the Tonypandy riots. Thereafter, bitter at not being offered a ministerial post and suffering from poor health, he retired from the Commons at the second 1910 election, aged fifty-four.

Margaret, meanwhile, by now in her mid-twenties, was busy making a name for herself as an active member of the Welsh branch of the WSPU. In 1910 she jumped on the running board of the Prime Minister's moving car; in 1913 she tried to blow up a postbox in Risca Road, Newport, and when she was sent to prison for three months for refusing to pay the fine she went on hunger strike. D.A. had immense confidence in his only child, initially paying her £1,000 a year to work in his offices in Cardiff docks, and then handing over his newspaper businesses and nearly twenty other companies (including Sanatogen) to her direct control. So inseparable did they become (despite her rather unfulfilling marriage to Sir Humphrey Mackworth in 1908) that when Lloyd George put D.A. to work as a British emissary to the United States in the First World War, he insisted on taking his daughter with him. (It was a decision that nearly cost them their lives: they travelled on the RMS *Lusitania* in May 1915 and only narrowly survived its sinking by a German U-boat. Margaret noted that the *Cardiff Evening News* had carried the headline 'Great National Disaster, "D.A." Saved.'[47]) In recognition of his wartime efforts D.A. was made a baron in 1916, and when he was offered an upgrade to a viscountcy at the start of 1918 he insisted that it should come 'with special remainder to his daughter and her heirs male'. So when he died a few months later on 3 July 1918, Margaret became the 2nd Viscountess Rhondda *suo jure*, in her own right. By now a woman of considerable fortune and undoubted character, she had no intention of leaving matters there. So, once the Sex Disqualification Removal Act, with its declaration that 'a woman shall not be disqualified by sex or marriage from the exercise of any public function', had been passed in 1919, she demanded the right to sit in the Lords. At first the Lords Committee of Privileges supported her plea, but when the misogynist Lord Chancellor, F. E. Smith, Lord Birkenhead, asked the committee to look again at the matter, they capitulated and resolved that since the letters patent granting the viscountcy entailed the seat (as opposed to the title) on heirs male, she was still barred. Margaret did not give up, thrusting a pre-prepared Bill into the hands of Nancy Astor's husband, the viscount, who presented it in the Lords year after year, and even got within spitting distance of a majority in 1925.

Then came a major piece of historical irony. The Sex Disqualification Act of 1919 had started life as a Labour, opposition Bill in the Commons and had been transposed into a rather reluctant government Bill in the Lords. But when, thirty years later, the virtually Labour-free House of Lords finally passed a resolution allowing women to take their seats in the upper house on 27 July 1949 by forty-five votes to twenty-seven, the Labour peers Addison, Stansgate and Jowitt voted against it and Labour refused to legislate for such a measure out of dislike for the hereditary principle. It was instead a Conservative peer, the 2nd marquess of Reading, who tabled the successful resolution. The issue was hardly to the fore when the Conservatives came to power in 1951, but in 1958 Harold Macmillan's government, which was well endowed with patricians, introduced a Life Peerages Act, allowing both men and women to be appointed life peers.

So it was that finally, nearly forty years after Viscountess Rhondda had been turned away, the first two women took their seats in the Lords. As Hansard put it, 'Stella, Marchioness Dowager of Reading, D.B.E., having been created Baroness Swanborough, of Swanborough in the County of Sussex, for life' and 'Barbara Frances, wife of George Percival Wright, Esquire (known as Barbara Wootton), having been created Baroness Wootton of Abinger, of Abinger Common in the County of Surrey, for life' were introduced. There was a further irony here. Stella Charnaud had been secretary to the Viceroy of India, Rufus Isaacs, the marquess of Reading, and had then married him when his first wife died. After a brief spell as Foreign Secretary in 1931, Reading had died in 1935 and been succeeded by his son from his first marriage, Gerald, the 2nd marquess – who moved the 1949 resolution of which his stepmother was to be the first political beneficiary.

The two women presented on 21 October 1958 could not have been more different. Stella was a large woman with a booming contralto voice and an imposing manner. Although she had certainly won her own independent spurs as the founder and chairman of the Women's Voluntary Service for Civil Defence (which became the WRVS in 1966), serving as vice-chair of the BBC and endowing several newer universities, she already had a title when she was made a baroness. By contrast, Barbara Wootton was an academic sociologist and criminologist, the petite daughter of two Cambridge classicists, who had been a conscientious objector in the Second World War and worked as a researcher for the TUC and the Labour party. Far from conventional, she was a humanist who supported doctor-assisted euthanasia and the legalization of cannabis, and referred to the new institution she had just joined as a 'creaking contrivance'. Stella was a wealthy woman, but Barbara worried about the cost of taking her seat. As she recounted in her autobiography,[48] it was her local car mechanic who suggested she speak to a peer in the neighbourhood who was rumoured to be ill, to ask if she might borrow his robes for her introduction. So it was that she joined the Lords clad in the ermine robes of the diminutive former Governor of the Bank of England, Thomas, Baron Catto.

The arrival of women life peers was a victory of sorts, but it was hardly egalitarianism sweeping all before it. One of the others in the first batch of women peers was Mary Curzon, who had inherited the title of Baron Ravensdale from her father, the former Viceroy, and was made Baroness Ravensdale for life to enable her to take her seat. And the last of the four ennobled in 1958 was Dame Katherine Elliott, who was not only the daughter of a baronet, but also the younger sister of Asquith's wife, Margot, and the widow of a former Conservative MP and minister. She had just failed to get elected to the Commons for her husband's former seat of Glasgow Kelvingrove, but a damehood and a seat in the Lords came in rapid succession, and she was to be the first woman to speak in the Lords since Queen Victoria.

Barbara Wootton ended her autobiography with an encomium on politics.

> Politics, they say, is the art of the possible. In half a century of public and professional life I have not found it so. The limits of the possible constantly shift, and those who ignore them are apt to win in the end. Again and again I have had the satisfaction of seeing the laughable idealism of one generation evolve into the accepted commonplace of the next. But it is from the champions of the impossible rather than the slaves of the possible that evolution draws its creative force.[49]

She could have been speaking specifically of the campaign for women's parliamentary emancipation. The female suffragists of the Victorian era passed without seeing women vote or sit in parliament. The early women MPs were reluctant to pursue women's issues and fought shy of anything that looked or sounded like feminism. Margaret, Viscountess Rhondda died three months before the Life Peerages Act gained royal assent, and the hereditary *suo jure* peeresses did not get to take their places in the Lords until 1963, when even that bastion of Conservatism, David Maxwell Fyfe, Lord Kilmuir, admitted that 'the exclusion of hereditary peeresses from this house is something of which we have all been secretly ashamed'.[50] Neither that minor reform, nor equal pay, nor free contraception and child care, nor legal abortion, nor even women's suffrage could ever have happened without the 'champions of the impossible'.

David Lloyd George, here seen assisting Herbert Asquith in handing out coronets and titles to wealthy supporters, is often typed as the most flagrant exemplar of the sale of honours, but when the House of Lords agreed in February 1914 that 'a contribution to Party funds should not be a consideration to a Minister when he recommends any name for an honour to His Majesty' both the Liberals and the Conservative and Unionist Party were highly active in the trade. The comment of one peer, that the motion was merely 'pious' and 'slightly Pharisaical', was proved right as the trade continued under Austen Chamberlain and Stanley Baldwin into the 1930s.

8

A Den of Thieves

THE FRONT PAGE OF THE *Daily Telegraph* on Thursday, 8 May 2009 threw
down the gauntlet, promising to disclose 'How Brown and his Cabinet
exploit expenses system'. It was to be the first of many days of searing
attacks. The next day junior ministers were in the firing line, and on
the Saturday it was the turn of David Cameron's shadow Cabinet and
a string of 'Tory grandees'. Over the weeks the spending habits of
hundreds of MPs were exposed to national ridicule, calumny and
righteous indignation.

MPs had brought it on themselves (ourselves) in more ways than
one. For decades the myth had been allowed to propagate that parliamentary allowances were another part of an MP's remuneration. A
modest allowance to meet MPs' accommodation costs had been introduced in 1971 as the result of a review by the independent Top Salaries
Review Body, but when it recommended four years later that MPs'
salaries be increased from £4,500 to £8,000 to keep up with raging
inflation, the Prime Minister Harold Wilson, understandably concerned about the effect on his national counter-inflation strategy,
offered an increase in MPs' pensions and in the allowance in exchange
for a much lower salary increase. It was a precedent his successors were
to follow. Just after the 1979 election the TSRB recommended a salary

of £12,000, but again the government baulked, and successive TSRB salary recommendations were either ignored or phased in while the Additional Costs Allowance was allowed to increase; and in 1985 MPs were allowed to reclaim mortgage interest payments. MPs' pay continued to be a fraught issue through the 1990s. Then, in 2001, a Senior Salaries Review Body report accepted that MPs 'receive lower salaries than those doing similarly weighted work in other parts of the public sector',[1] but proposed staging a pay rise. At this point backbench MPs took the matter into their own hands and, in the debate on the report, voted against the government for a 42 per cent increase in the ACA from £13,322 to £19,469, in line with overnight allowances for the House of Lords. MPs clearly felt undervalued and underpaid.

That was not all. MPs had been quietly encouraged to divide the annual allowance by twelve and submit a simple un-receipted monthly request for the sum, which was meant to cover the real costs of living in two places. By 2009 MPs recognized that such a system was disreputable, so some constraints had been imposed. The mileage allowance was slashed from 74.1p to 40p per mile. It was still possible to claim £400 a month for food and £250 for petty cash without any evidence, but for expenditure outside and above this receipts had to be provided.

The first story to break was that of Derek Conway, a lumbering Tory MP who had arrived in the Commons in 1983 and had served as a whip in John Major's government. Having lost his seat in 1997, he was back in 2001 for Edward Heath's old seat of Bexley and Sidcup despite being an ardent Eurosceptic. Conway's UKIP opponent in the 2005 election, Michael Barnbrook, then alleged that Conway had been employing his younger son Freddie as a parliamentary researcher, paid with taxpayers' money, while he was a full-time student at Newcastle University. When the Committee on Standards and Privileges reported on the case in January 2008, Conway was forced to repay £13,000 and suspended from the House for ten days, and David Cameron removed the Conservative whip. His ordeal was not over, though, for even as he angrily protested his innocence the Parliamentary Commissioner on Standards was investigating Conway's employment of his older, defiantly flamboyant son Henry, who had also been his father's paid researcher while a student. Yet again Conway was forced into repayment, this time of £3,758. At this point he announced he would not be standing for re-election. Public and parliament alike were scandalized, but neither had any idea that this skirmish was to be but a prologue to a far greater storm.

As the Freedom of Information Act began to bite, and after lengthy attempts to withhold details of MPs' expenses, including a legislative attempt to exempt MPs from the Act's provisions, the House authorities, led by the hapless Speaker, Michael Martin, set about collating all the material they had, just in case the Office of the Information Commissioner ruled it had to be published. Roomfuls of files, receipts and letters were scanned on to disk by a supposedly secret and secure company. Ironically, there was so much material that a newspaper would have needed a couple of juggernauts to steal it all, but with all the expenses claims made by MPs going back to 2003 on a single unexpurgated CD, the information was easily purloinable and usable.

For many members of the public the details proved pornographically fascinating. One MP had bought a shiny toilet seat. Another wondered whether his duck house might be covered. Yet another bought some eyeliner. Conway had claimed for a house that was 330 miles from his constituency. The *Telegraph* played its hand with consummate ease, demanding MPs respond to its accusations in double-quick time, releasing each day's story in time for the ten o'clock news and keeping up its campaign for months. MPs were exposed as slipshod, careless, morally dubious and downright dishonest – and, perhaps conveniently for the Tory-leaning *Telegraph*, the party of government took the lion's share of the blame. Soon few could distinguish between one MP's honest mistake and another's gross malfeasance, and the excuse that one had only followed the rules was laughed at as MPs had drafted the rules themselves. On the first day of the revelations the paper's editor, Charles Moore, had tarred every MP

PARLIAMENT: THE BIOGRAPHY

with the same brush: 'In any body of 650 or so people, there will always be some who cheat. The much more alarming thing that everyone now understands is that the entire system is a cheat.' If there were any justice, he challenged, there would be prosecutions and by-elections. There were certainly serious repercussions. The Speaker, tipped the wink in a phone call from Gordon Brown, was forced to resign. For a variety of reasons, the Home Secretary, the Local Government Secretary, the Minister for Employment, the Transport Secretary and the Exchequer Secretary to the Treasury all resigned as ministers prior to the 2010 election, and when the entry of the Liberal Democrats into the subsequent coalition government brought greater scrutiny to their accounts, the Chief Secretary to the Treasury, David Laws, was out of a job after just sixteen days in post. Six MPs – David Chaytor, Eric Illsley, Jim Devine, Elliot Morley, Margaret Moran and Denis MacShane – were charged under the Theft Act and either pleaded or were found guilty; and when Ian Gibson was expelled from the Labour party he resigned his Norwich seat, causing a by-election. At least another ten MPs openly stated that they would not stand for re-election in 2010, and many more were excised by the electorate in a general election that saw 117 seats change party and 232 MPs leave the House. The less scrutinized upper house suffered similar scandal, with the Conservative peers Lord Hanningfield and Lord Taylor of Warwick imprisoned for false accounting and three Labour peers, Lord Bhatia, Lord Paul and Baroness Uddin, suspended from the House and required to pay back substantial sums. Unlike the MPs, they all retained their seats.

None of this could possibly assuage public anger. Michael Martin, they pointed out, went to the House of Lords with a generous pension and Douglas Hogg, whose claim for £2,200 to clean his moat at Kettlethorpe Hall became an icon of the scandal, was mooted for a life peerage by David Cameron in 2011 (but was rejected by the House of Lords Appointments Commission). The very fact that hundreds of MPs were required to pay back significant amounts of money when an independent auditor was asked to review the whole cache of expenses merely proved to the public that the House had become a den of thieves.

Public anger was all the greater because this was hardly the first evidence of dodgy dealing in modern times. In the 1970s one former MP, Sir Herbert Butcher (National Liberal), and three sitting MPs, Albert Roberts (Labour), John Cordle (Conservative) and Reginald Maudling (Conservative), had been implicated in a corrupt network of financial deals and property developments which led to the imprisonment of John Poulson and T. Dan Smith. When the Poulson empire collapsed, Cordle resigned his seat and Maudling resigned as Home Secretary, but none of the MPs involved was prosecuted, even though Roberts had received a free house, Cordle had been on a £1,000 a year contract and both Maudling and his son had been on Poulson's books. The episode did have some lasting effect in the creation of the House of Commons Register of Financial Interests – but still the lesson had not been learned. In 1994 a similar scandal saw two Conservative MPs, Graham Riddick and David Tredinnick, suspended from the Commons for breaching the rules on payments for tabling parliamentary questions, and later that year two more Tories, Neil Hamilton and Tim Smith, were accused of taking cash from the then owner of Harrods, Mohammed Al-Fayed, at the generous rate of £2,000 a question. This last saga was battled out through the libel courts, the Court of Appeal, an official inquiry and a Standards and Privileges report which investigated Al-Fayed's wilder claims against twenty-five Members but found that five had breached the rules of the House on taking or declaring payments: Hamilton, Smith, Michael Brown, Sir Michael Grylls and Sir Andrew Bowden. All were already ex-MPs and so beyond the reach of Commons discipline. Such apparent impunity fed into the sense of pervasive sleaze and the landslide Labour victory of 1997, and Blair's willingness to exploit the matter created a sense that Labour would be different. It was not surprising that, a decade and more later, the public felt so let down.

But before we get too pious about modern parliamentary fraudsters, it is worth bearing in mind quite how important money has been in greasing the parliamentary system. From as early as the thirteenth century it was assumed that men would have to be paid to attend parliament, and in order to ensure this happened the king issued expenses writs demanding that the respective counties or boroughs pay the 'reasonable expenses' of their knights and burgesses for attending and travelling to and from parliament. This was not at first a fixed, predetermined sum. The City of London paid its burgesses ten shillings a day in 1296, but some communities baulked at the figures involved, others found it almost impossible to force those responsible to contribute, and it seems that in 1265 the knights for Yorkshire claimed *per diem* expenses for a suspiciously long period; so the middle ages saw the courts settle several legal disputes on parliamentary expenses (119 cases between 1377 and 1505). Following parliaments in both 1320 and 1322, for instance, the courts heard complaints that pairs of knights of the shire sought expenses of £20 for attending parliament, respectively for Lancashire and Derbyshire, 'whereas the community of the county could have had by their own election two sufficient men [*sufficientes homines*] to go to the parliament for ten marks or ten pounds'.[2] In view of these controversies, a universal rate was set in 1327: four shillings per day spent attending or travelling to parliament for a knight and two shillings for a burgess. This was a very handsome amount, as even when engaged on a military campaign a knight would only be paid two shillings per day, suggesting that from the very earliest times there was an assumption that if the king wanted men of quality to attend his parliament then he had to ensure they were properly rewarded. There were still complaints, though, for instance when the Lancashire sheriff sent his own nominees rather than allow a proper election in the county court in 1335 and even seized part of their expenses when they returned. Broadly speaking, this rate of pay survived into the seventeenth century, although London regularly paid considerably more, Bristol steadily increased its day rate to a noble (6s 8d) and Weymouth idiosyncratically paid its burgesses with five hundred mackerel in 1463.

By the time of the Restoration, though, MPs' pay had withered on the vine and ministerial office was so much more lucrative that men were prepared to attend gratis in the hope of preferment. The change was not universally welcomed. Samuel Pepys commented in his diary on 30 March 1668: 'At dinner . . . all concluded that the bane of the Parliament hath been the leaving off the old custom of the places [the counties and boroughs] allowing wages to those that served them in Parliament, by which they chose men that understood their business and would attend it, and they could expect an account from, which now they cannot.' But when Andrew Marvell died in 1678 he was reckoned to be the last MP to receive a parliamentary salary (from the borough of Kingston upon Hull), and although Thomas King complained that the borough of Harwich had not paid him his wages three years later, the practice remained defunct for more than two centuries.

One problem that Pepys did not foresee was that without any form of parliamentary pay members would seek other forms of recompense as ministers or loyal supporters of the crown in the shape of land, titles, sinecures, monopolies, pensions and perquisites that in today's climate would shame the hardest-skinned MP. As Macaulay put it:

> From the nobleman who held the White Staff and the Great Seal, down to the humblest tidewaiter and gauger, what would now be called gross corruption was practised without disguise and without reproach. Titles, places, commissions, pardons, were daily sold in the market overtly by the greatest dignitaries of the realm; in the 17th century a statesman who was at the head of affairs might easily, and without giving scandal, accumulate in no long time, an estate amply sufficient to support a dukedom.[3]

He was right. To take but one example, in fourteen years James I's favourite George Villiers racked up a knighthood, a barony, a viscountcy, an earldom, a marquessate and a dukedom for himself, distributed largesse to his vast 'connexion' of family, friends and allies, creamed off income from allocating monopolies and court patronage, acquired and elaborately accoutred the magnificent palatial homes of York House on the Strand, Burley on the Hill, New Hall near

Chelmsford, Wanstead House, Wallingford House by St James's Park and the Great House at Chelsea, and was granted lands in Buckinghamshire, Leicestershire, Rutland, Essex and London. When the Commons attempted to impeach him in the 1620s it complained about his holding several royal appointments simultaneously, but in his capacity as just one of them, Lord High Admiral (a post he had bought off the previous incumbent), he not only had the traditional rights to flotsam, jetsam and lagan and a tenth of the value of any enemy prize, but was extremely assiduous in claiming shipwrecks, all of which drew in £30,000–40,000 a year, a figure Buckingham's secretary Sir Edward Nicholas MP reckoned was 'more than a song to part with'.[4] Even one of his hangers-on, Sir James Bagg, an MP in each parliament from 1624 to 1628, managed to collect £28,253 from the sea in just five years.

Successive Stuart parliaments took understandable exception to such flagrant milking of the system, but Buckingham was hardly unique. Indeed, he stood in a long line of men who had prospered spectacularly as ministers and favourites. You only have to look at some of the palaces great parliamentarians raised for themselves to see how lucrative a ministerial career could be. Take Chatsworth House. The income that built both this and Hardwick Hall came from Bess of Hardwick's second marriage, in 1547, to Sir William Cavendish, MP for Thirsk, Treasurer of the Chamber and one of Thomas Cromwell's visitors of the monasteries, and her unhappy fourth marriage to George Talbot, the paranoid but landed 6th earl of Shrewsbury and Lord High Steward of Ireland, thereby ensuring the future estates of the dukes of Devonshire and of Newcastle. Likewise Audley End, formerly a Benedictine monastery, was given to Sir Thomas Audley in 1538 and was transformed into a great mansion by his grandson Thomas Howard, the earl of Suffolk. The former was Lord Chancellor; the latter, Lord Treasurer. So too the Cecils' remuneration for service as secretary of state and Lord High Treasurer to Queen Elizabeth and James I enabled William to refashion the family manor at Stamford as Burghley House, build the vast three-courtyard

Theobalds House near Cheshunt and make Cecil House in the Strand sumptuous enough for royal entertainment, and his son Robert to build the ultra-modern epitome of smart Jacobean domestic architecture, Hatfield House.

Even after the civil wars had attempted to weed out the enriching of royal favourites, such ostentatious displays of ministerial prosperity continued well into the eighteenth century. A grateful queen and nation garlanded the victor of the battle of Blenheim, John Churchill, as the duke of Marlborough, and granted him both the manor of Woodstock in Oxfordshire and hefty sums of cash to start the extravagantly proportioned Blenheim Palace; but it was as a court favourite of his wife's friend Queen Anne and thanks to his eighteen money-spinning years as Master-General of the Ordnance that he was able to complete it.

Often, ministerial office made rich men richer. Robert Walpole inherited estates worth £2,169 a year and made a tidy sum by extricating himself from the South Sea Bubble at just the right time, but the Palladian pile at Houghton Hall was his £200,000 present to himself after years as Secretary at War, Treasurer to the Navy, Paymaster to the Forces and First Commissioner of the Treasury, during which he also generously doled out lucrative posts to his three sons Robert, Edward and Horatio. Such ministerial ostentation was quite shameless. Not only did a senior minister expect to display his power and authority, but there was a sense of party rivals keeping up with one another. The Tory Nathaniel Curzon, who was made Baron Scarsdale in 1761 after a spell in the Commons, used his income as Chairman of Committees in the Lords to build the Palladian exemplar Kedleston Hall as a match for his Whig neighbour at Chatsworth, and while the original house of Wentworth Woodhouse near Rotherham was no cottage, by the time Thomas Watson-Wentworth, the first marquess of Rockingham, and his prime ministerial son the 2nd marquess, had finished with it, it had the longest façade of any private house in Europe and was an architectural paean to Whig hegemony. Even in the nineteenth century William

Cobbett pointed out that Liverpool received £7,000 as First Lord of the Treasury, £1,500 as Commissioner of Affairs in India, £4,100 as Warden of the Cinque Ports and £3,500 as Clerk of the Rolls in Ireland, and that thanks to his patronage his half-brother Cecil Cope Jenkinson received £2,000 as under-secretary at the Colonial and War Department and his cousin the dean of Worcester £2,000. Liverpool's salaries alone came to £16,100.

The very fact that ministerial office could bring such opulent rewards meant that it was a prize worth winning – and keeping. So once office began to depend less on the personal affections of the monarch and more on the ability to command a majority in parliament and thereby form an administration, the powers of patronage exercised by the First Lord of the Treasury on behalf of the crown became an essential part of the toolkit of government as ministerial office was effectively bought by doling out jobs, sinecures, pensions, titles and perquisites to MPs and peers.

The sheer scale of the patronage available to the crown in the eighteenth century was phenomenal. Across the royal household, the duchies of Lancaster and Cornwall, the county palatine of Lancaster, the earldom of Chester, and the offices of the pipe, the pells and the first fruits there were hundreds of well-upholstered niches into which a susceptible MP might be slipped without any expectation other than that he would vote for the government: in 1774 John Robinson reckoned there were 463 such sinecures. There was more money to be handed out unattached to offices: nearly £60,000 of it in secret service payments* every year, plus £95,447 in English pensions and £122,000 in Irish pensions. Hundreds of government contracts were awarded without any form of competitive tender or parliamentary scrutiny, and many (at least thirty-seven in 1761) went to mercantile MPs. Government loans on profitable terms were granted

---

* At this period, disbursements for undisclosed services that were rendered secretly, rather than payments for espionage.

to helpful financiers in parliament, and so many peers and MPs (at least eighty in 1787) benefited from advantageous leases on crown lands that as late as 1830 Daniel Harvey claimed in the Commons that the crown lands alone were 'quite sufficient to corrupt both houses of parliament'.[5] One person Harvey cited, the immensely wealthy baronet Sir Sampson Gideon MP, managed to embrace virtually all these forms of graft. For supporting the administrations led first by North and then by Pitt, he gained a cheap thirty-year lease on the manor of Waplow, profitable participation in several government loans, and a peerage as Baron Eardley in 1789. And on his own account he spread money and favours around like confetti at each of his elections as an MP.

All in all, it was a thoroughly corrupt trade that neutered parliament, and even before Robert Walpole took its exploitation to extremes many abhorred it. One particularly acerbic writer, Robert Crosfeild, argued that neither property nor liberty could be guaranteed 'so long as Members of Parliament are permitted to take Public Employments upon them, and wink at the ruin of those, who by the Constitution of this Government, they are obliged to protect'.[6] Indeed, following in the footsteps of Andrew Marvell, who had complained that there were upwards of 200 placemen in the Commons in 1692, a group of Whig independents, acting like their country party forebears and backed by the Tories who felt themselves excluded from office, ensured in 1700 that the Act of Settlement drawn up by the ruling Whig Junto stipulated that 'no Person who has an Office or Place of Profit under the King or receives a Pension from the Crown shall be capable of serving as a Member of the House of Commons'. By removing all office-holders from the Commons this held out the prospect of a complete presidentialist separation of the executive from parliament. However, the battle was not yet won, for the provisions of the Act were only to come into force once the Hanoverian succession began; so when the last of the Stuarts, Queen Anne, came to the throne in 1702 and Tories became ministers, the Whigs returned to the crease with a string of annual 'Place' Bills designed either wholly to eliminate or drastically to reduce the crown's power to corrupt parliament – and to do so immediately.

A piece of good fortune came their way when the government's Regency Bill, which sought to tidy up what would happen in the event of Queen Anne's death, arrived from the Lords in the Commons in January 1706. It was ripe for amendment to 'explain, regulate and alter' the Act of Settlement's provisions on offices of profit, especially given that the crown wanted its main provisions (laying down the terms for an interim government pending the arrival of the new Hanoverian monarch) enacted so badly that there would almost certainly be concessions. So while a leading non-court high Tory, Peter Freeman, moved that the total exclusion of placemen envisioned by the Act of Settlement be maintained, a group of country party Whigs led by Robert Eyres, Sir Richard Onslow, James Stanhope and Peter King, recognizing that this might leave the House suddenly denuded of ministers and facing more than a hundred by-elections, tabled their own amendment (which opponents called 'whimsical') to restrict the number of MP office-holders to forty. The politicking was intense and fluid, with Tory backbenchers like Sir Thomas Meeres supporting the 'whimsicals' even as Godolphin sought to have the Lords 'ruffle the clause pretty handsomely'.[7] The two-week tussle between the two Houses proved bruising as the court twisted arms and eventually persuaded some of the key supporters of the reform to back down. Onslow 'fainted at last in the pursuit',[8] Stanhope left for Spain and Eyres made a 'treacherous bargain' with the court, so that when King, Sir John Cropley and Sir William Ellys defended their clause on Monday, 18 February, they lost by eight votes. The 'bargain' was nonetheless a major court concession, as a replacement clause automatically excluded from the Commons all holders of newly created offices and a large number of existing office-holders, and made all the exclusions come into force not at the queen's death but at the end of the current session. True, this new scheme had a major get-out clause, as any MP barred by holding an office of profit from the crown was 'capable of being again elected, as if his place had not become void'.[9]

Since most elections were still uncontested, and the seat itself was as likely as the office of profit to be controlled by the crown, this was hardly an onerous requirement and, barring William Pole who lost his ministerial by-election in Devon in 1712 on being made Master of the Household, the vast majority of eighteenth-century placemen slipped back into the upholstery without much effort. Dissatisfied, the country party came back time and again with more exacting Place Bills during Anne's remaining years. One was subjected to an exceptional six divisions in the Commons but died in the Lords, and when in 1713 yet another came to its final hurdle (third reading in the Lords), the vote was tied and the Bill was lost. Had one more government-supporting bishop been delayed in getting to the vote or one more Tory peer supported the Bill, George I would have started his reign with a much diminished scope for patronage and Walpole might never have been able, in the words of one anonymous writer in 1731, to amass 'immense riches, not in the service of the crown, but by jobs, secret service, the sale of honours, places, pensions and bargains'.[10]

The next major attempt to deal with the grossly distorting power of royal patronage came from the Irishman Edmund Burke, who told the Commons just before Christmas 1779 that the source of all their grievances was 'the fatal and overgrown influence of the Crown'. Promising to introduce a Bill to abolish 'a quantity of influence equal to the places of fifty members of Parliament', he complained that this influence had 'insinuated itself into every creek and cranny in the kingdom'.[11] There was certainly plenty of material for him to complain about. The Commissioners of the Board of Trade included Edward Gibbon MP, who readily admitted that he was paid more than £700 a year and yet 'enjoyed many days and weeks of repose without being called away from my library to the office'.[12] So too the three clerks and three clerk comptrollers of the Board of the Green Cloth,* all of whom

* The Board, named after the green baize cloth on the table at which it sat, organized and audited royal travel, adjudicated on disputes in royal palaces, and licensed gambling and alcohol on royal premises. This last function was only abolished in 2004.

were MPs, received a handsome £1,018 a year between them for supporting the administration; the four gentlemen ushers of the Privy Chamber (£200) and its four grooms (£73), the three gentlemen ushers who were daily waiters (£150) and their eight quarterly counterparts (£50) together made up another nineteen MPs who were being remunerated for nominal service in the royal household; and the Master of the Jewel Office (£400 plus £80 for lodgings), the Keeper of the Great Wardrobe and the Groom of the Stole (£1,000) were all peers. One could make a very decent living out of these posts: Robert Manners, who sat in the Commons from 1784 to 1820, was also equerry and then clerk martial and avenor, and received £890 a year for twenty-eight years just for swearing in staff in the king's stables.

Burke's 'great and masterly' three-and-a-half-hour speech introducing his plan on 11 February 1780 was a mixture of conservatism and revolution. He was not worried about hereditary posts, or about the generous extant pensions; nor did he demand significant savings. It was 'the influence of the Crown' that he wanted to limit. Burke won the right to proceed with several Bills that day, but the coming debates were to prove that the public perception that the crown held sway over some 200 MPs was not exaggerated. True, John Dunning's motion 'that the influence of the Crown has increased, is increasing and ought to be diminished' was carried on 6 April in a late-night vote by 233 to 215, and a similar motion to render several places in the royal household incompatible with a Commons seat was also carried (by 215 to 213). But it was one thing to support theoretical principles, quite another to enact change. As Sir George Savile put it, a number of persons 'love well-sounding and constitutional maxims but hang an A[rse] at action'.[13] So a motion to delay was carried, and the abolition of both the entirely redundant third secretary of state (for America) and the whole department of the Great Wardrobe was lost. By the time prorogation killed all his measures Burke's only victory was the abolition of the Board of Trade.

Burke was not done yet, though. Appointed Paymaster-General (at £4,000 a year) in the new administration formed in 1782 under

Rockingham, he turned his old Bill into a financial measure relating to the national debt and the civil list, thereby claiming the financial privilege of the Commons for what he insisted was a Money Bill and therefore not subject to the Lords. The resultant bonfire of the sinecures was hardly a complete conflagration, but it put paid to 134 offices – and, just as significantly, it started a trend: another 144 were abolished by Shelburne, while Pitt consigned 765 revenue offices to history in 1789 and another 196 in 1798.

There were many who actively supported the 'old corruption'. Successive generations of ministerialists justified it, reckoning that without the power of patronage no government would be able to stand. One such MP, William Eden, who sat on the Board of Trade until it was abolished, complained that 'Burke's foolish Bill has made it a very difficult task for any set of men either to form or maintain an Administration',[14] and when Rockingham died after just three months and Shelburne's ministry lasted less than a year, the old Rockingham faction bemoaned that the new Prime Minister had 'a double list of candidates . . . impatient and clamorous for half the number of desirable places'.[15] Even well into the nineteenth century ministers spoke up for the old power of patronage. Far from decrying the influence of the crown, Thomas Grenville stated in 1809 that 'the influence of what they call corruption is, for practical purposes, too small rather than too great',[16] and Liverpool's Patronage Secretary Charles Arbuthnot urged colleagues in 1822 to vote against any measures to further limit patronage as 'it will be quite impossible for any set of men to conduct the government of this country, unless practices of this kind shall be successfully resisted'.[17] Eight years later the duke of Wellington took up the same feeble lament, wailing that 'no government can go on without some means of rewarding services. I have absolutely none!'[18]

By then, though, the campaign to limit the influence of the crown went in tandem with the wider reform movement, so the Grey government set up a Select Committee on the Reduction of Salaries. This resolved in 1834 'that anything in the nature of a sinecure office, with emoluments attached to it at the public charge, is alike indefensible in principle, pernicious as a means of influence and grievous as an undue addition to the general burthen of the nation'.[19] The committee declared the post of Ranger of St James's, the Green and Hyde Parks 'a sinecure, wholly useless to the Public';[20] it demanded that the Clerk of the Deliveries (£1,048) and the Lieutenant-General (£1,200) in the Ordnance be terminated; and it insisted that the Paymaster-General and the First Lord of the Admiralty lose their free residences. This was not just about saving money, for the committee worried that if ministerial salaries were fixed too low, 'a monopoly would be created in the hands of the wealthy' and argued that 'offices in a free country should not be put beyond the reach of men of moderate fortunes'.[21] It was a view shared by the Chancellor of the Exchequer, Sir Charles Wood, who argued: 'If the salaries of these offices were brought so low as to exclude the possibility of men of small fortune taking them, I conceive it would do a most irreparable injury to the public service, and great injustice to such parties.'[22] Nevertheless, the informal practice of ministers milking fees payable to their departments to make up their salaries, which had seen the Home Secretary's earnings rise to £8,733 in 1793 and the Foreign Secretary rake in £8,148 from a combination of 'various irregular sources', was ended, and a fixed salary of £5,000 attached to each office.

It had taken more than a century, but by abolishing most of the rotten boroughs, the pensions, the sinecures and secret service payments, and putting ministerial salaries on a properly audited footing, parliament had disentangled the knot of 'old corruption' that had strangled parliamentary freedom. No minister thereafter would earn a fortune out of being a minister; indeed, the originally generous figure of £5,000 remained virtually stagnant from 1830 to 1965, steadily eroded by inflation.

Bribery, in whatever form, was not the only way of ensuring a parliamentary majority. Roger Mortimer prevented Welsh royalists from attending parliament in 1327 by locking them up in a castle, Queen Elizabeth I enfranchised loyalist towns, and when in 1801, after a lifetime of political campaigning for others, the anti-ministerialist John Horne Tooke was elected for the rotten borough of Old Sarum, such was the hatred he had aroused in Pitt's brother-in-law Lord Temple that his lordship tried to have the new MP excluded from the Commons for having taken holy orders many years earlier. In the end the government drew up a Bill to exclude all clergy from the Commons, thereby putting paid to Horne Tooke's career. That exclusion was only repealed in 2001.

The subtle arts of organization and persuasion were also a vital part of the equation, based on two very simple principles. First: know your supporters. Nobody wanted to be in the position of Sir John Lowther in 1692, who worried that 'nobody can know, one day, what the House of Commons would do the next'.[23] So Thomas Cromwell kept lists of loyal supporters of Henry VIII's Reformation, Wolsey encouraged the Commons to divide physically when there was a vote so that his agents could see who his opponents were, Sir Arthur Heselrige acted as teller 167 times in the Long Parliament for the same reason, Sir Robert Paston produced a list of government adherents in 1673 and Shaftesbury drew up lists of Exclusionist MPs and peers while languishing in the Tower. Second: marshal your troops. The first known illustration of this principle in action dates from 1621, when James I wrote to allies demanding their attendance in parliament, sometimes underlining the request as often as six times. According to Pepys, his grandson Charles II got the Lord Chamberlain to send round to the theatres and brothels to drag MPs to parliament for a vote in 1666, and in September 1675 Sir Joseph Williamson, one of the two royal spokesmen in the Commons and secretary of state, wrote to a number of MPs informing them of the upcoming parliamentary session and requiring them to let him know as soon as they came to town.

In 1711 parliamentary management became an established part of the system when the post of secretary to the Treasury, which had existed on an informal basis since the days of Elizabeth I and had been formalized at the Restoration, was split in two. At first the existing secretary, William Lowndes, who had been in post since 1695 and had driven through radical reform of the financial system but had no clear party affiliation, took responsibility for purely financial matters while his junior devoted his energies to ensuring the preservation of the government's majority. Several of the men appointed to this post were close relatives or confidants of the senior ministers – Thomas Harley, Horatio and Edward Walpole, Stephen Fox – and successive occupants used all means at their disposal to win votes. They secured pensions, sinecures or secret service payments for loyalists, they found seats for their allies, they proffered perquisites for waverers and they mobilized their paid troops for key divisions. It was not work that anyone was proud of. John Scrope, the senior secretary for twenty-eight years from 1724 until his death, refused point blank to make any explanation of his use of secret service money to a Commons committee.

Soon the secretaries were referred to in fox-hunting terms as 'whippers-in', and government and opposition alike were equally assiduous in the activity. In 1742 Heneage Finch remarked in a letter that 'the Whigs for once in their lives have whipped in better than the Tories'.[24] and in 1769 Edmund Burke told the Commons that in trying to exclude John Wilkes the government had sent for their friends, 'whipping them in' from the north and from Paris. Treasury secretaries were a fixed and essential part of any government. One particular pairing was notably imaginative in a time of marked political futility: that of Grey Cooper and John Robinson, who worked together for twelve years from 1770. Cooper did well for himself, earning £5,500 out of his various sinecures, but his main responsibility was the management of financial business and the elections for the duchy of Cornwall. Robinson, by contrast, managed patronage appointments, secret service monies and elections, and would often act as teller in divisions, which in an era before published voting lists gave him a vital insight into precisely how an individual member voted. Since he also held the 'livre rouge', in which were detailed 'the means by which every individual attained his seat, and, in many instances, how far and through what channels he might prove accessible',[25] it was understandable that he was described as 'one of the most active and essential functionaries of the executive government'.[26]

By the time of the Reform Act whipping was seen as part of the standard machinery of government. On 23 July 1834 Francis Baring reckoned that since the 'notorious' system whereby one secretary had 'to do the jobbing, in fact the dirty work of the Government' had been in operation for the best part of a century it would never change 'until human nature was altered'.[27] Disraeli taunted Peel with it. Peel had once proclaimed that he had never joined in the anti-slavery cry and he would not now join in the cry for cheap sugar, yet only two years later he had forced his party to overturn its original vote on the sugar duties. 'It seems', chided Disraeli, 'that [his] horror of slavery extends to every place except the benches behind him . . . there the thong of the whip still sounds.'[28] And Henry Flood was even more acerbic about the whip in the Irish parliament, describing him as 'an incarnation of that evil principle which lives by the destruction of public virtue'.[29] But the whip (or 'patronage secretary') and his six assistants (entitled Lords of the Treasury, though confusingly they were not all lords) were so established a part of the furniture in the nineteenth-century Commons that both the government and the opposition whips were given offices in the new Palace. The Lords had whips as well – a notable example under Wellington being the Tory 6th earl of Shaftesbury, who hated philanthropy as fervently as his son espoused it. The government whip in the Commons was not always the Treasury secretary. Billy Holmes, for instance, was the Tory whip for thirty years up to 1841 but never held the post, which was taken successively by Wellington's confidant Charles Arbuthnot, by J. C. Herries and by Joseph Planta; yet *The Times* reckoned that Holmes dispensed 'the greater portion of that patronage which usually passes through the hands of the Secretary to the Treasury'.[30]

As for the practicalities, although in 1823 it was Castlereagh as Leader of the Commons who wrote a circular note to MPs (he would esteem it a personal favour if the Member could be in the House the following day at half past four o'clock and remain there until the division, which he expected to come 'in time to go away to dinner'[31]), by the middle of the century this became standardized as the 'whip', sent by the Treasury secretary and underlined once, twice or three times for added emphasis. One MP quipped that a four-line whip meant 'stay away at your own peril'. When sinecures, secret service money, pocket boroughs and pensions were severally abolished, the only elements of patronage still available to the Treasury secretary were the granting of honours and titles, and financial assistance with elections; but the government's seizure of 85 per cent of parliamentary time* gave the whips a new hold over their party MPs as it was they who drew up the weekly timetable, and so determined when an MP could be absent or go on holiday, and they who decided which MPs could sit on which committees. In the twentieth century this management of time and distribution would become an art in itself, especially in a closely balanced parliament. The number of whips in both houses grew, and the chief whip became a settled part of the political system.

One facet of the constitution has always put temptation in the Prime Minister's way – the infinite capacity of the House of Lords. Not only could the crown pack the Lords with suitable voting fodder, as when Pitt the Younger insisted on making 141 new Tory peers to balance the Whigs in 1783, but since, in the words of Lord John Russell, honours attracted 'the many who cannot be caught by the bait of covetousness [but] are caught by the bait of vanity',[32] the baubles of knighthoods, baronetcies and peerages could be every bit as effective as more straightforwardly financial inducements. Some of the peerage promotions were downright corrupt. Richard Temple-Nugent-

---

* A series of procedural reforms over the course of the nineteenth century handed control of Commons business to ministers. In 1811 precedence was given to government bills on Mondays and Fridays, in 1835 Wednesdays were added and debates on petitions were abolished, in 1854 the number of stages at which a bill could be debated was cut, in 1881 closure motions were created and in 1887 'guillotine' motions were initiated to curtail debate.

Brydges-Chandos-Grenville, as fat as his name was long, inherited his father's seat in the Lords as marquess of Buckingham in 1813, but made no bones about his hopes for a dukedom and in the early 1820s put his small coterie of ten or eleven MPs up for sale to the highest bidder. The fact that he was held in near-universal contempt – the Tory hostess Mrs Arbuthnot thought him odious, unpopular and 'utterly without talent or the respect of one human being'[33] – did not unduly trouble Lord Liverpool, who came up with the desired coronet in 1822 and offered Grenville's friends and relatives a suite of comfortable ministerial billets. The stratagem worked, and Liverpool formed a ministry with Grenville backing – but it drew many a barbed comment, including one from Sir Charles Bagot, who was glad that the Grenvilles had been taken into the government and had no objections to the head of the Grenville family getting a dukedom, but did 'see many to giving it to the actual blubber head who now reigns over them'.[34]

But even the shameless elevation of Richard Grenville pales into insignificance compared to the peerage profiteering of the post-war government of 1918–22, the blame for which history has dumped exclusively on the doorstep of Lloyd George. True, between 1917 and 1922 eighty-two peers were created under Lloyd George's premiership, and although many of these new creations were directly related to the war, for example generals and admirals, and many more consisted of the usual fare of law lords and former MPs, the list was supplemented by at least fourteen men who had paid for the privilege. The money did not go directly into the Prime Minister's pocket, nor did he make offers himself, but successive coalition Liberal chief whips, assisted by the failed actor and impresario turned political broker Maundy Gregory, and with the full connivance of Lloyd George, ensured that those who became 'subscribers' to the coalition Liberals could buy themselves a seat in the Lords. The thinking was simple. With the Liberal party proper in the hands of Asquith, Lloyd George had no party funds of his own, and his only prospect of continuing in office lay in building up funds to fight a general election. In private he actually argued 'that the sale of honours is the cleanest way of raising money for a political party'; but, as he moaned to anyone who would listen, 'you cannot defend it in public'. The entrepreneurial zeal with which Gregory approached his task was impressive. With a peerage going for £50,000, a baronetcy for £30,000 and a knighthood for £10,000, the Lloyd George Fund was able to bring in between two and three million pounds by 1922.

Some of the recipients raised more than a few eyebrows, especially as the next general election approached and Lloyd George's nominations became more outré. In the New Year's Honours list of 1921, for instance, the Newcastle shipbuilder Rowland Hodge was made a baronet, despite having been convicted just two years earlier for food hoarding. And then in June 1922 came the Birthday Honours, replete with extremely controversial peerages: for Sir Joseph Robinson, an 82-year-old South African millionaire who had swindled his own shareholders; for Sir William Vestey, a Liverpudlian meatpacker who had gone to South America to avoid taxes; for Samuel Waring, who had made a fortune in the war thanks to government contracts but had not paid back the creditors of his former bankrupt firm Waring and Gillow; for Sir Archibald Williamson, whose oil firm had done business with the enemy in the war; and for Sir Robert Borwick, whose sins were as minimal as his accomplishments (his company made custard powder). The public had no idea that all of them had bought their elevation, but there was such an outcry at these appointments that Robinson was persuaded not to accept the offer and the Prime Minister was forced to front a debate on the issue in the Commons on 17 July.

Lloyd George was not at his best on this occasion. He claimed that the war and the growing population had necessitated the recent increase in honours and that the political honours made up but a tiny proportion of the number granted. He was adamant that nobody should be excluded from a peerage because they had given money to a political party (a point echoed years later by Tony Blair) and suggested that the Prime Minister should expressly not be told who had given money to his party. He attempted to sound purposeful, suggesting that if honours had been sold 'it was a discreditable system. It ought never to have existed. If it does exist, it ought to be terminated, and if there were any doubt on that point, every step should be taken to deal with it.' Even so, his ambivalence shone through: 'But, seeing that this system – the system of reward for political services – is one which has obtained ... under the most distinguished leadership the country has ever seen, the country ought to consider very seriously before it brings it to an end.'[35]

Lloyd George was dissembling. But the honours scandal was not a one-man play. The Unionist leader Austen Chamberlain, summing up for the government as Leader of the House, cast doubt on 99 per cent of the rumours he had ever heard about the sale of honours, but confessed that he too had made recommendations for peerages and suggested that if he knew that a candidate had made a contribution to his party's funds 'that would be, to my mind, an additional claim'.[36] His predecessor, Bonar Law, had told the Commons categorically in 1919 that 'the Prime Minister has made, and will make, no recommendations to His Majesty as a reward for contributions to party funds'.[37] Yet the Unionists were every bit as deeply implicated as Lloyd George. Back in 1912 Bonar Law had netted £120,000–140,000 from the sale of honours for his party, and William Palmer, Lord Selborne, wrote to the Unionist leader in the Lords, Lansdowne, that 'to my certain knowledge honours have been hawked around by agents'.[38] If anything, the Unionists were the first out of the traps after the 1918 election as the Liberal chief whip, Freddy Guest, complained in June 1919 that 'Bonar [Law] has made a tidy pile for his party coffers with peerages for Sir Matthew Arthur, Sir Thomas Dewar and Sir William Tatem – we have only Sir Frederick Smith to date'.[39] Indeed, the two parties within the coalition were often in competition for potential candidates. The Unionist chairman Sir George Younger (who was made a baronet in 1911 and a viscount in 1923) complained directly to Bonar Law in 1921 that 'there must be a stop to Freddy [Guest] poaching our men', as he was certain that if he had got Frederick Mills a seat in the Lords he would have become a financial subscriber to the Unionist cause but that Guest had got there first with a baronetcy.[40] Clearly, what was at stake for the Unionists was not the principle, but the fact that they were losing out. Even the most voluble critic of the practice, the duke of Northumberland, complained to the Royal Commission on Honours which was set up in 1922 that 'both Mr Sale and Mr Clarence Smith are Conservatives. Why, therefore, should they be approached by . . . Lloyd George?'[41] The extent of Austen Chamberlain's dissembling to the Commons is betrayed by his correspondence with David Lindsay, the 27th earl of Crawford and Balcarres, who wrote to say that a Mr Murray would be happy to pay £10,000 for an honour. Far from decrying the practice, Chamberlain merely responded: 'The less I know about such offers the better. They should be made only to the whips!'[42] Of the six recipients of dubious peerages offered in 1922, three (Robinson, Waring and Borwick) had given money to the Unionists, not to Lloyd George.

The Unionists had one more trick up their sleeve when it came to the brouhaha in 1922, though. While the leadership kept their heads down, men like the nasty anti-semite Northumberland (who bore a grudge against Lloyd George for his comment in the 1909 budget discussions that 'a fully equipped duke costs as much to keep up as two Dreadnoughts, and dukes are just as great a terror – and they last longer'[43]) made lively and impassioned pleas to the royal commission, thereby giving the impression of Unionist sanctity. When the commission baldly stated in November that 'there is no doubt that there have been for some time, and recently in increasing numbers, persons who, for want of a better name, we may stigmatise as touts, who have been going about asserting that they were in a position to secure honours in return for specified payments',[44] the Unionists meekly agreed to act, and when Baldwin became Prime Minister he brought in the Honours (Prevention of Abuses) Act 1925 which made it a criminal offence to take money to procure 'the grant of a dignity or title of honour'.[45]

Maundy Gregory, meanwhile, had tried to diversify. He took over a hotel near Dorking where fashionable people could have a discreet dirty weekend, he joined the Catholic Church and did a brisk trade in papal honours, and he acted as an agent of the secret services. But he hadn't stopped selling British honours, just switched to work for the Conservatives. In 1928 he approached Sir George Lawson-Johnston about making a donation to the Conservative party in exchange for an honour. Scandalized, Sir George reported the matter to the party, specifically to its chairman from 1926 to 1930, Bonar Law's former secretary, J. C. C. Davidson MP, and its director of publicity, Joseph Ball. Anxious that Gregory was now out of control, these two officials then used Sir George as a stalking horse in an attempt to incriminate Gregory further with a view to a criminal prosecution under the Act of 1925. This was foiled, though, when it came to light that a Mr Broadbridge had approached the Conservatives' principal agent, Leigh Maclachlan, about buying a knighthood and had been put in touch with Gregory, who happily took £11,000 for the party. Ball then wrote to Davidson: 'I am satisfied that Maclachlan, without your knowledge or mine, has been working in close association with Maundy Gregory regarding the sale of honours,' adding without a trace of irony: 'This very much complicates the question of the prosecution.'[46] Since their party was clearly every bit as implicated in Gregory's corruption as Lloyd George had been, Ball and Davidson quietly let the matter drop.

Gregory eventually sailed too close to the wind, however. When he approached a Commander E. W. Billyard-Leake in January 1933, looking for £10,000 for a baronetcy, the commander went straight to the police and charges were brought under the new Act. Considering the terms in which Unionists such as Northumberland had condemned such practices ('the most shameless and cynical corruption'[47]), the reaction of Davidson and Ball to Gregory's impending prosecution was extraordinary. Instead of cooperating with the prosecuting authorities, Ball wrote to Davidson 'point[ing] out the dangers, in view of MG's past connection with the party, of this prosecution going forward', and on Stanley Baldwin's express instructions advised Gregory to flee the country. When this proved impossible, Davidson visited Gregory before his trial and begged him to plead guilty, and ensured that on his release after two months' imprisonment there was a pension waiting for him, along with a car to take him to a new home in France. A handwritten note from Baldwin in Ball's papers in the Bodleian dated 'January 19th 1934', around the time of Gregory's release, almost certainly refers to him and shows quite how frightened the party leadership was that the Conservatives' involvement in Gregory's nefarious activities would come out. Baldwin's note authorizes the expenditure, by Davidson and Ball, of £25,000 'for certain secret purposes' of which he and Lord Greenwood were aware and approved.[48] There have been few such flagrant examples of hypocrisy in British politics.

What is most remarkable about the Lloyd George honours scandal is not the brazenness of the corruption, nor the sums of money involved. The truly astounding fact is that although it was part of the malaise that led to the end of Lloyd George's premiership, it did little ultimate damage to his career. The newspapers, many of whose proprietors had been ennobled, were muted in their complaints, and while the Unionists were keen to seize the high moral ground for themselves, they were terrified of forcing every sinew of the patronage system out into the open. There were reasons why the story dangled round Lloyd George's neck. He was Prime Minister. He had amassed a large election fund, over which the divided Liberals fought. But most importantly, it was his tout, Gregory, who was (and is) the only person to have been convicted of selling honours; and it was that which made Lloyd George the face of the scandal. Gregory's office on the parliamentary estate, his flamboyance, his homosexuality and the strange death of his long-time live-in companion, the former musical actress Edith Rosse, all added to his notoriety – as did the strange matter of the former MP Victor Grayson.

Grayson had been elected as a young, handsome, bisexual and extremely articulate socialist with one of the thinnest majorities, just 153, in the Colne Valley by-election of 1907. Since that heady moment he had collapsed into alcoholism, lost his seat, edited the *Clarion*, migrated to America and New Zealand, been declared bankrupt back in England and been discharged unfit in the war. Yet somehow he had access to money, and the regular visitors at his plush new London flat in Bury Street were a motley crew, including the seamen's union MP Havelock Wilson, Horatio Bottomley – and Maundy Gregory, who may have been commissioned by MI5 to spy on him. For some unknown reason there was a falling out, and in September 1920, fully two years before the story broke nationally, Grayson told a public meeting in Liverpool that Lloyd George was selling honours and that this was 'a national scandal. It can be traced right down to 10 Downing Street, and to a monocled dandy with offices in Whitehall. I know this man, and one day I will name him.' A few days later Grayson was beaten up on the Strand and on the twenty-eighth he disappeared. Rumours have flourished ever since. Did Gregory murder both Grayson and Edith Rosse? Who had been paying for Grayson's new lifestyle? But the person who paid the reputational price was Lloyd George.

By chance, on the very day that Lloyd George stood up to defend himself, the House was notified of the imprisonment for fraud of another friend of Grayson's.

It is difficult to explain the phenomenon that was Horatio Bottomley, who was twice Liberal MP for Hackney South, first from 1906 to 1912 and then again from 1918 to 1922. Orphaned at the age of four, he grew up to live by his wits. He had some legitimate business interests, most notably the *Financial Times*, which he founded as a promotional exercise in 1888, but for the most part his financial dealings were drenched in dishonesty. A bankruptcy automatically disqualified him from sitting in the Commons in 1912, but he managed to rehabilitate himself thanks to a sustained campaign of brutal patriotism through the war, largely waged through another of his publications, *John Bull*. MacDonald and the Labour pacifists were excoriated and humiliated, the government was attacked for failing British servicemen, the Kaiser and his government were satirized as

'Germhuns' and a German resident in the UK was condemned as 'an unnatural beast – a human abortion'.[49] He demanded that anyone who found themselves being served by a German waiter after the war should 'throw the soup in his foul face'. It was all vile, demagogic stuff, but his populist oratory and his capacity to spot a political opportunity bought him a second chance in the 'coupon' election of 1918, when he won back his seat, this time sitting as an Independent. There was one thing that Bottomley enjoyed more than fame, and that was fortune, but as fast as he earned the large sums he commanded for writing or speaking on recruiting platforms, he spent them on wild gambling at the racecourse and on risky investments. Ever a megalomaniac, he constantly predicted a summons to the Palace to form a 'Business Government' and attempted to create his own party, the League of the People. In 1920 he even managed to secure the election of a journalistic colleague, Charles Palmer, who won the Wrekin by-election that February and telegraphed Bottomley with the result: 'Your great personality has won a famous victory.'[50] Palmer died later that year, but soon a small coterie of candidates entered the House as Independent Bottomley-backed 'Anti-Waste' members: Sir Thomas Polson, Major Christopher Lowther and Rear Admiral Murray Sueter. It felt as if Bottomley's political career might take off.

It was recklessness that brought him down. He had preyed on the credulous through a fraudulent and mismanaged financial scheme, the John Bull Victory Bond Club, which was no more than a lottery and therefore illegal. He had also alienated a former business associate, Reuben Bigland, by contemptuously refusing to back a ludicrous scheme to turn water into petrol. And when Bigland launched a campaign 'to unmask England's Greatest Living Humbug' by publishing thousands of copies of a stinging pamphlet attacking the Bond Club, Bottomley had decided to sue Bigland for libel and for demanding money with menaces. As with Dilke, such legal adventurism was doomed to fail. Bigland was acquitted of the charges, but in the process deliberately incriminated himself (and therefore Bottomley) of fraud and made it evident that the MP had perjured himself. Within days Bottomley was charged, and when he stood trial the following May the jury found him guilty in just twenty-eight minutes and the judge sentenced him to seven years' penal servitude. On 1 August 1922 parliament took its revenge when Austen Chamberlain read out a letter of contrition and moved the expulsion of the Member for Hackney South.

Even at the last Bottomley could take people in. One MP, Lieutenant-Colonel John Ward, gently rebuked Chamberlain for not moving Bottomley's expulsion 'with regret' and reckoned he could not allow him to be expelled 'without at least expressing my personal regret at the necessity'.[51] As one biographer put it, 'audacity, radiant good humour, ready unpretentious vulgarity, immediate generosity: all of these qualities combined to make him an immensely likeable personality to many people who had no interest in his dubious financial enterprises'.[52] For years Bottomley managed to maintain a reputation as a lovable rogue, doing a self-deprecatory auto-biographical music-hall turn. A story did the rounds that when the prison chaplain saw him mending mail bags he had asked: 'Sewing, Bottomley?' to which the former MP had replied: 'No, reaping.'

Bottomley was not the worst of the criminal fraudsters. That honour probably goes to the short, burly businessman Jabez Balfour, who was first elected MP in a three-way contest for the two Tamworth seats in 1880. When the second seat was abolished in 1885 and he failed to win the new seat of Croydon, where he lived, he tried to get himself elected for Walworth in 1886 and for Doncaster (where he had ambitiously bought the local *Gazette*) in 1888. Neither attempt succeeded, but when a vacancy suddenly occurred in Burnley in 1889 he proved that being a carpetbagger was no impediment for a man with the gift of the gab. By this time Balfour had made a lot of money as the linchpin in a string of dubious finance companies based on the Liberator Building Society, founded in 1868 by his brother-in-law, the Reverend Dawson Burns, with the laudable aim of enabling non-conformists to own their homes. But very soon after he was re-elected in 1892 one of his companies went under, owing more than £2 million.

PARLIAMENT: THE BIOGRAPHY

Suddenly the dominoes began to topple and, with the whole Balfour group of companies imperilled and his associates under arrest, he stood down as an MP in November and fled to Argentina. The long arm of the law managed to track him down in the form of a Metropolitan Police officer, Frank Castle Froest, who handcuffed him, bundled him on to a train and put him on a boat to England. There he stood trial and was sent to prison to do fourteen years of penal servitude as prisoner V460-14. Here was a true swindler, shameless in his fraudulence. As the *Westminster Gazette* put it: 'His religion and his philanthropy lent unction to his politics. His religion, his philanthropy and his politics gave sanction to his financial schemes. His eminence as a financier gave him weight as a politician, solidity as a philanthropist, consideration as a man of religion.'[53] Quite a trick.

Balfour and Bottomley were fraudsters, and the law dealt with them accordingly. So, too, Lord Chancellors Bacon, Macclesfield and Westbury were removed (in 1621, 1725 and 1865), Giles Mompesson was impeached in 1621, Speaker Trevor was driven from office in 1695, and several MPs were expelled for fraud over the centuries.

Here, though, is the problem. For when it comes to financial slipperiness the scimitar of public opinion has been wielded without consistency. There were many more corrupt MPs and peers than these. Trevor was engaging in a practice that many a predecessor had followed; Macclesfield, Bacon and even Mompesson were surrendered to the court of public opinion by masters (Walpole and Buckingham) who were every bit as corrupt as they; and senior ministers in every generation amassed fortunes from the public purse without so much as a raised eyebrow. In Westbury's case, the Commons even declared that they imputed no personal corruption to him, but in the highly charged atmosphere of the last days before the prorogation of parliament in 1865 Palmerston's attempt to adjourn the debate was frustrated by a sharp-tongued Disraeli out for a political scalp.

The truth is that throughout much of its formative history the whole parliamentary system was built on corruption, and even when the 'old corruption' had been swept away, political management persisted and the House of Lords remained a willing receptacle for prime ministerial patronage. Romantic illusions about the great public service ethic that supposedly infused the parliaments of yore are just one more parliamentary myth, and public wrath has often rained down unequally on lesser sinners.

Take the case of the MP for Pontypridd. On 20 December 1930 Margaret Mardy Jones and her twelve-year-old daughter boarded the Great Western Railway train at the Welsh town clutching two first-class tickets to London that her husband Thomas had sent her the day beforehand. Life had not been easy for Thomas. Born and educated up the valley in the Rhondda Fach, he started work in the mines at the age of twelve, and when his father was killed in a mining accident, as both of his grandfathers had been, he became the main breadwinner for a family of six. Yet he had made something of himself, gaining a place at Ruskin College, Oxford and, on his return to the Mardy pit in 1907, a promotion to the post of checkweighman. Further advances came. Having been an active lecturer for the ILP, he became parliamentary agent for the South Wales Miners' Federation in 1909, and when a by-election arose in Pontypridd in July 1922 owing to the Liberal Thomas Lewis's appointment as the party's Welsh whip, Mardy Jones won a celebrated and unexpected victory. A natural intellectual and a gifted economist, Mardy Jones might have enjoyed a lengthy parliamentary career had it not been for his wife's journey to London: for when she was questioned by the ticket inspectors about the fact that one of the two tickets was out of date, it became apparent that both tickets were non-transferable fares provided exclusively for the use of MPs. The inspectors told the police and early in the New Year they pressed charges, prompting Mardy Jones to resign as an MP the day before the case went to court on 6 February. He made some half-hearted excuses about being stuck in London on 19 December for a key vote on the Coal Mines Bill and needing some papers from Wales, but both he and his wife pleaded guilty. The magistrate was scathing, deploring an MP's involvement in such a case as 'disgraceful' and 'disgusting'.

Mardy Jones was foolish and wrong, and he was forced to leave parliament in disgrace, yet this was small change as historic parliamentary corruption went. As we have seen, corruption constantly infected the body politic in the nineteenth century. So the freemen of the City of York, having for some time demanded that candidates pay them half a guinea per vote, in 1807 increased their fee to one guinea, colloquially referring to the bribes as 'the Guineas'.[54] In Berwick-upon-Tweed similar payments were referred to as 'gooseberries', and in Kingston upon Hull they were charged at double the York price. Because bribing electors could be a very expensive business for a candidate, the two main parties would often come to an informal arrangement to avoid a contested election by taking one seat each in the two-member constituencies. Yet elections were also lucrative for electors, so sometimes they deliberately engineered a contest. Thus in the 1847 election the sitting Conservative MP for Bridgwater, Henry Broadwood, and the Liberal candidate, Charles Kemeys-Tynte, found their gentlemen's agreement to avoid the expense of a contest disrupted when local electors persuaded a Mr Serjeant Gazelee to stand, merely so as to continue the trade in votes. In 1870 Bridgwater's antics were considered so scandalous that the borough was disenfranchised, but this did not deter the voters of Barnstaple, who tried to advertise in *The Times* for a third candidate. It was only the newspaper's refusal to take part in 'bleeding the established parties'[55] that prevented the advertisement from being printed.

Seats themselves could be traded, too. In 1810 the borough constituency of Westbury was sold by the 5th earl of Abingdon to the 'borough-monger' Manneseh Lopes (who later represented the seat himself) for £75,000, and although the two seats at Camelford were for a long time in the direct gift of the duke of Bedford, in 1812 he sold the constituency to the earl of Darlington for £32,000. This particular trade ended with the Reform Act in 1832, but as late as the 1930s Sir Cuthbert Headlam bemoaned the fact that local Conservative

Associations would ask prospective candidates whether they would pay their own election expenses and how much they would give to the party annually, thereby effectively putting the seat up for sale to the highest bidder.

All of which puts Mardy Jones's crime in context. He was expelled from parliament, but Lloyd George sold peerages and ended up a peer of the realm, Bonar Law and Austen Chamberlain were parties to exactly the same trade but were never discovered, and Baldwin very successfully organized a cover-up of his party's involvement in 1934. The irony – and the depressing fact – is that often those who sinned most boldly got away with it.

" I THOUGHT ABOUT GOING
INTO POLITICS BUT I COULDN'T
KEEP UP WITH THE DRINKING "

Politics has always been a convivial and bibulous business. Seventeenth-century Westminster was well supplied with drinking venues, including a tavern known as Heaven and two riotous basement public houses known as Hell and Purgatory. Many MPs and peers, including Pitt the Younger, the marquess of Rockingham and Winston Churchill, drank to excess. At one key moment in the 1911 debates on the Parliament Bill, Asquith was so 'squiffy' at the dispatch box that he had to be carried out – but the freemasonry of the Commons ensured that the public never knew.

9

Tired and Emotional

TUESDAY, 2 MARCH 1976. A windy evening outside the Palace of Westminster. The 61-year-old former Foreign Secretary and deputy leader of the Labour Party, Lord George-Brown,* who had lost a battle with his party in the House of Lords earlier in the evening, had gone on television to announce that he was leaving the party and would henceforth sit on the cross benches. 'The Labour Party has become the establishment,' he claimed: 'It refuses freedom to individuals.'[1] He rambled, recounting that when his father joined the Dockers' Union back in 1898 his membership card was signed by Ben Tillett. And as he made his way back to the House of Lords, he fell over and landed spectacularly in the gutter, in full view of the assembled press photographers. Only the *Guardian* and the *Daily Mail* ran the photos the next day – *The Times*, the *Daily Express* and the *Daily Telegraph* were desperate to praise Brown so as to undermine the Prime Minister, Harold Wilson – but everyone presumed Brown was dead drunk

---

* Several MPs refused to assume the customary geographical title when they were appointed to the Lords. Garter King at Arms decided to create a new style for such baronies, hyphenating forename and surname to produce forms such as 'Lord George-Brown', 'Lord Duncan-Sandys', 'Lord Goronwy-Roberts' and 'Lord Selwyn-Lloyd'.

('whole-seas-over' in his Cabinet colleague Barbara Castle's words) as it was a barely concealed secret that he was an alcoholic. *The Times* openly declared its hand, averring that 'Lord George-Brown drunk is a better man than the Prime Minister sober',[2] but Castle was not alone in complaining that this was 'the worst [newspaper] leader I have ever read',[3] recalling what Wilson had put up with from his former deputy. The very term 'tired and emotional' had been coined by *Private Eye* to describe his pretty much constant state of inebriation, and he had a longstanding reputation for swaying between charming flirtatiousness and aggressive boorishness. His post-dinner tribute to the assassinated President Kennedy on ITV in 1963 (preceded by a near-fight in the green room with the actor Eli Wallach) was slurred and incoherent, and when Violet Bonham Carter was a panellist with him on the radio, she thought that she had never before 'met anyone so completely un-house-trained'.[4] Barbara Castle regularly commented on his state of intoxication in her diaries: he was 'roaring tight in the House' one night and 'auto-intoxicated' the next;[5] when he was 'high' he was offensively truculent, and at one meeting his speech was 'thick and belligerent'.[6] Unsurprisingly, when he was appointed Foreign Secretary in 1966 another colleague, Bill Rodgers, worried that 'you can't bully, bribe, charm and outwit the world's leaders and give them a drink at the end'.[7] He was right to worry. On Brown's overseas trips as Foreign Secretary his private secretary would warn the British ambassador that Brown was an alcoholic and that he would probably abuse him, his wife and all the embassy staff.

Brown was also notorious for alcohol-assisted impulsiveness. He tendered his resignation so frequently (reportedly as many as seventeen times) that Wilson told his officials to file each new letter with all the rest, and although he was often 'emotion-intoxicated, not drunk' (Castle again), his behaviour was certainly erratic on the night in March 1968 when he finally resigned as Foreign Secretary. Furious that Wilson had either deliberately or inadvertently excluded him from an important meeting, Brown corralled fellow right-wing ministers in the Commons and demanded that Wilson immediately set up a new round of meetings. Although he was heard to shout down the phone at Wilson, 'Now don't say that; don't say in my condition,' by the time they met at 1.30 a.m. he was more than emotional. Tony Benn recorded that 'George stood up and shrieked and bellowed and shouted abuse as he went round the table, then left the room'.[8] He stormed off to the Commons and when it came to the division at 4 a.m. Barbara Castle did not think that he was yet drunk, but he made it very clear that he was for voting for *her* government rather than *his*.

Neither of Brown's resignations left him a notably happy man. Although after 1968 he remained Labour's deputy leader until he lost his seat in 1970, he desperately begged Wilson to bring him back as Foreign Secretary – and after leaving the party in 1976 he slowly moved further to the right, penning vicious attacks on the trade unions for the *News of the World*, signing up to the Limehouse Declaration in 1981 and joining the Social Democratic Party four years later. On Christmas Eve 1982 he walked out on his wife and family to live with his secretary. By the end he had turned his back on nearly everything he had ever stood for and had become 'a fallen angel. He was one of the high-flying leaders of the Party and now earns his living attacking it.'[9] It is difficult not to agree with Tony Benn's assessment: 'One is torn between pity and loathing for a man who is ruined.'[10]

Brown may have been an egregious case, but he was by no means the only member of the Labour governments of the 1960s and 1970s to drink heavily. Indeed, according to Bernard Donoughue, head of the No. 10 Policy Unit, when problems mounted in late 1975 Wilson slugged back four brandies before Prime Minister's Questions on 25 October (and two after), downed another five before arriving in the House on the thirtieth, and performed badly after a boozy diplomatic lunch on 27 November. As Wilson's biographer Ben Pimlott argues, 'close aides were well aware of his increasing resort to the spirit bottle, especially before Question Time in the House'.[11]

In having recourse to the bottle under pressure, Wilson was in a well-established prime ministerial tradition. The highly strung, hypochondriac marquess of Rockingham also resorted to alcohol when he was frightened of speaking in parliament, although he clearly thought of it as medicinal, writing in 1769: 'I was from beginning to end, in a most violent agitation, and was obliged to speak notwithstanding, three times. I got a good draught of Madeira before I went to the House, and had a comfortable breathing of a vein, by Mr Adair's lancet afterwards.'[12] Henry Addington adopted a similar strategy to overcome crippling shyness, as the landscape artist Joseph Farington noted: 'He wants spirits and courage for his situation and though a temperate man, now drinks perhaps 20 glasses of wine at his dinner before he goes into the House of Commons to invigorate himself.'[13] In Rosebery's case the crutch was not alcohol, but drugs. So emotionally crippled was he by the death of his wife Hannah in 1890 (and confused thereafter by his own sexuality) that he used black-edged paper for all his correspondence throughout the remaining thirty-nine years of his life, and he described his feelings during his last year as Prime Minister in distressing terms: 'To lie night after night, staring wide awake, hopeless of sleep, tormented in nerves, and to realise all that was going on, at which I was present, so to speak, like a disembodied spirit, to watch one's own corpse as it were, day after day, is an experience which no sane man with a conscience would repeat.'[14] His answer was to resort to a dangerous tranquillizer, sulfonal, to help him sleep, and cocaine to bring him up to match performance in the Lords. The combination produced results, but at a price: Lord George Hamilton maintained that it made him 'brilliant for the moment, but exceptionally flabby and invertebrate for the rest of the day'.[15] So too Anthony Eden, a man of immense early promise, Churchill's suave post-war Foreign Secretary and prime ministerial victor of the 1955 election, struggled through the 1956 Suez crisis thanks to a medically prescribed daily diet of barbiturates to help him sleep and amphetamines to wake him up and keep him going through the day – and his own self-prescribed quantity of booze.

The Prime Minister furthest advanced in alcoholism, though, was Asquith, who turned up one evening for the committee stage of the

Welsh Church Bill, which was being taken through by Rufus Isaacs and Herbert Samuel, and promptly fell fast asleep. Sitting opposite, Balfour complained that the fate of the church was 'in the hands of two Jews who are entirely sober and one Christian who is very patently drunk'.[16] Sir Douglas Haig noted that Asquith's 'legs were unsteady, but his head was quite clear' when he visited his headquarters in September 1916, and Churchill called him 'supine, sodden and supreme'.[17] One Cabinet colleague (and also arch-enemy), Richard Haldane, warned him that he was drinking too much champagne in 1904; another, Sir Charles Hobhouse, complained that Asquith's failure to deal with Lloyd George in July 1909 was attributable to the fact that he had been drinking 'during the last week or two, pretty hard',[18] and at the height of the battle over the Parliament Bill, Lloyd George wrote home (in Welsh) that 'the Prime Minister came to the House last night in a very drunken state. The Tories behaved very honourably. Balfour begged [Alexander Murray, Master of] Elibank to take him home.'[19] He was not exaggerating. Hansard barely hints at the scene, but Asquith replied to one important opposition amendment with a speech that was both cursory and incomprehensible, and to another with a very lengthy discourse on everything under the sun other than the amendment in hand, so that when Balfour referred to the 'peculiar tone' he had adopted, 'the impossibility which he found in answering the arguments' and the 'very strange performance' he had given, most members must have been quietly sniggering to themselves.[20] By the time it came to the later divisions in the middle of the night Churchill, not Asquith, was leading for the government, as the Prime Minister had retired to bed. Churchill's conclusion was just as negative as Lloyd George's: 'On Thursday night the PM was vy bad: & I squirmed with embarrassment. He could hardly speak: & many people noticed his condition ... It is an awful pity, & only the persistent freemasonry of the House of Commons prevents a scandal.'[21] Asquith did have bouts of sobriety and even abstained for a while, but after the tragic death in action of their son Raymond on 15 September 1916 his wife came upon him weeping inconsolably in

Downing Street – and within weeks the 'freemasonry of the House of Commons', or at least of the Liberal party, had decided to replace him with Lloyd George.

In each of these cases alcohol was a crutch, a sustenance, a means of escape and a fount of self-confidence and courage. But it has also played a role in lubricating parliamentary proceedings and cementing political alliances. By its very nature, parliament has always been convivial. When the medieval kings gathered their early parliaments around their courts, food and drink were an essential part of the proceedings. Often medieval parliaments were deliberately held to coincide with religious feast days – such as the Deposition of Edward the Confessor (5 January), the Feast of St Hilary (13 January), the Purification (2 February), Michaelmas (29 September) or the Confessor's Translation (13 October). The parliament of 1290 coincided with two royal weddings and a great ball, and the Whitsun parliament of 1306 saw the religious festival celebrated along with the Feast of Swans, the investiture of Prince Edward and three hundred other knights, and three noble marriages. For the coronation of Edward II in 1308 three pipes were fitted in Westminster Hall to provide a continuous flow of, respectively, red wine, white wine and piment (wine with spices and honey), and the ten-week Good Parliament of 1376 ended with a feast for the knights of the shires, who invited some of the burgesses along.

Moreover, Westminster always had a good number of local hostelries – alehouses for the lower sort, inns for travellers, and taverns for the middling and better sort. Although the White Rose Tavern that sat next door to the house Geoffrey Chaucer occupied in Westminster in 1399 was demolished in 1502 to make way for Henry VII's chapel, by the time of James I the two basement passages under the Exchequer building and adjacent to Westminster Hall, known as Hell and Purgatory, were both in use as rough and riotous public houses, forming a theological trio with a tavern at the north end of Lindsay Lane (now Abingdon Street), known as Heaven. Since Hell had formerly been a debtors' prison and Purgatory retained the old ducking stools for scolds, neither was particularly salubrious, and although Pepys dined in Hell and it got a mention in both Samuel Butler's *Hudibras* and Ben Jonson's *The Alchemist*, the reputation of both taverns, with their mixed clientele of lawyers, jurors, lawyers' clerks, knights of the shires and burgesses, was rather seedy. It may be that it was here that the writer in the *Spectator* in 1711 witnessed the occasion on which 'my lord bishop swore he would throw [the land-lady] out at the window if she did not bring up more mild beer and . . . my lord duke would have a double mug of purl [ale made with wormwood]'.[22]

Beyond the immediate vicinity of Westminster, the multitude of London's taverns and coffee-houses played a key role in democratizing political life, with MPs and peers gathering as incipient political parties at Mistress Arundel's tavern in Poultney Lane, the King's Head on the corner of Chancery Lane and Fleet Street, or the White Horse off the Strand. The Whigs' Kit-Cat club first met at a pie-shop in Shire Lane, but soon moved to the Fountain in the Strand, and for several decades the Crown and Anchor just round the corner was the grand home of radicalism, hosting a birthday dinner with two thousand guests for Charles James Fox in 1798, sending a reforming delegation to the Prime Minister in the run-up to the Reform Act of 1832 and launching the People's Charter in 1837. These often raucous tavern societies were the precursors of the politically aligned dining clubs: the Reform, the Athenaeum and the National Liberal. Indeed, the first meetings of what later became the Carlton Club were held at the Thatched House Tavern in nearby St James's Street,* and it was said of another club which met on the same premises, the Dilettanti, that its 'nominal qualification [was] having been in Italy, and the real one, being drunk', its two leading members being the Master of the Horse, Charles Sackville, Lord Middlesex MP and the Chancellor of the Exchequer, Sir Francis Dashwood MP, 'who were seldom sober the whole time they were in Italy'.[23]

* See chapter 2 above.

But with the advent of sixteenth-century Puritanism, alcohol itself became political. When James VI of Scotland assumed the English crown in 1603, his parliament decided very swiftly to draw up a new statute 'to restrain inordinate haunting and tippling in Inns, Alehouses and other Victualling Houses'. The Act was abruptly authoritarian. Inns were for the relief and lodging of travelling people, not the 'harbouring of lewd and idle people, to spend and consume their money and their time in lewd and drunken manner'; so workmen were excluded, apart from an hour at lunchtime, and only legitimate travellers and their guests were to be admitted, on pain of a large (ten shillings) fine. Clearly, this one Act did not do the trick, as in 1606 parliament made another attempt to repress 'the odious and loathsome sin of drunkenness', which was reckoned to be the root and foundation of 'bloodshed, stabbing, murder, swearing, fornication, adultery . . . and the general impoverishing of many good subjects'. This new Act made drunkenness itself an offence, for the first time in English law – but it was as signal a failure as its predecessor, and parliament came back to the matter both in 1624 and in Charles I's first parliament, when an Act was passed 'for the further restraint of tippling'.

This was legislation of rank hypocrisy. Back in Scotland, King James had softened the Puritanism of the kirk, and it was not just the later Stuart political theorist Roger Coke who reckoned that 'the king was excessively addicted to hunting and drinking'.[24] James's queen, Anna of Denmark, also complained to the French envoy that 'the King drinks so much, and conducts himself so ill in every respect, that I expect an early and evil result'.[25] James's court was regularly criticized for its lewdness and drunkenness; a prominent group of MPs, including Richard Martin, John Hoskins, Christopher Brooke, Sir Robin Phelips and William Hakewill, were members of the Sireniacal Fraternity at the Mermaid Tavern or the 'convivium' based at the Mitre, where they could thrash out ideas, plan parliamentary business, indulge their liberty of speech and hone their wit; and John Pory got 'prettily well whittled' at a banquet laid on by Sir Edward Hoby in February 1607.[26]

The Puritans took a very dim view of all this. Ale and beer (ale brewed with hops) might in moderation be good, honest and indeed necessary, as clean drinking water was hard to come by. But William Vaughn preached in 1611 that alehouses 'breed conspiracies, combinations, common conjurations, detractions and defamations', and twenty years later Christopher Hudson maintained that they were the 'nests of Satan where the owls of impiety lurk and where all evil is hatched'.[27] Although such Puritan suspicion of alcohol of any kind was common before and during the Interregnum – in August 1647 Bulstrode Whitelocke recorded a petition to the Long Parliament from Devon against the undue election of burgesses who are 'strong in wine but weak in wisdom'[28] – Cromwell was more inclined to the regulation of alehouses and taverns and the suppression of drunkenness than the direct prohibition of alcohol. But with many royalists claiming (inaccurately) that he was the hypocritical killjoy son of a brewer, getting drunk, especially on French wine, became a sign of royalist patriotism.

So with the return of the monarchy came wine and exuberance. Indeed, the first Scottish parliament after the Restoration involved so much drunken revelry that it became known as the 'drunken' parliament, and Sir Walter Scott recounted that the members were frequently 'under the influence of wine, and they were more than once obliged to adjourn because the royal commissioner [John, 1st earl of Middleton] was too intoxicated to behave properly in the chair'.[29] It was the same back in London, where cavaliers ostentatiously disported themselves even in the Chamber, where, according to Pepys, on 19 December 1666 Sir Allen Broderick and Sir Allen Apsley 'did both come drunk the other day into the House and did both speak for half an hour together, and could not be either laughed or pulled, or bid to sit down and hold their peace'.[30] Many of the restored king's closest friends in the Lords threw restraint to the winds. It was said of the earl of Rochester that 'for five years together he was continually drunk',[31] and in 1682 a member of the Whig Junto, Thomas Wharton, got away with breaking into the church in Great Barrington, Gloucestershire, and relieving himself against the communion table and in the pulpit, being reprimanded for it only years later.

Even drink-fuelled violence was quietly condoned, as following the politicized trial of Edward Nosworthy MP in 1684 (for wishing at the height of the Exclusion crisis that the judges who had controversially convicted the Catholic Irishman Sir Edward Fitzharris of treason in 1681 might hang). After Nosworthy's acquittal on 14 October, the high-spirited jury, including several MPs – the foreman of the jury, Sir William Estcourt, the Tory Edmund Webb and the Whig Henry St John – retired late that night to the Globe Tavern in Fleet Street, having already downed several bottles of claret. Somehow St John got into a hot-tempered row with a former MP, Francis Stonehouse, who called him a fool, whereupon St John threw a bottle at him and ran at Estcourt with his sword drawn. Estcourt fell to the ground, where St John pummelled him into submission and Webb ran him through. St John and Webb were both found guilty of murder at the Old Bailey in December but managed to get pardoned. Clearly, well-placed Restoration gentlemen could disport themselves as they pleased under the influence of alcohol. Against such a background it is understandable that the independently minded self-confessed 'trimmer', George Savile, marquess of Halifax, complained about MPs' drinking habits after the Glorious Revolution in 1695: 'Great Drinkers are less fit to Serve in Parliament than is apprehended . . . Nothing is more frail than a Man too far engaged in wet Popularity . . . the vapours of Wine may sometimes throw out sparks of Wit, but they are like scattered pieces of Ore, there is no Vein to work upon.' [32]

The question was not just whether to drink, but what to drink, as although the wealthy could always afford expensive foreign wine, the constantly changing alliances with or against France, the Netherlands, Spain and Portugal led to parliamentary demands for tariffs as a form of political sanction or boycott;* that changed the price of imported wine, and that in turn changed people's drinking habits. So in 1675, at

* The term 'boycott' comes from a campaign run by Charles Stewart Parnell and the Irish National Land League in 1880 against the land agent to John Crichton, the 3rd Earl Erne, a Captain Charles Boycott.

a time when the opalescent court of Louis XIV lent fashionable lustre to all things French, nearly two-thirds of the wine imported to London came from France; but during the War of Spanish Succession (1703–12), when the Sun King became the enemy, 62 per cent of the wine quaffed in England and Wales came from Portugal, another 16 per cent from Spain and a mere 8 per cent from France. In a short space of time people had switched allegiance from French claret to 'a rough red table wine from the Douro Valley in northern Portugal',[33] port. This was no accident. The country party deliberately acted against French wine in 1679 in retribution for Charles II's secret deal with France – and the court party retaliated by adopting claret as their Tory tipple of choice and by denouncing those Whigs who supported the prohibition of French wines, like the earl of Shaftesbury, whose surname was Cooper (echoing the snobbish anti-ale slur against Cromwell). When William and Mary came to the throne, the Whig parliament again banned French imports and for a while Spain grabbed the lion's share of the English market; but when England, Portugal and the Netherlands united in asserting the claim of the Archduke Charles to the Spanish throne against the French, an accompanying treaty exchanged favourable terms for Portuguese wines in England and for English cloth in Lisbon. Dismayed Tories such as Charles Davenant managed to get the ban on claret overturned when they came to power in 1711, but the Whig bishop of Salisbury, Gilbert Burnet, complained that 'the interest of the nation lay against it so visibly, that nothing but the delicate palates of those who loved that liquor, could have carried such a motion through the two houses'.[34] To every Tory plea that people preferred claret came a Whig appeal to a patriotic hatred of France. As an anonymous poet put it in 1713:

> Be sometimes to your country true,
> Have once the public good in view;
> Bravely despise champagne at court
> And choose to dine at home on port.[35]

Whigs laughed at Tories for their toasting of the Jacobite king across the water with French-made claret. Far better, far more patriotic, was port. Such distinctions were to last well into the nineteenth century, with (Spanish) sherry stealing such a march that whereas in 1824 the 3rd earl of Ashburnham had 904 bottles of port in his cellar and just 283 of sherry, in 1831 his son the 4th earl had 1,213 bottles of sherry to just 335 of port. Neither, of course, was French, but even Gladstone in 1860 was criticizing those who still thought it 'an article of Christian faith, that an Englishman is not born to drink French wines'.[36]

Yet more controversy was provoked by the arrival from across the channel of a Dutch invention: gin. The precise date of gin's arrival in Britain is unknown, although 'geneva', the anglicized version of the Dutch 'genever', gets a mention in Philip Massinger's 1623 play *The Duke of Milan*. When all things Dutch achieved sudden popularity on the coat-tails of William of Orange in 1688, parliament deliberately promoted it as a potentially home-made alternative to French imports, and soon English distillers were manufacturing it in vast quantities. Then the law of unintended consequences kicked in with a vengeance, as rising incomes in the eighteenth century saw the consumption of gin rise and magistrates began to complain that it was 'the principal cause of all the vice and debauchery committed among the inferior sort of people'.[37] As gin flowed through the alleys of London the politicians grew fretful. A Gin Act was introduced in 1729, imposing a duty of two shillings a gallon and requiring distillers to take out a £20 annual licence, but a year later there were 7,000 gin shops in London alone and John, Lord Hervey complained that with people able to get dead drunk for a groat (fourpence), 'the whole town of London, and many towns in the country, swarmed with drunken people of both sexes from morning till night'.[38] Parliament's response came in 1736: the licence fee was increased to £50 and the duty to £1 per gallon. Suddenly, legally retailed gin was prohibitively expensive, and all the worst features of twentieth-century American Prohibition ensued. Gin distillers went underground, criminal enterprises took over the business, adulterated gin led to poisonings, there were extensive riots and the government's paid informers were attacked. Walpole, who had opposed the Act, was proved right: you couldn't legislate against the tastes of the people. In 1743 the 1736 Act was repealed with a system of magistrate-approved licences and moderate duties that encouraged more artisan distillation, and a final Gin Act of 1751 set the seal on a sensibly moderated system of licensing the sale of spirits.

Once again, this parliamentary preoccupation with the drinking habits of the poor was supremely hypocritical, as the eighteenth century saw parliament at its most alcoholic, many of the leading lights in both houses regularly drinking to utter excess. According to Gilbert Elliot in 1788, '[Charles James] Fox drinks what I would call a great deal . . . Sheridan excessively, and [Charles] Grey more than any of them.'[39] Certainly Fox glugged back a positively dangerous quantity, and when he died at fifty-six in 1806 his liver was found to be 'preternaturally hard' and 'almost entirely schirrous'.[40] His friend and ally Sheridan was a drinker of similar renown. Another convivialist and writer, Lord Byron, recalled a dinner at which Sheridan was 'first silent, then talky, then argumentative, then inarticulate, and then drunk,'[41] and Sheridan's wife Eliza reprimanded him when he failed to make it to the Commons one Monday due to a hangover: 'Would you have me say', she asked, '[that] drinking to that excess is not an abominable habit?'[42] His drinking got worse, too. Everyone thought he was drunk both when he made a 'very violent' speech in the Commons in the early hours of 21 January 1808, and again when he laid into William Windham on 12 April, but on 16 June that year he went too far. Even the brewer's son and leader of the Whigs, Samuel Whitbread, told Grey that Sheridan 'was so exceedingly drunk he could hardly articulate. A more disgraceful exhibition was seldom if ever witnessed.'[43]

Similar habits prevailed on the other side of the House. Pitt the Younger would regularly drink through the night and consume the equivalent of between one and a half and two modern bottles of strong wine at a single sitting. George Canning commented that Pitt had drunk 'I do not know how much Madeira' at one dinner, the *Morning Chronicle* cruelly noted that Pitt was 'observed, in walking to his carriage, to oscillate like his own bills',[44] and Sir William Napier maintained that when Pitt came home to dinner rather exhausted he 'seemed to require wine, port, of which he generally drank a bottle, or nearly so, in a rapid succession of glasses'.[45] Pitt would even get roaring drunk at a time of maximum political pressure – and then expect to perform well in the Chamber. One key such moment came in 1783 when he was the 23-year-old Chancellor of the Exchequer in Shelburne's ministry and had to reply to a vital debate on the peace treaty with France. A first debate on 17 February had led to a government defeat by sixteen votes; on the twenty-first Wilberforce recorded that Pitt drank so much port that he had to hold the door to Solomon's porch behind the Speaker's chair open with one hand, 'while vomiting during Fox's speech to whom he was to reply'.[46] He then gave a three-hour speech, lasting until four in the morning, which Wilberforce reckoned was a great success. Five years later, however, Pitt was completely incapacitated on at least one occasion as Prime Minister, and his drinking exploits with his friend Henry Dundas became notorious. As James Grant wrote in 1836, 'the practice of seeing double in the House, after a certain hour, is not new. It was quite common as far back as the days of Pitt and Dundas. They were in the habit of dialoguing each other after having dined together, as follows: Pitt – "I can't see the Speaker, Hal; can you?" Dundas – "Not see the Speaker, Billy! I see two!"'[46]

Members' excessive propensity for drink was not helped by the fact that when John Bellamy was appointed deputy housekeeper of the Lords and Commons in 1773 he created a kitchen-cum-tavern, connected to the lobby of the Commons by a long corridor, in which members could sit and down a few draughts or take tea or coffee. Bellamy's was no architectural gem – the main room was dominated by a roasting-jack and a gridiron hung over a large fire – but its major innovation was the posting of a man at the entrance who could relay news of who was speaking in the Chamber. So members of both houses could happily wine and dine until they heard the 'annunciator' declare that Mr Fox, Mr Pitt or Earl Grey was about to speak.*

This was a dramatic change. The old rules of the House of Commons had allowed some refreshment in the Chamber itself: the lobby of the Commons had an orange-seller who also sold biscuits, and the Prussian clergyman Karl Moritz noted in 1782 that MPs cracked nuts and ate oranges in the Chamber – indeed, when Henry Brougham made a six-hour speech on law reform on 7 February 1828 he sustained himself by regularly sucking on one of the oranges he had stored in his hat by his side. The radical MP Joseph Hume would be present in the Chamber for virtually every minute that the House sat and chewed on pears throughout the day, and in August 1880 the Irish nationalist Alexander Sullivan brought in a bag of buns for a 21-hour sitting and munched his way through 'a palpable supper'.[47]

But the advent of Bellamy's within the Palace precincts trans-formed parliament. Now one could spend the whole day within the Palace (although the story that Pitt the Younger expired with the words 'I think I could eat one of Bellamy's veal pies' on his lips is untrue). Along with much else, Bellamy's was burnt down in the conflagration of 1834, but when Barry's new Palace was completed the Lords and Commons gained a suite of ornate restaurants and bars, a smoking room and a tea room, including hierarchical dining rooms for Cabinet colleagues, junior ministers and other ranks. Personal preferences varied. Loulou Harcourt dined only at the Cabinet table and ordered very particularly. Many MPs and peers understandably liked to go home for dinner with their wives. Parnell preferred the anonymity of dining out with Kitty O'Shea. And Sir Richard Temple complained in 1886 that the dining rooms were far inferior to those of most gentlemen's clubs, a view echoed by the Scottish Liberal Sir John

---

* For much of its history, the Commons insisted that a member could not vote unless he was present in the Chamber to hear the vote being called. The 'annunciator' now takes the form of several television screens around the parliamentary estate that display the subject under debate, the name of the speaker and the length of time he or she has spoken.

Sinclair in 1872 (though his main complaint seemed to be that the division bell irritatingly interrupted dinner). But eating and dining together in neo-Gothic splendour became as central a part of being an MP as joining a club was essential to being a Victorian gentleman. This conviviality could be a tyrant, as those who eschewed it risked appearing aloof and at least one MP, Alfred Gathorne-Hardy, was widely reckoned to have missed out on promotion because he preferred his wife's company at dinner to that of his colleagues.

The inherent contradictions of nineteenth-century MPs' attitudes towards drinking are nicely exemplified by an incident in a vital no-confidence debate on 28 January 1840. The anxious Whig MP for Carlow Borough, Thomas Gisborne, was defending the Melbourne government when he broke down several times, asked for oranges and finally pleaded 'some physical inability'. According to Disraeli (who penned several eulogies to wine) the Tories thought he was drunk, but 'the Whigs say the fault was that he was not, and that when he is tipsy, and is not prepared, he is very good'.[48]

The result of these private and public inconsistencies was that parliament oscillated between liberalizing and restricting the sale of beer and spirits. In 1828 an Alehouse Act loosened the reins, and an 1830 Act openly boasted that it was 'expedient for the better supplying the public with Beer in England, to give greater facilities for the sale thereof', whereupon the nation rejoiced so much that they named many of the new public houses after the new King William. By 1871, though, the mood had changed under the influence of a growing temperance movement and, despite harbouring many a wealthy brewer in its midst, Gladstone's government attempted to bring in an Intoxicating Liquor (Licensing) Bill to curtail the drinking of the supposedly feckless poor. In response Bishop William Magee told the Lords that he thought 'it would be better that England should be free than that England should be compulsorily sober',[49] and the earl of Kimberley deplored the tendency to demand that the government 'remedy evils which I am satisfied cannot be remedied either by the police or by a still higher authority'.[50] Gladstone did not get his Bill first time out, but when it was passed the following year, it very effectively turned every alehouse in the country into a recruiting office for the Conservatives, who won the 1874 election on the promise of liberalization of the licensing laws. No wonder Gladstone felt he had been 'borne down in a torrent of gin and beer'.* By now the pattern had been established: the Liberals were for restrictive licensing, the Tories for slaking the popular thirst.

Despite the Chartists' origins in the Crown and Anchor, they too were keen to temper the alcoholic intake of the labouring classes, and by the turn of the twentieth century there was a multiplicity of non-conformist, Anglican and Catholic temperance societies. Many of the leading figures of the early Labour movement, including Keir Hardie, Arthur Henderson, George Lansbury, David Shackleton, Philip Snowden and Herbert Morrison, were dedicated teetotal campaigners against the demon drink. Some of this was personal. Hardie and Lansbury were scarred by the experience of alcoholic fathers, and Morrison was sent to spy on his father's drinking in the local pub by his mother. But for many it was the only way of rescuing the poor from poverty. As Hardie put it to a crowd, they 'robbed themselves of their manhood by swilling in a public house'.[51] Such was the antipathy to alcohol within the ILP that when a candidate stood down in 1895 to run a public house, he was viciously condemned, and as late as 1935 the Bermondsey GP and MP Alfred Salter claimed that 74 out of 154 Labour MPs were teetotal. For many others, though, temperance was both strategically foolhardy and personally unappealing. Ben Tillett, who was originally teetotal but lapsed into alcoholism, openly attacked his colleagues in 1908, maintaining that Henderson, Shackleton and Snowden had 'out-Heroded the worst ranters in denouncing their own class for supposed drunkenness and thriftlessness'.[52] The exchanges could be acerbic. Jimmy Thomas came under sustained attack from Snowden for spending one hundred and fifty days a year attending

* See page 70 above.

lunches and dinners, in the course of which, his critic calculated, 'he consumes nine gallons of champagne and his laundry bill for starched shirts comes to £18 a year'.[53] This was not the height of respectability to which Snowden thought a Labour man should aspire.

The otherwise hedonistic Lloyd George would have agreed. In the First World War he was convinced that alcohol would do more damage to Britain's chances of winning the war than German submarines, so in 1915 a Defence of the Realm Act stipulated a sharp restriction on pub opening hours that was maintained well into the late twentieth century. Such puritanism fed its way back into parliament: the chairman of the Commons Kitchen Committee, Sir James Agg-Gardner (himself a brewery owner), reckoned that MPs in the 1920s dined more wisely as 'the heavier wines formerly in vogue' had been supplanted by light French and German wines, lager beer and cider, and 'that rare as was then the appearance of inebriety, of recent years there has never been the slightest sign'.[54]

By the time of the Second World War, though, social attitudes had changed again. The Labour party had selected fewer and fewer abstentionists, the Liberals were a spent force, and at the national helm was one of the most enthusiastic drinkers parliament has seen, Winston Churchill. Many have tried to dismiss the accounts of Churchill's drinking as exaggerated. One of his many biographers, Roy Jenkins, argued that he was 'a sipper, not a guzzler'. But the pattern seems to have been sustained over many years. He took a first whisky and soda after breakfast (Eden noted that it was a 'stiff' one) and followed it up with champagne at lunch and brandy in the afternoon. He told his wife that he drank 'champagne at all meals and buckets of claret and soda in between'.[55] One official recorded that Churchill drank 'a good deal of champagne, port, brandy and Cointreau' at a lunch and ended it with two glasses of whisky and soda,[56] and at a meeting of the Defence Committee in 1944, Admiral Andrew Cunningham commented that Churchill was 'in no fit state to discuss anything – too tired and too much alcohol'.[57] President Roosevelt even commented when Churchill became Prime Minister that 'he supposed Churchill was the best man that England had, even if he was drunk half of his time'.[58] Churchill made no attempt to hide his drinking. Two of his most famous aphorisms openly confess his drunkenness. When Bessie Braddock accused him of being drunk as he left the Commons in 1946 he replied: 'Madam, you are ugly. In the morning I shall be sober.' And he maintained: 'I have taken more out of alcohol than it has taken out of me.'[59] Yet it is now uncontested that Churchill suffered from depression, and several of those closest to him were alcoholics pure and simple. The story of Churchill's closest personal friendship, with F. E. Smith, shows just how endemic heavy drinking was in parliamentary circles. Brought up in north-western middle-class wealth, and losing his father when he was just sixteen, F.E. was such a rapid success at the Bar that he was soon commanding £10,000 a year, and when he found himself a seat in the Commons in 1906 his maiden speech was received with rapturous acclaim. He and Churchill disagreed on everything – tariff reform, the 'people's budget', the Parliament Act – but, having both been denied membership of a dining society known as the Club, the pair set up their own, the Other Club, with the rule that 'Nothing in the rules or intercourse of the Club shall interfere with the rancour or asperity of party politics'.[60] It was an expensive business, coming in at £2 a meal every fortnight, but for Churchill and Smith, both of whom had something of the outsider about them, bibulous conviviality was an integral part of the political endeavour.

Not everyone cared for the aggressively opinionated and acute Lord Chancellor Birkenhead (as F.E. became in 1919). Margot Asquith wittily remarked that his brains 'appear to have gone to his head',[61] and when he campaigned in Churchill's stead in the general election of 1922, Winston being laid low with appendicitis, Clementine Churchill complained that Birkenhead was no use at all, as he was drunk. He made more enemies in the 1920s, thanks to rude attacks on Cabinet ministers as 'second-rate brains' and on Sir George Younger as 'the cabin boy', but by then he was well on the way to an early grave. In his early years he had been suave, lean and preternaturally muscular and healthy, but by the time he reached his fifties he was worn out and overweight. He died in 1930, aged just fifty-eight. His son, Frederick Winston, the 2nd earl, to whom Churchill was godfather, managed to rescue himself from alcoholism, but his godson Randolph Churchill also died of drink, aged fifty-seven. That Winston managed to survive to ninety betrays an iron constitution, but perhaps C. P. Snow got it right when he reckoned Churchill was not an alcoholic as no alcoholic could drink that much.

Later twentieth-century attitudes to alcohol continued to swing like a drunken pendulum as post-war, pre-television politics saw parliament get more alcoholic. In 1957, for instance, the *Spectator* alleged that on a trip to Venice the general secretary of the Labour party, Morgan Phillips, and two Labour MPs, Nye Bevan and Richard Crossman, 'puzzled the Italians by their capacity to fill themselves like tanks with whiskey and coffee'.[62] It was one thing to be drunk, or indeed to know that another MP was drunk, but since it was remarkably difficult to prove that someone was drunk after the event and being inebriated was considered a significant personal failing in polite society, the three sued the paper and won £2,500 each in damages. The story was true, however. Crossman wrote in his diary that Phillips 'drank steadily – I think mainly to avoid conversation – with the result that he got tiddly by midday and soaked by dinner time', and that he was 'dead drunk for most of the conference'.[63] They were not the only MPs to protest too much. In 1983 the minister at the dispatch box for a late-night debate on sex discrimination was the Conservative roué and exceptional diarist Alan Clark, who despite having only just been appointed a minister had done no preparation and made it very clear that he did not believe a word of the brief that he was reading out. MPs rapidly began to suspect that something was wrong as he got slower and slower; first Clare Short, then Michael Martin (a teetotaller) demanded that he speed it up a bit, and Dame Elaine Kellett-Bowman suggested that he might take a speed-reading course. It all got even more heated when Short suggested that he should either believe what he said or else resign, to which he imperiously replied that when she had been an MP a little longer she would appreciate that 'a certain separation between expressed and implied beliefs is endemic among those who hold office'. This prompted Short to rise on a point of order. 'I have read in the newspapers,' she said, 'that in the House one is not allowed to accuse another hon. Member of not being sober. However, I seriously put it to you that the Minister is incapable.'[64] Amid much fake outrage and screams of 'order', the Deputy Speaker forced her to apologize, but Clark later confessed in his diary that he had been to a wine tasting that evening where he had 'tasted' a bottle of '61 Palmer, plus 'for comparison' a bottle of the '75 before switching back to the '61, 'a really delicious Pichon Longueville', so that by the time he arrived in the Commons he was 'muzzy'.[65] Yet again the pre-television freemasonry of the House of Commons saved him from a scandal that would today almost certainly end a ministerial career.

Plenty of modern politicians have suffered far worse from alcohol's mastery of them. The attractive former television journalist Fiona Jones was just forty when she was elected as MP for the normally safe Conservative seat of Newark in 1997. Within weeks the Liberal Democrats complained to the police that the election expenses she filed did not represent the full amount that she had spent on the campaign and that she had therefore been fraudulently elected. A prosecution was brought under the Representation of the People Act 1983 and although the trial judge threw out most of the charges, Jones and her agent were convicted of 'corrupt practices' on 10 March 1999 and she was thereby deprived of her seat. No by-election writ was moved pending her appeal and on 15 April the conviction was quashed by the Court of Appeal. Two weeks later she took her seat in the Commons again. Thereafter she dwindled into alcoholic un-happiness; in 2001 she lost her seat, and in 2007 her husband found her dead at home surrounded by fifteen empty vodka bottles. The death certificate said she had died from 'alcoholic liver disease'.

She was not alone in falling victim to the bottle. Jamie Cann, the MP for Ipswich, was found guilty of drunk driving in 1998 and died of liver disease in October 2001. Charles Kennedy has now admitted that he was an alcoholic even before he became leader of the Liberal Democrats. Eric Joyce, the MP for Falkirk, was convicted of drunk driving in 2010, and although he apologized to the House on 4 July 2012 for a drunken assault on at least three MPs in the Strangers' Bar (for which he was fined but not imprisoned by the courts), he was banned from all the Palace's bars in 2013 following another drunken brawl.

Parliament's unsteady, inconstant and often downright hypocritical relationship with alcohol claimed one other victim, though. Garry Allighan was not an MP for long. A journalist by trade, he was elected for Gravesend in the Labour landslide of 1945, and in 1947 he wrote an article for the *World's Press News* in which he maintained that MPs had been divulging private information about other MPs to newspapers for cash or free drinks. There then ensued the most sustained piece of parliamentary self-righteousness imaginable. MPs protested in furious manner. The Committee on Standards and Privileges was forced to investigate this gross calumny and contempt of parliament, and when they in turn found that only two MPs had done any such thing, Evelyn Walkden and Allighan himself, demanded that the editor of the paper appear at the bar of the House, that Walkden apologize and that Allighan be suspended from the House for six months. The debate was irritable. True, Allighan did not help himself by giving what the committee called evidence 'of an evasive and contradictory nature', and retracting 'the allegation of insobriety which I made against unnamed Members' with ill grace.[66] But when the teetotaller Herbert Morrison moved the several motions as Leader of the House, he was ludicrously po-faced. In the end, 198 MPs decided that Allighan was 'guilty of dishonourable conduct which deserves to be severely punished' and 101, including Churchill, thought that he wasn't. He was permanently expelled, supposedly for 'corruptly accepting payment for the disclosure of information about matters to be proceeded with in Parliament obtained from other Members under the obligation of secrecy'.[67] In truth, though, he had merely broken the code of parliamentary *omertà* by revealing that sometimes MPs drank too much. No wonder Churchill could not bring himself to convict him.

DROPPING THE PILOT (BY FORCE IF NECESSARY)

Enoch Powell's maxim that 'all political lives, unless they are cut off in midstream at a happy juncture, end in failure' is not wholly accurate. Yet the manner of politicians' departing the political scene is rarely of their own choosing. Mirroring Sir John Tenniel's cartoon of Otto von Bismarck's enforced departure as Germany's Chancellor in 1890, Britain's first woman Prime Minister, Margaret Thatcher, is seen here being dropped from the ship of state by her Cabinet ministers, whom she unwisely consulted one by one in November 1990.

10

Post the Post-war Consensus

ON WEDNESDAY, 28 MARCH 1979 the leader of the opposition, Mrs Margaret Thatcher, rose to speak on a motion of no confidence in the Labour government of Jim Callaghan. The Commons was never her preferred stage. Harold Wilson and then Callaghan had regularly bested her at the twice-weekly Prime Minister's Questions,[1] and she had little of the magisterial ease or public-school swagger that the Commons likes. Her performance that Wednesday was pedestrian – so much so that not a single member tried to intervene during the thirty-one minutes she was speaking: she was heard in bored silence, and even she thought it no 'triumph of oratory'. But then, there was little need for parliamentary histrionics. All that mattered was the arithmetic, and in Thatcher's words, 'it would take more than rhetoric to persuade the unpredictable Members upon whose decisions the outcome depended'.[2]

The arithmetic was tight. In the two elections of 1974 the urbane, witty and fiercely clever Harold Wilson had won first the largest number of seats and then a diaphanous majority of three. But that had been shaved even thinner when the Labour MP John Stonehouse faked his own death, absconded to Australia and was arrested for insurance fraud on Christmas Eve 1974; and then Peter Bottomley won the Woolwich West by-election to take the seat from Labour on 26 June 1975. Even leaving aside the dire state of the economy (high unemployment, soaring inflation, many traditional British industries in collapse and a cap-in-hand trip to the International Monetary Fund in 1976), the government looked in danger as low-grade scandal circled Wilson's kitchen cabinet and the symptoms of tired decline became only too clear: personal enmities between key members, sharp Cabinet divisions over economic policy, and constant leaks. When Wilson suddenly resigned as Prime Minister in April 1976 (probably suffering from the early stages of Alzheimer's), and Callaghan defeated Michael Foot in the third round of the Labour leadership contest, the underlying political problems remained. Labour lost two more seats on 4 November 1976, when Stonehouse was convicted and when Fred Peart was unnecessarily promoted to the Lords to be its Leader. For a while the government attempted to live from hand to mouth, but when three more unforced errors (Roy Jenkins and David Marquand's appointments respectively as European Commissioner and *chef de cabinet*, and Reg Prentice's defection to the Conservatives) lost them more seats in early 1977, a pact was formed with the Liberals under David Steel, guaranteeing support in any vote of no confidence. By the autumn of 1978 that pact had lapsed and, with a general election inevitable by October 1979, Callaghan was reliant on the votes of the fourteen Scottish and Welsh Nationalist MPs and the two former Labour MPs Jim Sillars and John Robertson, who had broken off from Labour in 1976 to form the pro-devolution Scottish Labour party. Even so, had Callaghan gone to the country in late 1978, he might have won. His personal popularity ran far ahead of his party's, his policy of enforced wage restraint (which Thatcher, unlike most of her shadow Cabinet, opposed) had managed to bring inflation down from its peak of 20 per cent to single figures and, although unemployment was stubbornly high at 1.5 million, the economy was recuperating. But Callaghan calculated that the longer he waited the stronger the economy would be; so when the government lost a vote on its counter-inflation policy by two votes on 13 December he confidently tabled his own confidence motion the

Politics has always been a convivial pursuit. **Clockwise from top left**: **William Pitt the Younger** was so drunk before one of his most important speeches that he was violently sick behind the Speaker's chair. **Sir Francis Dashwood**, an eighteenth-century Chancellor of the Exchequer, was a member of the Dilettanti, renowned for being 'seldom sober'. **Roy Jenkins** described Winston Churchill as 'a sipper, not a guzzler', but enjoyed a bibulous lunch himself. And the euphemism 'tired and emotional' was coined expressly for **George Brown**, seen here collapsing on the night of his resignation from the Labour Party.

Above: Working-class MPs were one thing, professed socialists quite another: in the flamboyant 'Don Roberto' Cunninghame Graham, Westminster had its first avowed socialist, though decidedly non-proletarian, MP.

Above: Henry Broadhurst started his working life as a journeying stonemason on the Palace of Westminster but rose to be a junior minister in the Home Office in 1886 and sat as a Lib-Lab MP for a total of twenty-four years.

Below: Thanks to an electoral pact with the Liberals, twenty-nine Labour MPs were elected in the 1906 general election. They formed the parliamentary Labour party, which celebrated its centenary on 12 February 2006 (**below**).

Above: Archbishop William Temple (standing) first coined the term 'welfare state' and called the 1942 report by William Beveridge (seated, with Temple in Central Hall) an embodiment of 'the whole spirit of the Christian ethic in an Act of Parliament'.

Left: Labour's first Prime Minister, Ramsay MacDonald, arrives at the House of Commons on 1 October 1924. A week later he was toppled by a Liberal motion that was tantamount to a vote of no confidence.

Above: Although many expected Winston Churchill to repeat Lloyd George's 1918 success by winning the general election held immediately after the war in 1945, the mild-mannered Clement Attlee won a majority of 145.

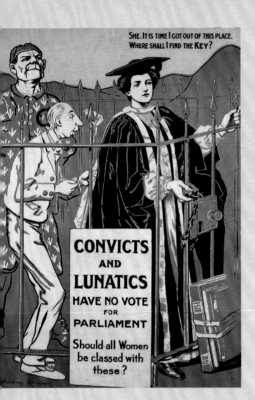

SHE. IT IS TIME I GOT OUT OF THIS PLACE. WHERE SHALL I FIND THE KEY?

CONVICTS
AND
LUNATICS
HAVE NO VOTE
FOR
PARLIAMENT

Should all Women
be classed with
these ?

PROCLAMATION.

Whereas the Nation depends for the progress and usefulness upon the work and services of women as well as of men ;

Whereas the State is organised for the mutual protection and cooperation of all its citizens, women as well as men ;

Whereas the development conduces the national building by means of taxes levied upon women as well as men ;

Whereas the women of the Nation have made clear their need for political rights, and their desire to possess the Parliamentary Vote ;

Since working women, not content to take home, are in special need of the protection of the Vote since legislation is daily saying more and more with their interests :

— the

EN'S FREEDOM LEAGUE

calls upon these women to remove the one disability which deprives qualified women of their just right of voting in the Parliamentary elections, and

DEMANDS

the removal the disabilities of the Franchise to Women on the same terms as it is, or may be extended to men.

The Nation can never be free until the law recognises and establishes

VOTES FOR WOMEN

THE DEMAND IS JUST   THE REFORM INEVITABLE

DELAY IS UNWISE AND UNJUST

Therefore in the Name of Liberty and Humanity the Women's Freedom League claims the Vote

THIS SESSION.

Above: On 28 October 1908 two suffragettes unfurled this banner from the Ladies' Gallery in the Commons and chained themselves to the grille, shouting 'Votes for women!'.

Left: Although women had played a significant role in politics for centuries, the Reform Act of 1832 entitled only 'ma persons' to vote. Women did not win the vote on an equal basis with men until 19

Conservative women MPs in 1931: Lady Iveagh, Irene Ward, Thelma Cazalet-Keir, Mavis Tate, Ida Copeland, Lady Astor, Sarah Ward, Florence Horsbrough, Mary Pickford, the Duchess of Atholl and Norah Runge.

Left: Margaret Mackworth inherited from her father her title as 2nd Viscountess Rhondda in her own right; but women only gained admittance to the Lords a month after she died in 1958, and *suo jure* peeresses had to wait until 1963.

Below: Many issues united women MPs across the party divide. A vote in favour of equal pay for teachers was overturned in the Second World War; here Irene Ward (Con), Barbara Castle (Lab) and Edith Summerskill (Lab) campaign for equal pay in 1954.

Below: On 22 November 1990, having already lost her own party's leadership, Britain's first woman Prime Minister, Margaret Thatcher, defeated a motion of no confidence, declaring as she gave her last speech in the Commons: 'I am enjoying this!'

Above left: Parliament has not been immune to fraud or corruption. Speaker Sir John Trevor was removed in 1695 for accepting a bribe to hasten along the City of London's Orphans Bill.

Above right: Before the secret ballot was introduced in 1872, election was regularly secured through bribing voters with cash or food and drink. This satire of 1722 shows the election carried by 'Bribery and the Devil'.

Right: The fraudster Jabez Balfour was an MP for nine years between 1880 and 1893, but in 1895 he was sentenced to fourteen years of penal servitude as prisoner V460-14.

parliament pro-rogued

Above: There was widespread public cynicism about political corruption long before the 'peerages for sale' scandal broke in 1922. This cartoon dates from before the First World War.

Right: In 1922 the Liberal MP Horatio Bottomley was imprisoned for fraud and perjury and expelled from the Commons. When the prison chaplain saw him mending mail bags he asked: 'Sewing, Bottomley?' to which the former MP replied: 'No, reaping.'

Left: On 18 July 1972 Reginald Maudling resigned as the Conservative Home Secretary over his involvement in a network of corrupt financial deals run by John Poulson. Two other MPs were involved: John Cordle (Conservative) and Albert Roberts (Labour).

The first two Asian MPs were both of Indian Parsi heritage. Dadabhai Naoroji (**right**) was Liberal MP for Finsbury Central from 1892 to 1895 and three times President of the Indian National Congress; Sir Mancherjee Merwanjee Bhownaggree (**left**) was elected as the Conservative member for North East Bethnal Green in 1895 and 1900.

Left: Another Indian of Parsi heritage, Shapurji Saklatvala, seen here addressing crowds in Trafalga Square on 'Unemployment Sunday' in 1922, was elected for Battersea North as a Communist with Labou backing in 1922 and 1923.

Below: In 1987 the first three black MPs were elected: Paul Boateng, Bernie Grant and Diane Abbott, seen here with Keith Vaz at the Labour party conference in Blackpool the following year.

next day. As Callaghan had secured the Ulster Unionists' votes in return for the creation of additional Northern Ireland seats in the Commons, Michael Foot confidently predicted 'that the vote of confidence will be carried tonight by a thumping majority, and when it is we shall come back after the next election – at a time chosen by the Prime Minister – with an even bigger majority'.[3] He was to prove a poor clairvoyant. Callaghan staved off defeat that night by ten votes, but then found himself at the mercy of events when months of strikes (which Labour ministers themselves dubbed a 'winter of discontent') gave the Tories unexpected succour, and the referendums on government plans for Scottish and Welsh devolution held on 1 March produced the worst of all possible results (in Scotland, a small majority in favour was baulked by a turnout short of the 40 per cent threshold that had been inserted into the Act thanks to two Labour rebels, Neil Kinnock and George Cunningham, and in Wales there was a four to one majority against the plans). As deeply riven by internal disputes on devolution as it was on the economy, the Labour government refused to push through the proposals, prompting the Scottish Nationalists to table a motion of no confidence for 28 March.

In the debate the customarily genial but occasionally caustic Callaghan was scathing about the opposition parties' tactics. The Tory chief whip, Humphrey Atkins, had 'scurried round to the Liberal Party to find out if it would vote for a motion of censure', the Liberals, 'spinning like a top', had assured him that they would and, thus fortified, the opposition had tabled their own vote of no confidence. In other words,

> once the Leader of the Opposition discovered what the Liberals and the SNP would do, she found the courage of their convictions. So, tonight, the Conservative Party, which wants the Act repealed and opposes even devolution, will march through the Lobby with the SNP, which wants independence for Scotland, and with the Liberals, who want to keep the Act. What a massive display of unsullied principle![4]

Whatever the theoretical numbers before a vote, the Commons can often produce a surprise as MPs succumb to last-minute blandishments, illness, their consciences or party loyalty. On this occasion there was a strike among Commons catering staff, so many Tory MPs went to their clubs or the Savoy to eat, and in between bouts of arm-twisting Thatcher and her close colleagues consumed two large hampers from Fortnum's in the opposition chief whip's office off the members' lobby. One Labour MP, Sir Alfred 'Doc' Broughton, was mortally ill but offered to travel from Yorkshire if necessary. Fearing that he might die en route, Callaghan vacillated, but by the time he asked him to make the journey it was too late. Meanwhile several MPs still had to decide how to vote, including the phalanx of Unionists and two Irish MPs sympathetic to Labour, Gerry Fitt and Frank Maguire, the latter of whom had yet to make his maiden speech. There was even a row between the two deputy chief whips over the convention that a mortally sick MP who could not vote would be paired by a fit MP who would abstain, a row that ended in Bernard Weatherill offering personally to pair with Broughton and Walter Harrison, for the government, releasing him from the deal as he knew it would end his counterpart's career.

When the division came at ten o'clock in the evening, nobody can have been certain of the result. The three Plaid Cymru members voted with Labour, as did Sillars and Robertson and two Unionists corralled by Roy Hattersley, so Mrs Thatcher initially thought she had lost by one vote. There was a rumour that the Tory chief whip had whispered an apology to his leader and that a Labour whip was looking cheerful. With the help of a bottle of whisky, Maguire was persuaded not to vote *against* the government, but Fitt (who said of Maguire that he was an Irish publican and 'could drink the whole government into oblivion') took offence at being bribed with gin by the Labour whips and refused to vote *with* the government, so neither of them made it into the lobbies. Broughton had stayed in Yorkshire, Weatherill had voted, and the entire corpus of the Conservative, Liberal and SNP members, along with eight Unionists, had marched through the lobby together.

There was just one vote in it, 311 to 310. When the Tory whip who had been counting in the Labour lobby appeared beside the Speaker's chair and held up his thumb Thatcher knew she had won, and as Conservatives cheered and a smattering of Labour members retaliated with 'The Red Flag', Callaghan announced he would be calling an election. He then went to his office to write to Broughton's wife that he had been quite right not to come. Broughton died a few days later.

Callaghan had joked in the debate that the minority parties had walked into a trap and that this was 'the first time in recorded history that turkeys have been known to vote for an early Christmas'.[5] The long election campaign running up to 3 May proved him right. The SNP lost nine of their eleven seats and Plaid Cymru lost one. But Callaghan, like Foot, was no clairvoyant. Thatcher managed to hang the winter of discontent round Labour's neck and remorselessly went for Labour's underbelly with her 'Labour isn't working' campaign. On the morning of 4 May the Conservatives had gained sixty-three seats, giving Mrs Thatcher a healthy 45-seat majority, and she became Britain's first female Prime Minister, thanks to the first ousting of a government by a Commons vote of censure since the ejection of MacDonald in 1924.

Mrs Thatcher's eleven and a half years in office have inspired fierce loyalty and intense hatred in equal measure. In the mining communities of England and Wales, for instance, it is still difficult to find a person who will speak well of her. Yet once she had got into her stride she was, for good or ill, as full of campaigning zeal as Attlee and his colleagues in 1945.

For all her fortitude and wilful determination, Margaret Thatcher was endowed with exceptional good fortune. True, she was heavily supported by her millionaire businessman husband Denis, but she was an outsider in a Tory party still dominated by money and the landed interest. The twentieth century had seen a series of Tory leaders from the major British public schools: four from Eton, two from Harrow and one each from Rugby and Glasgow High School. By contrast

Margaret Roberts, the daughter of a Grantham grocer, was a scholarship girl at the local grammar, and although she went to Oxford she studied not PPE or history but chemistry. Moreover, she was a woman in a party that had just seven female MPs in 1974.[6] After two attempts in 1950 and 1951, she was first elected in 1959 as MP for Finchley and showed early on that she had an independent mind, voting for the legalization of homosexuality and abortion before rising through the ranks, gaining junior office as a parliamentary under-secretary for pensions under Macmillan, and then joining Heath's Treasury team in opposition and his Cabinet as Secretary of State for Education in 1970. In 1975 luck helped her win the leadership of the Tory party, as Heath enjoyed much stronger support from his Cabinet than from his backbenchers. Thatcher had just one ideological ally, Keith Joseph, who waged a behind-stairs campaign to unseat Heath via a series of speeches after the first electoral defeat of 1974. Joseph too was an outsider, one of just two Jewish Conservative MPs, a man racked by indecision, painfully reticent and almost incoherent in interviews, more an intellectual than a politician, but he found a willing audience on the back benches of the Tory party and by the time of the October election he was the clear leader of the new Conservative right. When the second election came in October – and with it another, more definitive Tory defeat – Joseph was the front-runner. Then he over-reached himself in an exorbitant speech in Edgbaston on Saturday, 19 October 1974 decrying social protest as 'an excuse for antisocial behaviour' and bemoaning the threat to 'our human stock' from unmarried working-class mothers. This shrill outburst, in leaning towards the discredited pseudo-science of eugenics, attracted an equally high-pitched response that ensured that Joseph was consigned to the list of former future leaders of the Conservative party.

The way was clear for Thatcher, and when the chairman of the 1922 Committee, Sir Edward du Cann, decided not to stand, his wily supporter, the wartime hero and arch-conspirator Airey Neave, was recruited to run her campaign – on the understanding that she would not win, but that her candidacy might unseat Heath so that others could stand. After desperate attempts by Heath to avoid a contest, when Du Cann eventually held the ballot on 4 February Thatcher amassed a far more impressive than expected 130 votes, beating Heath by eleven and only narrowly missing out on the required majority as one other candidate, Sir Hugh Fraser, had sixteen votes. As expected, the second round held a week later saw a squad of grandees join the contest – Willie Whitelaw, Jim Prior and Geoffrey Howe – but Thatcher's vote held strong at 146 and she was elected with a clear majority. Had Heath stood down before Joseph's self-combustion, the outcome might have been very different.

Thatcher's luck stuck with her in office. In 1980 Labour elected as its leader a great author, orator and parliamentary performer: Michael Foot, who was already sixty-seven years old, had walked with a stick since a car crash in 1963 and seemed diminished rather than magnified by his job. His fissiparous party splintered: left-wingers led by Tony Benn demanded a renunciation of Callaghan's policies and the deselection of moderate or right-wing Labour MPs, and four former Cabinet ministers, Roy Jenkins, Shirley Williams, David Owen and William Rodgers, left Labour in early 1981 to found the Social Democratic Party. The internal rift widened when Benn challenged Denis Healey for the deputy leadership that summer, just as opinion polls were suggesting that although Thatcher's government was deeply unpopular, thanks to the rapid growth in unemployment, the new alliance of the SDP with the Liberals might beat Labour in a general election. Then came a further moment of Thatcherite good fortune, thanks to the crazed determination of General Galtieri to seize the Falkland Islands in early 1982 despite secret negotiations over their sovereignty already being under way. Her immediate decision to take them back – and Britain's successful prosecution of what was by any account a hazardous venture – helped Thatcher prove herself as a commander who could take brave decisions. Had the precise nature of the government's secret position prior to the invasion become known, or had the British fleet been delayed until the Falklands winter, again the story might have been very different; but as it turned out the election of 1983 proved to be an uneven contest between a battered Labour party riddled with internal enmity proffering a demented programme of unilateral nuclear disarmament, tax increases, abolition of the House of Lords, nationalization of the banks and withdrawal from the European Economic Community, and a resurgent Conservative party buoyed up by a return to economic growth and united behind a victorious war leader. The only surprise was that the 'longest suicide note in history', as Gerald Kaufman christened the Labour manifesto, did not enable the SDP to leapfrog Labour and become the official opposition. When the new Commons assembled on 15 June 1983, the first past the post system had given Thatcher 397 seats and a landslide majority of 144. Labour had won just 700,000 votes more than the Liberal–SDP Alliance, yet retained 209 seats to the Alliance's 23. Ironically, the architect of Labour's manifesto, Tony Benn, and one of the prime movers in the SDP, Shirley Williams, both lost their seats.

It was not just good fortune that gave Thatcher her three election victories. Like her predecessor, Edward Heath, she had schooled her vowels for the televisual era. She chose her enemies carefully, intentionally provoking the miners' strike of 1984 in order to replay the battle Heath had lost in 1973–4 with a new outcome. She had a clarity of purpose, too. Just as Labour had nationalized after the war, Thatcher privatized. Forty-four national concerns, including water, gas, electricity, British Telecom, Cable and Wireless, British Airways, Rolls-Royce and British Aerospace, were all sold off. There were three major reforms of employment law following Jim Prior's replacement as Secretary of State for Employment by the more abrasively free-marketeering Norman Tebbit in September 1981. VAT was increased from 8 per cent to 15 per cent in the first budget, income tax rates were cut (initially from 33 to 30 per cent and 83 to 60 per cent on earned income, and from 98 to 75 per cent on unearned income) and the whole tax system was simplified. Mass deregulation was implemented with the abolition of controls on prices, incomes, dividends, industrial development and foreign exchange. It was a clear – divisively clear – programme with a 'take it or leave it' insouciance to it.

*

The first policy that the Thatcher government brought forward, though, was far from divisive. On 25 June 1979 the new Leader of the House, who was a noted 'wet' and had the camp but pious air of an Anglo-Catholic vicar, Norman St John Stevas, moved the creation of twelve parliamentary select committees, one for each department of state. His claim that these represented the 'most important parliamentary reforms of the century' was an exaggeration.[7] Both the Lords and the Commons had used committees for centuries. The Commons had demanded joint 'communing' committees with the Lords as far back as the 1380s, members were selected to form ad hoc committees to consider specific issues in the early 1400s, and one of the first agenda items at Tudor parliaments was the creation of standing committees to consider grievances, petitions, privileges and elections. Their use had developed over the centuries. For the most part only supporters of a Bill were allowed to sit on its committee, but on occasion the committee was used as a means of establishing consensus, as when the Commons selected a committee to debate the Bill in Restraint of Appeals under Thomas Cromwell's guidance in 1533. In the 1590s another innovation was introduced, 'general' committees – later known as 'committees of the whole House' – which sat in the Chamber. All MPs were allowed to participate and, unlike in main debates, could speak more than once under less stringent rules and in the absence of the Speaker. In time the Committee of Supply and of Ways and Means,* which determined expenditure and taxation, came to be conducted on this basis (and much later any constitutional matter was treated similarly).

Some sixteenth-century members made their political names as conspicuous committee-men. In 1593 Robert Wroth chaired a committee that considered separate Bills on the stealing of oxen, the assize of bread and the deprivation of Bishop Bonner; on casks,

---

* The budget is ostensibly debated in a Ways and Means Committee of the whole House, which is why the budget statement is chaired not by the Speaker but by the Deputy Speaker, the chairman of Ways and Means.

brewers, jurors, alien retailers, weirs, cordage and coopers. Knighted in 1597, he arrived at the 1604 parliament with a seven-point plan, and two committees were set up specifically charged with drawing up the necessary new laws. This became the established pattern, so that when the House fretted about the operation of the poor law in 1696, it set up a committee including more than fifty named MPs to 'inspect laws relating to the poor; and to prepare, and bring in, a Bill, or Bills, for explaining and better execution thereof, and for the better relief and employment of the poor'.[8] Little came of this, but when Henry Blaake (*sic*), a Wiltshire MP, introduced a Bill 'for supplying some defects in the laws now in force for the relief of the poor of this kingdom' on 11 March 1697, it too was committed to sixty-five MPs, including 'all the members for Gloucester, Southampton and Wilts, and for the principality of Wales',[9] for consideration before being enacted with a small amendment from the Lords.

In the eighteenth century the use of committees to scrutinize and draft legislation was extended with the invention of the committee of inquiry, which became an established piece of parliamentary furniture. Notable reports on gaols (1729–30), on the Charitable Corporation (1732), on madhouses (1763), on India (1781–3) and on the poor law attracted much public attention and led to significant changes in the law; and the enthusiasm for this way of going about things continued well into the nineteenth century, with an average of forty such inquiries set up every year between 1801 and 1817.

The Victorian era brought two further committee innovations. Members had been complaining about the lack of scrutiny of crown expenditure for centuries, but it was not until 1861 that Gladstone succumbed to a very insistent member, Sir Francis Baring, the wealthy evangelical former Chancellor of the Exchequer. Baring, who had first made his mark in the Commons on the Select Committee on Middlesex Pauper Lunatics in 1827 and was soon to be made a baron when he retired from the Commons in 1865, argued that a permanent Commons committee could help the government make savings; so when Gladstone moved that a Committee of Public Accounts, supported by an Auditor-General, be set up 'for the examination of the accounts showing the appropriation of the sums granted by Parliament to meet the public expenditure',[10] Baring was the obvious choice for its first chairman. The second Victorian committee innovation also came about thanks to badgering, albeit of a different kind: in 1882, with the Irish members waging guerrilla warfare on the floor of the Commons, it was decided that public Bills* would be considered by one of two committees rather than in the main Chamber. These initial 'standing' committees lapsed by the end of the century, but in 1906 four similar committees were formed and a system was created that, with some changes, lasted until 2006.

So, for all his boasting, St John Stevas was building on an established tradition. Indeed, a Labour predecessor of his as Leader of the House, Richard Crossman, had tentatively introduced six thematic committees in the 1966 government, and Heath had created an Expenditure Committee with six sub-committees. Nevertheless, it was under Thatcher that a report commissioned by the Callaghan government was implemented with the creation of select committees expressly charged with scrutinizing the full panoply of the executive. The motion in 1979 was carried by a large majority, 248 to 12, but not all St John Stevas' colleagues were impressed. There were ten divisions that evening, and traditionalists objected that the new committees would detract from the central role of the Chamber. Somewhat ironically, the strongest opponent, Gerald Kaufman, who argued against 'strangling parliament in a skein of Committees'[11] and unusually joined Dennis Skinner in the Noe lobby, ended up serving as

---

* The Bible of parliamentary procedure describes the two classes of Bills as follows: public Bills 'relate to matters of public policy and are introduced directly by members of the House', whereas private Bills 'are for the particular interest or benefit of any person or persons, public company or corporation, or local authority and are solicited by the parties themselves who are interested in their promotion, being founded upon petitions'. The latter are distinct from private members' Bills. See Erskine May, *Treatise on the Law, Privileges, Proceedings and Usage of Parliament*, 21st edn, London, Butterworth, 1989, p. 439.

chairman of the National Heritage and Culture Media and Sport Select
Committees for thirteen years.

Few now doubt, though, that the creation of select committees
was an entirely positive development in the Commons. Further
changes – salaries for those appointed to chair them, introduced in
2005, and the election of chairpersons by secret ballot of the whole
House from 2010 – gave them a degree of independence from both
the executive and the party whip that has shifted much public interest
in parliament to the committee corridor. The former Labour Home
Secretary Merlyn Rees said in 1979 that 'we should not clap ourselves
to death when we move forward',[12] but the St John Stevas reforms were
a success.

One element of the constitution that the Thatcher government had
no intention of touching was the House of Lords. Ever since the
Parliament Act of 1911, whose preamble had balefully intimated that
'it is intended to substitute for the House of Lords as it at present exists
a Second Chamber constituted on a popular instead of hereditary
basis', but that 'such substitution cannot be immediately brought into
operation', there had been intermittent calls for reform.

One tiny reform had even come to pass, thanks to a horrific
accident. On 15 August 1935 Edward Russell, the 26th Baron de
Clifford, was involved in a car crash at three o'clock in the morning
which led to the death of another man, George Hopkins. Ironically,
the lanky young peer had devoted his maiden speech in the House of
Lords to the issue of road safety, but the police charged him with
manslaughter and he was initially sent for trial to the Old Bailey. Ever
since 1341, though, peers of the realm had had to be tried for any
crime classified as a felony, such as manslaughter, by their fellows and
not in a common court. There had been so few such 'trials by peers'
(just forty-four since 1500) that although the Lord Chancellor at the
time of de Clifford's arrest, Viscount Sankey, said the very idea had
'outlived its usefulness' and was an unnecessary 'expenditure of
judicial time and public money',[13] nobody had done anything about

the stipulation. Yet history had proved it manifestly unjust. When Philip Herbert, 7th earl of Pembroke, and Charles, 3rd Baron Cornwallis, were arraigned for viciously lynching two commoners in 1678, they were merely found guilty of manslaughter, which enabled them to claim the 'privilege of peerage' according to which, since 1547, for any felony other than treason or murder a peer would receive no punishment for a first offence. The same extreme leniency was granted to three peers who severally killed men in duels in 1699 and 1765;[14] and when James Brudenell, the 7th earl of Cardigan, threatened to claim the privilege in 1841, he was unanimously acquitted of a duelling murder on a technicality. 'Privilege of peerage' was then abolished, but it took a case of truly exceptional barbarity for a peer to be convicted of murder – as when Laurence Shirley, 4th earl of Ferrers, who had already been excommunicated and deprived of his estates for his brutal treatment of his wife Mary, killed the man in whom his estates had been vested, John Johnson, in January 1760. For once the House of Lords sentenced the peer to execution at Tyburn and insisted that he be hanged like a commoner and surgically anatomized like a criminal.

Yet even in 1935 a peer could not waive his right to trial by his co-equals; so the House of Lords fashioned a trial, which took place as soon as practicable after the general election, in the Royal Gallery on 12 December, with the new Lord Chancellor Douglas Hogg, Viscount Hailsham, presiding, having been appointed Lord High Steward for the day. There was a full hour of pomp and circumstance, a roll call of peers and a debate about whether peers who were not wearing cocked hats could participate before de Clifford could be tried 'by God and my peers', but the trial itself was brief, his lawyer arguing implausibly but effectively that being on the wrong side of the road was no evidence of criminal negligence. When the peers returned from a brief debate, they pronounced their individual judgments one by one, starting with the most junior baron. The contingent of Italians who had come to support de Clifford, a well-known supporter of Mosley's Fascists, were delighted with the not guilty verdict. At the end of the proceedings Hailsham ceremonially broke his white staff of office in two, proclaiming himself rather pleased with the glorious upholding of ancient tradition, but the ensuing public outcry led to demands for repeal of the 1341 statute. The Lords made one attempt the following year and when they tried again in 1948, by adding section 30 to the Criminal Justice Act, the whole system was abolished.

Calls for wider reform continued, and in an attempt to conserve as much of the traditional House as possible, Harold Macmillan's government brought in the Life Peerages Act of 1958, allowing both men and women to be made barons for life. Then came one of those strange quirks of fate by which adjustments in the constitutional settlement have so often come about. On 17 November 1960 the veteran Labour politician William Wedgwood Benn, who had been Secretary for India from 1929 to 1931, died. Benn had accepted a viscountcy in 1942 on the understanding that his eldest son Michael, who was considering the priesthood, had no desire to sit in the Commons and would therefore not object to inheriting a peerage; but when Michael was killed in the Second World War, the succession fell to Viscount Stansgate's next son, Anthony, who was utterly dedicated to politics, being elected as Stafford Cripps's successor in Bristol East in 1950 aged twenty-five (and taking his seat as the youngest member of the House). Stansgate's death automatically disqualified Anthony from the Commons, but it did not per se prevent him from standing in the subsequent by-election on 4 May 1961. Benn won 70 per cent of the vote and increased his majority, but when the courts determined that he was ineligible to be elected, his Conservative opponent Malcolm St Clair was declared the MP. Hugh Gaitskell, the Labour leader, suggested that Benn should now give up and get his wife to stand instead, but when Gaitskell died in February 1963 and was replaced by Wilson, the pressure for reform grew, and in a desire to sort out a couple of other anomalies Macmillan's government brought forward another Peerages Act, which allowed Stansgate to disclaim his peerage and become plain Tony Benn MP again.*

* The Act also ended the ban on female peers taking their seats in their own right, and abolished the elections for Scottish representative peers by incorporating the whole Scottish peerage.

It was to be a double-edged reform for the Conservatives, as when Macmillan resigned on health grounds in October that year (unnecessarily, as it turned out), two of his potential successors were hereditary peers: Quintin Hogg, the 2nd Viscount Hailsham, who was Leader in the Lords and initially Macmillan's preferred successor, and Alec Douglas-Home, the 14th earl of Home, who was Foreign Secretary. There then followed a strange aristocratic minuet. Hailsham announced on 10 October that he would disclaim his peerage and seek to return to the Commons just before going off to the Conservative party conference in Blackpool, where he campaigned furiously and, according to some, 'vulgarly', for the leadership. Since the Conservative party still had no formal election for leader,* it was left to Macmillan to recommend a successor to the queen, and after some inaccurate soundings among Conservative MPs he plumped for Home, who was asked by the queen to form a government on 18 October. The following day Home became Prime Minister, and four days later he followed Hailsham's example and disclaimed his several titles. This left him with a seat in neither House, a snag overcome by persuading the Conservative candidate for the Kinross and West Perthshire by-election to be held on 7 November, George Younger (the heir to another Scottish hereditary title), to stand aside. Parliament dutifully waited until the by-election was over before it reconvened, with Alec Douglas-Home MP at the helm (something one cannot imagine happening again). There was one further piece of the ballet to endure, though, as the MP for St Marylebone, the former England rugby player Sir Wavell Wakefield, was prevailed upon to go to the Lords so that in December Hailsham, now plain Quintin Hogg, could step into the Commons seat his father had held in the 1920s. (The noble quadrille was completed when Edward Heath put Hogg back in the Lords in 1970 as a life peer and in 1974 Home followed suit.)

Both disclaimed Tory peers won their seats in 1963, but the whole rigmarole played badly with the public, and in the 1964 general

---

* That was only introduced for the leadership election in 1965.

election campaign Wilson was convincingly able to portray the Conservatives as out of touch. There are other reasons why the Conservatives lost in 1964. The Profumo affair spread an air of scandal over the government, and the Tory party seemed ill at ease with itself after Macmillan's dramatic cull of Cabinet ministers in 1962 and divided after the mass rebellion over Edward Heath's Bill to abolish resale price maintenance. But without the 1963 Act Macmillan would have been forced to choose a commoner as leader, probably his Deputy Prime Minister, Rab Butler, and although Butler could be laconic in the way of many essentially good-natured politicians, his reputation as a successful Home Secretary and his Macmillanite brand of 'one nation' Toryism might well have made the difference in the election that saw Wilson ease ahead by just 0.7 per cent of the national vote and win a majority of only four seats. The Leader of the House, Iain Macleod, made the point: 'We were now proposing to admit that after twelve years of Tory Government no one amongst the 363 members of the party in the House of Commons was acceptable as Prime Minister.'[15] It was hardly a declaration of self-confidence.

The two Macmillan Peerages Acts were to change the House of Lords in other ways, too. Successive prime ministers used the new power of patronage with relish (or abandon): Macmillan added 84 life peers, Douglas-Home made 29 in just one year, Wilson appointed 141 in his first period in office and a further 80 in his second, and Callaghan 58. By these standards Heath was abstemious, restricting himself to just 45 new peers between 1970 and 1974.

Who were these new peers? Politicians, in the main. Senior government ministers had often found their way to the Lords towards the end of a career in the Commons, and it became standard practice in the twentieth century that prime ministers should receive an earldom or barony on retirement – an honour refused by only four out of eighteen: Churchill, Heath, Major and Blair. Every Foreign Secretary from the marquess of Reading to Douglas Hurd was either already a peer or subsequently ennobled, apart from Ernest

Bevin and Tony Crosland, both of whom died in office as MPs. Of the thirty-six Home Secretaries between 1900 and 1997, eleven became viscounts, seventeen were made barons, one resigned (Reginald Maudling), one remains in ministerial office (Ken Clarke) and just three others never made it to the Lords, including Reginald McKenna who constantly refused a peerage in the hope that he might return some day as Chancellor of the Exchequer. Hundreds of MPs took up the offer of elevation to the upper house. By 2007, 470 of them had been ennobled, representing 40 per cent of the total as against just 131 industrialists and 88 from academia. These were partisan figures, many having been schooled in the whips' offices along the corridor. Indeed, only one of the nineteen Conservative chief whips between 1900 and 1997 did not become a peer – Edward Heath – and every Labour chief whip since the Second World War, up to and including Hilary Armstrong, has either died in office as an MP (or, in Donald Dewar's case, as First Minister of Scotland) or been sent to the Lords.

This new influx of peers changed both the tempo of the upper house and its style of business, as its more sedentary and deferential atmosphere gave way to explicitly political activism. In the 1950–1 session, the Lords sat on only 100 days and for an average of just less than three hours. By 2006–7 the figures were much higher: 146 sitting days and an average length of six and three-quarter hours. Attendance rose, too, from an average of a mere 86 in 1950 to 411 in 2006, and there was more questioning of ministers, more general debate, and more political partisanship. In short, the Lords came to look and sound more and more like the Commons.

One element that did not change was the political make-up of the Lords. Rosebery had noted that Conservative governments had little need to reform a House that had an inbuilt Conservative majority, and with the demise of the Liberals that majority became ever more evident, so by 1970 the Conservatives had 468 peers, against 120 for Labour and a paltry 38 for the Liberals and Lib Dems. Even if the opposition joined forces with all 110 cross-benchers, they could easily be outnumbered by Conservatives. What was more, the new more active Chamber chose to make its affiliation ever more evident by staying its hand against Tory legislation but wreaking havoc with Labour's. Thus Conservative governments were defeated just eleven times between 1959 and 1964, and twenty-six times between 1970 and 1974. Admittedly, Mrs Thatcher saw the number of defeats rise during her three terms, but still the number never topped seventy-two a term. By contrast, no Labour government saw fewer than a hundred Lords defeats a year, and the 1974–9 government was overturned on 353 occasions – roughly once every second sitting day.

Even if Thatcher had believed in Lords reform, though, she or any Prime Minister might have been chary of attempting it after the experience of Harold Wilson who, following cross-party talks, on 3 February 1969 moved second reading of a Bill that would exclude future hereditary peers, establish a two-tier structure of salaried, voting peers and unpaid, non-voting ones, reduce the number of bishops and restrict the powers of the House of Lords. Despite the measure's having the support of the opposition front bench in the shape of both Maudling and Douglas-Home (who argued that the Lords had become virtually dysfunctional by virtue of its 'overwhelming built-in Conservative majority'[16]), the debate was lively. Some Labour members clamoured for nothing less than full abolition of the Lords, and a larger number of Tories were concerned by the undermining of the hereditary peers. Michael Foot, at this stage a backbencher, led the rebellious charge in a scathing *tour de force*, declaring that the new second chamber would be 'a Heath Robinson House of Lords, a contraption that would fall to pieces', and pouring scorn on 'a second Chamber selected by the Whips. A seraglio of eunuchs.' Under the proposals, he argued, everything would depend on the cross-benchers, who would hold the balance of votes, and in a national crisis the country would have to await 'a falsetto chorus from these political castrati' who 'would be the final arbiters of our destiny in our new constitution'.[17]

For all his wit, the Bill sailed through its second reading by 285 votes to 135, but a week later it hit heavy weather, battered by squalls of organized dissent. First MPs on both sides raised a string of points of order that lasted a full hour; then, supposedly while debating the first amendment, members dilated at length on the history of heredity, on princes of the blood royal, on hereditary bummarees,* on the validity of the Bill's preamble . . . and by the end of the day just one amendment had been voted on and not even the first clause had been agreed. So it went on. The government had hoped to get the Bill through its committee stage in five days on the floor of the House, but Foot, together with Robert Sheldon and Eric Heffer on the Labour side and John Boyd-Carpenter, Nicholas Ridley, Sir Brandon Rhys Williams and Enoch Powell from the Tory back benches, waged a relentless war of attrition, contriving to have proceedings of the committee suspended on 18 February, tying the chair up with vexatious points of order again for two hours on 18 March, and ensuring that the Bill progressed no further than clause five (out of thirteen) by the middle of April. Richard Crossman, the Leader of the House, who had main responsibility for the Bill, had never managed to get the wholehearted backing of the Cabinet: Denis Healey thought him 'a heavyweight intellect with a lightweight judgement',[18] and Barbara Castle complained that he had 'a fatal habit of getting carried away by short-term enthusiasms for a piece of work on which he is engaged and tends to lose sight of the rabbit'.[19] But while Wilson was reluctant to ditch the Bill when just twenty-five Labour MPs had voted against it and it enjoyed the arithmetical cushion of the Conservative front bench, he was conscious that at this rate it would take another twenty-four days to get through and would eclipse the rest of the government's programme. The normal tactic at this point would have been to introduce a guillotine motion, but this option was ruled out when the opposition said they would not support any such timetable. Wilson felt he had little choice, and on 17 April, after a fraught

---

* Like a seat in the Lords, a licence to operate as a meat porter at Smithfield Market was passed down through the generations.

Cabinet debate, he told the House that the government was abandoning the measure so as to concentrate its efforts on Barbara Castle's Industrial Relations Bill. One minister could not help pointing out the irony that the Labour government was abandoning 'a Bill to limit the power of the peers in favour of a Bill to limit the freedom to strike'.[20]

The end result? With Labour unable to deliver Lords reform in the 1970s and the Conservatives unwilling to do so in the 1980s, when Tony Blair became Prime Minister in 1997 there were 1,330 peers, 750 of them hereditary, and 26 bishops still in the House alongside 21 non-royal dukes, 27 marquesses, 150 earls and 82 viscounts.

Wilson did not achieve reform of the Lords and Thatcher was either indifferent or opposed to it, but there were two other constitutional reforms that steadily crept upon Westminster: Britain's participation in a new European political architecture, and the advent of the referendum.

The vociferousness of modern British Euroscepticism might suggest that the UK was always reluctant to be drawn into Europe, but as often as not in the aftermath of the Second World War it was British politicians who led the calls for bodies that might guarantee the protection of human rights and prevent another conflict. In 1946 Churchill mused in a speech in Zurich that we might need something like a 'United States of Europe', albeit one of which Great Britain would not be part. A year later his son-in-law Duncan Sandys, also a Conservative MP, helped create the United European Movement, and in May 1948 Churchill presided over a congress of all the international movements for European unity in The Hague, which was attended by Sandys, Harold Macmillan and the wartime Solicitor-General Sir David Maxwell Fyfe and concluded with a call for a political, economic and monetary union of Europe. When the Labour government negotiated the Treaty of London that created the Council of Europe, drawing together within it the UK, France, Italy, Norway, Sweden, Denmark, Ireland and the Benelux countries in May 1949, Maxwell

Fyfe became the chairman of the legal committee of its parliamentary assembly and, perhaps influenced by his experience of interrogating Hermann Goering at the Nuremberg trials, drew up an uncompromising European Convention on Human Rights by which all Council members are bound.

Further attempts at cementing peace through political and economic union were to follow. The French foreign minister Robert Schumann called for a customs union and then, in May 1950, for a High Authority and Assembly for the shared European administration of the two key industries vital to war. A year later the European Coal and Steel Community was formed, with France and Germany at its heart, but the UK excluded. Six years later the European Economic Community and the European Atomic Energy Community were also established, each with a High Authority (or Commission) and an Assembly. Realizing the value of economic cooperation, a separate grouping of European countries created the European Free Trade Association in 1960, and four of the EFTA countries then applied for membership of the Communities: Ireland, Denmark, Norway and the UK. The French president, General de Gaulle, vetoed Britain's applications and the three Communities decided to merge into one body with a European Commission and European Parliament.

The merger was implemented in 1967, whereupon Harold Wilson renewed Britain's bid for membership along with the other three countries the day after a debate in the Commons on 10 May in which the reapplication was endorsed by 487 to 26. The ensuing UK negotiations were completed by the Conservative Prime Minister Edward Heath, an ardent Europeanist who told the Commons in October 1971 that throughout his political career he had had the vision 'of a Britain in a united Europe; a Britain which would be united economically to Europe' and that he had worked for Britain to be 'a member of a Europe which is united politically, and which will enjoy lasting peace and the greater security which would ensue.'[21] This time Labour had found a spurious reason to vote against the measure, so the vote was tighter – 356 to 244 – and the ensuing parliamentary debates over the ratification of the accession treaty that had been signed on 22 January saw forty-seven divisions in the Commons on the European Communities Bill. At second reading Heath only managed to scrape through with a majority of eight by turning the vote into a matter of confidence in his government. When it came to third reading on 13 July, the Solicitor-General, Sir Geoffrey Howe, was faced with sustained barracking by Labour MPs on the question of UK law being superseded by European law, but was able to quote from Labour's own white paper advocating membership in 1967, which had stated: 'If this country became a Member of the European Communities it would be accepting Community Law . . . The constitutional innovation would lie in the acceptance in advance as part of the law of the United Kingdom of provisions to be made in the future by instruments issued by Community institutions – a situation for which there is no precedent in this country.' Howe went further, making it clear that 'we cannot accept Community obligations contingently'. He pointed out that the decision to join the Communities was itself an act of parliamentary sovereignty and that 'a decision to share power to the common advantage is an enhancement rather than a loss of sovereignty; and for so long as we remain a member of the Communities, pooling decisions in the interests of Europe as a whole rather than looking to the narrow interests of a single State, that, too, will be a deliberate and continuing exercise of national sovereignty'.[22] Peter Shore, who was as personally ideologically opposed to membership as Howe was committed, responded for Labour in words that might issue from Nigel Farage in 2014, complaining that the Bill seeks 'to change the whole course of our parliamentary history' and that 'the power to make the laws of England is being deliberately transferred by the Bill to authorities outside our own land, responsible to no one in it'.[23] Yet after a thoroughly pro-European maiden speech by Norman Lamont, the Bill got its third reading by 301 to 284 and passed without amendment through the Lords, courtesy of the Conservatives' inbuilt hereditary majority. On 1 January 1973 the UK acceded to the European Communities alongside Ireland and Denmark.

When Wilson won the year's second general election in October 1974, the inherent inconsistencies in Labour's position became only too clear. His answer was to resort to a constitutional innovation every bit as significant as membership of the European Community. The idea of a referendum had been anathema to most British politicians. Clement Attlee had said referendums were inimical to British traditions, and Thatcher later favourably cited his reference to them as the 'device of demagogues and dictators'. Because referendums were thought to undermine parliamentary government, the British had insisted that West Germany's post-war constitution render such votes either illegal or impracticable. Yet the other three applicant countries had held referendums in 1972; Ireland and Denmark had enthusi-astically voted 'yes' (respectively 83.1 per cent and 63.3 per cent), but Norway had voted 'no'. In the eyes of those who were opposed to mem-bership, this wholly invalidated the UK's reliance on the parliamentary process of ratification, so when the Conservative MP Neil Marten moved an amendment to the Bill in April 1972 demanding a refer-endum, he got the support of the Labour shadow Cabinet. Roy Jenkins promptly resigned as Labour's deputy leader in protest; but, hemmed in by a divided party and noting the effectiveness of the referendum held in Northern Ireland in 1973 on whether it should remain in the UK or join the Republic of Ireland, Wilson committed Labour in the 1974 manifesto to a renegotiation of British EEC membership followed by a binding decision by the British people 'at the ballot box'. Wilson then commenced an entirely cosmetic process of renegotiation, staged with the other member states; declaring this successful in March, he then carried a Commons motion to continue membership by 396 to 170 on 9 April 1975 (and 262 to 20 in the Lords on the twenty-second), and called the referendum for 5 June. Labour was still divided, with Michael Foot, Tony Benn and Barbara Castle opposing Jenkins, Denis Healey and Jim Callaghan; but with all the other major parties almost unanimously supportive of continued membership the 'yes' camp emerged victorious with 67.3 per cent of the vote.

The two referendums of 1973 and 1975 proved an innovation more popular than might have been suspected. Callaghan called referendums on Scottish and Welsh devolution, as did Tony Blair in Scotland, Wales, London and the north-east of England, and on the Good Friday agreement in Northern Ireland. The coalition government called one on adopting the alternative vote for parliamentary elections in 2011 (it was heavily defeated) and agreed to a Scottish referendum on independence to be held on 18 September 2014. The 55:45 result against Scottish independence did not permanently resolve that matter, nor did the 1975 referendum end the European debate. Each further step of integration was contested at increasing volume. In 1986 Thatcher took the Single European Act through parliament (in the shape of the European Communities (Amendment) Bill), thereby replacing unanimity with qualified majority voting in many decisions on the single European market. With a large Conservative majority she could fend off the likes of Teddy Taylor and Neil Hamilton from her own side as well as the official opposition, and the Bill comfortably passed second reading by 319 to 160; but when John Major attempted to ratify the Treaty of Maastricht in 1993, the parliamentary battle was so intense that one vote was lost and others might have gone the same way had it not been for the Labour MP John Smith's decision to ignore the Labour whip.

Prime ministers spend a great deal of their time in office considering how to hold on to it, but rarely does any one of them leave the stage voluntarily and at a time of his or her own choosing. The list of twentieth-century departures is sad. Balfour lost his own seat in the 1906 Liberal landslide, his 69-year-old successor Campbell-Bannerman had to resign after a series of heart attacks in 1908 and died nineteen days later, and Asquith, having been ousted from the premiership in 1916, also found himself without a seat in 1918. Similarly, when a visibly exhausted and often incoherent MacDonald agreed a timetable to hand over power to Stanley Baldwin after George V's Silver Jubilee celebrations in 1935, he too lost his seat in Seaham in the general election, and although he returned as MP for the Combined Scottish Universities in 1936, by the end of the year he was dead. Neville Chamberlain was a bit more fortunate – he was retained in the Cabinet after leaving Downing Street in 1940 – but he too failed to last the year out; and both Eden and Macmillan resigned through ill-health.

There were a few political resurrections in these decades. MacDonald, Baldwin, Churchill and Wilson all returned after losing an election, while Balfour and Douglas-Home both lost general elections but later returned to government as Foreign Secretary. But the earnest expectation of a return to the front line has often soured the fading years of a political career. Think of Lloyd George. Removed as Prime Minister of the National government by the Carlton Club vote of Conservative MPs, he had no real party to fall back on but hung around the Commons like Banquo's ghost. Even Churchill, whose modern popularity is assured, knew the vicissitudes of politics, as he lost his seat more often than any other member, being understandably deselected by the Tories in Oldham when he joined the Liberals, losing his ministerial by-election in 1908 and coming a poor fourth in Dundee in 1922 (a contest during which, as he reflected, he lost his seat, his party and his appendix). Although he retired as Prime Minister owing to ill-health, having suffered a series of strokes in 1955, he remained an MP until 1964, by which time, in his eighties, he could only attend the House in a wheelchair. Given that Wilson's decision was made for him by the advance of Alzheimer's, that leaves only Baldwin relinquishing office entirely voluntarily, in 'a blaze of affection', a fortnight after George VI's coronation in May 1937. He was lucky. His policy towards Germany and Italy and his very slow adoption of rearmament had already been attacked by a few brave souls, but it had not yet been exposed as appeasement. When he attended the unveiling of a statue of George V in 1947 he was so deaf and so uncertain of his place in public life that he had to ask whether the crowd was booing him. In fact they were cheering.

The most brutal despatch of the century was that of Thatcher.

She had courted controversy and had gained enemies. By 1990, although she had won three general elections, she was less popular than her party, and her speech to the College of Europe in Bruges in 1988, in which she preached against what she called a 'European super-state exercising a new dominance from Brussels', had been viewed askance by some of her own Cabinet who had agreed with her in favour of joining the European Economic Community in 1973, had voted yes with her in the referendum of 1975 and had pushed her Single European Act through parliament in 1986. The lion-haired self-made millionaire Michael Heseltine had already jumped ship in 1986, when he stormed out of the Cabinet as Defence Secretary straight into an impromptu press conference – and had been sharpening his talons on the back benches ever since. Less fiery members of the Cabinet had been snarled at, antagonized and undermined, including the Chancellor, Nigel Lawson, and the Foreign Secretary, Sir Geoffrey Howe, both of whom supported Britain joining the European Exchange Rate Mechanism, a policy Thatcher derided.

The happiness of Cabinet ministers is not a prerequisite of success for a government; nor is it essential that they all get on with one another. Nevertheless, Thatcher's weakness lay in personnel manage-ment, and in July 1989, with public opinion turning sharply against the government over the recently dreamt up 'Community Charge', she compounded her problems with a reshuffle in which Howe was demoted to the less significant post of Leader of the House and given the entirely honorific title of Deputy Prime Minister. Then Lawson's patience snapped. He told Thatcher in October that she had to choose between her Chancellor and her private economic adviser, the lugubrious free-wheeling free-market fanatic, Sir Alan Walters – and resigned. The government's ratings in the opinion polls continued to slide, and when it came to the annual contest bizarrely allowed for under the Tory party rules dreamt up by Douglas-Home in 1965 (which had enabled Thatcher to unseat Heath), a hitherto unknown backbench Tory MP, Sir Anthony Meyer, put up a challenge. Meyer knew he could not win, and once the Thatcherite press had finished with him he was portrayed as so pro-European and soft on crime, immigration and welfare that he might as well have been a member of the Labour party (in fact, he did later join the Liberal Democrats), and yet thirty-three Tory MPs preferred him to Thatcher – and a further twenty-seven either spoilt their ballot papers or refused to vote. For any ordinary leader this would have been a moment to reach out to colleagues. In Thatcher's mindset, though, it was only when a battle was being fought that the blood was up and the outcome worth the winning. Revolution was in the air, too. In Berlin the borders between East and West were opened, in Czechoslovakia, in Poland and in Hungary the communists were driven from office, and in South Africa Nelson Mandela was released. Thatcher, with her Manichean vision of right and wrong and her passion for free markets and 'sound money', felt herself a part of these momentous events, a woman of destiny who could persuade or cajole people into her way of thinking. This lady was not for turning.

It was the most mild-mannered of Cabinet ministers, though, who dealt the final blow, when the demoted Howe, the last man standing from Thatcher's first Cabinet, resigned on 1 November 1990, following the Prime Minister's declaration at the European Council meeting the previous weekend in Rome that Britain would neither join the single currency nor declare a date for joining the European Exchange Mechanism. Howe's resignation letter was generous to a fault, and his intention not to make any public statement until the House met again after the State Opening, which was planned for Wednesday 7 November, was reinforced by the fact that he entirely lost his voice. So at first Thatcher seemed to have got away with another bout of mild political turbulence – and the challenge might have subsided, had it not been for two things. First, it was yet again that time of year when the rules of the Conservative party required anyone wishing to contest the leadership to have a nomination lodged with the chairman of the 1922 Committee. The deadline was noon on 15 November – and Heseltine was canvassing support for a far more serious challenge than

Meyer's. Second, and more importantly, Howe not only regained his voice, but, infuriated by Downing Street press briefings against him and wound up by colleagues and friends telling him that he had been 'sadly provoked',[24] he decided to make a personal statement to the Commons on the last day of the queen's speech debate, Tuesday 13 November, just after Prime Minister's Questions, when the Chamber would be packed.

Howe, having expressly resolved that his speech must not be a 'damp squib', delivered a softly spoken but ferocious nineteen-minute broadside. He took his metaphorical cue from Thatcher, who had boasted at the Lord Mayor's Banquet the night before: 'I am still at the crease, though the bowling has been pretty hostile of late. And in case anyone doubted it, can I assure you there will be no ducking the bouncers, no stonewalling, no playing for time. The bowling's going to get hit all round the ground. That is my style.'[25] Quite the reverse, suggested Howe. In fact, he said, Thatcher's position on Europe was 'rather like sending your opening batsmen to the crease only for them to find, the moment the first balls are bowled, that their bats have been broken before the game by the team captain'. He criticized her 'finger-wagging' and argued that her actions were directly against the national interest. Gasps of amazement that the most loyal of Thatcher allies should be twisting the knife so determinedly gave way to a queasy silence on the Tory benches when Howe ended with an incitement to others. 'I have done what I believe to be right for my party and my country. The time has come for others to consider their own response to the tragic conflict of loyalties with which I have myself wrestled for perhaps too long.'[26]

In a different era, a Prime Minister might have survived this mauling. But a year earlier the Commons had reluctantly decided to allow television cameras into the Chamber, and in 1990 the arrangement was made permanent. So the great British public could see Howe calmly, unhistrionically, making his point. That evening the news was dominated by images of Lawson nodding in agreement, and of Thatcher, pinched and all icy defiance ('tense from top to toe', recalled

Major). The next morning Heseltine announced that he intended to stand in the contest that was billed for Tuesday the twentieth. The campaign to secure both a majority of the 372 Conservative MPs and a clear 15 per cent (or 56-vote) margin began. Neither side was well run, but Thatcher played it particularly badly, squandering the natural advantage she enjoyed in that no Cabinet minister could publicly nominate Heseltine. She could hardly disclaim her least popular policy, the poll tax, as Heseltine did, but she came across as slightly unhinged when she likened Heseltine's views 'to some of the Labour Party policies' and 'the philosophy in the Soviet Union'.[27] Even the logistics went badly, as her campaign manager George Younger was stuck for much of the time in Scotland and her PPS, Peter Morrison, was too lethargic, complacent or drunk to lobby colleagues ardently enough or garner accurate information (or even, on the afternoon of the day before the first poll, to stay awake).

Thatcher did have one bit of bad luck, although it was rather of her own making. She decided not to stay in London to pursue waverers but to go to Paris for a three day post-communism jamboree and she was there, staying at the British Embassy, when the result of the first ballot came. She had 204 votes to Heseltine's 152. It was a victory of sorts, but not enough. Sixteen MPs had abstained, so, just as Heath had fallen short in 1975, she needed four votes more for the required majority. Another round would be held and nominations had to be in by noon on Thursday. Thatcher immediately found a BBC reporter and declared she would stand, but instead of returning to Britain that night she joined European leaders at the ballet. 'I fight on. I fight to win,'[28] she told the press back in London on the Wednesday, but by then she had lost vital hours and the tide of Cabinet opinion was already flowing rapidly away from her. If she had gathered them together she might still have been able to intimidate her ministers into supporting her, but when she summoned them one by one that afternoon they flattered her but made it clear they would not support her. 'Treachery with a smile on its face',[29] she later called it.

The following morning at seven-thirty she succumbed, tearfully telling the Cabinet and demanding that they 'stop Heseltine'. This they dutifully did when on the twenty-seventh John Major defeated Heseltine by 185 votes to 131, with Douglas Hurd running a distant third on 56. In theory Major fell short of the required 15 per cent margin by two votes, but Heseltine and Hurd immediately withdrew.

According to Thatcher, one minister who had urged her to continue the fight – the raffish, roguish Alan Clark – had gone on to argue 'that I should fight on even though I was bound to lose because it was better to go down in a blaze of glorious defeat than go gentle into that good night'. She suggests that since she had 'no particular fondness for Wagnerian endings, this lifted my spirits only briefly', yet there was something of the *Twilight of the Gods* about her 'defenestration'. She saw it in operatic terms. Howe was 'poisonous', he had 'deliberately set out to bring down a colleague in this brutal and public way' and had engaged in 'a final act of bile and treachery'.[30] The Cabinet, including those closest to her, had deserted her so completely that she could not even muster 'a credible campaign team';[31] and she told Woodrow Wyatt that the party had 'sold her down the river'.[32]

Like every self-cast tragic hero, Thatcher staged a final moment of resilient defiance when she came to the Commons the day after resigning to reply to a no-confidence motion. A Liberal Democrat, Alan Beith, asked whether she would continue in her campaign against the single currency and she picked up on a sarcastic heckle from Dennis Skinner that she was going to be governor of the European Central Bank. 'What a good idea! I hadn't thought of that,' she replied, before going into a passionate attack on 'a federal Europe by the back door', stopping only to draw breath: 'Now, where was I? I am enjoying this.'[33] She ended with characteristic self-assertion:

There is something else which one feels. That is a sense of this country's destiny: the centuries of history and experience which ensure that, when principles have to be defended, when good has to be upheld and when evil has to be overcome, Britain will take up arms. It is because we on this side have never flinched from difficult decisions that this House and this country can have confidence in this Government today.[34]

She was right; the Conservatives won the vote by 120. The following Tuesday she answered her last – her 7,501st – Prime Minister's Question, and the next morning she took her tearful farewell of Downing Street. When Heath was ejected in 1974 a Tory MP took pity on his homelessness and lent him a flat; Thatcher went to a very unlived-in executive house in Dulwich.

SELECTING THE 92 HEREDITARIES TO REMAIN

Parliament remains ripe for reform. Since 1999 the only hereditary peers entitled to attend the House of Lords have been two hereditary postholders and ninety others elected for life by their fellows. In a recent hereditary by-election following the death of Hugh Mackay, the 14th Lord Reay, Geoffrey, the 5th Baron Browick, defeated Douglas Hogg, the former Conservative minister and 3rd Viscount Hailsham, and twenty-one other peers after sixteen transfers of votes.

Epilogue

WHEN JOHN BONHAM CARTER, the Liberal member for Winchester, rose to second the loyal address following the state opening of parliament on Tuesday, 3 February 1852, it was not quite the first time that Barry and Pugin's new House of Commons had been put to use, as MPs had been so eager to try it out that they had held a couple of sessions in it the previous August; but it still felt spick and span. The new Palace was not universally popular. When Barry first completed the Commons in 1850, Disraeli argued that, since no profession had ever yet succeeded in Britain until it had furnished 'an example', it was time the government considered hanging an architect, so as to 'put a stop to such blunders in future'.[1] Joseph Hume complained that 'the money they had expended upon [the Commons] was enough to have provided golden seats for the Members; but yet it was utterly unfit for its purpose' and that 'any schoolboy would be flogged for designing such a place'.[2] The complaints had led to a substantial refit and the installation of a false ceiling that cut off half the windows, further reduced the number of seats and required yet more artificial lighting. But even after these works had been done (which so upset Barry that he never visited the Commons again), MPs were still unhappy. Hume complained that the atmosphere was now completely unbearable and that the whole Palace was lit up like the Red Lion in Brentford. Others moaned about the lack of seats for the 658 MPs, about the stuffiness of the gas-lit Chamber, and the acoustics (as did Glenda Jackson on being asked to compare parliament to the theatre many years later, declaring the Commons 'under-rehearsed and badly lit and the acoustic is terrible'[3]). Bonham Carter, though, referred to it in glowing terms, praising the fact that in constructing the new building, the architect 'had not laid the hands of wanton destruction on the old'.[4] His was the historic plea of the traditionalist for evolution not revolution. What impression would Bonham Carter get if he were to visit parliament today? Has there been a revolution since 1852? And if so, has it been for the better?

Leaving aside the obvious sartorial and technological changes, and the fact that the Commons had to be rebuilt again after its bombing in the Second World War, Bonham Carter would certainly notice some dramatic differences. In his day Ireland sent 100 MPs; now Northern Ireland gets just eighteen, and five of them, Sinn Féin members, do not take their seats. Scotland has its own parliament, and Northern Ireland and Wales have powerful assemblies. There are women in parliament, and not just observers obscured behind a grille: 142 in the Commons and 181 in the Lords, though there is not yet one on the bench of bishops. The Commons is more ethnically diverse, too. The first Indian MP, the president of the Indian National Congress, Dadabhai Naoroji, was elected as a Liberal as long ago as 1892, to be followed by the Conservative Mancherjee Bhownaggree in 1895 and the Communist Shapurji Saklatvala in 1922; and in 1987 Bernie Grant, Paul Boateng and Diane Abbott were returned as the first black MPs. There are now twenty-seven ethnic minority MPs and, following on from the first Indian peer, Satyendra Prasanna Sinha, who was appointed in 1919, forty-two ethnic minority peers.[5]

On the whole members' finances are more constrained today. There are some very wealthy MPs and peers: Lord Ashcroft is reputed to be worth £1.2 billion, Lord Ballyedmond – at the time of his death in a helicopter accident early in 2014 – £860 million, Lord Sainsbury

£400 million, Lord Heseltine £264 million, Lord Fink £130 million, Richard Benyon £125 million, Lord Deighton £95 million, Lord Drayson and Zac Goldsmith £75 million apiece and Adam Afriyie £50 million. In 2010 the *Daily Mail* reckoned that twenty-three out of twenty-nine Cabinet ministers owned investments worth more than £1 million. The register of members' financial interests shows that in 2011/12 Gordon Brown made £900,000 for his several charities, David Miliband made £410,171 out of speeches, the two barristers Geoffrey Cox and Stephen Phillips earned £405,729 and £329,297 respectively, Sir Malcolm Rifkind made £246,359 out of farming and consultancy work, David Blunkett made £241,151 out of a combination of journalism and directorships, and eighteen MPs earned more than £100,000 outside parliament. Yet whereas a Victorian needed a significant private income or an additional job to be an MP and many peers had extensive landed interests, the vast majority of today's MPs rely entirely on their parliamentary salaries, and they have become more professional and more career-oriented, running fully staffed, taxpayer-funded offices in both Westminster and their constituencies.

There has been some constitutional change. The term 'His Majesty's Opposition' was first coined in 1826 by the radical MP for Westminster, John Cam Hobhouse, in a Commons debate on ministerial salaries,[6] and the concept of an alternative government in waiting was already well established by 1852, but the post of leader of the opposition was not officially recognized until 1937, when the Ministers of the Crown Act added it to the ministerial payroll (to be followed in 1975 by the leader of the opposition in the Lords, the opposition chief whips in both houses and up to two deputy chief whips in the Commons) and left the decision as to who precisely it was to the Speaker. Since 1975 both houses have also provided financial assistance to opposition parties in the form of 'Short money' and 'Cranborne money', totalling £7,064,324.38 for the six opposition parties in the Commons in 2013/14, and £627,518 for Labour and the cross-benchers in the Lords. In 1852 most constituencies had two MPs, often from different parties; now every member is a singleton. Then, clergy (apart from non-conformists) were barred from the Commons; since 2001, ordination has been no bar to election. Attendances are higher, as, aware that no British MP has been returned unopposed since the 1945 general election when Liverpool Scotland and Rhondda West saw no contest, MPs have become far more constituency-focused.[7] Where once they returned to their patches at the end of the parliamentary season, if at all, now they do advice surgeries, knock on doors and open village fetes in their constituencies every weekend. In order to get their names in the press or their faces on television, they speak and sit in the Commons more often; and sharp questions in the committee corridor and clever TV interviews on College Green have become as important as speeches in the Chamber. Those speeches, too have changed. Often there are so many wishing to say their piece that the Speaker sets and enforces a strict time limit of between three and fifteen minutes (a 21st-century innovation); certainly two-hour addresses with elaborate rhetorical flourishes and lengthy classical allusions are a thing of the past, today's MPs preferring to raise matters of direct concern to their constituents as pithily as possible, just before issuing a press release. Correspondence and case work now take up many hours of an MP's working week.

There have been significant changes in political tone, too. Although the Victorians enjoy a reputation for mawkish sentiment-ality, modern MPs are far more sentimental than their forebears; since the Iraq War the Commons always acknowledges the death of a member of the armed forces at Prime Minister's Questions, it marks the death of a member (often repeatedly and at length), and local catastrophes are always brought to the floor of the House, something that rarely happened in 1852. The Commons is more deferential to the royal family today. Notwithstanding Disraeli's astute management of the queen, Victorian criticism of the royals in the Commons was fairly common, and civil list debates could be rowdy. By contrast, recent debates on financing the Palace have been extraordinarily circumspect, and any direct criticism of a member of the royal family has been expressly forbidden by the rules of the House since 1887, when Charles Conybeare was told by the Chair, Henry Raikes, that he was not allowed to suggest that the popularity of the royal family was 'rapidly waning' or that members of the royal family should be forced to pay rent and water rates, as he 'must speak respectfully of the Royal Family in debate'.[8] Religion, once the dominant feature of so many parliamentary skirmishes, plays far less significant a role than in the days of parliamentary battles over Catholic and Jewish emancipation, although many MPs are active in their respective faith communities and both the Commons and the Lords start each day with prayers according to the Book of Common Prayer. Modern technology has made a dramatic difference, enabling constituents to contact MPs by email and through automated online campaigns, and MPs to publicize their views or their opponents' voting records on Twitter and Facebook.

The daily business is followed far more rigidly, always starting with an hour of questions to a department's ministers and finishing with a half-hour debate on the subject of an individual member's choice, apart from on a Friday when private members' Bills are being considered. Timetable motions are agreed for nearly every piece of business in the Commons apart from finance Bills, so late-night sittings are extremely rare. Some days have been set aside for specific topics, such as opposition-led debates, but since 2010 a Backbench Business Committee has determined the topic for debate on days allocated to it by the government. Private members' Bills were an important part of the equation right up until the 1960s, when Bills on abortion, homosexuality and the death penalty were advanced by individual MPs rather than the government, but where once a solitary MP could trammel up the government's timetable, today the government only ever loses control of the agenda when the Speaker permits a member to pose an 'urgent question' to a minister or allows an emergency debate on a matter of national significance or a reference to the Committee of Privileges. Victorian prime ministers regularly led second reading debates on key legislation and answered questions just like any other minister without a specific slot. But since Harold

Macmillan introduced it in 1961, Prime Minister's Questions has proved the dramatic highlight of the political week and a very audible (and now visible) means of holding the government to account – or at least of shouting at or for it. Departmental select committees, especially since their chairmen started to be elected by the whole House in 2010, have become a steadily more important way of holding the feet of the powerful to the fire.

Yet the Commons has become far more timid about asserting its own authority. In the nineteenth century the House regularly used its historic powers to punish a contempt of parliament by a non-member. As late as 1880 it imprisoned the former naval lieutenant Charles Grissell for publicly suggesting that he could 'control' a Commons committee on the building of a new bridge over the Thames. His audacity (he fled to Boulogne until the eve of the end of the parliamentary session and left his lawyer to sweat in the cell in the clock tower) undoubtedly contributed to the Commons' determination to have him arrested on his return, but that was the last time the Commons used its power to arrest a non-member (the free-thinking MP Charles Bradlaugh was also put in the clock tower cell for refusing to swear the oath in 1880). The Commons last used its power to fine in 1666, and has not forced anyone to appear at the bar of the House since 24 January 1957, when the editor of the *Sunday Express*, John Junor, was made to apologize profusely for an article that had suggested MPs had been avoiding petrol rationing. By contrast, it took intense provocation by the Maxwell brothers in January 1992 to persuade the Social Security Select Committee to seek a warrant from the Sergeant-at-Arms to require their attendance at the committee, Rebekah Brooks refused with impunity to attend the Culture, Media and Sport Committee in the 2005–10 parliament to discuss phone hacking, and when Rupert and James Murdoch at first suggested that they would not give evidence to the inquiry on phone hacking at the *News of the World* in 2011 MPs even worried whether the Commons had any power of compulsion. Eventually the deputy Sergeant-at-Arms delivered a formal summons to News International and they capitulated, but even when it was revealed that dozens of MPs and peers had had their phones hacked the Committee on Standards and Privileges considered only that this 'could *potentially* be a contempt' and urged that 'the House should assert its privileges *sparingly*'.[9] A claim by the Culture Committee that three News International employees had lied to the committee has still to be resolved.

As for the House of Lords, a woman, Baroness D'Souza, currently sits on the Woolsack, as Lord Speaker* rather than Lord Chancellor (who happens to be an MP, Chris Grayling), the Supreme Court has superseded the Lords as the highest legal tribunal in the land, and the skirmishes that led to the Parliament Acts of 1911 and 1949 and the introduction of life peers have rendered the upper house both less significant than its cousin down the corridor and more political than ever (thanks to the way peers are paid for attendance, the daily ministerial question time is far better populated in the Lords than in the Commons). In 1852 the largest landowners were all members of the Lords, but since the majority of hereditary peers were removed in 1999, the likes of the dukes of Buccleuch, Atholl, Westminster and Northumberland have departed the scene and only the dukes of Montrose and Norfolk (the Earl Marshal) remain. Once drawn exclusively from the landed and hallmarked families of Britain and Ireland, its membership might now seem rather brash and arriviste to Bonham Carter, with its collection of broadcasters, businessmen and former MPs. Although many peers have other jobs and the rules on the declaration of interests are less stringent than in the Commons, a significant number of the most active peers rely on their pensions and an untaxed daily allowance, set at £300, as their only income.

Most notably, although the 1852 bench of bishops included the sons of a woollen-draper, a clerk, a captain in the marines, a master in chancery and an innkeeper,[10] as well as several offspring of clergy (only the bishop of Rochester, George Murray, the grandson of the duke of Atholl, could really be counted an aristocrat), thanks to the church's

* The Lord Speaker does not vote.

historic endowments the very fact of being a Victorian bishop made you wealthy. By contrast today's bishops are far poorer, their palaces invariably taken up with the clutter of diocesan offices. The bishops have changed in other ways, too. The four Irish and four Welsh bishops left when their respective churches were disestablished, and the twenty-six longest-serving diocesan bishops of the Church of England now sit alongside the leaders of other faiths and denominations, including former presidents of Methodist Conference and the Chief Rabbi.

The Scottish and Irish representative peers have gone, and in 1999 the vast majority of the hereditary peers were excluded. Now they can stand either for the Commons (and one has successfully done so: John Sinclair, 3rd Viscount Thurso, MP for Caithness, Sutherland and Easter Ross), or for a rump of ninety seats, held for life, in the Lords (there are two more kept specifically for the ceremonial officers of state, the Lord Great Chamberlain and the Earl Marshal). Although this was meant to be a temporary measure pending fuller reform of the Lords, bizarre by-elections among the hereditary peers come along fairly regularly as individuals die. So, for instance, in the by-election in July 2011 following the death of Geoffrey Russell, the 4th Lord Ampthill, the television director Charles, 5th Viscount Colville of Culross, defeated John Seymour, the 19th duke of Somerset, in the fifteenth round of voting; and when Michael, the loathsome 7th earl of Onslow, died, his son and heir Rupert came eighth down a list that included the descendants of two twentieth-century prime ministers and was headed by the Lloyd's underwriter Thomas, 4th Baron Ashton of Hyde.

Full democratic reform of the Lords has proved as elusive as ever. The disagreement between Tony Blair's chief whip, Hilary Armstrong, and his Leader of the House, Robin Cook, and a wider split in Labour's ranks meant that the supposed second stage of reform never materialized under Labour, although the Commons voted in favour of a wholly elected second chamber in March 2007 by 337 votes to 234. The Coalition government's Bill fared no better, winning a second reading on 10 July 2012 by the even larger majority of 462 to 124 but being dropped when 91 Conservatives voted against the whip. So parliament is left with an 800-person house of patronage, full of political appointees who take a party whip, plus twenty-six bishops and ninety-two hereditary peers. There are those who argue that this is a house of expertise, but many peers have substantial business interests which they pursue in tandem with their membership of the legislature; and the most worrying facet of this vast, emboldened house is that its power is circumscribed only by its members' capacity for self-denial. Since the Cranborne–Addison convention, whereby the Lords would not vote down legislation adumbrated in the governing party's manifesto, is now effectively defunct and nobody has yet been able to agree a means of codifying the relationship between the two Houses in law, prime ministers are keen to ensure themselves a majority by appointing more and more peers. Since 2010 David Cameron has appointed 122 new peers, at the fastest rate in history. This galloping inflation is unsustainable; and the uncertainty over the respective powers of the Commons and Lords will not hold.

One major constitutional change has affected both houses. Britain's membership of the European Economic Community since 1973 and subsequently of the European Union, enacted in statute law (like every other constitutional revolution since Thomas Cromwell) in the shape of the European Communities Act 1972, has meant that some UK law-making is a transposition of legislation drafted by the European Commission and battled over by the European Council and European Parliament. Some fret about the Westminster parliament's loss of sovereignty and many exaggerate the proportion of such legislation (in 2010 the House of Commons library estimated that between 1997 and 2009 just 6.8 per cent of statutes and 14.1 per cent of statutory instruments had stemmed from EU legislation, a figure far lower than Eurosceptics suggest), but the truth is that some EU measures are slipped through via unamendable secondary legislation, and in consequence parliament scrutinizes EU legislation too little and too late to make a difference. The remedy for this lies entirely in MPs and peers' own hands. Others complain even more that the rulings of the European Court of Human Rights infringe British sovereignty. Yet the United Kingdom was a founding signatory of the Convention, and a British lawyer, later the Conservative Home Secretary, David Maxwell Fyfe, drafted it. Its transposition into UK law via the Human Rights Act 1998 meant that most British appeals under the Human Rights Convention could be resolved in UK courts. Here too the remedy, if remedy is needed, is in parliament's hands; the UK could, if it chose to, resile from the Court, abandon the Convention and leave the Council of Europe. It would cost the UK its international reputation for upholding the rule of law, but it could do so, if it so chose.

Some things feel very settled. In the Stuart era it was still not uncommon for a Bill to have several readings, but the pattern of three readings, with a committee and report stage in each House, has been followed for more than 300 years. The House of Lords occasionally tries to meddle with the Commons' financial privilege, but gets rebuffed. Members of both houses refer to one another in the third person, and they vote slowly and laboriously by walking through a lobby (MPs get eight minutes before the doors are locked, peers get eleven). The respective numbers needed for a quorum in the Commons (a hundred) and the Lords (thirty) and the rules governing what happens when a vote is tied, have remained unchanged for decades. A government is always formed by virtue of commanding a majority in the Commons. Ministers are appointed and dismissed by the Prime Minister, not the monarch (although they are still officially ministers of the crown, and the Prime Minister plays far less of a role in the appointment of bishops than formerly). Some provisions have changed: since the Fixed Term Parliaments Act 2011, each parliament lasts five years and elections are held on the first Thursday in May, unless a government loses a vote of confidence and no alternative can be formed within a fortnight. Some of the more recondite traditions remain, such as the Commons Petitions Bag at the back of the Speaker's chair, and the old right enjoyed by members of the Lords to enter a protest against a decision of the House in the *Journal*, which was used extensively by the opposition in the early eighteenth century, was resorted to after the passing of the Great Reform Act and was last used by Norman Tebbit on 16 July 1998.

Some significant characteristics of parliament have barely changed at all. First, although heredity is almost defunct (only six hereditary peerages having been granted since 1965, three of them to royals, two to men who died without male issue and one to Harold Macmillan, whose grandson the 2nd earl of Stockton is not in the Lords), family is every bit as important as ever. Some of the oldest parliamentary families have modern scions: Jane Bonham Carter follows her grandmother Violet, her father Mark and her uncle Jo Grimond in sitting as a life peer; Clement Attlee's grandson John has inherited his earldom and sits as a Conservative elected hereditary peer; Richard Drax has a small legion of parliamentary antecedents that includes Sir Christopher Plunkett, who became an Irish peer in 1439, and Thomas Ernle, who hosted a meeting of Exclusionists in 1686 that led to the Glorious Revolution; George Osborne is the heir to the Irish baronetcy probably sold to Sir Richard Osborne in 1629 and has at least five direct antecedents who were members of the Irish parliament; Theresa Villiers' ancestors include George Villiers, the 4th earl of Clarendon, who was Foreign Secretary three times, his father Thomas Hyde Villiers, who was Secretary of the Board of Control, and the longest ever sitting MP, Charles Pelham Villiers; Sir George Young is the sixth of the baronets of Formosa Place and can list eight predecessors as MPs on his father's side and another dozen on his mother's, including the Victorian Tory 'Ultra' Sir Edward Knatchbull, his Liberal son Edward Knatchbull-Hugessen and Sir Norton Knatchbull; and David Cameron's antecedents include a host of dukes, marquesses and royals. When Richard Benyon was elected for Newbury in 2005 he was following in a family tradition that included his father Bill, who was a Conservative MP for twenty-two years; three other Richard Benyons who were MPs; William Henry Fellowes, who was an MP from 1796 to 1830; Fellowes' two grandsons, William and Ailwyn, respectively a whip in Salisbury's government and President of the Board of

Agriculture under Balfour; William Gascoyne-Cecil, the eccentric bishop of Exeter, plus the former prime minister the marquess of Salisbury and the whole Cecil dynasty; and in the further reaches of the family the royalist hero of the siege of Basing House John Paulet, 5th marquess of Winchester, who acquired the house in Berkshire named after the Speaker (twice: 1497 and 1510) Sir Thomas Englefield, in which Richard Benyon lives today. Most impressively, Laura Sandys can look back to her father Duncan; her grandfather George; the star of the Jacobean parliaments, Sir Edwin Sandys; his knighted brothers Miles and Samuel; their father Edwin, the archbishop of York; and a quartet of fourteenth-century knights of the shire, Sir John Sandys, Sir Walter, Sir Thomas and, in 1377, Richard del Sandys.

Others have more recent family connections. The Paymaster-General, Francis Maude, holds the job his father Angus held in Mrs Thatcher's first government; Robin Walker is MP for the seat his father, the Cabinet minister Peter Walker, held from 1961 to 1992; Jacob Rees-Mogg's father William, the former editor of *The Times*, sat as a cross-bench peer from 1988 to his death in 2012; Ben Gummer's father and uncle are both peers; and on the Labour side Tristram Hunt's father was made a life peer in 2000 and Hilary Benn's father Tony, his grandfather William Wedgwood Benn and his great-grandfathers Sir John Benn and Daniel Holmes were all MPs. With the twentieth-century advent of women in both houses there are new-style family connections as well. Peter Bottomley's wife Virginia was a Conservative MP and Secretary for Education, and is now a baroness; his niece, Kitty Ussher, was a Labour MP. Bernard Jenkin's father and wife are both peers. There are several parliamentary couples: Harriet Harman and Jack Dromey, Ed Balls and Yvette Cooper, Jo Swinson and Duncan Hames, and the twin sisters Angela and Maria Eagle, are all in the Commons; Geoffrey and Elspeth Howe and Alan Howarth and Patricia Hollis are in the Lords. All of which proves that although familial connections no longer necessarily give someone an advantage in politics, the very fact of being born into a political family may incline an individual to stand for parliament.

Second, politics is every bit as confrontational as it was in 1852. Heckling, put-downs and crafty vituperation that just avoid the censure of the Speaker for being 'unparliamentary' are still the order of the day. Blair tells Hague that the 'jokes are good but the judgement less so'. Cameron shakes his head at Blair and says 'you were the future, once'. Brown claims Cameron's policy on inheritance tax was 'dreamed up on the playing fields of Eton'. Cameron attacks Miliband as the 'croupier in the casino when the bank went bust'.[11] In the week that the Prime Minister changed his policy on alcohol pricing, Miliband asks whether there is *anything* that Cameron could organize in a brewery. Some decry this. They want a more adult debate, and this last parliament has been the noisiest, the most raucous and the least consensual in living memory. Yet the very architecture of the Commons, where MPs face each other in an overcrowded room with too few seats, demands confrontation. A recorded abstention, although theoretically possible if you walk through both lobbies, is frowned on and has been ruled out of order.* So British parliaments have always been adversarial in style, and today's jibes are little different in essence from Disraeli comparing Peel's smile to the silver fittings on a coffin, or Cobbett calling Pitt the Younger 'that great snorting bawler',[12] or Lloyd George dismissing Balfour as 'not a man but a mannerism',[13] or Allen Adams describing Mrs Thatcher as a 'sex-starved boa constrictor',[14] or Michael Foot referring to Norman Tebbit as a 'semi-house-trained polecat',[15] or the dismissal of Sir John Lowther as 'an empty piece of misplaced eloquence'.[16] This is knockabout, Punch and Judy, pantomime, what you will.

In defence of today's politicians, their behaviour is very rarely as bad as in previous eras. In 1920 the Irish nationalist MP Joe Devlin was assaulted by John Morton, in 1923 Robert Murray and Walter

---

*When a member inadvertently votes in both lobbies, he or she is meant to explain the matter to the House. In the Lords, however, a peer who inadvertently votes in the wrong lobby can have that vote corrected, and if a peer votes in both lobbies their name is subsequently removed from both lists and their vote is disregarded.

Guinness got into a tussle over the treatment of ex-servicemen, and in 1976 Michael Heseltine started swinging the mace around when Wilson's government controversially won a procedural motion by a single vote. There are fewer staged displays of disorder today, too, of the kind seen when the mining MPs expressed their fury that none of them had been called on 25 June 1926, or Labour MPs forced the Speaker to suspend the session by shouting at Sir Philip Cunliffe-Lister on 16 November 1927, or when Prime Minister's Questions were suspended in 1972 as Labour MPs repeatedly bellowed 'Heath out', or when the budget was disrupted in 1988. Occasionally, much to the public's disgust, modern parliamentary belligerence spills over into deliberately coordinated bullying and the Speaker's requests for 'Order, order' sound plaintive and ineffectual. Yet the Commons is also a crucible (as, increasingly, is the Lords) in which a member's mettle is proved and their argument tested. Indeed, those occasions when the House is of one accord and dissent falls silent have often proved our biggest mistakes, and we should relish the fact that few other democracies are so fierce in their scrutiny of politicians or fearless in their disregard for the personal sensitivities of the powerful.

Yet there is a paradox in this, as parliament's debates over the war in Iraq proved. On the one hand, parliament triumphed; Tony Blair had to face members every week and win a public vote in the run-up to the war, whereas George W. Bush never once faced such a congressional grilling and the Spanish Prime Minister, José María Aznar, also sent troops to Iraq but got away with a secret ballot in the Cortes. Yet the fact that Iain Duncan Smith, the leader of the opposition, was even more supportive of the war than many government MPs meant that the vote was never in doubt (the Commons voted 412 to 149 in support of war on 18 March 2003), and parliamentary scrutiny of the conduct of the war was pitifully inadequate. When it came to the vote on the possibility of a military intervention in Syria on 29 August 2013, the ghosts of that parliamentary failure on Iraq (and the twentieth-century appeasement of Franco, Hitler, Mussolini and Milosevic) were evident as MPs, hastily recalled from recess, quietly resolved to vote down both the opposition's amendment (by 332 to 220) and the government's motion (by 285 to 272). For the first time since 1782 the crown had lost a vote on its foreign policy. Parliament had decided to decide nothing, David Cameron immediately declared that 'the British Parliament, reflecting the views of the British people, does not want to see British military action',[17] President Obama had to cancel any plans he had for immediate military intervention and President Putin seized the initiative while Syrians continued to die.

Third, long after the sun set on the empire, the British remain just as preposterously self-regarding as ever, and self-aggrandizing myths about parliament abound. Witness Nigel Evans referring in his resignation statement as deputy Speaker to the people who put him in 'the mother of Parliaments',[18] an inaccurate and frequently misquoted and misapplied phrase. Such myths have been endemic in British history, as the critic and historiographer royal Thomas Rymer pointed out in the early eighteenth century, when he rightly scoffed at the respected Jacobean jurist and MP Sir Edward Coke for claiming that the word 'parliament' came from 'parler le ment', meaning to speak one's mind. 'He might as honestly have taught us', wrote Rymer, 'that "firmament" is "firma mentis" (a farm for the mind) and "fundament" the bottom of the mind.'[19] The same applies to false parliamentary etymologies attributed to 'toe the line', 'in the bag' and 'sit on the fence', none of which applies to the Commons Chamber.

The truth is that parliament is very far from perfect. Some things have gone backwards. When Edmund Burke campaigned against the 'old corruption', his concern was that the government had 150 placemen in receipt of a government salary, pension or other form of emolument in the Commons. The number was subsequently cut dramatically and MPs had to fight by-elections if they were appointed as ministers. Yet in December 2012 the Commons payroll, including ministers, parliamentary private secretaries, and official and unofficial whips stood at exactly 140 – and the by-election requirement was done away with in 1926. The power of patronage that is thereby afforded to the government and opposition is immense. Whips already existed in

1852, but they were few in number and roughly 80 per cent of votes saw some cross-party voting. Today the number of significant rebellions is comparatively tiny and the government has a complement of eighteen whips in the Commons.[20] The government alone decides when parliament sits, when it adjourns and when it is prorogued. Only government legislation and government business gets priority on the order paper. Only a government minister can table or vary a charge to the public purse. And it still has trips, titles and honours to dangle in front of the ambitious or the vain, including seats in the House of Lords that last for life even if one has been imprisoned for perjury, arson, dangerous driving or fraud (as present peers have been). All too often it feels less like a parliament of the free-born and more as if, in the words that Shakespeare put into the mouth of John of Gaunt, Britain's democracy 'is now leased out'. Parliament is less a legislature or a vent for the people's grievances than a gene-pool for government.

The journalist and historian George Barnett Smith wrote in 1892 that 'the people of England regard with just pride the venerable system of Parliamentary Government under which it is their happiness to live'.[21] Few hold parliament in such veneration today. Recent polling suggests that the predominant emotion that has driven down turnout in elections is not apathy but anger towards MPs and parties that break their promises. Yet parliamentary democracy, evolved by time, fashioned by chance and adapted by experience, still places the possibility of an ever better system in our own hands. Free and fair elections, reform by statute rather than by force, government for the many without forgetting the few, the liberty of the individual made possible by the collective endeavour, not arbitrary tyranny but the rule of law, the shared sovereignty of the people – these are worth taking pride in, protecting and enhancing.

That great radical Sir John Hobhouse MP was mistaken to declare on the passage of the Reform Act in 1832: 'Thus ends this great national exploit. The deed is done.'[22] Today, the most dangerous myth of all is that the process of reform is over. That great national exploit will never be complete.

Tables of Office-holders, Electoral Contests and Parliamentary Composition

Presiding Officers and Speakers of the House of Commons

Date	Name	Constituency	Notes
1258	Peter de Montfort		*Styled* Prolocutor
1327	William Trussell		*Joint spokesman of Commons and Lords, styled* Procurator
1332	Henry Beaumont		*Joint spokesman of Commons and Lords*
1332	Sir Geoffrey le Scrope		*Ditto*
1340, 1343	William Trussell		
1347–8	William de Thorpe		
1351–2	William de Shareshull		
1361–3	Sir Henry Green		
1376	Sir Peter de la Mare	Herefordshire	
1377	Sir Thomas Hungerford	Wiltshire	*The first to be styled Speaker*
1377	Sir Peter de la Mare	Herefordshire	
1378	Sir James Pickering	Westmorland	
1380	Sir John Guildesborough	Essex	
1381–2	Sir Richard Waldegrave	Suffolk	
1383	Sir James Pickering	Yorkshire	
1394–8	Sir John Bussy	Lincolnshire	*Beheaded*
1399	Sir John Cheyne	Gloucestershire	
1399	John Dorewood	Essex	
1401–2	Sir Arnold Savage	Kent	
1402	Sir Henry Redford	Lincolnshire	
1404	Sir Arnold Savage	Kent	

Presiding Officers and Speakers cont.

Date	Name	Constituency	Notes
1404	Sir William Sturmy	Devon	
1406	Sir John Tiptoft	Huntingdonshire	*First Speaker to be made a baron*
1407–11	Thomas Chaucer	Oxfordshire	
1413	William Stourton	Dorset	
1413	John Doreward	Essex	
1414	Sir Walter Hungerford	Wiltshire	
1414–15	Thomas Chaucer	Oxfordshire	
1415	Sir Richard Redman (or Redmayne)	Yorkshire	
1416	Sir Walter Beauchamp	Wiltshire	
1416–19	Roger Flower	Rutland	
1420–1	Roger Hunt	Bedfordshire	
1421	Thomas Chaucer	Oxfordshire	
1421–2	Richard Baynard	Essex	
1422	Roger Flower	Rutland	
1423–4	Sir John Russell	Herefordshire	
1425	Sir Thomas Walton	Bedfordshire	
1426	Sir Richard Vernon	Derbyshire	
1427–8	Sir John Tyrrell	Hertfordshire	
1429–30	Sir William Alington I	Cambridgeshire	
1431	Sir John Tyrrell	Essex	
1432	Sir John Russell	Herefordshire	
1433	Roger Hunt	Huntingdonshire	
1435	John Bowes	Nottinghamshire	
1437	Sir John Tyrrell	Essex	
1437	William Burley	Shropshire	
1439–42	William Tresham	Northamptonshire	
1445	William Burley	Shropshire	
1447	William Tresham	Northamptonshire	
1449	Sir John Say	Cambridgeshire	
1449	Sir John Popham	Hampshire	
1449	William Tresham	Northamptonshire	*Murdered in 1450*

Date	Name	Constituency	Notes
1450	Sir William Oldhall	Hertfordshire	
1453–4	Thomas Thorpe	Essex	*Imprisoned and, in 1461, beheaded*
1454	Sir Thomas Charlton	Middlesex	
1455–6	Sir John Wenlock	Bedfordshire	
1459	Sir Thomas Tresham	Northamptonshire	*Beheaded in 1471*
1460	John Green	Essex	
1461–2	Sir James Strangeways	Yorkshire	
1463–8	Sir John Say	Hertfordshire	
1472–8	William Alington II	Cambridgeshire	
1483	John Wood (or Wode)	Surrey	
1484	William Catesby	Northamptonshire	*Beheaded in 1485*
1484–6	Sir Thomas Lovell	Northamptonshire	
1487–8	Sir John Mordaunt	Bedfordshire	
1489–90	Sir Thomas Fitzwilliam	Lincolnshire	
1491–2	Sir Richard Empson	Northamptonshire	*Beheaded in 1510*
1495	Sir Robert Drury	Suffolk	
1497	Sir Thomas Englefield	Berkshire	
1504	Edmond Dudley	Staffordshire	
1510	Sir Thomas Englefield	Berkshire	*Beheaded in 1510*
1512–13	Sir Robert Sheffield	Lincolnshire	
1515	Sir Thomas Nevill	Kent	
1523	Sir Thomas More	Middlesex	*Beheaded in 1535*
1529–33	Sir Thomas Audley	Essex	
1533–6	Sir Humphrey Wingfield	Great Yarmouth	*The first Speaker for a borough seat*
1536	Sir Richard Rich	Colchester	
1539–40	Sir Nicholas Hare	Norfolk	
1542–4	Sir Thomas Moyle	Peterborough	
1545–52	Sir John Baker	Huntingdonshire	
1553	Sir James Dyer	Cambridgeshire	
1553	John Pollard	Oxfordshire	
1554	Sir Robert Broke	City of London	

Presiding Officers and Speakers cont.

Date	Name	Constituency	Notes
1554–5	Sir Clement Higham	West Looe	
1555	John Pollard	Chippenham	
1558	Sir William Cordell	Suffolk	
1559	Sir Thomas Gargrave	Yorkshire	
1563	Thomas Williams	Exeter	
1566–7	Richard Onslow	Steyning	
1571	Sir Christopher Wray	Ludgershall	
1572–6	Sir Robert Bell	Lyme Regis	
1581–3	Sir John Popham	Bristol	
1584–7	Sir John Puckering	Carmarthen and then Gatton	
1588–9	Sir Thomas Snagge	Bedford	
1592–3	Sir Edward Coke	Norfolk	
1597–8	Sir Christopher Yelverton	Northamptonshire	
1601	Sir John Croke	City of London	
1603–11	Sir Edward Phelips	Somerset	
1614	Sir Randolph Crewe	Saltash	
1621–2	Sir Thomas Richardson	St Albans	
1623–5	Sir Thomas Crewe	Aylesbury and then Gatton	
1625–6	Sir Heneage Finch	City of London	
1628–9	Sir John Finch	Canterbury	*Impeached in 1640*
1640	Sir John Glanville	Bristol	
1640–7	William Lenthall	Woodstock	
1647	Henry Pelham	Grantham	
1647–53	William Lenthall	Woodstock	
1653	Revd Francis Rous	Devon	
1654–5	William Lenthall	Oxfordshire	
1656–8	Sir Thomas Widdrington	Northumberland	
1657	Bulstrode Whitelocke	Buckinghamshire	
1658–9	Chaloner Chute	Middlesex	
1659	Sir Lislebone Long	Wells	
1659	Thomas Bampfylde	Exeter	

Date	Name	Constituency	Notes
1659–60	William Lenthall	Oxfordshire	
1660	William Say	Camelford	
1660	Sir Harbottle Grimston	Colchester	
1661–71	Sir Edward Turnour	Hertford	
1672	Sir Job Charlton	Ludlow	
1673	Sir Edward Seymour	Totnes	
1678	Sir Robert Sawyer	Wycombe	
1678–9	Sir Edward Seymour	Totnes	
1679	Sir William Gregory	Weobley	
1680–1	Sir William Williams	Chester	
1685–7	Sir John Trevor	Denbigh	
1688–9	Henry Powle	Windsor	
1689–95	Sir John Trevor	Yarmouth, Isle of Wight	*Expelled in 1695 for taking a bribe*
1695–8	Paul Foley	Hereford	
1698–1700	Sir Thomas Littleton	Woodstock	
1701–5	Robert Harley	New Radnor	
1705–7	John Smith	Andover	
1708–10	Sir Richard Onslow	Surrey	
1710–13	William Bromley	Oxford University	
1714–15	Sir Thomas Hanmer	Suffolk	
1715–27	Sir Spencer Compton	Sussex	
1728–61	Arthur Onslow	Surrey	
1761–70	Sir John Cust	Grantham	
1770–80	Sir Fletcher Norton	Guildford	
1780–9	Charles Wolfran Cornwall	Winchelsea and then Rye	*Died in office*
1789	William Wyndham Grenville	Buckinghamshire	
1789–1801	Henry Addington	Truro and then Devizes	*The last Speaker to remain an MP after leaving the chair*
1801–2	Sir John Mitford	Northumberland	

Presiding Officers and Speakers cont.

Date	Name	Constituency	Notes
1802–17	Charles Abbot	Woodstock and then Oxford University	
1817–34	Charles Manners Sutton	Scarborough and then Cambridge University	
1835–9	James Abercromby	Edinburgh	
1839–57	Charles Shaw Lefevre	North Hampshire	
1857–72	John Evelyn Denison	North Nottinghamshire	
1872–84	Henry Bouverie William Brand	Cambridgeshire	
1886–95	Arthur Wellesley Peel	Warwick and Leamington	
1895–1905	William Court Gully	Carlisle	
1905–21	James William Lowther	Penrith and then Penrith and Cockermouth	
1921–8	John Henry Whitley	Halifax	
1928–43	Edward Algernon Fitzroy	Daventry	
1943–51	Douglas Clifton Brown	Hexham	
1951–9	William Shepherd Morrison	Cirencester and Tewkesbury	
1959–65	Sir Harry Hylton Foster	Cities of London and Westminster	
1965–71	Dr Horace King	Southampton Itchen	
1971–6	John Selwyn Lloyd	Wirral	
1976–83	Thomas George Thomas	Cardiff West	
1983–92	Bernard Weatherill	Croydon North East	
1992–2000	Betty Boothroyd	West Bromwich West	
2000–9	Michael John Martin	Glasgow Springburn, then Glasgow North East	
2009–	John Bercow	Buckingham	

Prime Ministers and First Lords of the Treasury

Date of taking office	Date of leaving office	Name and personal title	Office title and other notes
8 May 1702	11 Aug. 1710	Sidney Godolphin, 1st earl of Godolphin	*Lord High Treasurer*
30 May 1711	30 Jul. 1714	Robert Harley, 1st earl of Oxford	*Lord High Treasurer*
17 Sept. 1714	12 Dec. 1716	Charles Townshend, Baron Townshend	*Northern Secretary*
13 Oct. 1714	19 May 1715	Charles Montagu, 1st earl of Halifax	*First Lord of the Treasury*
23 May 1715	10 Oct. 1715	Charles Howard, 3rd earl of Carlisle	*First Lord of the Treasury*
10 Oct. 1715	12 Apr. 1717	Robert Walpole	*First Lord of the Treasury*
12 Apr. 1717	21 Mar. 1718	James Stanhope, 1st Viscount Stanhope	*First Lord of the Treasury*
21 Mar. 1718	4 Apr. 1721	Charles Spencer, 3rd earl of Sunderland	*First Lord of the Treasury*
4 Apr. 1721	11 Feb. 1742	Sir Robert Walpole	*First Lord of the Treasury and Prime Minister*
16 Feb. 1742	2 Jul. 1743	Spencer Compton, 1st earl of Wilmington	*Died in office*
27 Aug. 1743	7 Mar. 1754	Henry Pelham	
16 Mar. 1754	16 Nov. 1756	Thomas Pelham-Holles, 1st duke of Newcastle	*Succeeded his younger brother*
16 Nov. 1756	25 Jun. 1757	William Cavendish, 4th duke of Devonshire	
2 Jul. 1757	26 May 1762	Thomas Pelham-Holles, 1st duke of Newcastle	
26 May 1762	16 Apr. 1763	John Stuart, 3rd earl of Bute	
16 Apr. 1763	13 Jul. 1765	George Grenville	
13 Jul. 1765	30 Jul. 1766	Charles Watson-Wentworth, 2nd marquess of Rockingham	
30 Jul. 1766	14 Oct. 1768	William Pitt the Elder, 1st earl of Chatham	*Chatham was Lord Privy Seal; the duke of Grafton was First Lord of the Treasury*
14 Oct. 1768	28 Jan. 1770	Augustus Fitzroy, 3rd duke of Grafton	
28 Jan. 1770	22 Mar. 1782	Frederick North, Lord North	

Prime Ministers and First Lords of the Treasury cont.

Date of taking office	Date of leaving office	Name and personal title	Office title and other notes
27 Mar. 1782	1 Jul. 1782	Charles Watson-Wentworth, 2nd marquess of Rockingham	*Died in office after just 14 weeks*
4 Jul. 1782	2 Apr. 1783	William Petty, 2nd earl of Shelburne	
2 Apr. 1783	19 Dec. 1783	William Henry Cavendish Bentinck, 3rd duke of Portland	
19 Dec. 1783	14 Mar. 1801	William Pitt the Younger	*Youngest Prime Minister*
17 Mar. 1801	10 May 1804	Henry Addington	
10 May 1804	23 Jan. 1806	William Pitt the Younger	*Died in office*
11 Feb. 1806	31 Mar. 1807	William Wyndham Grenville, 1st Baron Grenville	
31 Mar. 1807	4 Oct. 1809	William Henry Cavendish Bentinck, 3rd duke of Portland	
4 Oct. 1809	11 May 1812	Spencer Perceval	*Assassinated in 1812*
9 Jun. 1812	10 Apr. 1827	Robert Banks Jenkinson, 2nd earl of Liverpool	*Longest serving Prime Minister of the United Kingdom*
10 Apr. 1827	8 Aug. 1827	George Canning	*Died in office after 119 days*
31 Aug. 1827	22 Jan. 1828	Frederick John Robinson, 1st Viscount Goderich	
22 Jan. 1828	22 Nov. 1830	Arthur Wellesley, 1st duke of Wellington	
22 Nov. 1830	16 Jul. 1834	Charles, 2nd Earl Grey	
16 Jul. 1834	17 Nov. 1834	William Lamb, 2nd Viscount Melbourne	*The last Prime Minister to be dismissed by an incoming king (William IV)*
17 Nov. 1834	9 Dec. 1834	Arthur Wellesley, 1st duke of Wellington	*Caretaker*
10 Dec. 1834	18 Apr. 1835	Sir Robert Peel	
18 Apr. 1835	30 Aug. 1841	William Lamb, 2nd Viscount Melbourne	
30 Aug. 1841	30 Jun. 1846	Sir Robert Peel	
30 Jun. 1846	23 Feb. 1852	Lord John Russell	
23 Feb. 1852	19 Dec. 1852	Edward Geoffrey Smith-Stanley, 14th earl of Derby	

Date of taking office	Date of leaving office	Name and personal title	Office title and other notes
19 Dec. 1852	6 Feb. 1855	George Hamilton Gordon, 4th earl of Aberdeen	
6 Feb. 1855	20 Feb. 1858	Henry John Temple, 3rd Viscount Palmerston	
20 Feb. 1858	12 Jun. 1859	Edward Geoffrey Smith Stanley, 14th earl of Derby	
12 Jun. 1859	18 Oct. 1865	Henry John Temple, 3rd Viscount Palmerston	
29 Oct. 1865	28 Jun. 1866	John, 1st Earl Russell	
28 Jun. 1866	27 Feb. 1868	Edward Geoffrey Smith Stanley, 14th earl of Derby	
27 Feb. 1868	3 Dec. 1868	Benjamin Disraeli	
3 Dec. 1868	20 Feb. 1874	William Ewart Gladstone	
20 Feb. 1874	23 Apr. 1880	Benjamin Disraeli, 1st earl of Beaconsfield	
23 Apr. 1880	23 Jun. 1885	William Ewart Gladstone	
23 Jun. 1885	1 Feb. 1886	Robert Arthur Talbot Gascoyne Cecil, 3rd marquess of Salisbury	*Salisbury was Leader in the Lords; the First Lord of the Treasury was Stafford Northcote, 1st earl of Iddesleigh*
1 Feb. 1886	25 Jul. 1886	William Ewart Gladstone	
3 Aug. 1886	15 Aug. 1892	Robert Arthur Talbot Gascoyne Cecil, 3rd marquess of Salisbury	*Between January 1887 and August 1892 two other men held the post of First Lord of the Treasury: W. H. Smith and Salisbury's nephew Arthur Balfour*
15 Aug. 1892	5 Mar. 1894	William Ewart Gladstone	
5 Mar. 1894	25 Jun. 1895	Archibald Philip Primrose, 5th earl of Rosebery	
25 Jun. 1895	12 Jul. 1902	Robert Arthur Talbot Gascoyne Cecil, 3rd marquess of Salisbury	*Although he was the last Prime Minister to serve his term in the Lords, the First Lord of the Treasury was Arthur Balfour*

Prime Ministers and First Lords of the Treasury cont.

Date of taking office	Date of leaving office	Name and personal title	Office title and other notes
12 Jul. 1902	5 Dec. 1905	Arthur Balfour	*Succeeded his uncle*
5 Dec. 1905	7 Apr. 1908	Henry Campbell-Bannerman	*Liberal*
7 Apr. 1908	27 May 1915	Herbert Henry Asquith	*Liberal minority*
27 May 1915	7 Dec. 1916	Herbert Henry Asquith	*Coalition*
7 Dec. 1916	23 Oct. 1922	David Lloyd George	*Coalition*
23 Oct. 1922	22 May 1923	Andrew Bonar Law	*Conservative*
22 May 1923	22 Jan. 1924	Stanley Baldwin	*Conservative*
22 Jan. 1924	4 Nov. 1924	Ramsay MacDonald	*Labour minority*
4 Nov. 1924	5 Jun. 1929	Stanley Baldwin	*Conservative*
5 Jun. 1929	24 Aug. 1931	Ramsay MacDonald	*Labour minority*
24 Aug. 1931	7 Jun. 1935	Ramsay MacDonald	*National Government*
7 Jun. 1935	28 May 1937	Stanley Baldwin	*National Government*
28 May 1937	10 May 1940	Neville Chamberlain	*National Government*
10 May 1940	23 May 1945	Winston Churchill	*Wartime Coalition*
23 May 1945	26 Jul. 1945	Winston Churchill	*Caretaker*
26 Jul. 1945	26 Oct. 1951	Clement Attlee	*Labour*
26 Oct. 1951	6 Apr. 1955	Winston Churchill	*Conservative*
6 Apr. 1955	10 Jan. 1957	Anthony Eden	*Conservative*
10 Jan. 1957	19 Oct. 1963	Harold Macmillan	*Conservative*
19 Oct. 1963	16 Oct. 1964	Alec Douglas-Home (14th earl of Home until 1963)	*Conservative*
16 Oct. 1964	19 Jun. 1970	Harold Wilson	*Labour*
19 Jun. 1970	4 Mar. 1974	Edward Heath	*Conservative*
4 Mar. 1974	5 Apr. 1976	Harold Wilson	*Labour*
5 Apr. 1976	4 May 1979	James Callaghan	*Labour*
4 May 1979	28 Nov. 1990	Margaret Thatcher	*Conservative*
28 Nov. 1990	2 May 1997	John Major	*Conservative*
2 May 1997	26 Jun. 2007	Tony Blair	*Labour*
26 Jun. 2007	11 May 2010	Gordon Brown	*Labour*
11 May 2010		David Cameron	*Coalition*

Lord Chancellors and Keepers of the Great Seal since 1214

Dates of office	Name and clerical office
1214–16	Richard Marsh, archdeacon of Northumberland
1226	Ralph Neville, bishop of Chichester
1240	Richard le Gras, abbot of Evesham
1242	Ralph Neville, bishop of Chichester
1244	Silvester de Everdon, archdeacon of Chester
1246	John Mansel, provost of Beverley
1247	Sir John Lexington
1248	John Mansel, provost of Beverley
1249	Sir John Lexington
1250	William of Kilkenny, archdeacon of Coventry
1255	Henry Wingham, bishop of London
1260	Nicholas of Ely, archdeacon of Ely
1261	Walter de Merton, archdeacon of Bath
1263	Nicholas of Ely, archdeacon of Ely
1263	John Chishull, archdeacon of London
1264	Thomas Cantilupe, archdeacon of Stafford
1265	Ralph Sandwich
1265	Walter Gifford, bishop of Bath and Wells
1266	Godfrey Gifford, archdeacon of Wells
1268	John Chishull, dean of St Paul's
1269	Richard Middleton, archdeacon of Northumberland
1272	Walter Merton, archdeacon of Bath
1274	Robert Burnell, archdeacon of York and bishop of Bath and Wells
1292	John Langton, canon of Lincoln
1302	William Greenfield, dean of Chichester
1305	William of Hamilton, dean of York
1307	Ralph Baldock, bishop of London
1307	John Langton, bishop of Chichester
1310	Walter Reynolds, bishop of Worcester
1314	John Sandall, bishop of Winchester
1318	John Hotham, bishop of Ely
1320	John Salmon, bishop of Norwich

Lord Chancellors and Keepers of the Great Seal cont.

Dates of office	Name and clerical office
1323	Robert Baldock, archdeacon of Middlesex
1326	William Airmyn, bishop of Norwich, acting keeper of the seal, jointly with Henry Cliff
1327	John Hotham, bishop of Ely
1328	Henry Burghersh, bishop of Lincoln
1330	John Stratford, bishop of Winchester
1334	Richard Bury, bishop of Durham
1335	John Stratford, archbishop of Canterbury
1337	Robert Stratford, bishop of Chichester
1338	Richard Bintworth, bishop of London
1340	John Stratford, archbishop of Canterbury
1340	Robert Stratford, bishop of Chichester
1340	Sir Robert Bourchier
1341	Sir Robert Parving
1343	Sir Robert Sadington
1345	John Offord, dean of Lincoln
1349	John Thoresby, bishop of Worcester
1356	William Edington, bishop of Winchester
1363	Simon Langham, bishop of Ely
1367	William Wykeham, bishop of Winchester
1371	Sir Robert Thorpe
1372	Sir John Knyvet
1377	Adam Houghton, bishop of St David's
1378	Richard Scrope, lord Scrope of Bolton
1380	Simon Sudbury, archbishop of Canterbury
1381	Hugh Segrave
1381	William Courtenay, bishop of London
1381	Richard Scrope, lord Scrope of Bolton
1382	Robert Braybrooke, bishop of London
1383	Michael de la Pole, later earl of Suffolk
1386	Thomas Arundel, bishop of Ely
1389	William Wykeham, bishop of Winchester
1391	Thomas Arundel, archbishop of York

Dates of office	Name and clerical office
1396	Edmund Stafford, bishop of Exeter
1399	Thomas Arundel, archbishop of Canterbury
1399	John Scarle, archdeacon of Lincoln
1401	Edmund Stafford, bishop of Exeter
1403	Henry Beaufort, bishop of Lincoln
1405	Thomas Langley, dean of York
1407	Thomas Arundel, archbishop of Canterbury
1410	Sir Thomas Beaufort
1412	Thomas Arundel, archbishop of Canterbury
1413	Henry Beaufort, bishop of Winchester
1417	Thomas Langley, bishop of Durham
1424	Henry Beaufort, bishop of Winchester
1426	John Kemp, archbishop of York
1432	John Stafford, bishop of Bath and Wells
1450	John Kemp, archbishop of York
1454	Richard Neville, earl of Salisbury
1455	Thomas Bourchier, archbishop of Canterbury
1456	William Waynflete, bishop of Winchester
1460	George Neville, bishop of Exeter
1467	Robert Stillington, bishop of Bath and Wells
1470	George Neville, archbishop of York
1473	Laurence Booth, bishop of Durham
1474	Thomas Rotherham, bishop of Lincoln
1475	John Alcock, bishop of Rochester
1475	Thomas Rotherham, bishop of Lincoln
1483	John Russell, bishop of Lincoln
1485	Thomas Rotherham, archbishop of York
1485	John Alcock, bishop of Worcester
1487	John Morton, archbishop of Canterbury
1500	Henry Deane, bishop of Salisbury and archbishop of Canterbury
1504	William Warham, archbishop of Canterbury
1515	Thomas Wolsey, archbishop of York
1529	Sir Thomas More

Lord Chancellors and Keepers of the Great Seal cont.

Dates of office	Name and clerical office
1533	Sir Thomas Audley
1544	Thomas, Baron Wriothesley
1547	William Paulet, Lord St John
1547	Richard Rich, Lord Rich
1551	Thomas Goodrich, bishop of Ely
1553	Stephen Gardiner, bishop of Winchester
1556	Nicholas Heath, archbishop of York
1558	Sir Nicholas Bacon
1579	Sir Thomas Bromley
1587–91	Sir Christopher Hatton
1592	Sir John Puckering
1596	Sir Thomas Egerton, later Baron Ellesmere
1617	Sir Francis Bacon, later Baron Verulam
1621	John Williams, bishop of Lincoln
1625	Sir Thomas Coventry
1640	Sir John Finch
1641	Edward, Baron Lyttleton
1645	Sir Richard Lane
1653	Sir Edward Herbert
1658	Sir Edward Hyde, later Lord Hyde and earl of Clarendon
1667	Sir Orlando Bridgeman
1672	Anthony Ashley-Cooper, earl of Shaftesbury
1673	Sir Heneage Finch, later Baron Finch
1682	Sir Francis North, later Baron Guildford
1685	George, Baron Jeffreys
1693	Sir John Somers, later Baron Somers
1700	Sir Nathan Wright
1705	William Cowper, later Baron Cowper
1710	Sir Simon Harcourt, later Baron Harcourt
1714	William, Baron Cowper
1718	Thomas, Baron Parker, later earl of Macclesfield
1725	Peter, Baron King

Dates of office	Name and clerical office
1733	Charles Talbot, Lord Talbot of Hensol
1737	Philip Yorke, Baron Hardwicke
1757	Sir Robert Henley, later Baron Henley
1766	Charles Pratt, Baron Camden
1770	Charles Yorke
1771	Henry Bathurst, Baron Apsley
1778–92	Edward Thurlow, Baron Thurlow
1793	Alexander Wedderburn, Baron Loughborough
1801	John Scott, Baron Eldon
1806	Thomas Erskine, Baron Erskine
1807	John Scott, Lord Eldon
1827	John Singleton Copley, Baron Lyndhurst
1830	Henry Brougham, Baron Brougham and Vaux
1834–5	John Singleton Copley, Baron Lyndhurst
1836	Charles Pepys, Baron Cottenham
1841	John Singleton Copley, Baron Lyndhurst
1846	Charles Pepys, Baron Cottenham
1850	Thomas Wilde, Baron Truro
1852	Edward Burtenshaw Sugden, Baron St Leonards
1852	Robert Rolfe, Baron Cranworth
1858	Frederic Thesiger, Baron Chelmsford
1859	John Campbell, Baron Campbell
1861	Richard Bethell, Baron Westbury
1865	Robert Rolfe, Baron Cranworth
1866	Frederic Thesiger, Baron Chelmsford
1868	Hugh, Baron Cairns
1868	William Page Wood, Baron Hatherley
1872	Frederic Thesiger, Baron Chelmsford
1874	Hugh, Baron Cairns
1880	Frederic Thesiger, Baron Chelmsford
1885	Hardinge Giffard, Baron Halsbury
1886	Farrer, Baron Herschell

Lord Chancellors and Keepers of the Great Seal cont.

Dates of office	Name and clerical office
1886	Hardinge Giffard, Baron Halsbury
1892	Farrer, Baron Herschell
1895	Hardinge Giffard, Baron Halsbury
1905	Robert Reid, Baron Loreburn
1912	Richard, Viscount Haldane
1915	Stanley, Baron Buckmaster
1916	Robert, Baron Finlay
1919	F. E. Smith, Baron Birkenhead
1922	George, Viscount Cave
1924	Viscount Haldane
1924	Viscount Cave
1928	Douglas Hogg, Baron Hailsham
1929	John Sankey, Baron, later Viscount Sankey
1935	Douglas Hogg, Viscount Hailsham
1938	Frederick Maugham, Baron Maugham
1939	Thomas Inskip, Viscount Caldecote
1940	John, Viscount Simon
1945	William Jowitt, Baron Jowitt
1951	Gavin Simonds, Baron, later Viscount Simonds
1954	David Maxwell Fyfe, Viscount Kilmuir
1962	Reginald Manningham-Buller, Baron Dilhorne
1964	Gerald, Baron Gardiner
1970	Quintin Hogg, Baron Hailsham of St Marylebone
1974	Frederick Elwyn-Jones, Baron Elwyn-Jones
1979	Baron Hailsham of St Marylebone
1987	Michael, Baron Havers
1987	James, Baron Mackay of Clashfern
1997	Derry, Baron Irvine of Lairg
2003	Charles, Baron Falconer of Thoroton
2007	Jack Straw
2010	Kenneth Clarke
2012	Chris Grayling

Composition of select pre-1707 Scottish parliaments or 'Three Estates'

Date	Clergy	Nobles	Burgesses	Shires	Officers of state	Total
1290	46	62	0	0	0	108
1469	23	54	22	0	0	99
1540	25	21	8	0	3	57
1681	12	57	60	57	4	190

Contested seats in general elections from the Act of Union 1707 to the Reform Act 1832

Date	No. of constituencies contested
30 Apr. – 7 Jul. 1708	121[*]
2 Oct. – 16 Nov. 1710	153
22 August – 12 Nov. 1713	110
22 Jan. – 9 Mar. 1715	c.120
19 Mar. – 9 May 1722	154
14 August – 17 Oct. 1727	114
22 Apr. – 6 June 1734	c.130
30 Apr. – 11 June 1741	94
26 June – 4 August 1747	62
18 Apr. – 20 May 1754	62
25 Mar. – 5 May 1761	53
16 Mar. – 6 May 1768	83
5 Oct. – 10 Nov. 1774	95
6 Sept – 18 Oct. 1780	76
30 Mar. – 10 May 1784	87
16 June – 28 Jul. 1790	92
25 May – 29 June 1796	66
5 Jul. – 28 Aug. 1802[†]	97

---

[*] Out of 314 constituencies.
[†] The Act of Union with Ireland increased the number of constituencies from 314 to 380.

Contested seats in general elections cont.

Date	No. of constituencies contested
29 Oct. – 17 Dec. 1806	87
4 May – 9 June 1807	102
5 Oct. – 10 Nov. 1812	96
10 June – 4 Aug. 1818	120
6 Mar. – 14 Apr. 1820	93
7 June – 12 Jul. 1826	112
29 Jul. – 1 Sept 1830	128
28 Apr. – 1 June 1831	125

United Kingdom general elections since 1832: dates, size of electorate and uncontested seats

Date	Size of electorate	No. of MPs elected unopposed
8 Dec. 1832 – 8 Jan. 1833	812,938	275
6 Jan. – 6 Feb. 1835	845,776	236
24 Jul. – 18 Aug. 1837	1,004,664	337
29 Jun. – 22 Jul. 1841	1,017,379	367
29 Jul. – 26 Aug. 1847	1,106,514	255
7–31 Jul. 1852	1,184,689	283
27 Mar. – 24 Apr. 1857	1,235,530	328
28 Apr. – 18 May 1859	1,271,900	379
11–24 Jul. 1865	1,350,404	303
17 Nov. – 7 Dec. 1868	2,484,713	212
31 Jan. – 17 Feb. 1874	2,753,142	187
31 Mar. – 27 Apr. 1880	3,040,050	109
21 Nov. – 18 Dec. 1885	5,708,030	43
1–27 Jul. 1886	5,708,030	224
4–26 Jul. 1892	6,160,541	63
13 Jul. – 7 Aug. 1895	6,330,519	189
1–24 Oct. 1900	6,730,935	243
12 Jan. – 8 Feb. 1906	7,264,608	114

since 1832

Date	Size of electorate	No. of MPs elected unopposed
15 Jan. – 10 Feb. 1910	7,694,741	75
3–19 Dec. 1910	7,709,981	163
Sat. 14 Dec. 1918	21,392,322	107
Weds. 15 Nov. 1922	20,874,456	57
Thurs. 6 Dec. 1923	21,283,061	50
Weds. 29 Oct. 1924	21,730,988	32
Thurs. 30 May 1929	28,854,748	7
Tues. 27 Oct. 1931*	29,952,361	67
Thurs. 14 Nov. 1935	31,374,449	40
Thurs. 5 Jul. 1945	33,240,391	3
Thurs. 23 Feb. 1950	34,412,255	4
Thurs. 25 Oct. 1951	34,919,331	0
Thurs. 26 May 1955	34,852,179	0
Thurs. 8 Oct. 1959	35,397,304	0
Thurs. 15 Oct. 1964	35,894,054	0
Thurs. 31 Mar. 1966	35,957,245	0
Thurs. 18 Jun. 1970	39,342,013	0
Thurs. 28 Feb. 1974	39,753,863	0
Thurs. 10 Oct. 1974	40,072,970	0
Thurs. 3 May 1979	41,095,649	0
Thurs. 9 Jun. 1983	42,192,999	0
Thurs. 11 Jun. 1987	43,180,753	0
Thurs. 9 Apr. 1992	43,240,084	0
Thurs. 1 May 1997	43,784,559	0
Thurs. 7 Jun. 2001	44,401,238	0
Thurs. 5 May 2005	44,245,939	0
Thurs. 6 May 2010	45,533,536	0

* Since then general elections have, by tradition rather than by statute, been held on a Thursday. The last by-election not held on a Thursday was the Hamilton by-election on 31 May 1978, held on a Wednesday so as to avoid a clash with the opening match of the World Cup.

Membership of the House of Commons, 1295–2010

Date	England	Wales	Scotland	Ireland	*Total*
1295	292*	0	0	0	*292*
1384	252	0	0	0	*252*
1510	296	0	0	0	*296*
1542	311	27	0	0	*338*
1601	440	27	0	0	*467*
1659	480	27	30	30	*567*
1660	480	27	0	0	*507*
1678	486	27	0	0	*513*
1708	486	27	45	0	*558*
1801	486	27	45	100	*658*
1821	484	27	45	100	*656*
1832	468	32	53	105	*658*
1885	461	34	72	103	*670*
1918	492	36	74	105	*707*
1922	492	36	74	13	*615*
1945	517	36	74	13	*640*
1950	506	36	71	12	*625*
1955	511	36	71	12	*630*
1974	516	36	71	12	*635*
1983	523	38	72	17	*650*
1992	524	38	72	17	*651*
1997	529	40	72	18	*659*
2005	529	40	59	18	*646*
2010	533	40	59	18	*650*

* The 1295 Parliament included 148 members of the non-episcopal clergy.

Membership of the House of Lords, 1295–2014

Date	Bishops	Abbots	Hereditary	Scottish	Irish	Life	Total
1295	21	99	c.64	0	0	0	c.184
1510	21	27	37	0	0	0	85
1545	26[*]	0	50	0	0	0	76
1603	26	0	55	0	0	0	81
1661	26	0	132	0	0	0	158
1707	26	0	168	16	0	0	210
1801	30[†]	0	272	16	28	0	374
1936	26[‡]	0	681	16	17	8[§]	748
1959	26	0	810	16[**]	1[††]	31	884
1984	26	0	775	0	0	178	979
1992	26	0	777	0	0	402	1205
2005	26	0	92	0	0	606	724
2014	26	0	92	0	0	666	784

[*] Henry VIII abolished the monasteries and created six new dioceses, five of which survived.

[†] Four Irish bishops joined the Westminster parliament from 1801 until the disestablishment of the Church in Ireland in 1871.

[‡] The Welsh Church was disestablished in 1920 and the four Welsh bishops were replaced by additional English bishops.

[§] All four were law lords appointed for life under the Appellate Jurisdiction Act 1876.

[**] The last Scottish representative peers sat until 31 Jul. 1963, when the whole Scottish peerage was amalgamated into the UK peerage.

[††] No further Irish representative peers were elected after 1919, but as they were elected for life, the last to remain a member was Francis Needham, 4th earl of Kilmorey, who died on 11 January 1961.

Women Members of Parliament

Date	Commons	Lords[*]
1918	1	0
1922	2	0
1923	8	0
1924	4	0
1929	14	0
1931	15	0
1935	9	0
1945	24	0
1951	17	0
1964	29	26
1979	19	56
1992	60	75
1997	120	87
2014	147	192

[*] Figures taken from Dods annual listings.

Notes

Prologue

1 Earl Leslie Griggs, ed., *Collected Letters of Samuel Taylor Coleridge*, Oxford, Clarendon Press, 2000, vol. 1, p. 569.
2 John Thomas Smith, *Antiquities of Westminster*, London, Thomas Bensley, 1807, p. vi.
3 Basil Ferrey, *Recollections of A. N. Welby Pugin and his Father, Augustus Pugin*, London, Edward Stanford, 1861, p. 95.

Chapter 1: The Voice of a Nation

1 This was only repealed by the Doctrine of the Trinity Act 1813.
2 George Thomas Keppel, earl of Albemarle, *Memoirs of the Marquis of Rockingham*, London, Richard Bentley, 1852, vol. 2, p. 117.
3 Horace Twiss, *The Public and Private Life of Lord Chancellor Eldon*, London, John Murray, 1844, vol. 2, p. 356.
4 William Cobbett, *The Parliamentary History of England*, vol. 33, London, Hansard, 1818, col. 684.
5 Cited in R. G. Thorne, ed., *The House of Commons 1790–1820*, London, History of Parliament Trust, 1986, vol. 5, p. 375.
6 Robert Isaac Wilberforce, *The Life of William Wilberforce*, London, John Murray, 1839, vol. 3, p. 298.
7 Edmund Burke, *Works*, 9 vols, London, Little, Brown, 1839, vol. 3, pp. 18–19.
8 Ibid., vol. 1, p. 253.
9 William Cobbett, ed., *Parliamentary Debates*, London, Hansard, 1812, vol. 14, pp. 1053–4.
10 Ibid., p. 775.
11 *A Year's Residence in the United States of America*, para. 290, cited in Richard Ingrams, *The Life and Adventures of William Cobbett*, London, HarperCollins, 2005, p. 74.
12 Ingrams, *The Life and Adventures of William Cobbett*, p. 74.
13 Lord Robert Auckland, ed., *The Journal and Correspondence of William, Lord Auckland*, London, Spottiswoode, 1802, vol. 4, p. 269.
14 Wilberforce, *The Life of William Wilberforce*, p. 411.
15 Thomas Moore, ed., *The Life of Lord Byron*, London, John Murray, 1844, pp. 676–7.
16 BL Add. MS Wilson Papers 30111, fo. 71, cited in Arthur Aspinall, 'The coalition ministries of 1827', *English Historical Review*, vol. 42, no. 168 (Oct. 1927), p. 533.

17 Lytton Strachey and Roger Fulford, eds, *The Greville Memoirs*, London, Macmillan, 1938, vol. 1, p. 208.

18 Henry Reeve, ed., *The Greville Memoirs: A Journal of the Reigns of King George IV and King William IV*, Longmans, Green, London, 1875, vol. 3, p. 148.

19 G. D. H. Cole and M. Cole, eds, *Cobbett's Rural Rides*, London, Peter Davies, 1930, vol. 1, p. 42.

20 Edward, Lord Brabourne, ed., *Letters of Jane Austen*, London, Bentley, 1884, vol. 2, pp. 273–4.

21 *Hansard's Parliamentary Debates, Commons* (*HC*), 24 March 1829, vol. 20, cols 728–80.

22 Cited in Edward Pearce, *Reform*, London, Jonathan Cape, 2003, p. 61.

23 Lt-Gen. Charles Grey, *Some Account of the Life and Opinions of Charles, Second Earl Grey*, London, Richard Bentley, 1861, p. 192.

24 William Carpenter, *Peerage for the People*, London, William Carpenter, 1837, p. 34.

25 Benjamin Disraeli, *Tancred, or The New Crusade*, London, Frederick Warne, 1866, p. 51.

26 Henry Holland, *Further Memoirs of the Whig Party: 1807–1821*, London, John Murray, 1905, p. 283.

27 *HC*, 1 March 1831, vol. 2, col. 1077.

28 Strachey and Fulford, eds, *The Greville Memoirs*, vol. 2, p. 123.

29 *HC*, 1 March 1831, vol. 2, col. 1084.

30 Ibid., col. 1191.

31 Ibid., col. 1198.

32 *HC*, 3 March 1831, vol. 2, col. 1353.

33 Lord Henry Brougham, *The Lord Chancellor's Speech on Parliamentary Reform*, London, Ridgway, 1831, p. 91.

34 Hugh Elliott, ed., *The Letters of J. S. Mill*, London, Longmans et al., 1910, vol. 1, pp. 4, 7.

35 *HC*, 12 Oct. 1831, vol. 8, col. 599.

36 *Hansard's Parliamentary Debates, Lords* (*HL*), 13 April 1832, vol. 12, col. 444.

37 Abraham Kriegel, ed., *The Holland House Diaries 1831–1840*, London, Routledge & Kegan Paul, 1977, p. 168.

38 E. A. Smith, *Lord Grey, 1764–1845*, Oxford, Clarendon Press, 1990, p. 277.

39 John Cam Hobhouse, *Recollections of a Long Life*, 6 vols, ed. Lady Dorchester, Cambridge, Cambridge University Press, 1910, vol. 4, p. 242.

40 Alan G. Hill, ed., *The Letters of William and Dorothy Wordsworth*, Oxford, Oxford University Press, 1967, vol. 5, pp. 500–1.

41 Smith, *Lord Grey*, p. 278.

Chapter 2: A Liberal and a Conservative

1 John Morley, *Life of Gladstone*, London, Macmillan, 1903, vol. 1, p. 101.

2 National Library of Scotland, Ellice MSS, Grey to Ellice, 3 Sept. 1833.

3   Henry Reeve, ed., *The Greville Memoirs: A Journal of the Reigns of King George IV and King William IV*, London, Longmans, Green, 1875, vol. 3, p. 109.

4   Ibid., p. 76.

5   *Quarterly Review*, Jan. 1830.

6   *Edinburgh Review or Critical Journal*, vol. 62, 1836, p. 171.

7   Sir Charles Petrie and Alistair Cooke, *The Carlton Club 1832–2007*, London, Carlton Club, 2007, p. 11.

8   Paul Langford, et al., eds, *The Writings and Speeches of Edmund Burke*, Oxford, Clarendon Press, 1981, vol. 2, p. 314.

9   Ibid., p. 317.

10 Goulburn MSS Acc. 319, box 40, Peel to Goulburn, 3 Sept. 1834, cited in Philip Salmon, *Electoral Reform at Work: Local Politics and National Parties, 1832–1841*, Woodbridge, Boydell, 2002, p. 52.

11 W. T. Haly, ed., *The Opinions of Sir Robert Peel*, London, n.p., 1850, p. 393.

12 Cited in Norman Gash, *Politics in the Age of Peel*, Hassocks, Harvester, 1977, p. 418.

13 Benjamin Disraeli, *Lord George Bentinck: A Political Biography*, London, Colburn, 1852, p. 69.

14 G. W. E. Russell, *Collections and Recollections by One Who Has Kept a Diary*, London, Smith, Elder, 1898, p. 191.

15 Disraeli, *Lord George Bentinck*, p. 316.

16 Ibid., pp. 315–16.

17 *HC*, 21 Feb. 1842, vol. 60, col. 779.

18 Spencer Walpole, *The Life of Lord John Russell*, London, Longmans, Green and Co., 1889, vol. 1, p. 369.

19 *The Times*, 25 Oct. 1869, p. 7.

20 *HC*, 18 Feb. 1828, vol. 18, col. 523.

21 Cited in John Charmley, *A History of Conservative Politics since 1830*, Basingstoke, Palgrave Macmillan, 2008, p. 20.

22 *HC*, 28 Feb. 1845, vol. 78, col. 154.

23 *HC*, 17 March 1845, vol. 78, col. 1028.

24 *HC*, 22 Jan. 1846, vol. 83, col. 116.

25 *HC*, 28 Feb. 1845, vol. 78, cols 154–5.

26 *HC*, 22 Jan. 1846, vol. 83, col. 123.

27 John Russell Vincent, ed., *Disraeli, Derby and the Conservative Party*, Brighton, Harvester, 1978, p. 1.

28 Lord Redesdale, ed., *Memories, by Lord Redesdale, 1867–76*, London, 1915, vol. 1, p. 534.

29 Angus Hawkins, *The Forgotten Prime Minister: The 14th Earl of Derby*, Oxford, Oxford University Press, 2008, vol. 2, p. 122.

30 Cited in Charmley, *A History of Conservative Politics since 1830*, p. 39.

31 *HC*, 16 Dec. 1852, vol. 123, col. 1653.

32 Ibid., cols 1655–6.

33 Vincent, ed., *Disraeli, Derby and the Conservative Party*, p. 89.
34 *HC*, 16 Dec. 1852, vol. 123, col. 1667.
35 Ibid., cols 1692–3.
36 Stuart J. Reid, *Life and Letters of the First Earl of Durham*, London, Longmans, Green & Co., 1906, vol. 2, pp. 3–4.
37 Millicent Garrett Fawcett, *Life of the Right Hon. Sir William Molesworth*, London, Macmillan, 1901, p. 74.
38 *The Times*, 16 June 1887, p. 6, cited in George Woodbridge, *The Reform Club 1836–1978*, London, privately printed, 1978, p. 1.
39 Fawcett, *Life of the Right Hon. Sir William Molesworth*, p. 71.
40 Walpole, *The Life of Lord John Russell*, vol. 2, p. 144.
41 Vincent, ed., *Disraeli, Derby and the Conservative Party*, p. 77.
42 *HC*, 25 June 1850, vol. 112, col. 444.
43 BL Add. MSS 48582, Palmerston letter books, Palmerston to Bruce, 26 Nov. 1860, cited in E. D. Steele, *Palmerston and Liberalism, 1855–1865*, Cambridge, Cambridge University Press, 1991, p. 94.
44 Shaftesbury papers, BP (SHA/PD/7), diary, 21 June 1859, cited in Steele, *Palmerston and Liberalism*, p. 95.
45 Maurice Cowling, *1867: Disraeli, Gladstone and Revolution – The Passing of the Second Reform Bill*, Cambridge, Cambridge University Press, 1967, p. 290.
46 *HC*, 13 March 1866, vol. 182, cols 147–9.
47 Ibid., col. 218.
48 Disraeli Papers, Hughenden MSS B/CC/S/367, Derby to Disraeli, 9 Oct. 1866.
49 Cited in Richard Aldous, *The Lion and the Unicorn: Gladstone vs. Disraeli*, London, Pimlico, 2007, p. 174.
50 Cited in Bill Cash, *John Bright, Statesman, Orator, Agitator*, London, I. B. Tauris, 2012, p. 125.
51 Alexander Ewald, *The Right Hon. Benjamin Disraeli, Earl of Beaconsfield, K.G., and His Times*, London, W. Mackenzie, 1882, vol. 2, p. 61.
52 *HC*, 15 July 1867, vol. 188, col. 1540.
53 *HL*, 22 July 1867, vol. 188, col. 1803.
54 Ibid., col. 1845.
55 John Brooke and Mary Sorenson, eds., *The Prime Ministers' Papers: W. E. Gladstone*, London, HMSO, 1971, vol. 1, p. 95.
56 Hawkins, *The Forgotten Prime Minister*, vol. 2, p. 386.
57 Thomas Babington Macaulay, *Edinburgh Review*, April 1839; also publ. in *Critical and Historical Essays Contributed to the Edinburgh Review*, Leipzig, Bernhard Tauchnitz, 1850, vol. 3, p. 252.
58 Reginald Wilberforce, *Life of the Right Reverend Samuel Wilberforce*, London, John Murray, 1881, vol. 2, p. 349.
59 *HC*, 11 May 1864, vol. 175, col. 324.
60 George Nathaniel Curzon (marquess of), *Modern Parliamentary Eloquence*, London, Macmillan, 1913, p. 25.

61 William Ewart Gladstone, *Political Speeches in Scotland, November and December 1879*, Edinburgh, Andrew Elliot, 1879, p. 148.

62 W. F. Monypenny and G. E. Buckle, *The Life of Benjamin Disraeli, 1910–20*, vol. 5, p. 191.

63 Morley, *Life of Gladstone*, vol. 2, p. 495.

64 *HL*, 9 July 1866, vol. 184, col. 736.

65 J. Vincent, ed., *The Derby Diaries, 1869–1878*, Cambridge, Cambridge University Press, 1995, p. 337, entry for 23 Oct. 1876.

66 Andrew Roberts, *Salisbury: Victorian Titan*, London, Phoenix, 2000, pp. 151–2.

67 Lady Gwendolen Cecil, *Life of Robert, Marquis of Salisbury*, London, Hodder & Stoughton, 1921, vol. 2, p. 171.

68 Vincent, ed., *The Derby Diaries*, pp. 522, 523.

69 William Ewart Gladstone, *Diaries*, Oxford, Clarendon Press, 1982, vol. 8, p. 462, entry for 16 Feb. 1874.

70 Monypenny and Buckle, *The Life of Benjamin Disraeli*, vol. 2, p. 862.

71 *HC*, 2 May 1876, vol. 228, col. 2024.

72 Ibid., col. 2037.

73 *The Times*, 21 Nov. 1835.

74 Derby MSS Box 159, Gen. Grey to Derby, 28 Oct. 1866, cited in Cowling, *1867*, p. 287.

75 Robert Leader, *Life and Letters of John Arthur Roebuck*, London, Arnold, 1897, p. 312.

76 Monypenny and Buckle, *The Life of Benjamin Disraeli*, vol. 2, p. 709.

Chapter 3: Extravagant and Erring Spirits

1 Stephen Gwynn, *The Life of the Rt Hon. Sir Charles W. Dilke*, London, John Murray, 1917, vol. 2, p. 192.

2 Ibid.

3 Cited in David Nicholls, *Sir Charles Dilke: The Lost Prime Minister*, London, Hambledon Press, 1995, p. 178.

4 Ibid., p. 229.

5 Gilbert Burnet, *Some Passages of the Life and Death of the Right Honourable John Earl of Rochester, who died the 26th of July, 1680*, London, n.p., 1680, p. 38.

6 Robert Latham and William Mathews, eds, *The Diary of Samuel Pepys*, London, Bell & Hyman, 1971, vol. 4, pp. 209–10.

7 Ibid., vol. 8, p. 596.

8 Lord Shaftesbury to Evelyn Ashley, 6 Jan. 1876, cited in Evelyn Ashley, *The Life of Henry John Temple, Viscount Palmerston*, London, R. Bentley, 1876, vol. 2, p. 316.

9 Cited in Michael Brock and Edwin Montagu, eds, *H. H. Asquith, Letters to Venetia Stanley*, Oxford, Oxford University Press, 1982, p. 12.

10 *HC*, 3 Feb. 1881, vol. 258, col. 72.

11 Cited in Frank Callanan, *The Parnell Split, 1890–91,* New York, Syracuse University Press, 1992, p. 41.

12 *National Press,* 11 March 1891.

13 William Pulteney, *A Proper Reply to a Late Scurrilous Libel,* London, n.p., 1731, cited in Rictor Norton, *Mother Clap's Molly House: The Gay Subculture in England, 1700–1830,* London, Gay Men's Press, 1992, p. 149.

14 Lewis Saul Benjamin, ed., *The Life and Letters of William Beckford of Fonthill,* London, Duffield, 1910, p. 187.

15 Cited in Percy Fitzgerald, *The Book Fancier,* London, Sampson Low, Marston Searle & Rivington, 1887, p. 230.

16 Cited in Regenia Gagnier, *Idylls of the Marketplace,* Stanford, Stanford University Press, 1986, p. 206.

17 Edward David, ed., *Inside Asquith's Cabinet, from the Diaries of Charles Hobhouse,* London, John Murray, 1977, p. 229.

18 S. Hignett, *Brett: From Bloomsbury to New Mexico – A Biography,* London, Hodder & Stoughton, 1984, p. 31.

19 Cited in James Lees-Milne, *The Enigmatic Edwardian,* London, Sidgwick & Jackson, 1986, p. 176.

20 Paula Byrne, *Mad World: Evelyn Waugh and the Secrets of Brideshead,* London, HarperCollins, 2009, p. 322.

21 Cited in Richard Ellman, *Oscar Wilde,* London, Hamish Hamilton, 1987, p. 426.

22 Peter Stansky, *Sassoon: The Worlds of Philip and Sybil,* New Haven, Yale University Press, 2003, pp. 79–80.

23 *HC,* 7 June 1988, vol. 134, col. 788.

24 Matthew Parris, *Chance Witness,* London, Penguin, 2002, p. 298.

25 Nick Smart, ed., *The Diaries and Letters of Robert Bernays, 1932–1939: An Insider's Account of the House of Commons,* Lampeter, Edwin Mellen Press, 1996, pp. 292, 317.

26 *HC,* Northern Ireland Grand Committee, 17 June 2008, col. 19.

27 *Minutes of Evidence Taken Before the Royal Commission on Divorce,* London, HMSO, 1912, vol. 3, p. 515.

28 *Aberdeen Journal,* 20 Nov. 1943.

Chapter 4: The End of Aristocracy

1 The distribution of seats among the respective parties is often attributed differently, thanks to the election of several minor party members loosely affiliated to the main parties, but the point stands that the arithmetic was tight as Gladstone could not rely on more than half of the 670 seats.

2 Lady Gwendolen Cecil, *Life of Robert, Marquis of Salisbury,* London, Hodder & Stoughton, 1921, vol. 3, p. 302.

3 Some give the figures as 341 to 311, but this is to ignore the two tellers on either side.

4   William Ewart Gladstone, *Diaries*, Oxford, Clarendon Press, 1982, vol. 13, p. 4, entry for 15 July 1892.

5   *HC*, 11 May 1882, vol. 269, col. 517.

6   George, Viscount Goschen, *Essays and Addresses on Economic Questions*, London, Edward Arnold, 1905, vol. 3, p. 22.

7   Cited in David Cannadine, *The Decline and Fall of the British Aristocracy*, London, Macmillan, 1992, p. 214.

8   Ibid.

9   Andrew Roberts, *Salisbury: Victorian Titan*, London, Phoenix, 2000, p. 319.

10 Cited in P. Smith, *Disraelian Conservatism and Social Reform*, London, Routledge & Kegan Paul, 1967, p. 217.

11 Robin Harcourt Williams, ed., *The Salisbury–Balfour Correspondence*, Ware, Hertfordshire Record Society, 1988, p. 348.

12 Kenneth Rose, *Curzon: A Most Superior Person*, London, Macmillan, 1985, p. 120.

13 Lord Ernest Hamilton, *Forty Years On*, London, Hodder & Stoughton, 1922, p. 203.

14 Keith Robbins, *Sir Edward Grey: A Biography of Lord Grey of Fallodon*, London, Cassell, 1971, p. 358.

15 Rose, *Curzon*, p. 379.

16 Ibid.

17 Cited in Cannadine, *The Decline and Fall of the British Aristocracy*, p. 189.

18 Montgomery Hyde, *The Londonderrys: A Family Portrait*, London, Hamish Hamilton, 1979, p. 180.

19 Cited in Cannadine, *The Decline and Fall of the British Aristocracy*, p. 198.

20 Philip Guedalla, *The Queen and Mr Gladstone*, London, Hodder & Stoughton, 1933, vol. 1, p. 206.

21 *Saturday Review*, 16 Dec. 1905.

22 Jamie Camplin, *The Rise of the Rich*, London, St Martin's Press, 1979, p. 117.

23 Contrary to several reports, although Lloyd George did make this comment, it was to the assistant secretary of the Cabinet, Thomas Jones, in 1922 and it was not repeated in the tribute debate on Balfour's death on 20 March 1930, in which Lloyd George was extremely magnanimous to his former sparring partner. See Thomas Jones, *Whitehall Diary*, ed. Keith Middlemas, London, 1969, vol. 1, p. 201.

24 Lloyd George speech at Kircaldy, 27 Oct. 1905, cited in John Grigg, *Lloyd George: The People's Champion*, London, Penguin, 1978, p. 90.

25 *HL*, 27 Nov. 1908, vol. 197, cols 894–5.

26 Octavius Francis Christie, *Transition to Democracy*, London, Routledge, 1934, p. 267.

27 Edward David, ed., *Inside Asquith's Cabinet, from the Diaries of Charles Hobhouse*, London, John Murray, 1977, p. 118.

28 *HC*, 29 April 1909, vol. 4, col. 548.

29 George Peel, ed., *Sir Robert Peel, from his Private Papers*, London, John Murray, 1899, vol. 2, p. 224.

30 Cecil, *Life of Robert, Marquess of Salisbury*, vol. 2, p. 25.

31 *HC*, 25 June 1907, vol. 176, col. 1245.

32 Cited in Roy Jenkins, *Mr Balfour's Poodle*, Macmillan, London, 1999, p. 76.

33 Ibid.

34 *Annual Register*, 1909, p. 221.

35 *HL*, 22 Nov. 1909, vol. 4, col. 735.

36 Ibid., col. 750

37 *HL*, 23 Nov. 1909, vol. 4, col. 842.

38 *HL*, 22 Nov. 1909, vol. 4, col. 806.

39 *HL*, 29 Nov. 1909, vol. 4, col. 1193.

40 *HL*, 25 Nov. 1909, vol. 4, cols 1085–6.

41 *HL*, 24 Nov. 1909, vol. 4, col. 949.

42 *HL*, 29 Nov. 1909, vol. 4, cols 1152–3.

43 *HC*, 14 April 1910, vol. 16, col. 1549.

44 *HC*, 2 March 1911, vol. 22, col. 567.

45 Cited in Jenkins, *Mr Balfour's Poodle*, p. 214.

46 *HC*, 24 July 1911, vol. 28, col. 1467.

47 Roy Jenkins maintains that this was at the behest of Margot Asquith, who was in the Ladies' Gallery.

48 Halsbury may well have been quoting Lord Lyndhurst, who had used the same words in the Lords in 1853, and had then lost the vote. Halsbury's remark is cited in George Dangerfield, *The Strange Death of Liberal England*, London, Serif, 1997, p. 54.

49 *HC*, 7 Aug. 1911, vol. 29, col. 796.

50 *HL*, 9 Aug. 1911, vol. 9, col. 917.

51 Ibid., col. 914.

52 Ibid., col. 934.

53 *HL*, 10 Aug. 1911, vol. 9, col. 999.

54 Roy Jenkins incorrectly asserts that Edward Glyn, the bishop of Peterborough, voted with the diehards. Since he was the brother of three Liberal politicians, George, the 2nd Lord Wolverton, Sidney and Pascoe, all of whom supported Gladstone on home rule, it is extremely unlikely that he would have done so, but Hansard is clear that neither he nor his Conservative nephew, Frederick, the 4th Baron Wolverton, voted.

55 Cited in Kenneth Rose, *The Later Cecils*, London, Harper & Row, 1975, p. 242.

56 Ibid., p. 238.

57 *HC*, 8 Aug. 1911, vol. 29, cols 980–2.

58 *HL*, 9 Aug. 1911, vol. 9, col. 914.

59 Rose, *The Later Cecils*, p. 321.

60 Cited in Cannadine, *The Decline and Fall of the British Aristocracy*, p. 214.

61 Simon Haxey, *Tory MP*, London, Victor Gollancz, 1939, p. 172.

62 *HL*, 24 Nov. 1909, vol. 4, col. 939.

Chapter 5: Two Houses at War

1   R. Coupland, ed., *The War Speeches of William Pitt the Younger*, Oxford, Oxford University Press, 1915, pp. 53–4.

2   R. J. Q. Adams, *Bonar Law*, London, John Murray, 1999, pp. 108–9.

3   John Horgan, *Parnell to Pearse*, Dublin, Brown & Nolans, 1948, p. 198.

4   *HC*, 7 March 1917, vol. 91, cols 448–9.

5   *HC*, 3 Aug. 1914, vol. 65, col. 1831.

6   Ibid., col. 1838.

7   Ibid., col. 1847.

8   David Hamer, *John Morley: Liberal Intellectual in Politics*, Oxford, Oxford University Press, 1968, p. 57.

9   *HC*, 5 Aug. 1914, vol. 65, col. 1963.

10 Cited in John Turner, 'The House of Commons and the executive in the First World War', *Parliamentary History*, vol. 10, no. 2 (1991), p. 300.

11 Asquith to Venetia Stanley, 15 Sept. 1914, in Michael Brock and Edwin Montagu, eds, *H. H. Asquith, Letters to Venetia Stanley*, Oxford, Oxford University Press, 1982, p. 239.

12 *HC*, 17 May 1915, vol. 71, col. 2105.

13 Ibid., col. 2107.

14 Ibid., col. 2110.

15 Cited in Cameron Hazlehurst, *Politicians at War*, London, Jonathan Cape, 1971, p. 275.

16 Hobhouse to Runciman, 28 May 1915, cited in John Turner, *British Politics and the Great War*, New Haven, Yale University Press, 1992, p. 62.

17 Charles to Mary Trevelyan, 21 May 1915, cited in Hazlehurst, *Politicians at War*, pp. 286–7.

18 Philip Snowden, *Autobiography*, London, Ivor Nicholson & Watson, 1934, pp. 394–5.

19 Chamberlain to Herbert Samuel, 9 April 1916, cited in Turner, 'The House of Commons and the executive in the First World War', p. 303.

20 Catherine Bailey, *The Secret Rooms*, London, Viking, 2012.

21 *HC*, 20 July 1915, vol. 73, col. 1408.

22 Willoughby de Broke to Lord Boutwood, July 1916, cited in Turner, *British Politics and the Great War*, p. 116.

23 *HC*, 8 Nov. 1916, vol. 87, col. 364.

24 *HC*, 4 April 1917, vol. 92, col. 1363.

25 *HC*, 6 July 1917, vol. 95, col. 1495.

26 Ibid., col. 1543.

27 Cited in Turner, 'The House of Commons and the executive in the First World War', p. 306.

28 *HC*, 9 May 1918, vol. 105, col. 2373.

29 Nigel Keohane, *The Party of Patriotism: The Conservative Party and the First World War*, Farnham, Ashgate, 2010, p. 58.

30 Robert Self, ed., *The Neville Chamberlain Diary Letters*, Aldershot, Ashgate, 2000, vol. 1, p. 260.

31 Long to Law, 17 July 1918, cited in Keohane, *The Party of Patriotism*, p. 58.

32 *HC*, 14 March 1938, vol. 333, col. 52.

33 Ibid., col. 95.

34 *HC*, 3 Oct. 1938, vol. 339, cols 149–50, quoting Tawney from *Manchester Guardian*, 22 September 1938.

35 *HC*, 2 Aug. 1939, vol. 350, cols 2431–2.

36 Ibid., col. 2494.

37 Ibid., col. 2444.

38 *HC*, 1 Sept. 1939, vol. 351, cols 126–33.

39 Ibid., col. 133.

40 *HC*, 2 Sept. 1939, vol. 351, col. 280.

41 *HC*, 3 Sept. 1939, vol. 351, col. 292.

42 Kevin Jefferys, *The Churchill Coalition and Wartime Politics, 1940–45*, Manchester, Manchester University Press, 1991, p. 16.

43 A. J. P. Taylor, ed., *Off the Record: W. P. Crozier, Political Interviews 1933–1944*, London, Hutchinson, 1973, p. 156.

44 Nigel Nicolson, ed., *Harold Nicolson: Diaries and Letters 1939–1945*, London, Collins, 1966, p. 74, entry for 30 April 1940.

45 *HC*, 7 May 1940, vol. 360, col. 1094.

46 Ibid., col. 1116.

47 Amery diary, entry for 7 May 1940, cited in Jefferys, *The Churchill Coalition and Wartime Politics*, p. 23.

48 *HC*, 7 May 1940, vol. 360, col. 1150.

49 *HC*, 8 May 1940, vol. 360, col. 1265.

50 Ibid., col. 1266.

51 Ibid., col. 1289.

52 Ibid., col. 1308.

53 Ibid., col. 1348.

54 Ibid., col. 1362.

55 Robert Rhodes James, ed., *Chips: The Diaries of Sir Henry Channon*, London, Weidenfeld & Nicolson, 1993, p. 247.

56 John Colville, *The Fringes of Power: Downing Street Diaries, 1939–1955*, London, Hodder & Stoughton, 1985, entry for 10 May 1940, p. 122.

57 Ibid.

58 Rhodes James, *Chips*, p. 252.

59 *HC*, 13 May 1940, vol. 360, col. 1502.

60 *HC*, 4 June 1940, vol. 361, col. 796.

61 *HC*, 18 June 1940, vol. 362, cols 60–1.

62 Jefferys, *The Churchill Coalition and Wartime Politics*, p. 47.

63 Ben Pimlott, ed., *The Second World War Diary of Hugh Dalton*, London, Jonathan Cape, 1986, p. 42, entry for 18 June 1940.

64 Rhodes James, *Chips*, p. 260.

65 Ibid., p. 262.

66 Pimlott, ed., *The Second World War Diary of Hugh Dalton*, p. 67, entry for 30 July 1940.

67 Keith Feiling, *The Life of Neville Chamberlain*, London, Macmillan, 1946, p. 451.

68 George Orwell, 'The lion and the unicorn', in S. Orwell and I. Angus, eds, *The Collected Essays, Journalism and Letters of George Orwell*, London, Penguin, 1970, vol. 2, p. 86.

69 *HC*, 5 Nov. 1940, vol. 365, col. 1299.

70 Patrick Donner, *Crusade: A Life against the Calamitous Twentieth Century*, London, Sherwood, 1984, p. 249, quoting Churchill: 'I say today that unless the right hon. Gentleman changes his policy and methods and moves without the slightest delay, he will be as great a curse to this country in time of peace, as he was a squalid nuisance in time of war' (*HC*, 6 Dec. 1945, vol. 416, col. 2544).

71 *HC*, 2 Aug. 1939, vol. 350, col. 2495.

72 Rhodes James, *Chips*, p. 307.

73 *HC*, 6 May 1941, vol. 371, col. 766.

74 Rhodes James, *Chips*, p. 304, entry for 7 May 1941.

75 Ibid., pp. 317–18, entries for 20–2 Jan. 1942.

76 Kevin Jefferys, ed., *Labour and the Wartime Coalition: From the Diary of James Chuter Ede*, London, Historians' Press, 1987, p. 320, entry for 15–18 Feb. 1942.

77 *HC*, 1 July 1942, vol. 381, col. 228.

78 Ibid., col. 247.

79 *HC*, 2 July 1942, vol. 381, col. 528.

80 *HC*, 8 Sept. 1942, vol. 383, col. 112.

81 Pimlott, ed., *The Second World War Diary of Hugh Dalton*, p. 490, entry for 8 Sept. 1942.

82 Quoted in Andrew Chandler, 'The Church of England and the obliteration bombing of Germany in the Second World War', *English Historical Review*, vol. 108, no. 429 (1993), p. 926.

83 Ibid., p. 928.

84 *Chronicle of Convocation*, London, Church of England, 1941, p. 1.

85 Jeremy Crang and Paul Addison, eds, *Firestorm: The Bombing of Dresden, 1945*, London, Pimlico, 2006, p. 189.

86 *HL*, 9 Feb. 1944, vol. 130, cols 741, 744.

87 *HC*, 3 Aug. 1914, vol. 65, col. 1838.

88 Nobody bothered to point out that his being attended by four other Harrovian ministers – Leo Amery, J. T. C. Moore-Brabazon, David Margesson and Geoffrey Lloyd – might suggest ministerial office as one of the privileges that needed to be more widely distributed. The speech is in Charles Eade, ed., *The Unrelenting Struggle: War Speeches of Winston Churchill*, London, Little, Brown, 1941, p. 20.

89 Janet Beveridge, *Beveridge and his Plan*, London, Hodder & Stoughton, 1954, p. 135.

90 *HC*, 12 Nov. 1942, vol. 385, col. 138.

91 Pimlott, ed., *The Second World War Diary of Hugh Dalton*, p. 632, entry for 6 Sept. 1943.

92 Jefferys, *The Churchill Coalition and Wartime Politics*, p. 122.

93 Pimlott, ed., *The Second World War Diary of Hugh Dalton*, p. 865, entry for 28 May 1945.

94 The whole speech is reproduced in David Cannadine, ed., *Blood, Toil, Tears and Sweat: Winston Churchill's Famous Speeches*, London, Cassell, 1989, pp. 270–7.

95 Roy Jenkins, ed., *Purpose and Policy: Selected Speeches of C. R. Attlee*, London, Hutchinson, 1947, p. 3.

96 *HC*, 15 May 1945, vol. 410, col. 2307.

97 John Maynard Keynes, *Essays in Biography*, London, Macmillan, 1933, p. 36.

98 Michael Foot, *Loyalists and Loners*, London, Collins, 1986, p. 142.

99 *Daily Express*, 17 Sept. 1936

100 Winston Churchill to Clementine Hozier, 27 April 1908, cited in Randolph S. Churchill, *Winston Churchill: Young Statesman, 1901–1914*, London, Heinemann, 1967, pp. 260–1.

101 *The Times*, 11 June 1926, cited in Martin Pugh, '"Queen Anne is dead": the abolition of ministerial by-elections, 1867–1926', *Parliamentary History*, vol. 21, no. 3 (2002), p. 366, to which I am indebted for this section.

102 Figures from D. Butler and G. Butler, eds, *Twentieth-Century British Political Facts, 1900–2000*, 8th edn, Basingstoke, Macmillan, 2000, p. 71.

Chapter 6: The Dignity of Labour

1 Henry Broadhurst, *The Story of His Life from a Stonemason's Bench to the Treasury Bench*, Hutchinson, London, 1901, p. 29.

2 Ibid., p. 312.

3 HMC *Egmont Diary*, vol. 1, p. 87.

4 Zygmunt Bauman, *Between Class and Elite*, Manchester, Manchester University Press, 1972, p. 124.

5 Kenneth O. Morgan, *Labour People*, Oxford, Oxford University Press, 1987, p. 75.

6 Cited in Chris Bryant, *Possible Dreams: A Personal History of the Christian Socialists*, London, Hodder & Stoughton, 1997, p. 91.

7 *HC*, 1 Feb. 1887, vol. 310, col. 445.

8 *HC*, 4 May 1892, vol. 4, col. 108.

9 George Robinson, *The Duty of the Age*, London, John James Bezer, 1852.

10 *Church Reformer*, vol. 8, no. 8, Aug. 1888.

11 Charles Gore, *Christianity and Socialism*, CSU pamphlet no. 24, London, Mowbray, 1908.

12 *The Twentieth Century*, vol. 45 (Nineteenth Century and After Ltd, 1899), p. 25.

13 Henry Pelling, *The Origins of the Labour Party, 1880–1900*, Oxford, Oxford University Press, 1966, p. 205.

14 BL Add MSS 46337, John Burns's diary, 26 Sept. 1915.

15 Cited in Martin Pugh, *Speak for Britain!, A New History of the Labour Party*, London, Bodley Head, 2010, p. 60.

16 *HC*, 10 Aug. 1911, vol. 29, col. 1383.

17 Col. Arthur Lee, speaking ibid., col. 1385.

18 Robert Self, ed., *The Neville Chamberlain Diary Letters*, Aldershot, Ashgate, 2000, vol. 2, p. 412.

19 David Cannadine, *G. M. Trevelyan: A Life in History*, London, HarperCollins, 1992, p. 11.

20 *HC*, 12 Feb. 1924, vol. 169, col. 773.

21 Jennie Lee, *Tomorrow is a New Day*, London, Penguin, 1939, p. 144.

22 Trades Union Congress, *Congress Report, 1925*, London, TUC, pp. 363–4.

23 James Klugmann, *History of the Communist Party of Great Britain*, London, Laurence & Wishart, 1968, vol. 1, p. 182. His arrest was reported to the Commons on 11 Nov. 1920.

24 Labour Party archives, PLP minutes, 20 June 1923.

25 Philip Snowden, *Autobiography*, London, Ivor Nicholson & Watson, 1934, vol. 2, pp. 595–6.

26 *HC*, 30 Sept. 1924, vol. 177, col. 16.

27 *HC*, 8 Oct. 1924, vol. 177, col. 513.

28 Bodleian Library MSS, Joseph Ball papers, MS Eng. c. 6652.

29 Robert Rhodes James, *Memoirs of a Conservative: J. C. C. Davidson's Memoirs and Papers, 1910–1937*, London, Weidenfeld & Nicolson, 1969, p. 272.

30 Ibid., p. 199.

31 *HC*, 9 Dec. 1924, vol. 179, col. 62.

32 *HL*, 2 July 1929, vol. 75, col. 14.

33 Ibid., col. 45.

34 *HC*, 29 Oct. 1929, vol. 231, col. 3.

35 Both are paraphrases of Herbert Morrison and Oswald Mosley responding to the debate.

36 David Kirkwood, *My Life of Revolt*, London, G. G. Harrap, 1935, p. 248.

37 Lauchlan MacNeill Weir, *The Tragedy of Ramsay MacDonald*, London, Secker & Warburg, 1938, p. 383.

38 *HC*, 8 Sept. 1931, vol. 256, col. 8.

39 Ibid., col. 28.

40 Ibid., col. 40.

41 David Howell, *MacDonald's Party*, Oxford, Oxford University Press, 2002, pp. 417–18.

42 *HC*, 10 Nov. 1931, vol. 259, col. 59.

43 The numbers looked even better when one added in the three ILP Glaswegian members, James Carmichael, Campbell Stephen and John McGovern, and the one Common Wealth MP, Ernest Millington, all of whom had joined the Labour party by the end of 1947.

44 Kevin Jefferys, ed., *Labour and the Wartime Coalition: From the Diary of James Chuter Ede*, London, Historians' Press, 1987, p. 229, entry for 28 July 1945.

45 James Callaghan, *Biography*, cited in Malcolm Pearce and Geoffrey Stewart, eds, *British Political History 1867–2001*, Abingdon, Routledge, 1992, p. 443.

46 *HC*, 16 Aug. 1945, vol. 413, col. 95.

47 Ibid., col. 113.

48 *Forward*, 27 July 1946.

49 *HL*, 16 Aug. 1945, vol. 137, col. 52.

50 *HL*, 4 Nov. 1946, vol. 261, col. 66.

51 R. J. Minney, *Viscount Addison: Leader of the Lords*, London, Odhams, 1958, p. 53.

52 Jean Mann, *Woman in Parliament*, London, Odhams, 1962, p. 13.

53 The remaining two-member seats in 1945 were Antrim, Blackburn, Bolton, Brighton, City of London, Derby, Down, Dundee, Fermanagh and Tyrone, Norwich, Oldham, Preston, Southampton, Stockport and Sunderland. All these were elected by the first two past the post system, while the university seats were elected by single transferable vote. In 1945 these were Cambridge (2), Combined English (2), Dublin, London, National, Oxford (2), Queen's Belfast, Scotland and Wales. Plural voting allowed a voter affiliated to one of the relevant universities to vote both in their home constituency and the university seat, and property owners to vote both where they lived and where the property lay.

54 Hewitson was the last MP elected in 1945, as when the Labour MP for Kingston-upon-Hull Central, Walter Windsor, died on 29 June the poll was deferred until 19 July and the result was announced on 9 August.

55 *HC*, 7 April 1949, vol. 463, col. 2270.

56 *HC*, 2 April 1946, vol. 421, col. 1213.

57 Pugh, *Speak for Britain!*, p. 290.

58 Vincent Brome, *Aneurin Bevan: A Biography*, London, Longmans, Green, 1953, p. 189.

59 *HC*, 10 April 1951, vol. 486, cols 851–2.

60 *HC*, 23 April 1951, vol. 487, col. 43.

61 John Boyd-Carpenter, *Way of Life*, London, Sidgwick & Jackson, 1980, p. 79.

62 *Merthyr Pioneer*, 2 Oct. 1915.

63 *Woman's Dreadnought*, 2 Oct. 1915.

64 H. Tessell Tiltman, *James Ramsay MacDonald*, London, Jarrolds, 1929, p. 104.

65 Weir, *The Tragedy of Ramsay MacDonald*, pp. 85–6.

66 Clement Attlee, *As it Happened*, London, Heinemann, 1954, p. 74.

67 Correlli Barnett, *The Audit of War*, London, Macmillan, 1987, p. 267.

Chapter 7: A Woman in the House

1 Adrian Fort, *Nancy: The Story of Lady Astor*, Oxford, Oxford University Press, 2012, p. 171.

2 *Daily Express*, 2 Dec. 1919.

3 Patricia Hollis, *Jennie Lee*, Oxford, Oxford University Press, 1997, p. 37.

4 Sir Henry Morris-Jones, *Doctor in the Whips' Room*, London, Robert Hale, 1955, p. 159.

5 *Manchester Guardian*, 2 Dec. 1919.

6 Sir Henry Spelman, ed., *Concilia, Decreta, Leges, Constitutiones in re Ecclesiasticarum Orbis Britannici*, London, n.p., 1639, p. 190.

7 Sir Henry Savile, ed., *Rerum Anglicarum Scriptores post Bedam*, London, n.p., 1596, repr. Frankfurt, 1601, p. 862.

8 Respectively in John Selden, *Tituli Honorum*, Frankfurt, Jeremy Schrey, 1696, p. 729, and Bulstrode Whitelocke, *Notes upon the King's Writ*, London, W. Strahan, 1766, vol. 1, pp. 479–80.

9 The full Latin text can be found in Sir T. C. Banks, ed., *Baronia Anglica Concentrata*, Ripon, William Harrison, 1844, vol. 1, p. 33; it is referred to in Thornhagh Gurdon, *The History of the High Court of Parliament*, London, n.p., 1731, vol. 1, p. 202.

10 Lord Wharncliffe, ed., *The Letters and Works of Lady Mary Wortley Montagu*, London, Richard Bentley, 1837, vol. 2, p. 249.

11 William Prynne, *Brevia Parliamentia Rediviva*, London, n.p., 1662, pp. 152, 153.

12 Cited in P. W. Hasler, ed., *The House of Commons 1558–1603*, London, HMSO, 1981, vol. 1, p. 252.

13 Samuel, Heywood, *A Digest of the Law Respecting County Elections; Containing the Duty and Authority of the High Sheriff . . . and the Mode of Proceeding at County Elections*, London, n.p., 1790, p. 256.

14 Cited in Peter Thomas, *The House of Commons in the Eighteenth Century*, Oxford, Oxford University Press, 1971, pp. 148–9.

15 John Hatsell, *Precedents of Proceedings in the House of Commons*, London, Payne, Cadell, Davies, 1796, vol. 2, p. 172.

16 Augustus Hare, ed., *Life and Letters of Maria Edgeworth*, London, Arnold, 1894, vol. 2, pp. 66–7.

17 Stephen King-Hall and Ann Dewar, *History in Hansard*, London, Constable, 1952, p. 197.

18 *HC*, 20 June 1848, vol. 99, col. 950.

19 *HC*, 20 May 1867, vol. 187, col. 820.

20 In fact the main problem was that the Irish nationalist MPs had decided to vote against the Bill.

21 *HC*, 25 June 1912, vol. 40, col. 217.

22 Second reading in the Commons on 4 November and in the Lords on 12 November; royal assent on 21 November.

23 'A woman shall not be disqualified by sex or marriage from being elected to or sitting or voting as a Member of the Commons House of Parliament.'

24 Justin McCarthy, ed., *The Inner Life of the House of Commons by William White*, London, Fisher Unwin, 1897, p. 5.

25 *The Living Age*, 17 April 1926, p. 154.

26 Ibid., p. 152.

27 *HC*, 24 Feb. 1920, vol. 125, col. 1621.

28 Ibid., col. 1624.

29 Edith Picton-Turbevill, *Life is Good: An Autobiography*, London, F. Muller, 1939, p. 233.

30 A. P. Herbert, *Independent Member*, London, Methuen, 1950, p. 39.

31 *HC*, 1 Dec. 1969, vol. 792, col. 948.

32 Quoted by Richard Needham in *Honourable Member*, London, P. Stephens, 1983. There is, however, no record of the comment in Hansard, so unless it was made during a wartime secret session, it may be apocryphal.

33 *Western Morning News*, 4 Nov. 1919.

34 Oliver Lyttelton, *The Memoirs of Lord Chandos*, London, Bodley Head, 1962, p. 324.

35 *HC*, 20 March 1962, vol. 656, col. 216.

36 Hollis, *Jennie Lee*, p. 36.

37 Jean Mann, *Woman in Parliament*, London, Odhams, 1962, p. 18.

38 Ibid., p. 25.

39 Clement Attlee, 'The attitudes of MPs and active peers', *Political Quarterly*, vol. 30, no. 1 (1959), p. 31.

40 Norman Mackenzie and Jean Mackenzie, eds, *Diary of Beatrice Webb*, London, Virago, 1984, vol. 4, p. 357.

41 Margaret Bondfield, *A Life's Work*, London, Hutchinson, 1948, p. 37.

42 Geoffrey Searle, *A New England: Peace and War 1886–1918*, Oxford, Oxford University Press, 2004, p. 461.

43 Picton-Turbervill, *Life is Good*, p. 94.

44 Nancy Astor, *My Two Countries*, London, Doubleday, 1923, p. 52.

45 Anne Perkins, *Red Queen*, London, Macmillan, 2003, p. 99.

46 Leah Manning, *A Life for Education*, London, Victor Gollancz, 1970, p. 203.

47 Angela V. John, *Turning the Tide: The Life of Lady Rhondda*, Swansea, Parthian, 2013, p. 131.

48 Barbara Wootton, *In a World I Never Made*, London, Allen & Unwin, 1967, p. 131.

49 Ibid., p. 279.

50 *HL*, 28 March 1963, vol. 248, col. 288.

Chapter 8: A Den of Thieves

1 Review Body on Senior Salaries, *Review of Parliamentary Pay and Allowances*, Report No. 48, Cmnd 4997-I, March 2001, para 2.11.

2 G. H. Tupling, *South Lancashire in the Reign of Edward II*, Manchester, Chetham Society, 1949, ser. 3, vol. 1, p. 119.

3 Thomas Babington Macaulay, *History of England*, London, Longman, Green, Brown, 1858, vol. 1, pp. 309–10.

4 PRO, SP 16/539/17, cited in Thomas Cogswell, Richard Cust and Peter Lake, eds, *Politics, Religion and Popularity in Early Stuart England*, Cambridge, Cambridge University Press, 2002, p. 111.

5 *HC*, 30 March 1830, vol. 23, col. 1067.

6 Robert Crosfeild, *A Vindication of the Constitution of the English Monarchy, and the Just Rights of the People*, London, n.p., 1703, p. 9.

7 Geoffrey Holmes, 'The attack on the influence of the crown 1702–1716', *Historical Research*, vol. 39, no. 99 (1966), p. 56.

8 Chevening MSS, 19 Feb. 1706, cited ibid., p. 58.

9 6 Anne, c. 41, s. 26.

10 William Coxe, *Memoirs of the Life and Administration of Sir Robert Walpole, Earl of Orford*, London, Cadell & Davies, 1800, vol. 3, p. 301.

11 Paul Langford, et al., eds, *Writings and Speeches of Edmund Burke*, Oxford, Oxford University Press, 1981, vol. 3, p. 471.

12 Cited in F. P. Lock, *Edmund Burke*, Oxford, Oxford University Press, 1998, vol. 1, pp. 457–8.

13 Ibid., p. 460.

14 William Eden, Lord Auckland, *Journal and Correspondence*, London, R. Bentley, 1861, vol. 1, p. 12.

15 J. E. Norton, ed., *The Letters of Edward Gibbon*, London, Cassell, 1956, vol. 2, p. 341.

16 HMC *Drogmore MSS*, vol. 9, p. 296.

17 *HC*, 15 March 1822, vol. 6, col. 1174.

18 Arthur Wellesley, duke of Wellington, *Despatches, Correspondence and Memoranda of Field-Marshal Arthur, Duke of Wellington*, London, John Murray, 1867, vol. 7, pp. 286–7.

19 Cited in Archibald Foord, 'The waning of "the influence of the crown"', *English Historical Review*, vol. 62, no. 245 (Oct. 1947), p. 500.

20 *HC* 1830–31 (322), *Report of the Select Committee on the Reduction of Salaries*, p. 9.

21 Ibid., p. 4.

22 *HC* 1850 (611), *Report from the Select Committee on Official Salaries*, p. 13.

23 *Calendar of State Papers Domestic*, 1691–2, p. 410.

24 Peter Thomas, *The House of Commons in the Eighteenth Century*, Oxford, Clarendon Press, 1971, p. 114.

25 H. B. Wheatley, ed., *The Historical and the Posthumous Memoirs of Sir Nathaniel William Wraxall*, London, Bickers & Son, 1884, vol. 3, p. 236.

26 Sir N. William Wraxall, *Memoirs of My Own Time*, London, Cadell & Davies, 1815, vol. 1, p. 559.

27 *HC*, 23 July 1834, vol. 25, col. 391.

28 George Henry Jennings, *An Anecdotal History of Parliament*, London, H. Cox, 1883, p. 317.

29 Ibid., p. 194.

30 *The Times*, 28 Jan. 1851.

31 A. Aspinall, 'English party organization in the early nineteenth century', *English Historical Review*, vol. 41, no. 168 (1926), p. 399.

32 Lord John Russell, *An Essay on the History of the English Government and Constitution*, London, Longman, Hurst, 1823, p. 422.

33 J. V. Beckett, *The Rise and Fall of the Grenvilles: Dukes of Buckingham and Chandos, 1710 to 1921*, Manchester, Manchester University Press, 1994, p. 110.

34 Ibid., p. 108.

35 *HC*, 17 July 1922, vol. 156, cols 1765–6.

36 Ibid., col. 1856.

37 *HC*, 28 May 1919, vol. 116, col. 1367.

38 Parliamentary archive, Bonar Law papers, BL 26/3/21.

39 Lloyd George papers, F/21/3/24, cited in Andrew Cook, *Cash for Honours: The Story of Maundy Gregory*, Stroud, History Press, 2008, p. 328.

40 Parliamentary archive, Bonar Law papers, BL/100/1/2, 2 Jan. 1921.

41 Cambridge University Library MSS, Templewood Papers, Part 1, Box 2, File 11, Paper 32, p. 11, cited in Andrew Cook, *Cash for Honours*, p. 98.

42 Both letters in the Austen Chamberlain papers at the University of Birmingham, AC/26/4/38 and 39.

43 *The Times*, 11 Oct. 1909.

44 *Report of the Royal Commission on Honours*, Cmd. 1789, Dec. 1922, para. 21.

45 Honours (Prevention of Abuses) Act 1925, c. 72, s. 1.1.

46 Bodleian Library MSS, Joseph Ball papers, MS Eng. c. 6657 fo. 153.

47 Cambridge University Library MSS, Templewood Papers, Part 1, Box 2, File 11, Paper 32, pp. 1–2, cited in Cook, *Cash for Honours*, p. 107.

48 Bodleian Library MSS, Joseph Ball papers, MS Eng. c. 6657 fo. 109.

49 Julian Symonds, *Horatio Bottomley*, London, Cresset, 1955, p. 166.

50 Ibid., p. 221.

51 *HC*, 1 Aug. 1922, vol. 157, col. 1288.

52 Symonds, *Horatio Bottomley*, pp. 65–6.

53 Cited in David McKie, *Jabez: The Rise and Fall of a Victorian Rogue*, London, Atlantic, 2004, p. 255.

54 *Report from the Select Committee on York City Election Bribery Petition*, 1835, p. 4.

55 Charles Seymour, *Electoral Reform in England and Wales: The Development and Operation of the Parliamentary Franchise, 1832–1885*, London, 1915, p. 176.

Chapter 9: Tired and Emotional

1   *The Times*, 3 March 1976.
2   Ibid., 4 March 1976.
3   Barbara Castle, *The Castle Diaries*, London, Weidenfeld & Nicolson, 1980, vol. 2: *1970–76*, p. 669, entry for 3 March 1976.
4   Mark Pottle, ed., *Daring to Hope: The Letters and Diaries of Violet Bonham Carter*, London, Weidenfeld & Nicolson, 2000, p. 140.
5   Barbara Castle, *The Castle Diaries*, London, Weidenfeld & Nicolson, 1980, vol. 1: *1964–70*, p. 29, entry for 13 April 1965.
6   Ibid., p. 95, entry for 18 Jan. 1966
7   Bill Rodgers, *Fourth among Equals*, London, Politico's, 2000, p. 96.
8   A. Benn, *Office without Power: Diaries, 1968–72*, London, Hutchinson, 1989, p. 45.
9   A. Benn, *Conflicts of Interest: Diaries, 1977–80*, London, Hutchinson, 1990, p. 508.
10 A. Benn, *Against the Tide: Diaries, 1973–76*, London, Hutchinson, 1989, p. 526.
11 Ben Pimlott, *Harold Wilson*, London, HarperCollins, 1992, p. 675.
12 University of Nottingham, Portland MS, PwF 9117.
13 James Greig, ed., *The Farington Diary*, London, Hutchinson, 1923, vol. 2, p. 100.
14 R. O. A. Crewe-Milnes, *Lord Rosebery*, London, Harper, 1931, vol. 2, pp. 586–7.
15 BL, India Office MSS, EUR F 111/162, Lord George Hamilton to Lord Curzon of Kettleston, 5 March 1903.
16 Alan Clark, ed., *A Good Innings: The Private Papers of Viscount Lee of Fareham*, London, John Murray, 1974, p. 98.
17 Stephen Koss, *Asquith*, London, Allen Lane, 1976, p. 187.
18 Edward David, ed., *Inside Asquith's Cabinet, from the Diaries of Charles Hobhouse*, London, John Murray, 1977, p. 79.
19 Kenneth O. Morgan, ed., *Lloyd George: Family Letters*, Cardiff, University of Wales Press, 1973, p. 155.
20 *HC*, 20 April 1911, vol. 24, cols 1056, 1112.
21 Randolph S. Churchill, *Winston Churchill: Young Statesman, 1901–1914*, London, Heinemann, 1967, p. 344.
22 *Spectator*, no. 88, Monday, 11 June 1711.
23 Horace Walpole, *The Letters of Horace Walpole, Earl of Orford: Including Numerous Letters Now First Published from the Original Manuscripts*, ed. J. Wright, Philadelphia, Lea & Blanchard, 1842, vol. 1, p. 317.
24 Roger Coke, *A Detection of the Court and State of England*, London, A. Bell, 1697, p. 71.
25 Pauline Croft, *King James*, Basingstoke, Palgrave Macmillan, 2003, p. 56.
26 N. E. McClure, ed., *Letters of John Chamberlain*, American Philosophical Society, 1939, vol. 1, p. 243.

27 Mark Holt, ed., *Alcohol: A Social History*, Oxford, Berg, 2006, p. 35.

28 Bulstrode Whitelocke, *Memorials of the English Affairs*, London, J. Tomson, 1732, p. 262.

29 Sir Walter Scott, *Tales of a Grandfather*, Edinburgh, Cadell & Co., 1829, p. 178.

30 Samuel Pepys, *The Concise Pepys*, London, Wordsworth Editions, 1997, p. 477.

31 Christopher Wordsworth, ed., *Ecclesiastical Biography*, London, Rivington, 1839, vol. 4, p. 596.

32 George Savile, 'Some Cautions offered to the Consideration of those who are to chuse Members to serve for the Ensuing Parliament', 1695, in Walter Raleigh, ed., *The Complete Works of George Savile, First Marquess of Halifax*, Oxford, Clarendon Press, 1912, p. 146.

33 Charles Ludington, 'The politics of wine in England, 1660–1714', in A. Smyth, ed., *A Pleasing Sinne*, Cambridge, D. S. Brewer, 2004, p. 91.

34 Gilbert Burnet, *History of his own Time*, London, W. Smith, 1840, vol. 2, p. 864.

35 Ludington, 'The politics of wine in England', p. 103.

36 *HC*, 10 Feb. 1860, vol. 156, col. 847.

37 Patrick Dillon, *The Much-lamented Death of Madam Geneva*, London, Headline, 2003.

38 John Wilson Croker, ed., *The Memoirs of John, Lord Hervey*, London, John Murray, 1848, vol. 2, p. 139.

39 Emma, Countess Minto, ed., *Life and Letters of Sir Gilbert Elliot*, London, Longmans, Green, 1874, vol. 1, p. 189.

40 L. G. Mitchell, *Charles James Fox*, Oxford, Oxford University Press, 1992, p. 97.

41 Thomas Moore, ed., *Letters and Journals of Lord Byron*, London, John Murray, 1833, vol. 1, pp. 634–5.

42 National Library of Ireland, Le Fanu Papers, N2975, cited in Fintan O'Toole, *A Traitor's Kiss*, London, Granta, 1997, p. 207.

43 Arthur Aspinall, ed., *The Later Correspondence of George III*, Cambridge, Cambridge University Press, 1968, vol. 4, p. 12.

44 George Pellew, ed., *The Life and Correspondence of the Rt Hon. Henry Addington*, London, John Murray, 1847, vol. 1, p. 91.

45 H. A. Bruce, ed., *The Life of General Sir William Napier*, London, John Murray, 1864, vol. 1, p. 30.

46 James Grant, *Random Recollections of the House of Commons*, London, J. J. Cox, 1836, pp. 378–9.

47 T. P. O'Connor, *Gladstone's House of Commons*, London, Ward & Downey, 1885, p. 88.

48 Ralph Disraeli, ed., *Lord Beaconsfield's Correspondence with his Sister, 1832–1852*, London, John Murray, 1886, p. 150.

49 *HL*, 2 May 1872, vol. 211, col. 86.

50 Ibid., col. 91.

51 Caroline Benn, *Keir Hardie*, London, Hutchinson, 1992, p. 51

52 Ben Tillett, *Is the Parliamentary Labour Party a Failure?*, London, Twentieth Century Press, 1908, p. 13.

53 Henry Phillpott, T*he Right Hon. J. H. Thomas*, London, S. Low, Marston and Co., 1932, p. 5.

54 Sir James Agg-Gardner, *Some Parliamentary Recollections*, London, J. Burrow and Co., 1927, pp. 86–7.

55 Clive Ponting, *Winston Churchill*, London, Sinclair-Stevenson, 1995, pp. 287–8.

56 David Carlton, *Anthony Eden*, London, Allen Lane, 1981, p. 328.

57 British Library MSS, Cunningham diary, 6 July 1944, cited in Ponting, *Winston Churchill*, p. 620.

58 Harold Icke's diary, 12 May 1940, cited in Ponting, *Winston Churchill*, pp. 497–8.

59 The latter comment is cited by Collin Brooks in his chapter in Charles Eade, ed., *Churchill the Conversationalist*, London, Hutchinson, 1953, p. 248. As for the Braddock story, like many statements attributed to Churchill, there is some uncertainty about its precise provenance. Although Churchill's bodyguard, Ronald Golding, confirmed it to Richard Langworth for his collection of quotations *Churchill by Himself: The Definitive Collection of Quotations* (New York, Public Affairs, 2011), it has been attributed to several earlier MPs, including Sir Stafford Northcote and Dr Charles Tanner.

60 John Campbell, *F. E. Smith, First Earl of Birkenhead*, London, Jonathan Cape, 1983, p. 270.

61 Ibid., p. 616.

62 *Spectator*, 1 March 1957.

63 Richard Crossman, *The Backbench Diaries*, London, Hamish Hamilton, 1981, pp. 632, 631, entry for 22 Nov. 1957.

64 *HC*, 20 July 1983, vol. 46, col. 483.

65 Alan Clark, *Diaries 1983–92*, London, Weidenfeld & Nicolson, 1993.

66 *HC*, 30 Oct. 1947, vol. 443, cols. 1097, 1096.

67 Ibid., col. 1199.

Chapter 10: Post the Post-war Consensus

1 Held for fifteen minutes on Tuesday and Thursday afternoons until Tony Blair summarily changed the pattern to a single thirty-minute session every Wednesday.

2 Margaret Thatcher, *The Path to Power*, London, HarperCollins, 1995, p. 432.

3 *HC*, 14 Dec. 1978, vol. 960, col. 1044.

4 *HC*, 28 March 1979, vol. 965, col. 471.

5 Ibid.

6 The numbers would not rise much during her leadership: there were eight in 1979, thirteen in 1983 and just seventeen in 1987.

7   *HC*, 25 June 1979, vol. 969, col. 35.
8   *House of Commons Journals*, 31 Oct. 1696, vol. 11, p. 573.
9   *House of Commons Journals*, 13 March 1697, vol. 11, p. 738.
10 Standing Orders of the House of Commons, HMSO, 2012, no. 148.
11 *HC*, 25 June 1979, vol. 969, col. 178.
12 Ibid., col. 51.
13 *The Times*, 5 Feb. 1936.
14 Charles Mohun, 4th Baron Mohun, and Edward Rich, 3rd Earl of Holland, both in 1699; and William Byron, 5th Baron Byron, in 1765.
15 Iain Macleod, 'The Tory leadership', *Spectator*, 17 Jan. 1964.
16 *HC*, 3 Feb. 1969, vol. 777, col. 149.
17 Ibid., cols 90, 88, 89.
18 Denis Healey, *The Time of My Life*, Harmondsworth, Penguin, 1990, p. 108.
19 Barbara Castle, *The Castle Diaries*, London, Weidenfeld & Nicolson, 1980, vol. 1: *1964–70*, p. 183, entry for 1 Feb. 1968.
20 PRO CAB 128/44 Part One, 18th Conclusions, 16 April 1969, cited in Peter Dorey and Alexandra Kelso, *House of Lords Reform since 1911: Must the Lords Go?*, London, Palgrave, 2011, p. 166.
21 *HC*, 28 Oct. 1971, vol. 823, cols 2211–12.
22 *HC*, 13 July 1972, vol. 840, cols 1873–5.
23 Ibid., col. 1881.
24 The archbishop of Canterbury, Robert Runcie, was among the many who wrote in such terms to Howe: see Geoffrey Howe, *Conflict of Loyalty*, London, Macmillan, 1994, p. 657.
25 John Campbell, *Margaret Thatcher: The Iron Lady*, London, Jonathan Cape, 2003, p. 718.
26 *HC*, 13 Nov. 1990, vol. 180, cols 461–5.
27 *The Times*, 19 Nov. 1990.
28 *The Times*, 22 Nov. 1990.
29 Michael Crick, *Michael Heseltine: A Biography*, London, Hamish Hamilton, 1997, p. 349.
30 Margaret Thatcher, *The Downing Street Years*, London, HarperCollins, 1993, pp. 85, 840.
31 Ibid., p. 855.
32 Woodrow Wyatt, *The Journals*, London, Macmillan, 1992, vol. 2, p. 400, entry for 23 Nov. 1990.
33 *HC*, 22 Nov. 1990, vol. 181, col. 451.
34 Ibid., col. 453.

Epilogue

1   *HC*, 2 Aug. 1850, vol. 113, col. 739.
2   Ibid., col. 728.
3   Chris Bryant, *Glenda Jackson: The Biography*, London, HarperCollins, 1999, p. 250.

4   *HC*, 3 Feb. 1852, vol. 119, col. 76.
5   Two more have taken a permanent leave of absence so as not to be required to pay British taxes.
6   Hobhouse inherited his father's baronetcy in 1831 and, after serving in Grey and Melbourne's ministries, joined the Lords as Baron Broughton in 1851. He never used the often added word 'loyal', his precise words being: 'It is said to be hard on His Majesty's Ministers to raise objections of this character but it is more hard on His Majesty's Opposition to compel them to take this course.' Hansard, 10 April 1826, vol. 15, col. 135, adds that the House laughed at the idea.
7   In Ireland four seats were uncontested in 1951: Armagh, Londonderry, and North and South Antrim.
8   *HC*, 21 March 1887, vol. 312, col. 1061. Erskine May now insists that 'reflections must not be cast in debate on the conduct of the Sovereign, the heir to the throne, or other members of the royal family, the Lord Chancellor, the Governor-General of an independent territory, the Speaker, the Chairman of Ways and Means, Members of either House of Parliament, or judges of the superior courts of the United Kingdom'. Erskine May, *Parliamentary Practice*, 24th edn, London, Butterworth, 2011, pp. 443–4.
9   Standards and Privileges Committee, 14th Report of Session 2010–12, *Privilege: Hacking of Members' Mobile Phones*, ss. 52 & 58 (italics added).
10 Respectively, Thomas Musgrave (York), John Graham (Chester), Ashurst Gilbert (Chichester), Henry Pepys (Worcester) and Henry Phillpotts (Exeter).
11 Respectively, *HC*, 15 Feb. 2006, vol. 442, col. 1414; 7 Dec. 2005, vol. 440, col. 861; 2 Dec. 2009, vol. 501, col. 1103; and 6 March 2013, vol. 559, col. 950.
12 William Cobbett, *Political Register*, London, Cobbett, 1823, vol. 47, col. 664.
13 John Grigg, *Lloyd George: The People's Champion*, London, Penguin, 1978, p. 90.
14 *HC*, 31 March 1988, vol. 130, col. 1283.
15 *HC*, 2 March 1978, vol. 945, col. 668.
16 G. de F. Lord, ed., *Poems on Affairs of State: Augustan Satirical Verse, 1660–1714*, 7 vols, New Haven, Yale University Press, 1963, vol. 2, p. 211.
17 *HC*, 29 Aug. 2013, vol. 556, col. 1556.
18 *HC*, 11 Sept. 2013, vol. 567, col. 980.
19 Matthew Giancarlo, *Parliament and Literature in Late Medieval England*, Cambridge, Cambridge University Press, 2007, p. 22.
20 Government whips in the Lords play a different role as departmental spokespeople.
21 George Barnett Smith, *History of the English Parliament*, London, Ward, Lock, Bowden, 1892, vol. 1, p. 1.
22 John Cam Hobhouse, *Recollections of a Long Life*, 6 vols, ed. Lady Dorchester, Cambridge, Cambridge University Press, 1910, vol. 4, p. 242.

Bibliography

Periodicals

Daily Mail
Daily Telegraph
Edinburgh Review or Critical Journal
English Historical Review
Gentleman's Magazine
Historical Research
Manchester Guardian
Pall Mall Gazette
Parliamentary History
Parliamentary History of England (William Cobbett)
Political Quarterly
Spectator
The Times
Time and Tide

Archives, Manuscripts and Online Resources

Bodleian Library MSS
British History Online: www.british-history.ac.uk
British Library MSS
Cambridge University Library MSS
Historic Hansard 1803–2005 Online: hansard.millbanksystems.com
Historical Manuscripts Commission Reports
   HMC *Drogmore MSS*
   HMC *Egmont Diary*
History of Parliament Online: www.historyofparliamentonline.org
Lambeth Palace Library
National Archives at Kew
Oxford Dictionary of National Biography Online: www.oxforddnb.com
Parliamentary Archives

Published Works

Adams, R. J. Q., 'Andrew Bonar Law and the fall of the Asquith Coalition: the December 1916 Cabinet crisis', *Canadian Journal of History*, vol. 32, no. 2 (1997), pp. 185–200
— *Bonar Law*, London, John Murray, 1999

Addison, Paul, *Churchill on the Home Front 1900–1955*, London, Jonathan Cape, 1992

— *The Road to 1945: British Politics and the Second World War*, London, Pimlico, 1994

Adonis, Andrew, *Making Aristocracy Work: The Peerage and the Political System in Britain 1884–1914*, Oxford, Clarendon Press, 1993

Agg-Gardner, Sir James, *Some Parliamentary Recollections*, London, J. Burrow and Co., 1927

Aldous, Richard, *The Lion and the Unicorn: Gladstone vs. Disraeli*, London, Pimlico, 2007

Ashley, Evelyn, *The Life of Henry John Temple, Viscount Palmerston*, 2 vols, London, R. Bentley, 1876

Aspinall, Arthur, 'The coalition ministries of 1827', *English Historical Review*, vol. 42, no. 168 (Oct. 1927), pp. 533–59

— 'English party organization in the early nineteenth century', *English Historical Review*, vol. 41, no. 168 (1926), pp. 389–411

— ed., *The Later Correspondence of George III*, 5 vols, Cambridge, Cambridge University Press, 1968

Astor, Nancy, *My Two Countries*, London, Doubleday, 1923

Attlee, Clement, *As it Happened*, London, Heinemann, 1954

— 'The attitudes of MPs and active peers', *Political Quarterly*, vol. 30, no. 1 (1959), pp. 29–32

Auckland, Robert, Lord, ed., *The Journal and Correspondence of William, Lord Auckland*, 5 vols, London, Spottiswoode, 1802

Bailey, Catherine, *The Secret Rooms*, London, Viking, 2012

Baker, Arthur, *The House is Sitting*, London, Blandford, 1958

Baldwin, Oliver, *The Questing Beast*, London, Grayson & Grayson, 1935

Ball, Stuart, ed., *Parliament and Politics in the Age of Churchill and Attlee: The Headlam Diaries*, London, Royal Historical Society, 1999

Banks, Sir T. C., ed., *Baronia Anglica Concentrata*, Ripon, William Harrison, 1844

Barnes, John, and Nicholson, David, eds, *The Leo Amery Diaries*, 2 vols, London, Hutchinson, 1980

Barnett, Correlli, *The Audit of War*, London, Macmillan, 1987

Barnett Smith, George, *History of the English Parliament*, 2 vols, London, Ward, Lock, Bowden, 1892

Bauman, Zygmunt, *Between Class and Elite*, Manchester, Manchester University Press, 1972

Beckett, J. V., *The Rise and Fall of the Grenvilles: Dukes of Buckingham and Chandos, 1710 to 1921*, Manchester, Manchester University Press, 1994

Benjamin, Lewis Saul, ed., *The Life and Letters of William Beckford of Fonthill*, London, Duffield, 1910

Benn, A., *Office without Power: Diaries, 1968–72*, London, Hutchinson, 1989.

— *Against the Tide: Diaries, 1973–76*, London, Hutchinson, 1989

— *Conflicts of Interest: Diaries, 1977–80*, London, Hutchinson, 1990

Bevan, Aneurin, *In Place of Fear,* London, Heinemann, 1952

Beveridge, Janet, *Beveridge and his Plan,* London, Hodder & Stoughton, 1954

Biffen, John, *Inside the House of Commons,* London, Grafton, 1989

Blake, Robert, *The Conservative Party from Peel to Churchill,* London, Eyre & Spottiswoode, 1970

— *Disraeli,* London, Methuen, 1969

— *The Unknown Prime Minister: The Life and Times of Andrew Bonar Law, 1858–1923,* London, Eyre & Spottiswoode, 1955

Bogdanor, Vernon, ed., *The British Constitution in the Twentieth Century,* Oxford, Oxford University Press, 2003

Bondfield, Margaret, *A Life's Work,* London, Hutchinson, 1948

Bonham Carter, Violet, *Winston Churchill as I Knew Him,* London, Eyre, Spottiswoode & Collins, 1965

Boyd-Carpenter, John, *Way of Life,* London, Sidgwick & Jackson, 1980

Brabourne, Edward, Lord, ed., *Letters of Jane Austen,* vol. 2, London, Bentley, 1884

Brightfield, Myron, *John Wilson Croker,* Berkeley, University of California Press, 1940

Broadhurst, Henry, *The Story of his Life from a Stonemason's Bench to the Treasury Bench,* London, Hutchinson, 1901

Brock, Michael, *The Great Reform Act,* London, Hutchinson, 1973

Brock, Michael, and Montagu, Edwin, eds, *H. H. Asquith, Letters to Venetia Stanley,* Oxford, Oxford University Press, 1982

Brome, Vincent, *Aneurin Bevan: A Biography,* London, Longmans, Green, 1953

Brooke, John and Sorenson, Mary, eds, *The Prime Ministers' Papers: W. E. Gladstone,* 4 vols, London, HMSO, 1971

Brougham, Henry, Lord, *The Lord Chancellor's Speech on Parliamentary Reform,* London, Ridgway, 1831

Brown, David, *Palmerston: A Biography,* New Haven, Yale University Press, 2013

Brown, George, *In My Way,* London, Book Club Associates, 1970

Bruce, H. A., ed., *The Life of General Sir William Napier,* 2 vols, London, John Murray, 1864

Bryant, Chris, *Glenda Jackson: The Biography,* London, HarperCollins, 1999

— *Possible Dreams: A Personal History of the Christian Socialists,* London, Hodder & Stoughton, 1997

Burke, Edmund, *Works,* 9 vols, London, Little, Brown, 1839

Burnet, Gilbert, *History of his own Time,* 3 vols, London, W. Smith, 1840

— *Some Passages of the Life and Death of the Right Honourable John Earl of Rochester, who died the 26th of July, 1680,* London, n.p., 1680

Butler, D. and Butler, G., eds, *Twentieth-Century British Political Facts, 1900–2000,* 8th edn, Basingstoke, Macmillan, 2000

Byrne, Paula, *Mad World: Evelyn Waugh and the Secrets of Brideshead,* London, HarperCollins, 2009

Callanan, Frank, *The Parnell Split, 1890–91*, New York, Syracuse University Press, 1992

Campbell, John, *F. E. Smith, First Earl of Birkenhead*, London, Jonathan Cape, 1983

— *Margaret Thatcher: The Iron Lady*, London, Jonathan Cape, 2003

Camplin, Jamie, *The Rise of the Rich*, London, St Martin's Press, 1979

Cannadine, David, ed., *Blood, Toil, Tears and Sweat: Winston Churchill's Famous Speeches*, London, Cassell, 1989

— *The Decline and Fall of the British Aristocracy*, London, Macmillan, 1992

— *G. M. Trevelyan: A Life in History*, London, HarperCollins, 1992

Cannon, John, *Parliamentary Reform 1640–1832*, Cambridge, Cambridge University Press, 1973

Carlton, David, *Anthony Eden*, London, Allen Lane, 1981

Carpenter, William, *Peerage for the People*, London, William Carpenter, 1837

Cartland, Barbara, *Ronald Cartland*, London, Collins, 1942

Cash, Bill, *John Bright, Statesman, Orator, Agitator*, London, I. B. Tauris, 2012

Castle, Barbara, *The Castle Diaries*, 2 vols, London, Weidenfeld & Nicolson, 1980

'Cato', *Guilty Men*, London, Victor Gollancz, 1940

Catterall, Peter, ed., *The Macmillan Diaries*, 2 vols, London, Macmillan, 2003, 2011

Cecil, Lady Gwendolen, *Life of Robert, Marquis of Salisbury*, 2 vols, London, Hodder & Stoughton, 1921

Chambers, James, *Palmerston: The People's Darling*, London, John Murray, 2004

Chandler, Andrew, 'The Church of England and the obliteration bombing of Germany in the Second World War', *English Historical Review*, vol. 108, no. 429, 1993, pp. 920–46

Charmley, John, *A History of Conservative Politics since 1830*, Basingstoke, Palgrave Macmillan, 2008

Christie, Octavius Francis, *Transition to Democracy*, London, Routledge, 1934

Churchill, Randolph S., *Winston Churchill: Young Statesman, 1901–1914*, London, Heinemann, 1967

Clark, Alan, *Diaries 1983–92*, London, Weidenfeld & Nicolson, 1993

— ed., *A Good Innings: The Private Papers of Viscount Lee of Fareham*, London, John Murray, 1974

Cockett, Richard, *The Twilight of Truth: Chamberlain, Appeasement and the Manipulation of the Press*, London, Weidenfeld & Nicolson, 1989

Cogswell, Thomas; Cust, Richard; and Lake, Peter, eds, *Politics, Religion and Popularity in Early Stuart England*, Cambridge, Cambridge University Press, 2002

Coke, Roger, *A Detection of the Court and State of England*, London, A. Bell, 1697

Cole, G. D. H. and Cole, M., eds, *Cobbett's Rural Rides*, 3 vols, London, Peter Davies, 1930

Colville, John, *The Fringes of Power: Downing Street Diaries, 1939–1955*, London, Hodder & Stoughton, 1985

Cook, Andrew, *Cash for Honours: The Story of Maundy Gregory*, Stroud, History Press, 2008

Coupland, R, ed., *The War Speeches of William Pitt the Younger*, Oxford, Oxford University Press, 1915

Cowling, Maurice, *1867: Disraeli, Gladstone and Revolution – The Passing of the Second Reform Bill*, Cambridge, Cambridge University Press, 1967

— *The Impact of Labour 1920–1924*, Cambridge, Cambridge University Press, 1971

Coxe, William, *Memoirs of the Life and Administration of Sir Robert Walpole, Earl of Orford*, 3 vols, London, Cadell & Davies, 1800

Crang, Jeremy, and Addison, Paul, eds, *Firestorm: The Bombing of Dresden, 1945*, London, Pimlico, 2006

Crewe-Milnes, R. O. A., *Lord Rosebery*, 2 vols, London, Harper, 1931

Crick, Michael, *Michael Heseltine: A Biography*, London, Hamish Hamilton, 1997

Croft, Pauline, *King James*, Basingstoke, Palgrave Macmillan, 2003

Croker, John Wilson, ed., *The Memoirs of John, Lord Hervey*, 2 vols, London, John Murray, 1848

Crosfeild, Robert, *A Vindication of the Constitution of the English Monarchy, and the Just Rights of the People*, London, n.p., 1703

Crossman, Richard, *The Backbench Diaries*, London, Hamish Hamilton, 1981

Curtis, Sarah, ed., *The Journals of Woodrow Wyatt*, 3 vols, London, Macmillan, 1992

Curzon, George Nathaniel (marquess of), *Modern Parliamentary Eloquence: The Rede Lecture*, London, Macmillan, 1913

Dabhoiwala, Faramerz, *The Origins of Sex: A History of the First Sexual Revolution*, London, Allen Lane, 2012

Dangerfield, George, *The Strange Death of Liberal England*, London, Serif, 1997

Davenport-Hines, Richard, *The Macmillans*, London, Mandarin, 1993

David, Edward, ed., *Inside Asquith's Cabinet, from the Diaries of Charles Hobhouse*, London, John Murray, 1977

Dell, Edmund, *The Chancellors*, London, HarperCollins, 1996

Dillon, Patrick, *The Much-lamented Death of Madam Geneva*, London, Headline, 2003

Disraeli, Benjamin, *Lord George Bentinck: A Political Biography*, London, Colburn, 1852

— *Tancred, or The New Crusade*, London, Frederick Warne, 1866

Disraeli, Ralph, ed., *Lord Beaconsfield's Correspondence with his Sister, 1832–1852*, London, John Murray, 1886

Donner, Patrick, *Crusade: A Life against the Calamitous Twentieth Century*, London, Sherwood, 1984

Dorey, Peter, and Kelso, Alexandra, *House of Lords Reform since 1911: Must the Lords Go?*, London, Palgrave, 2011

Drewry, G. ed., *The New Select Committees: A Study of the 1979 Reforms*, Oxford, Clarendon Press, 1989

Dugdale, Blanche, *Arthur James Balfour, First Earl of Balfour*, 2 vols, London, Hutchinson, 1936

Dutton, David, *Anthony Eden: A Life and Reputation*, London, Arnold, 1997

— *Austen Chamberlain: Gentleman in Politics*, Bolton, Ross Anderson, 1985

Eade, Charles, ed., *The Unrelenting Struggle: War Speeches of Winston Churchill*, London, Little, Brown, 1941

Eden, William, Lord Auckland, *Journal and Correspondence*, 2 vols, London, R. Bentley, 1861

Elliott, Hugh, ed., *The Letters of J. S. Mill*, 2 vols, London, Longmans et al., 1910

Ellman, Richard, *Oscar Wilde*, London, Hamish Hamilton, 1987

Ewald, Alexander, *The Right Hon. Benjamin Disraeli, Earl of Beaconsfield, K.G., and His Times*, 2 vols, London, W. Mackenzie, 1882

Fawcett, Millicent Garrett, *Life of the Right Hon. Sir William Molesworth*, London, Macmillan, 1901

Feiling, Keith, *A History of the Second Tory Party 1714–1832*, London, Macmillan, 1938

— *The Life of Neville Chamberlain*, London, Macmillan, 1946

Fielding, Steven, *The Labour Party*, Basingstoke, Palgrave Macmillan, 2003

Fitzgerald, Percy, *The Book Fancier*, London, Sampson Low, Marston Searle & Rivington, 1887

Foord, Archibald, 'The waning of "the influence of the crown"', *English Historical Review*, vol. 62, no. 245 (Oct. 1947), pp. 484–507

Foot, Michael, *Loyalists and Loners*, London, Collins, 1986

— *Aneurin Bevan*, London, Victor Gollancz, 1997

Foot, Paul, *The Vote, How it was Won and How it was Undermined*, London, Viking, 2005

Fort, Adrian, *Nancy: The Story of Lady Astor*, Oxford, Oxford University Press, 2012

Foster, R. F., *Lord Randolph Churchill: A Political Life*, London, Clarendon Press, 1981

Fraser, Lady Antonia, *Perilous Question: The Drama of the Great Reform Bill 1832*, London, Weidenfeld & Nicolson, 2013

Fraser, Peter, *Lord Esher: A Political Biography*, London, Hart-Davis MacGibbon, 1973

Gagnier, Regenia, *Idylls of the Marketplace*, Stanford, Stanford University Press, 1986

Gardiner, Juliet, *Wartime Britain 1939–1945*, London, Headline, 2004

Gash, Norman, *Lord Liverpool: The Life and Political Career of Robert Banks Jenkinson, Second Earl of Liverpool 1770–1828*, London, Weidenfeld & Nicolson, 1984

— *Mr Secretary Peel: The Life of Sir Robert Peel*, 2 vols, London, Longman, 1961, 1972

— *Politics in the Age of Peel*, Hassocks, Harvester, 1977

— *Reaction and Reconstruction in English Politics 1832–1852*, Oxford, Clarendon Press, 1965

Giancarlo, Matthew, *Parliament and Literature in Late Medieval England*, Cambridge, Cambridge University Press, 2007

Gilmour, David, *Curzon*, London, Papermac, 1994

Gladstone, William Ewart, *Diaries*, 12 vols, Oxford, Clarendon Press, 1982

— *Political Speeches in Scotland, November and December 1879*, Edinburgh, Andrew Elliot, 1879

Gore, Charles, *Christianity and Socialism*, CSU pamphlet no. 24, London, Mowbray, 1908

— ed., *Lux Mundi*, London, John Murray, 1989

Goschen, George, Viscount, *Essays and Addresses on Economic Questions*, 3 vols, London, Edward Arnold, 1905

Grant, James, *Random Recollections of the House of Commons*, London, J. J. Cox, 1836

Graves, Pamela, *Labour Women*, Cambridge, Cambridge University Press, 1994

Greig, James, ed., *The Farington Diary*, 8 vols, London, Hutchinson, 1923

Grey, Lt-Gen. Charles, *Some Account of the Life and Opinions of Charles, Second Earl Grey*, London, Richard Bentley, 1861

Grigg, John, *Lloyd George: The People's Champion*, London, Penguin, 1978

Guedalla, Philip, *The Queen and Mr Gladstone*, London, Hodder & Stoughton, 1933

Gurdon, Thornhagh, *The History of the High Court of Parliament*, 2 vols, London, n.p., 1731

Gwynn, Stephen, *The Life of the Rt Hon. Sir Charles W. Dilke*, 2 vols, London, John Murray, 1917

Hague, William, *William Wilberforce: The Life of the Great Anti-Slave Trade Campaigner*, London, HarperCollins, 2007

Haly, W. T., ed., *The Opinions of Sir Robert Peel*, London, n.p., 1850

Hamer, David, *John Morley: Liberal Intellectual in Politics*, Oxford, Oxford University Press, 1968

Hamilton, Lord Ernest, *Forty Years On*, London, Hodder & Stoughton, 1922

Hamilton, Lord George, *Parliamentary Reminiscences and Reflections*, 2 vols, London, John Murray, 1916, 1922

Hamilton, M. A., *Arthur Henderson*, London, Heinemann, 1938

Hare, Augustus, ed., *Life and Letters of Maria Edgeworth*, London, Arnold, 1894

Harris, Kenneth, *Attlee*, London, Weidenfeld & Nicolson, 1982

Harris, Sir Percy, *Forty Years in and out of Parliament*, London, Melrose, 1947

Harris, Robin, *The Conservatives: A History*, London, Bantam, 2011

— *Not for Turning*, London, Bantam, 2013

Harvey, Ian, *To Fall Like Lucifer*, London, Biteback, 2011

Hasler, P. W., ed., *The House of Commons 1558–1603*, London, HMSO, 1981 (History of Parliament Online)

Hatsell, John, *Precedents of Proceedings in the House of Commons*, London, H. Hughs, 1781

Hattersley, Roy, *The Edwardians*, London, Little, Brown, 2004

Hawkins, Angus, *The Forgotten Prime Minister: The 14th Earl of Derby*, 2 vols, Oxford, Oxford University Press, 2007–8

— *Parliament, Party and the Art of Politics in Britain, 1855–59*, London, Macmillan, 1987

Haxey, Simon, *Tory MP*, London, Victor Gollancz, 1939

Hazlehurst, Cameron, 'Asquith as Prime Minister, 1908–1916', *English Historical Review*, vol. 85, no. 336 (July 1970), pp. 502–31

— *Politicians at War*, London, Jonathan Cape, 1971

Healey, Denis, *The Time of My Life*, Harmondsworth, Penguin, 1990

Hennessy, Peter, *The Prime Minister: The Office and its Holders since 1945*, London, Allen Lane, 2000

Herbert, A. P., *Independent Member*, London, Methuen, 1950

Hetherington, S. J., *Katherine Atholl: Against the Tide*, Aberdeen, Aberdeen University Press, 1989

Heywood, Samuel, *A Digest of the Law Respecting County Elections; Containing the Duty and Authority of the High Sheriff . . . and the Mode of Proceeding at County Elections*, London, n.p., 1790

Hibbert, Christopher, *Disraeli: A Personal History*, London, HarperCollins, 2004

Hignett, S, *Brett: From Bloomsbury to New Mexico – A Biography*, London, Hodder & Stoughton, 1984

Hill, Alan G., ed., *The Letters of William and Dorothy Wordsworth*, Oxford, Oxford University Press, 1967

Hinde, Wendy, *George Canning*, London, Collins, 1973

Hobhouse, John Cam, *Recollections of a Long Life*, ed. Lady Dorchester, 6 vols, Cambridge, Cambridge University Press, 1910

Holland, Henry, Baron, *Further Memoirs of the Whig Party: 1807–1821*, London, John Murray, 1905

Hollis, Patricia, *Jennie Lee*, Oxford, Oxford University Press, 1997

Holmes, Geoffrey, 'The attack on the influence of the crown 1702–1716', *Historical Research*, vol. 39, no. 99 (1966), pp. 47–68

Holmes, Richard, *Wellington: The Iron Duke*, London, Harper Perennial, 2007

Holt, Mark, ed., *Alcohol: A Social History*, Oxford, Berg, 2006

Howarth, Patrick, *Questions in the House*, London, Bodley Head, 1956

Howe, Geoffrey, *Conflict of Loyalty*, London, Macmillan, 1994

Howell, David, *MacDonald's Party*, Oxford, Oxford University Press, 2002

Hurd, Douglas, and Young, Edward, *Disraeli, or The Two Lives*, London, Weidenfeld & Nicolson, 2013

Hurd, Douglas, *Robert Peel: A Biography*, London, Phoenix, 2007

Hyde, Montgomery, *The Londonderrys: A Family Portrait*, London, Hamish Hamilton, 1979

Ingrams, Richard, *The Life and Adventures of William Cobbett*, London, HarperCollins, 2005

Iremonger, F. A., *William Temple*, Oxford, Clarendon Press, 1948

Jackson, Patrick, ed., *Loulou: Selected Extracts from the Journals of Lewis Harcourt (1880–1895)*, Madison, NJ, Fairleigh Dickinson University Press, 2006

Jay, Richard, *Joseph Chamberlain: A Political Life*, Oxford, Clarendon Press, 1981

Jefferys, Kevin, *The Churchill Coalition and Wartime Politics, 1940–45*, Manchester, Manchester University Press, 1991

— ed., *Labour and the Wartime Coalition: From the Diary of James Chuter Ede*, London, Historians' Press, 1987

Jenkins, Roy, *Mr Balfour's Poodle*, London, Macmillan, 1999

— *Nine Men of Power*, London, Hamish Hamilton, 1974

— *Sir Charles Dilke: A Victorian Tragedy*, London, Collins, 1958

— *Winston Churchill*, London, Macmillan, 2001

— ed., *Purpose and Policy: Selected Speeches of C. R. Attlee*, London, Hutchinson, 1947

Jennings, George Henry, *An Anecdotal History of Parliament*, London, H. Cox, 1883

Jennings, Louis J., ed., *The Correspondence and Diaries of the Late Right Honourable John Wilson Croker*, 3 vols, London, John Murray, 1884

John, Angela V., *Turning the Tide: The Life of Lady Rhondda 1883–1958*, Swansea, Parthian, 2013

Jones, Mervyn, *A Radical Life: The Biography of Megan Lloyd George, 1902–66*, London, Hutchinson, 1991

Jones, Thomas, *Whitehall Diary*, 3 vols, ed. Keith Middlemas, London, Oxford University Press, 1969

Jupp, Peter, *The Governing of Britain, 1688–1848*, London, Routledge, 2006

Kellner, Peter, *Democracy*, London, Hamish Hamilton, 2009

Keohane, Nigel, *The Party of Patriotism: The Conservative Party and the First World War*, Farnham, Ashgate, 2010

Keppel, George Thomas (earl of Albemarle), *Memoirs of the Marquis of Rockingham*, 2 vols, London, Richard Bentley, 1852

Keynes, John Maynard, *Essays in Biography*, London, Macmillan, 1933

King-Hall, Stephen, and Dewar, Ann, *History in Hansard*, London, Constable, 1952

Kirkwood, David, *My Life of Revolt*, London, Harrap, 1935

Klugmann, James, *History of the Communist Party of Great Britain*, 2 vols, Laurence & Wishart, 1968

Koss, Stephen, *Asquith*, London, Allen Lane, 1976

Kriegel, Abraham, ed., *The Holland House Diaries 1831–1840*, London, Routledge & Kegan Paul, 1977

Langford, Paul et al., eds, *The Writings and Speeches of Edmund Burke*, 9 vols, Oxford, Oxford University Press, 1981

Lansbury, George, *My Life*, London, Constable, 1928

Latham, Robert, and Mathews, William, eds, *The Diary of Samuel Pepys*, 11 vols, London, Bell & Hyman, 1971

Leader, Robert, *Life and Letters of John Arthur Roebuck*, London, Arnold, 1897

Lee, Jennie, *Tomorrow is a New Day*, London, Penguin, 1939

— *My Life with Nye*, Harmondsworth, Penguin, 1980

Lees-Milne, James, *The Enigmatic Edwardian*, London, Sidgwick & Jackson, 1986

Lock, F. P., *Edmund Burke*, 3 vols, Oxford, Oxford University Press, 1998

Lockhart, J. G., *Cosmo Gordon Lang*, London, Hodder & Stoughton, 1949

Lucy, Sir Henry William, *A Diary of the Salisbury Parliament, 1886–92*, London, Cassell, 1892

— *Lords and Commoners*, London, Fisher Unwin, 1921

— *Memories of Eight Parliaments*, London, Heinemann, 1908

Lyttelton, Oliver, *The Memoirs of Lord Chandos*, London, Bodley Head, 1962

Macaulay, Thomas Babington, *History of England*, 5 vols, London, Longman, Green, Brown, 1858

McCarthy, Justin, ed., *The Inner Life of the House of Commons by William White*, London, Fisher Unwin, 1897

McClure, N. E., ed., *Letters of John Chamberlain*, 2 vols, Philadelphia, American Philosophical Society, 1939

MacDonagh, Michael, *The Reporters' Gallery*, London, Hodder & Stoughton, 1913

Mackenzie, Norman, and Mackenzie, Jeanne, eds, *Diary of Beatrice Webb*, 4 vols, London, Virago, 1984

McKie, David, *Jabez: The Rise and Fall of a Victorian Rogue*, London, Atlantic, 2004

Macleod, Iain, *Neville Chamberlain*, London, Muller, 1961

Macnamara, J. R. J., *The Whistle Blows*, London, Eyre & Spottiswoode, 1938

MacNeill Weir, Lauchlin, *The Tragedy of Ramsay MacDonald*, London, Secker & Warburg, 1938

Mann, Jean, *Woman in Parliament*, London, Odhams, 1962

Manning, Leah, *A Life for Education*, London, Victor Gollancz, 1970

Mansbridge, A., *Edward Stuart Talbot and Charles Gore*, London, Dent, 1935

Marlow, Joyce, ed., *Votes for Women: The Virago Book of Suffragettes*, London, Virago, 2000

Marquand, David, *Ramsay MacDonald*, London, Jonathan Cape, 1977

Maxwell, Sir Herbert, ed., *The Creevey Papers: A Selection from the Correspondence and Diaries of the Late Thomas Creevey MP*, 3 vols, London, John Murray, 1904

Middlemas, Keith, ed., *Thomas Jones' Whitehall Diary*, 2 vols, Oxford, Oxford University Press, 1969

Minney, R. J., *Viscount Addison: Leader of the Lords*, London, Odhams, 1958

Minto, Emma, Countess, ed., *Life and Letters of Sir Gilbert Elliot*, 3 vols, London, Longmans, Green, 1874

Mitchell, L. G., *Charles James Fox*, Oxford, Oxford University Press, 1992

— *Lord Melbourne 1779–1848*, Oxford, Oxford University Press, 1997

Monypenny, W. F., and Buckle, G. E., *The Life of Benjamin Disraeli*, 6 vols, London, John Murray, 1910–20

Moore, Charles, *Margaret Thatcher: The Authorized Biography*, vol. 1: *Not for Turning*, London, Allen Lane, 2013

Moore, Thomas, ed., *Letters and Journals of Lord Byron*, 2 vols, London, John Murray, 1833

— *The Life of Lord Byron*, London, John Murray, 1844

Morgan, Kenneth O., *Callaghan: A Life*, Oxford, Oxford University Press, 1997

— *Labour People*, Oxford, Oxford University Press, 1987

— ed., *Lloyd George: Family Letters*, Cardiff, University of Wales Press, 1973

Morley, John, *Life of Gladstone*, 3 vols, London, Macmillan, 1903

Morris-Jones, Sir Henry, *Doctor in the Whips' Room*, London, Robert Hale, 1955

Needham, Richard, *Honourable Member*, London, P. Stephens, 1983

New, Chester, *Lord Durham: A Biography of John George Lambton, 1st Earl Durham*, Oxford, Oxford University Press, 1929

Nicholls, David, *Sir Charles Dilke: The Lost Prime Minister*, London, Hambledon Press, 1995

Nicolson, Nigel, *Portrait of a Marriage*, Chicago, University of Chicago Press, 1998

— ed., *Harold Nicolson: Diaries and Letters 1939–1945*, London, Collins, 1966

Norman, Jess, *Edmund Burke: Philosopher, Politician, Prophet*, London, Collins, 2013

Norton, J. E., ed., *The Letters of Edward Gibbon*, 3 vols, London, Cassell, 1956

Norton, Philip, ed., *Parliament in the 1980s*, Oxford, Oxford University Press, 1985

Norton, Rictor, *Mother Clap's Molly House: The Gay Subculture in England, 1700–1830*, London, Gay Men's Press, 1992

O'Connor, T. P., *Gladstone's House of Commons*, London, Ward & Downey, 1885

O'Leary, Cornelius, *The Elimination of Corrupt Practices in British Elections, 1868–1911*, Oxford, Oxford University Press, 1962

Olson, Lynne, *Troublesome Young Men*, London, Bloomsbury, 2007

Orwell, S., and Angus, I., eds, *The Collected Essays, Journalism and Letters of George Orwell*, 4 vols, London, Penguin, 1970

O'Toole, Fintan, *A Traitor's Kiss*, London, Granta, 1997

Parris, Matthew, *Chance Witness*, London, Penguin, 2002

Pearce, Edward, *The Lost Leaders*, London, Little, Brown, 1997

— *Reform*, London, Jonathan Cape, 2003

Pearce, Malcolm, and Stewart, Geoffrey, eds, *British Political History 1867–2001*, Abingdon, Routledge, 1992

Peel, George, ed., *Sir Robert Peel, from his Private Papers*, London, John Murray, 1899

Pellew, George, ed., *The Life and Correspondence of the Rt Hon. Henry Addington*, 2 vols, London, John Murray, 1847

Pelling, Henry, *The Origins of the Labour Party, 1880–1900*, Oxford, Oxford University Press, 1966

Perkins, Anne, *Red Queen*, London, Macmillan, 2003

Pethick-Lawrence, Frederick William, *Fate Has Been Kind*, London, Hutchinson, 1942

Petrie, Sir Charles, and Cooke, Alistair, *The Carlton Club 1832–2007*, London, Carlton Club, 2007

Phillips, Gordon, *The Rise of the Labour Party 1893–1931*, London, Routledge, 1992

Phillpott, Henry, *The Right Hon. J. H. Thomas*, London, S. Low, Marston and Co., 1932

Picton-Turbevill, Edith, *Life is Good: An Autobiography*, London, F. Muller, 1939

Pimlott, Ben, *Harold Wilson*, London, HarperCollins, 1992

— *Hugh Dalton*, London, Jonathan Cape, 1985

— ed., *The Second World War Diary of Hugh Dalton*, London, Jonathan Cape, 1986

Ponting, Clive, *Winston Churchill*, London, Sinclair-Stevenson, 1995

Porritt, E., and Porritt, A. G., *The Unreformed House of Commons*, 2 vols, Cambridge, Cambridge University Press, 1909

Postgate, Raymond, *The Life of George Lansbury*, London, Longmans, Green, 1951

Pottle, Mark, ed., *Daring to Hope: The Letters and Diaries of Violet Bonham Carter*, London, Weidenfeld & Nicolson, 2000

Prest, John, *Lord John Russell*, London, Macmillan, 1972

Prynne, William, *Brevia Parliamentia Rediviva*, London, n.p., 1662

Pugh, Martin, *Electoral Reform in War and Peace 1906–1918*, London, Routledge & Kegan Paul, 1978

— '"Queen Anne is dead": the abolition of ministerial by-elections, 1867–1926', *Parliamentary History*, vol. 21, no. 3 (2002), pp. 351–66

— *Speak for Britain! A New History of the Labour Party*, London, Bodley Head, 2010

— *The Tories and the People, 1880–1935*, Oxford, Blackwell, 1985

Pulteney, William, *A Proper Reply to a Late Scurrilous Libel*, London, n.p., 1731

Radice, Giles, *The Tortoise and the Hares*, London, Politico's, 2008

Raleigh, Walter, ed., *The Complete Works of George Savile, First Marquess of Halifax*, Oxford, Clarendon Press, 1912

Ramsden, John, *The Age of Balfour and Baldwin, 1902–1940*, London, Longman, 1978

— *The Age of Churchill and Eden, 1940–1957*, London, Longman, 1995

— *An Appetite for Power: A History of the Conservative Party since 1830*, London, HarperCollins, 1998

— *The Winds of Change: Macmillan to Heath, 1957–1975*, London, Longman, 1996

Reckitt, M. B., *Maurice to Temple*, London, Faber, 1946

Redesdale, Lord, ed., *Memories, by Lord Redesdale, 1867–76*, vol. 1, London, Hutchinson, 1915

Reeve, Henry, ed., *The Greville Memoirs: A Journal of the Reigns of King George IV and King William IV*, 3 vols, London, Longmans, Green, 1875

Reid, Stuart J., *Life and Letters of the First Earl of Durham*, 2 vols, London, Longmans Green & Co., 1906

Rhodes James, Robert, *Churchill: A Study in Failure 1900–1939*, London, Weidenfeld & Nicolson, 1970

— *Robert Boothby: A Portrait of Churchill's Ally*, New York, Viking, 1991

— ed., *Chips: The Diaries of Sir Henry Channon*, London, Weidenfeld & Nicolson, 1993

— *Memoirs of a Conservative: J. C. C. Davidson's Memoirs and Papers, 1910–1937*, London, Weidenfeld & Nicolson, 1969

Richards, Peter, *The Backbenchers*, London, Faber, 1972

Robbins, Keith, *Sir Edward Grey: A Biography of Lord Grey of Fallodon*, London, Cassell, 1971

Roberts, Andrew, '*The Holy Fox': The Life of Lord Halifax*, London, Phoenix, 1997

— *Salisbury: Victorian Titan*, London, Phoenix, 2000

Robinson, George, *The Duty of the Age*, London, John James Bezer, 1852

Robinson, W. Sydney, *Muckraker: The Scandalous Life and Times of W. T. Stead, Britain's First Investigative Journalist*, London, Robson, 2012

Rodgers, Bill, *Fourth among Equals*, London, Politico's, 2000

Rose, Kenneth, *The Later Cecils*, London, Harper & Row, 1975

— *Curzon: A Most Superior Person*, London, Macmillan, 1985

Rush, M., *The Role of the Member of Parliament since 1868: From Gentleman to Players*, Oxford, Oxford University Press, 2001

— ed., *Parliament and Pressure Politics*, Oxford, Oxford University Press, 1990

Russell, G. W. E., *Collections and Recollections by One Who Has Kept a Diary*, London, Smith, Elder, 1898

Russell, Lord John, *An Essay on the History of the English Government and Constitution*, London, Longman, Hurst, 1823

Salmon, Philip, *Electoral Reform at Work: Local Politics and National Parties, 1832–1841*, Woodbridge, Boydell, 2002

Savile, George, 'Some Cautions offered to the Consideration of those who are to chuse Members to serve for the Ensuing Parliament', n.p., 1695

Savile, Sir Henry, ed., *Rerum Anglicarum Scriptores post Bedam*, London, n.p., 1596, repr. Frankfurt, 1601

Scott, Sir Walter, *Tales of a Grandfather*, Edinburgh, Cadell, 1829

Searle, Geoffrey, *A New England; Peace and War 1886–1918*, Oxford, Oxford University Press, 2004

Selden, John, *Tituli Honorum*, Frankfurt, Jeremy Schrey, 1696

Self, Robert, ed., *The Neville Chamberlain Diary Letters*, 3 vols, Aldershot, Ashgate, 2000

Shenton, Caroline, *The Day Parliament Burned Down*, Oxford, Oxford University Press, 2012

Skidelsky, Robert, *Politicians and the Slump: The Labour Government of 1929–1931*, London, Macmillan, 1967

Smart, Nick, ed., *The Diaries and Letters of Robert Bernays, 1932–1939: An Insider's Account of the House of Commons*, Lampeter, Edwin Mellen Press, 1996

Smith, E. A., *Lord Grey, 1764–1845*, Oxford, Clarendon Press, 1990

Smith, P., *Disraelian Conservatism and Social Reform*, London, Routledge & Kegan Paul, 1967

Smyth, A., ed., *A Pleasing Sinne*, Cambridge, D. S. Brewer, 2004

Snowden, Philip, *Autobiography*, London, Ivor Nicholson & Watson, 1934

Spelman, Sir Henry, ed., *Concilia, Decreta, Leges, Constitutiones in re Ecclesiasticarum Orbis Britannici*, London, n.p., 1639

Steele, E. D., *Palmerston and Liberalism, 1855–1865*, Cambridge, Cambridge University Press, 1991

Stewart, Graham, *Burying Caesar: Churchill, Chamberlain and the Battle for the Tory Party*, London, Weidenfeld & Nicolson, 1999

Strachey, Lytton, and Fulford, Roger, eds, *The Greville Memoirs*, 8 vols, London, Macmillan, 1938

Summerskill, Edith, *A Woman's World*, London, Heinemann, 1967

Symonds, Julian, *Horatio Bottomley*, London, Cresset, 1955

Taylor, A. J. P., ed., *Off the Record: W. P. Crozier, Political Interviews 1933–1944*, London, Hutchinson, 1973

Temple, William, *Christianity and the Social Order*, London, Penguin, 1942

Thatcher, Margaret, *The Downing Street Years*, London, HarperCollins, 1993

— *The Path to Power*, London, HarperCollins, 1995

Thomas, Peter, *The House of Commons in the Eighteenth Century*, Oxford, Oxford University Press, 1971

Tillett, Ben, *Is the Parliamentary Labour Party a Failure?*, London, Twentieth Century Press, 1908

Tiltman, H. Tessell, *James Ramsay MacDonald*, London, Jarrolds, 1929

Townsend, William Charles, *History of the House of Commons, from the Convention Parliament of 1688–9 to the Passing of the Reform Bill in 1832*, 2 vols, London, Henry Colburn, 1843–4

Trevelyan, George Macaulay, *Lord Grey of the Reform Bill*, London, Longmans, 1929

Turner, John, *British Politics and the Great War*, New Haven, Yale University Press, 1992

— 'The House of Commons and the executive in the First World War', *Parliamentary History*, vol. 10, no. 2 (1991), pp. 297–316

Twiss, Horace, *The Public and Private Life of Lord Chancellor Eldon*, 2 vols, London, John Murray, 1844

Vincent, J., ed., *The Derby Diaries, 1869–1878*, Cambridge, Cambridge University Press, 1995

Vincent, J., ed., *Disraeli, Derby and the Conservative Party*, Brighton, Harvester, 1978

Walker, Christopher J., *Oliver Baldwin: A Life of Dissent*, London, Arcadia, 2003

Walkland, S. A., ed., *The House of Commons in the Twentieth Century*, Oxford, Oxford University Press, 1979

Walpole, Horace, *The Letters of Horace Walpole, Earl of Orford: Including Numerous Letters Now First Published from the Original Manuscripts*, ed. J. Wright, Philadelphia, Lea & Blanchard, 1842

Walpole, Spencer, *The Life of Lord John Russell*, 2 vols, London, Longmans, Green & Co., 1889

Ward, John Towers, *Sir James Graham*, London, Macmillan, 1967

Watts, Cedric, and Davies, Laurence, *Cunninghame Graham: A Critical Biography*, Cambridge, Cambridge University Press, 1979

Weir, Lauchlan MacNeill, *The Tragedy of Ramsay MacDonald*, London, Secker & Warburg, 1938

Wellesley, Arthur, duke of Wellington, *Despatches, Correspondence and Memoranda of Field-Marshal Arthur, Duke of Wellington*, 7 vols, London, John Murray, 1867

Westcott, Brooke Fosse, *Social Aspects of Christianity*, London, Macmillan, 1888

Wharncliffe, Lord, ed., *The Letters and Works of Lady Mary Wortley Montagu*, 2 vols, London, Richard Bentley, 1837

Wheatley, H. B., ed., *The Historical and the Posthumous Memoirs of Sir Nathaniel William Wraxall*, 5 vols, London, Bickers & Son, 1884

Wheen, Francis, *Tom Driberg: His Life and Indiscretions*, London, Chatto & Windus, 1990

Whitelocke, Bulstrode, *Memorials of the English Affairs*, London, J. Tomson, 1732

— *Notes upon the King's Writ*, London, W. Strahan, 1766

Wilberforce, Reginald, *Life of the Right Reverend Samuel Wilberforce*, 3 vols, London, John Murray, 1881

Wilberforce, Robert Isaac, *The Life of William Wilberforce*, 3 vols, London, John Murray, 1839

Williams, Robin Harcourt, ed., *The Salisbury–Balfour Correspondence*, Ware, Hertfordshire Record Society, 1988

Wilson, Trevor, 'The coupon and the British general election of 1918', *Journal of Modern History*, vol. 36, no. 1 (March 1964), pp. 28–42

Woodbridge, George, *The Reform Club 1836–1978*, London, privately printed, 1978

Wootton, Barbara, *In a World I Never Made*, London, Allen & Unwin, 1967

Wordsworth, Christopher, ed., *Ecclesiastical Biography*, 6 vols, London, Rivington, 1839

Wraxall, Sir N. William, *Memoirs of My Own Time*, 2 vols, London, Cadell & Davies, 1815

Wyatt, Woodrow, *The Journals*, vol. 2, London, Macmillan, 1992

Illustrations

Every effort has been made to trace copyright holders. Any who have been
overlooked are invited to get in touch with the publishers.

Endpapers (hardback edition only)

'Plan of the principal floor of the Palace of Westminster' by Charles Barry,
1840s–50s.

Images in the text

p. x: Part of the south side of St Stephen's Chapel, detail of 'Interior Views of St
Stephen's Chapel, recorded before the enlargement of the House of Commons in
1800; including sections of carved screen wall and stone work', engraved illustration to *Antiquities of Westminster* by J. T. Smith, 1807: © The Trustees of the
British Museum.

p. 6: 'A memento of the great public question of reform', etching and aquatint
'Designed and engraved exclusively for the Bell's New Weekly Messenger, and
delivered gratis. April 15, 1832': © The Trustees of the British Museum.

p. 42: 'Papa Cobden taking Master Robert for a free trade walk', cartoon by
Richard Doyle, *Punch*, 10 March 1845.

p. 78: Cover of *Crawford Divorce Case (Verbatim Report.) Illustrated with portraits of Sir Charles Dilke and others concerned.* Pamphlet by F. Henning, 1886:
Lilly Library, University of Indiana.

p. 114: 'Awful scene of gloom and dejection, when the ministry heard of the
Lords' decision to refer the budget to the country', cartoon by Edward Tennyson
Reed, *Punch*, 24 November 1909.

p. 148: Grave of Captain Harold Cawley MP (killed in action on 24 September
1915), near Cape Helles: © Marion Doss.

p. 194: 'Don't Keir-Hardie, M.P. for 'Am', cartoon by Harry Furniss, *Punch*,
20 August 1892.

p. 236: Ladies' Gallery, House of Commons, illustration by Paul Renouard, *The
Graphic*, 22 July 1893: © Illustrated London News Ltd/Mary Evans.

p. 266: 'The Chance of a Lifetime', cartoon by Leonard Raven Hill, *Punch*, 28
December 1910.

Illustration sections

Credits read from top left clockwise for each spread.

First section

'Cupid out of place', cartoon by Ebeneezer Landells from *Punch*, 4 December 1841; William Lygon, 7th earl of Beauchamp, as Governor of New South Wales, 1900, photograph by Freeman & Co.: State Library of New South Wales; J. R. J. Macnamara electioneering, 14 April 1934: © TopFoto.co.uk; *Daily Mirror*, front page, 24 May 1973: mirrorpix.

Second section

'Auspicium melioris aevi', satirical print, 17 March 1788: © The Trustees of the British Museum; *Sir Francis Dashwood in Oriental Dress*, West Wycombe Park, Bucks: photo National Trust, by permission of Sir Edward Dashwood, Bt; Roy Jenkins, cartoon by Gerald Scarfe, *The Times*, 6 January 2003: copyright © Gerald Scarfe; Lord George-Brown, 2 March 1976: Getty Images.

'The working-man Member', caricature by 'Spy' of Henry Broadhurst from *Vanity Fair*, 9 August 1894; R. B. Cunninghame Graham at the Scottish National Party Bannockburn Day annual demonstration, 1935: © Pictorial Press Ltd/Alamy; William Temple, archbishop of Canterbury (right) and William Beveridge, Central Hall, Westminster, 1 August 1943: Getty Images; Labour party election campaign, 12 May 1955: REX/Associated Press; Labour party MPs in the Chamber of the House of Commons, 2006: Terry Moore; Ramsay MacDonald arriving at the House of Commons, 1 October 1924: REX/Daily Mail.

'Convicts and lunatics have no vote for Parliament', suffragette poster by Emily J. Harding Andrews, c.1912: © Pictorial Press/Alamy; suffragette banner, October 1908: Parliamentary Archives HC/SA/SJ/3/1; Margaret Haig Mackworth, 2nd Viscountess Rhondda, photograph by Bassano, 6 May 1937: National Portrait Gallery, London; Irene Ward, Barbara Castle and Edith Summerskill campaigning for women's rights, 6 March 1954: J. Wilds/Keyston/Getty Images; Margaret Thatcher, House of Commons, 22 November 1990: © Richard Baker/Alamy; Lady Iveagh, Irene Ward, Thelma Cazalet-Keir, Mavis Tate, Ida Copeland, Lady Astor, Sarah Ward, Florence Horsbrough, Mary Pickford, duchess of Atholl and Norah Runge on the House of Commons Terrace, 1931.

Rt Hon. Sir John Trevor, portrait, English School: Palace of Westminster Collection; 'The Prevailing Candidate, or the Election carried by Bribery and the Devil', anonymous satirical print, 1722: © The Trustees of the British Museum; 'Parliament pro-rogued', postcard by Cynicus, c.1910: fotolibra; Horatio Bottomley in the 1920s: REX/Daily Mail; *Daily Mirror*, front page, 26 September 1972: mirrorpix; 'Jabez Balfour in the Bow Street cells', illustration by Charles Sheldon, *Black and White*, 11 May 1895.

Sir Mancherjee Merwanjee Bhownaggree, platinum print by Sir John (Benjamin) Stone, 1897: National Portrait Gallery, London; Dadabhai Naoroji, c.1890: Getty Images; Shapurji Saklatvala, addressing crowds in Trafalgar Square on 'Unemployment Sunday', 1922: © PA Archive/ Press Association Images; Paul

Boateng, Bernie Grant, Keith Vaz and Diane Abbott, at the Labour party conference, Blackpool, 5 October 1988: PA/PA Archive/Press Association.

Index

Guardian, 301
Guest, Freddy, 289, 290
Guest, Sir Ivor (Baron Wimborne), 126–7
Guild of St Matthew, 198
Guilford, Francis North, 6th earl of, 129
Guinness, Sir Arthur (Baron Ardilaun), 126
Guinness, Walter, 369–70
Gulland, John, 154
Gumley, Samuel, 13
Gummer, Ben, 368

habeas corpus, 4, 23, 36
Hackney, 64; Hackney South, 295
Hague, William, 369
Haig, Douglas, 1st Earl, 106, 305
Haigh, Mervyn, bishop of Coventry, 184
Hailsham, Douglas Hogg, 1st Viscount, 270, 337–8
Hailsham, Douglas Hogg, 3rd Viscount, 356
Hailsham, Quintin Hogg, 2nd Viscount, 168, 339
Hakewill, William, 308
Haldane, Richard Haldane, 1st Viscount, 131, 134, 260, 305
Halifax, Edward Wood, 1st Earl and 3rd Viscount, 125, 174–5, 177
Halifax, George Savile, marquess of, 310
Hall, Glenvil, 168
Hall, Sydney, 128
Halsbury, Hardinge Giffard, earl of, 143, 144
Hames, Duncan, 368
Hamilton, Lord Ernest, 125
Hamilton, Lord George, 133, 304
Hamilton, Mary, 258
Hamilton, Neil, 271, 348
Hammond, Anthony, 240
Hampden, John, 21*n*
Hampden, Renn Dickson, bishop of Hereford, 59
Hampden Clubs, 21*n*
Hampshire, HMS, 159
Hampson, Keith, 110
Hanningfield, Paul White, Baron, 270
Hansard, 35, 39, 90, 142, 218, 263
Harcourt, Lewis ('Loulou'), 102–4, 246, 315
Harcourt, Sir William, 102, 130, 131
Hardie, Agnes, 255
Hardie, George, 255
Hardie, James Keir, *194*, 201–4, 206, 207, 233–4, 261, 317
Hardwick Hall, Derbyshire, 274
Hare, John, 209
Harley, Thomas, 284
Harman, Harriet, 368

Harmsworth, Alfred, *see* Northcliffe, Viscount
Harmsworth, Harold, *see* Rothermere, Viscount
Harmsworth, St John, 89, 90
Harris, Arthur ('Bomber Harris'), 185
Harrison, Walter, 328
Harrowby, Lord, 24
Harrow East, 105
Hart, Judith, 252
Hartington, marquess of, *see* Devonshire, 8th *and* 10th dukes of
Hartlebury Castle, Worcestershire, 129
Hartlepool, 64
Hartman, Mrs, 89
Hartshorn, Vernon, 210
Harvey, Daniel, 277
Harvey, Edmund, 151
Harvey, Ian, 105–6
Harwich, 273
Hastings, Sir Patrick, 212
Hatfield House, Hertfordshire, 275
hats, wearing of, 249–50
Hatsell, John, 242
Hattersley, Roy, 328
Hawarden Castle, Wales, 68, 69, 117, 120
Hawkesbury, Robert Jenkinson, 2nd Lord, *see* Liverpool, 2nd earl of
Hawkestone family, 13
'Hay, Ian', 113
Headlam, Arthur, bishop of Gloucester, 184
Headlam, Sir Cuthbert, 298–9
Headlam, Stewart, 198
Healey, Denis, 331, 343, 347
Healy, Tim, 91, 92
Heath, Sir Edward (Ted), 259, 268, 332; his Bill to abolish retail price maintenance, 340; creates Expenditure Committee, 335; makes life peers, 340; puts Hogg in Lords, 339; refuses peerage, 340, 341; and Europe, 345–6; and Labour, 370; and Jellicoe, 94, 95; defeated by Mrs Thatcher, 330–1, 350, 355
Heathcoat-Amory, Patrick, 168
Heber, Richard, 100
Heffer, Eric, 343
Hell (tavern), 306–7
Hellfire Club, 14
Henderson, Arthur: teetotal, 317; wins 1903 by-election, 205; wartime posts, 154, 160, 207; threatens resignation, 156; death of son, 148; visits Russia, 163; resigns, 163; in MacDonald's government, 210; becomes Foreign Secretary, 215; opposes MacDonald, 218, 317

Rowntree, Arnold, 151
Royal Commission on Honours (1922), 290
royal family, criticism of the, 360–1
Royal Scots Fusiliers, 6th Battalion of, 161
Royal Titles Act (1876), 71, 75
Royce, William, 208
Rugby School, 128, 157, 329
Rumbold, Thomas, 18
Runciman, Hilda, 255
Runciman, Walter, 1st Viscount Runciman of
   Doxford, 255
Russell, Sir Charles, 250
Russell, Frank Russell, 2nd Earl, 213
Russell, Lord John Russell, 1st Earl 19n, 59; and
   parliamentary reform, 19, 32, 34–5, 36, 37,
   38; invents 'episcopal elevator', 59, 130; and
   Irish church, 51; uses term 'liberal', 54n;
   resigns, 52; his government, 53–4, 59, 122;
   supports Peel in corn law repeal, 51, 52;
   becomes anti-Catholic bigot, 59; forced to
   resign by Palmerston, 59; in Aberdeen's
   government, 59–60; becomes Palmerston's
   Foreign Secretary, 61; becomes Prime
   Minister, 61–2; defeated by 'Abdullamites',
   62; on peerages, 286
Russell, Mabel, 254
Russia/Soviet Union, 70, 71, 228; declares war
   on Turkey, 72, 73; Bolshevik Revolution
   (1918), 163, 211; and First World War, 168,
   169, 181, 182
Rutland, Cicely, countess of, 240
Rutland, Henry Manners, 8th duke of, 137
Rutland, John Manners, 9th duke of, 157
Ryder, Richard, 9
Rye, 21
Ryle, Herbert, bishop of Winchester, 144
Rymer, Thomas, 371

Sacramental Test Act (1828), 59
Sadler, Michael, 77
Sainsbury, David, Baron Sainsbury of Turville,
   358
St Albans: diocese, 130
St Asaph: diocese, 130
St Clair, Malcolm, 338
St Ives: by-election (1928), 255
St John, Henry, 310
St John Stevas, Norman, 333, 335, 336
St Marylebone, 339
St Stephen's, Chapel of, x, 1–3, 7, 236
Saklatvala, Shapurji, 211, 358
salaries, MPs', 10, 206–7, 267–8, 272–3, 275–6,
   279–82, 359, 371
Salford North, 199

Salisbury, 17
Salisbury, Georgina Gascoyne-Cecil (née
   Alderson), marchioness of, 115
Salisbury, James Gascoyne-Cecil, 2nd marquess
   of, 46, 115
Salisbury, James Gascoyne-Cecil, 4th marquess
   of (formerly Viscount Cranborne), 123,
   125, 143, 144, 146–7, 166
Salisbury, Robert Cecil, 1st earl of, 115, 275
Salisbury, Robert Arthur James ('Bobbety')
   Gascoyne-Cecil, 5th marquess of (formerly
   Viscount Cranborne), 171, 185, 224, 225
Salisbury, Robert Arthur Talbot
   Gascoyne-Cecil, 3rd marquess of (formerly
   Viscount Cranborne), 4, 115–16, 368;
   opposes Franchise Bill (1867), 63–4; and
   father's affair with Lady Derby, 72;
   supports Disraeli's foreign policy, 71, 72–3;
   and 1880 election, 73; becomes Prime
   Minister, 82, 84, 88, 115, 116; resignation,
   117; opposes Irish home rule, 118, 119,
   120; forms Unionist coalition government,
   120, 121, 122, 367; Cabinets, 123; bemoans
   end of aristocracy, 123–4; accused of
   conspiring with Lord Arthur Somerset,
   101; on the Lords, 126, 136; and Hardie,
   202; hands premiership to Balfour, 132;
   death, 145
Salisbury, Robert Michael Gascoyne-Cecil, 7th
   marquess of (Viscount Cranborne; Baron
   Cecil of Essendon), 52n
Salmon, Sir Isidore, 177
Salter, Alfred, 317
Samuel, Sir Herbert, 162, 166, 217, 218n, 249,
   305
Sandford, George, 66
Sandwich, Edward Montagu, 3rd earl of, 240
Sandwich, Elizabeth Montagu, countess of, 240
Sandys, Duncan, 169, 301n, 344, 368
Sandys, Edwin, 368
Sandys, Sir Edwin, 368
Sandys, George, 368
Sandys, John, 368
Sandys, Sir John, 368
Sandys, Laura, 368
Sandys, Miles, 368
Sandys, Richard del, 368
Sandys, Samuel, 368
Sandys, Sir Thomas, 368
Sandys, Sir Walter, 368
Sankey, John Sankey, 1st Viscount, 209, 217,
   219, 336
San Stefano, Treaty of (1878), 73
Sassoon, Sir Philip, 106, 109

Vavasour, Sir Henry, 239

Vavasour, Margaret, 239

Velázquez, Diego: *The Rokeby Venus*, 246

Venables-Vernon-Harcourt, Edward, archbishop of York, 39

Vesey-Fitzgerald, William, 28

Vestey, Sir William, 1st Baron, 288

Victoria, Queen, 46, 60, 66, 70, 71, 75, 81, 83, 87, 126, 135, 360

Villiers, Charles Pelham, 50, 61, 367

Villiers, Theresa, 367

Villiers, Thomas Hyde, 367

voting rights, 4, 12, 17–20, 36, 40, 62, 63–5, 81, 121, 135, 161; and registration campaigns, 46, 47, 48; and secret ballots, 58, 63, 69, 77; 'faggot votes', 74 *and n*; postal voting, 227; *see also* Catholic emancipation; women

Vyvyan, Sir Richard, 28, 29, 35, 36

Wakefield 65; diocese, 130

Wakefield, Wavell, 1st Baron, 339

Walcheren expedition (1809), 10 *and n*, 156n

Wales, 12, 37, 123, 358; devolution referendum, 327, 348

Walkden, Evelyn, 322

Walker, Peter, 368

Walker, Robin, 368

Wall, Charles Baring, 100

Wallach, Eli, 302

Waller, Gary, 96

Wallington Hall, Northumberland, 209

Wallsend, 253; by-election (1926), 257

Wall Street Crash (1929), 215

Walpole, Sir Edward, 275, 284

Walpole, Horace, 98

Walpole, Horatio, 1st Baron, 86, 275, 284

Walpole, Sir Robert (1st earl of Orford), 9n, 21, 45n, 86, 97, 98, 249, 275, 277, 279, 296

Walpole, Robert (son), *see* Orford, 2nd earl of

Walpole, Spencer, 63

Walsh, Stephen, 210

Walsingham, Sir Francis, 240

Walters, Sir Alan, 350

Walters, Catherine, 88

Walters, Tudor, 161–2

Walworth, 295

Wandsworth, Sydney Stern, Baron, 127

Wansbeck, 197

War of Spanish Succession (1703–12), 311

Ward, Dame Irene, 251, 253

Ward, Lieutenant-Colonel John, 295

Ward, Sarah, 253

Wardlaw-Milne, Sir John, 182–3

Wardle, Colonel Gwyllym, 9–10

Waring, Samuel, 1st Baron, 288, 290

Waring and Gillow (firm), 288

Watson, Richard, bishop of Llandaff, 34

Waugh, Evelyn: *Brideshead Revisited*, 104–5

Wavell, Field Marshal Archibald, 181

Ways and Means Committee, 333 *and n*

Weatherill, Bernard, 328

Webb, Beatrice, 200, 210, 257

Webb, Edmund, 310

Webb, Sidney, 200, 209, 210, 233

Wedgwood, Josiah, 151, 161, 172, 174, 185

Weir, Lauchlan MacNeill, 217

'welfare state', 186

welfare system, 136, 186, 211, 226, 230; *see also* pensions

Wellesley, Richard, Marquess Wellesley, 11 *and n*

Wellington, Arthur Wellesley, 1st duke of, 4, 21; and Burdett, 10–11; in Cabinet with Liverpool and Canning, 25, 26; refuses to serve under Canning, 26, 27; as Prime Minister, 9n, 27, 28, 31; episcopal appointments, 29, 33, 34; drives through Catholic emancipation, 77; bemoans his lack of patronage, 281; opposed to parliamentary reform, 30, 31, 39–40; resigns, 31; appears as character witness for homosexual, 100; and Croker, 41; and Peel, 47, 49; resigns Leadership of the House, 52; supports Peel in corn law repeal, 53

Wells, 98; palace, 128

Welsh Church Act (1914), 150, 304–5

Wendover, 16, 21

Wentworth Woodhouse, nr Rotherham, 275

Wesley, Charles, 13

Wesley, John, 13

Westbury, 29, 298

Westbury, Richard Bethell, 1st Baron, 296

Westcott, Brooke Fosse ('the Miners' Bishop'), 201

West Ham South, 201

Westminster, 65, 359

Westminster, Gerald Grosvenor, 6th duke of, 363

Westminster, Hugh Grosvenor, 2nd duke of, 104, 105, 142

Westminster Gazette, 297

Wetherell, Sir Charles, 35

Weymouth, 272

Wharton, Thomas, 309

Whateley, Richard, archbishop of Dublin, 34

Whigs, 6, 11, 13, 20, 25, 26, 27, 28, 30, 33, 57, 58, 76, 77, 130, 241, 277–8; and Peel, 51, 53; and wine imports, 311–12; *see also*

Chris Bryant is a British Labour Party politician who has been the Member of Parliament for the Rhondda since 2001 and was the Minister for Europe and the Deputy Leader of the House of Commons in the previous Labour government. He was one of the two leading MPs who fought to expose the phone-hacking scandal at Rupert Murdoch's News International. Before entering parliament he was a priest in the Church of England. His previous books include biographies of Sir Stafford Cripps and Glenda Jackson.

Parliament: The Biography
Volume 1: Ancestral Voices

Chris Bryant

THE HISTORY OF PARLIAMENT is the history of the United Kingdom itself. It has a cast of thousands. Some were ambitious, visionary and altruistic. Others were hot-headed, violent and self-serving. Few were unambiguously noble. Yet their rowdy confrontations, their campaigning zeal and their unstable alliances framed our nation.

This first of two volumes takes us on a 500-year journey from Parliament's earliest days in the thirteenth century through the turbulent years of the Wars of the Roses and the upheavals of the Civil Wars, and up to 1801, when Parliament emerged in its modern form.

Chris Bryant tells this epic tale through the lives of the myriad MPs, lords and bishops who passed through Parliament. It is the vivid, colourful biography of a cast of characters whose passions and obsessions, strengths and weaknesses laid the foundations of modern democracy.

'Admirably comprehensive'
NEW STATESMAN

'Remarkably readable'
KEN CLARKE

'Magnificent'
LEO MCKINSTRY, EXPRESS

'Wonderful'
MARY BEARD

'Fascinating'
TIMES LITERARY SUPPLEMENT